DEUTERONOMY AND CITY LIFE

A Form Criticism of Texts with the Word CITY ('îr) in Deuteronomy 4:41-26:19

Don C. Benjamin

UNIVERSITY
PRESS OF
AMERICA

LANHAM • NEW YORK • LONDON

Copyright © 1983 by

University Press of America,™ Inc.

4720 Boston Way
Lanham, MD 20706

3 Henrietta Street
London WC2E 8LU England

ISBN (Perfect): 0-8191-3139-3
ISBN   (Cloth): 0-8191-3138-5

Library of Congress Number: 83-3609

DEDICATION

FOR

Peter J. Hinde, O. Carm., who gave me the
exciting vision of the christian as an urban
person in Washington, D.C. in 1964-5;

AND

Matt J. Ewing, O. Carm., and the other
priests and people with whom I lived and
worked in South Central Los Angeles in
1969-78.

--- THEIR FAITH IN THE CITY MADE A BELIEVER
OUT OF ME!

April 25, 1977

iii

ACKNOWLEDGEMENTS

Rolf P. Knierim, Professor of Old Testament at the
Claremont Graduate School (Claremont, CA), chaired
the supervisory committee for my PhD dissertation.
This book is based on the research submitted to
him and Professors William H. Brownlee, now retired,
and James A. Sanders in 1981. I am grateful to
each of them for developing my interest in the
Bible, but I am especially grateful to Dr. Knierim
who as my teacher and director showed me so many
new and exciting possibilities in Old Testament
interpretation.

I also wish to thank T.R. Reckling, III, President
of the Turner Charitable Foundation and Clyde J.
Verheyden, Secretary of the Turner Foundation, for
their continuing interest in the Department of
Religious Studies at Rice University, Houston,
Texas, where I teach. Their recommendation of our
department to the Turner Foundation allowed us to
receive a grant which the department used in part
to prepare *Deuteronomy and City Life* for publication.

Finally, I wish to thank Jo Monaghan, I am only one
of the many scholars and students for whom Jo typed
research during her years at Rice University. She
has an admirable way of erasing the tediousness of
preparing a manuscript with her careful attention
to detail and a wonderful sense of humor.

TABLE OF CONTENTS

LIST OF CHARTS

CHAPTER I

INTRODUCTION

. *The Hebrew Bible and the New Testament*[1]

The Hebrew Bible is a Miscarriage of History

Many Christians consider the Hebrew Bible obsolete, an *old testament*. During the second century CE, Marcion contrasted the loving and merciful Jesus of Christianity with the legalistic, capricious, violent, vindictive and tyrannical Yahweh of Israel.[2] According to Marcion, Christianity, the religion of love, is incompatible with Judaism, the religion of law.[3]

Unlike Marcion who sees no value in the Hebrew Bible for the Christian, Bultmann considers it an important preparation for the gospel. For Bultmann, the Hebrew Bible is a story of failure and frustration. Israel tries to save herself through the prerogatives she enjoys under the covenant as the people of Yahweh. She cannot. This sobering lesson, according to Bultmann, encourages the Christian to trust *only* in the mercy of Jesus. Bultmann's theology indirectly relates the Old Testament to the New Testament, but it fails to develop the more direct promises in the Hebrew Bible,[4] on which the hope of the New Testament is based.

Theoretically, few Christians devaluate the Hebrew Bible as emphatically as Marcion. Many, however, do share Bultmann's conviction that although the Hebrew Bible is clearly revelation, it is impossibly legalistic. Yet in either case, most consider the Hebrew Bible to have little, if any, influence on their own lives. This popular brand of Marcionism continues to deprive Christians of the benefit of Israel's experience of the city, and how that experience affected her understanding of Yahweh and her community life.

The Hebrew Bible is a Primer for the New Testament

Most Christian scholars consider the Hebrew Bible a primer for Christianity, a source book of theological terms or significant themes.[5] For example, Strathmann introduces his article on the meaning of *city* for the *Theological Dictionary of the New Testament* with a study of the Greek translations of the Hebrew Bible and the other religious writings of the Jews.[6]

According to Strathmann, the city in the Hebrew Bible is both a blessing and a curse. As a fortification in which Israel could feel secure, and as a gift freely given by Yahweh to Israel, the city is a blessing.

> Then we turned and went up the way to Bashan; and Og the king of Bashan came out against us, he and all his people, to battle at Edrei. But the Lord said to me, 'Do not fear him; for I have given him and all his people and his land into your hand; and you shall do to him as you did to Sihon the king of the Amorites, who dwelt at Heshbon'. So the Lord our God gave into our hand Og also, the king of Bashan and all his people; and we smote him until no survivor was left to him. And we took all his cities at that time--there was not a city which we did not take from them-- sixty cities, the whole region of Argob, the kingdom of Og in Bashan. All these were cities fortified with high walls, gates, and bars, besides very many unwalled villages. And we utterly destroyed them as we did to Sihon the king of Heshbon, destroying every city, men, women and children. (Dt 3:1-6)[7]

But cities often became temptations to self-confidence and human arrogance. Thus the city was not only a blessing, it was often a curse!

> Now the whole earth had one language and few words. And as men migrated from the east, they found a plain in the land of Shinar and settled there. And they said

2

to one another, 'Come let us make bricks,
and burn them thoroughly.' And they had
brick for stone and bitumen for mortar.
Then they said, 'Come let us build ourselves a city, and a tower with its top
in the heavens, and let us make a name
for ourselves, lest we be scattered abroad
upon the face of the whole earth. And
the Lord came down to see the city and
the tower, which the sons of men had built.
And the Lord said, 'Behold, they are one
people, and they have all one language;
and this is only the beginning of what
they will do; and nothing that they propose
to do will now be possible for them.
(Gn 11:1-6)

In the New Testament, according to Strathmann, the city
is neither a blessing, nor a curse. Here the city has
no political connotations. The city is neither a
cultural, nor an administrative, nor a juridical
institution. The city in the New Testament is simply
a safe place to live![8]

Strathmann contrasts the Hebrew $\hat{i}r$ with the Greek
polis from the literatures of the two cultures. However, he does not compensate for the fact that Greek
literature is extremely philosophical; the Hebrew Bible
is not. Greek literature abstracts the values of the
city and its cultural functions. The Hebrew Bible
tells the story of Yahweh's dealings with Israel, without reflecting philosophically on social institutions.

Strathmann also assumes Israel is a desert people,
completely uncomfortable in the urban culture of Canaan.
He accepts this nomadic ideal while admitting Israel
built and lived in cities![9] It is unnecessary, however,
to assume that Israel was nomadic or that she was
militarily weaker than Bashan or Sihon to understand
Dt 3:1-6. Even in Israel's military and political
and urban prime, the prophets challenged her to trust
completely in Yahweh, who alone was the cause of victory. Furthermore, the focus of Dt 3:1-6 need not be
on the city as an overwhelming military fortification,
but on the city as Israel's inheritance (*nahalâ*)--a
gift from Yahweh. Finally, the city in Dt 3:1-6 need
not have been destroyed because it was contaminated,
but rather offered to Yahweh as a sacrifice.

Although Strathmann's conclusions are questionable,

3

his view of the relationship between the Hebrew Bible
and the New Testament is clear. The theological
terms and significant themes of Israel are the theological terms and significant themes of Christianity.

However, this understanding of the relationship
between the testaments is a one-way street. Influence
flows *only* from Israel to Christianity. The New
Testament use of theological terms and significant
themes from the Hebrew Bible is irrelevant for the
theology of the Hebrew Bible. Many contemporary·
theologians of the Hebrew at least theoretically admit
that the theological terms and significant themes of
Christianity influence Israel.[10] Unfortunately, no
one has attempted a study of the effect which the New
Testament might have on the theology of the city in
the Hebrew Bible, and most studies of the Hebrew Bible
still analyze the city without any reference to the
New Testament.

The structure of such theologies is standard.
They compare the root for the Hebrew word with roots
in other Ancient Near Eastern languages. Hulst, for
example, observes that the root *'îr* in Hebrew,
Ugaritic and Phoenician means *city*.[11] In Old Arabic,
the root means *mountain*. The relationship of *'îr* and
the Sumerian root *uru* is not clear. However, in
every language, *'îr* indicates a *fortification*. The
root *qîr* in Hebrew, Moabite, Aramaic also means *city*;
however, the settlement is *unfortified*.[12] Both *'îr*
and *qîr* occur in compounds such as *city of the palms*
in Dt 34:3; Ju 1:16, 3:13 and *city of the scribes* in
Jos 15:15-16.

Such theologies also assemble statistics on the
word's use. Hulst counts 678 examples of the root *'îr*
in the Hebrew Bible. The root occurs most often in
Jeremiah (79 times) and Joshua (70 times). The root
appears 30 times in Deuteronomy, but not at all in
Hosea, Obadiah, Haggai and Malachai.

Such theologies then define the word on the basis
of these examples. Hulst observes that the variation
in cities was great. For example, Dt 3:5 contrasts
cities with high walls, towers and bolted gates, with
settlements fortified by only a fence to ward off wild
animals.[13] Like the root *âlu* in Akkadian, whose cog-
nate in Hebrew means *tent*, *'îr* can also mean a camp.[14]

Originally, according to Hulst, the Israelites

4

occupied very primitive sites in Palestine; however,
during the monarchy, these former nomads became en-
thusiastic converts to urban life. He shares
Strathmann's conclusions that for Israel the city was
primarily a place of protection and not a cultural,
economic, spiritual or political institution. The
city afforded protection not only to its citizens, but
to those who lived around the city as well. Only in
the course of time, according to Hulst, did the
Israelites abandon their semi-nomadic ways for urban
life.

Finally, such theologies consider a word's
connotations as well as its precise definition.
According to Hulst, Gn 4:17--a notice that *Cain*
founded the city--could be the Yahwist's negative
judgment, if not outright rejection of the city as a
fit place for Israelites to live. The tower of Babel
story in Gn 11:1-9 associates the city with humanity's
search for security, domination, power and rebellion
against Yahweh. The story of Sodom and Gomorrah in
Gn 18 may show how at home repulsive sins are in the
city.[15] According to this assessment of the city,
urban life leads to a breakdown of family relationships and encourages immoral behavior; the prophets
condemn the city for its corruption, and the Rechabites
(Je 35:6-10) are a rebellion against sedentary
culture.[16] Wallis summarizes this anti-urban attitude,
by arguing that Israel never had a positive or
acceptable bond with the city.[17]

However, Hulst points out that this completely
negative judgment of the city does not do justice to
the Hebrew Bible. The *city* established in Gn 4:17 may
be a safe rallying place for nomads in times of
trouble, and thus recall a positive and not a negative
assessment of the city by Israel.[18] Genesis 11:1-19
neither condemns the building of the city itself, nor
praises the city as Yahweh's creation. For the Hebrew
Bible, the city is simply accepted as a clearly human
accomplishment. However, Yahweh acknowledges this
accomplishment by approving Israel's confiscation of
the cities in Canaan.[19]

> And when the Lord your God brings you into
> the land which he swore to your fathers,
> to Abraham, to Isaac, and to Jacob, to give
> you, with great and goodly cities, which
> you did not build, and houses full of all
> good things, which you did not fill, and

cisterns hewn out, which you did not hew,
and vineyards and olive trees, which you
did not plant, and when you eat and are
full, then take heed lest you forget the
Lord, who brought you out of the land of
Egypt, out of the house of bondage.
(Dt 6:10-12)

Living in houses was not a sin in itself, but it was
dangerous because frequently it led Israel into sin.
Certainly the prophets may have had cultural or rural
prejudices against the city, but in the final analysis
their judgments are religious. They condemn not the
city, but self-sufficiency, misuse of power and
domineering economic systems as rebellions against
Yahweh. The sin was not the city itself, nor its
walls, nor its towers, but the trust urbanites frequently placed in these fortifications.[20]

. . . a nation . . . from afar . . . shall
besiege you in all your towns, until your
high and fortified walls, in which you
trusted, come down throughout all your
land; and they shall besiege you in all your
towns throughout all your land, which the
Lord your God has given you. (Dt 28:49+
52-3)

Israel must trust not in the security of what humanity
is able to achieve, but only in the security which
Yahweh can give.

Unless the Lord builds the house,
  those who build it labor in vain.
Unless the Lord watches over the city
  the watchman stays awake in vain.

It is vain that you rise up early
  and go late to rest
  eating the bread of anxious toil;
  for he gives to his beloved in sleep.

Lo, sons are a heritage from the Lord,
  the fruit of the womb a reward.
Like arrows in the hand of a warrior
  are the sons of one's youth.

Happy is the man
  who has his quiver full of them!
He shall not be put to shame

6

when he speaks with his enemies in the gate.
(Ps 127)

The assumption that it is only the Hebrew Bible
which influences the New Testament, and not the New
Testament which influences the Hebrew Bible is apparent
in each part of the study. The etymology, the statistics, the definitions and the connotations are all
done without reference to the New Testament. This is
a theology limited to the literature of the Hebrew
Bible.

Even in Grelot's entry in the *Dictionary of
Biblical Theology* is careful to keep the influence
flowing in only one direction.[21] Despite the treatment of the city in both the Hebrew Bible and the New
Testament in consecutive articles, no evaluation of
the impact which New Testament usage should have on
the Hebrew Bible interpretation is mentioned.

Grelot concludes that Israel alternated between
urban and semi-nomadic styles of life. Israel did not
invent the city, it is present in the epoch
primeval.[22] However, the great urban empires of
Mesopotamia emerge only after the flood.[23] According
to Grelot, Israel's ancestors appear in this great
urban age, although as a non-urban people.

Terah took Abram his son and Lot the son
of Haran, his grandson and Sarai his
daughter-in-law, his son Abram's wife,
and they went forth together from Ur of
the Chaldeans to go into the land of
Canaan; but when they came to Haran, they
settled there. (Gn 11:31)

Israel's Egyptian period was urban, and only after the
exodus does Israel take up what Grelot describes as
her *traditional nomadic life in the steppes.*[24] The
settlement is another urban period, with only the
Rechabites clinging to a non-urban form of life.

On the basis of this survey, Grelot argues that
the urban tradition of the Hebrew is ambivalent. True,
the city is a refuge from raiding parties and warring
armies. True, the city is the site of sanctuaries
dedicated to Yahweh. But the city is also an occasion
of sin. He considers the age of the ancestors, which
may have lasted 100 years, and the desert wandering,
which may have lasted 40 years as *the* formative period
for Israel. That is questionable. He also considers

7

the Israel of these two times naturally nomadic. That
is also questionable. What is not questionable is that
Grelot considers the theology which developed from
these alternating periods of nomadic and urban life to
have profoundly influenced the New Testament. Although
the New Testament developed entirely within an urban
civilization, Grelot argues that it was as ambivalent
as the Hebrew Bible toward the city.[25] Therefore, he
can conclude that the Biblical and not the Hebrew
Bible's theology of the city is ambivalent.

The Hebrew Bible is a Paradigm for New Testament

The Hebrew Bible is not only a source book of
theological terms and significant themes appearing in
the New Testament; it also introduces persons, events
and institutions from which analogies have been drawn
by Christians in order to understand what God is doing
in their time. The persecuted and prophetic Jesus of
Peter's Jerusalem sermon corresponds to the persecuted
and prophetic Moses of Exodus. Both stand between God
and God's people and make the relationship between the
two possible and productive. The crucifixion of
Jesus, according to 1 C 5:7 corresponds to the sacrifice of the pascal lamb in Ex 12. The community of
Christians who consider themselves ransomed, adopted,
and undeserving corresponds to the slaves of Egypt who
considered themselves children of Yahweh without having
deserved the honor. This form of interpretation, on
which a relationship between the testaments is based,
is called *typology*.[27]

The original tradition--Moses, the passover, the
people of Yahweh--is called a *type*. The subsequent
tradition--Jesus, the crucifixion, the church--is
called an *anti-type*. Types are not symbols of general
and abstract religious truths. Moses is not an
elaborate metaphor of self-sacrifice; nor the passover
meal an image of intimacy; nor the people of Yahweh a
coded abstract of community. Types are concrete
historical actions performed by Yahweh; anti-types
affirm that once again God is acting in concrete and
historical ways in human history. God does not repeat
actions in human history, therefore type and anti-type
are never identical. Typology exists not because human
history runs in a circle, repeating itself over and
over again; typology exists because of a conviction
shared by Jews and Christians that God is faithful to

8

his word. Committed to an ongoing relationship with humanity, God continues to do things to enrich that relationship; things similar to what have been done in time past. The relationship is dynamic and each new act not only fulfills the past, it opens the present to a future fulfillment.

The person with whom urban typology is connected in the Hebrew Bible is David; the institution is Jerusalem. Named after the fortification around which the city of Jerusalem was built, it is called *Zion theology*.[28] Originally *Zion* or *Sion* was the Jebusite stronghold captured by Joab for David.[29] In 1 K 8:1 (=2 C 5:2), *Zion* is the lower city. Solomon moves the ark from here to the temple. Later, *Zion* included not only the temple, but the entire metropolitan area as well.[30] The name *Zion* has retained its sacred character throughout the subsequent history of Israel, always signifying the historical and religious connection between the people and the city of Jerusalem.

Like those who consider the Hebrew Bible a primer or a paradigm for the New Testament, *Deuteronomy and City Life* assumes that both testaments contain a continuous record of the activity of one God in human life. Thus, *Deuteronomy and City Life* assumes that if Yahweh established precedents in Israel for dealing with humanity through the city and through urban institutions, any urban theology needs an understanding and appreciation of these precedents to remain authentically Christian.[31]

But, although *Deuteronomy and City Life* agrees with those who see the need to evaluate not only the impact of the Hebrew Bible on the New Testament, but the impact of the New Testament on the Hebrew Bible, it makes no attempt to do either here. Certainly passages like the parable of the prodigal son in Lk 15:11-32 could be used to exegete a city text like the legal instruction concerning an incorrigible son from an urban family in Dt 21:18-21, and vice versa. However, studying the influence of these city texts on the New Testament would make this study too long, and there is still no accurate method by which to apply material from the New Testament to the interpretation of the Hebrew Bible. So a study of the impact which these city texts have on the New Testament, and which the New Testament has on these city texts has been postponed.

The Hebrew Bible and The City

The city was not only a fit place for the people of Yahweh to dwell; it was a fit symbol of Yahweh himself. The believer in Ps 46 praying: *A mighty fortress is our God*, as well as the believer in Ps 23 praying: *The Lord is my shepherd* both use urban images: for one Yahweh is a city; for the other a city ruler.[32] Since feeding and protecting are the responsibilities of both shepherds and kings, the king was often called a shepherd in the Ancient Near East.[33]

In each period of Hebrew history--the migration, the settlement, the monarchy, the exile and the post-exile--the city played an important role in Israel's understanding of herself and her god.[34] Zabulon and Issachar at first indenture themselves to cities and then revolt against their urban overlords. The destruction of Hazor may have occurred at their hands. Judah, on the other hand, acts differently with the city. She is never a slave to any city, but through the city of Hebron, she governs her territory. Ephraim does not conquer, but does influence the ancient city of Shechem, while David and Solomon make full use of the city as a political and military tool to govern their empire.[35] But despite the contributions which these cities made to Israel, many still consider biblical religion an exclusively rural religion which cities threaten to destroy. The prejudice is ancient and ingrained.

The Yahwist theologians whose tradition (J) is the backbone of the Hebrew Bible, lived in the city. The leisure, education, art and economy of Jerusalem supported their work. Nonetheless, they denied the city was ever Israel's home. For the Yahwist, neither the epoch primeval nor the time of the ancestors was urban. *In the beginning*, according to the Yahwist, Yahweh gave Israel a garden, not a city. Only her stubbornness forced Israel to live in the city. Cities were the homes of murderers like Cain, braggarts like the citizens of Babel, and savages like the people of Sodom. For the Yahwist, Israel's story is the exodus of Abraham from the cities of Mesopotamia: the exodus of Moses from the cities of Egypt and the victory of Joshua over the cities of Canaan. Models of Hebrew piety did not live in

10

cities. In the cities, the lives of Abraham and Isaac
are threatened. The vocations of Sarah and Rebecca
are compromised; and Yahweh's promise that the ancestors will have a family is endangered.[36] To the city,
Jacob loses his favorite son, Joseph, as a slave. In
the cities, Moses sees only suffering and death, and
Joshua witnesses Yahweh's power to destroy. David conquered cities and built palaces, but he was still
Jesse's shepherd son. Israel is a people who either
abandons cities or destroys them.[37]

Somehow, this ancient critique of the city by the
Yahwist became a dogma, and three thousand years
later, only those who flee the city or destroy it find
a companion in Israel and can use her Bible as a guide.
The urban community considers itself illegitimate,
since presumably the city can teach nothing about God,
nor provide a suitable place for the people of God to
dwell.

In the United States, this prejudice took on
critical proportions during the immigrations in the
19th century. Since their anti-urban bias so
seriously affected the life and mission of religious
communities in the United States, Neuhaus assigns them
the special role of correcting the damage done.[39]
The National Federation of Priests' Councils repeated
that challenge to the Roman Catholic community in
the pastoral: *Hear the Cry of Jerusalem.*[40]

Nonetheless, attitudes toward the city in the 20th
century continue to be ambiguous.[41] Cox celebrates
the freedom which the city bestows upon its citizens,
and invites them to embrace the discipline which
living in the city requires.[42] Martin believes that
serious research on the city in the Bible would re-
veal a hope-filled and loving attitude toward the
city.[43] Yet, Ellul extends the curse of Cain to the
city which he founded (Gn 4:17), and therefore concludes that for the Bible, the city is an impossible
living arrangement.[44]

The goal of *Deuteronomy and City Life*

The material it studies

To challenge the assumption that Biblical religion is exclusively a rural religion, *Deuteronomy and City Life* studies ten texts:

Dt 6:10-19   A parenesis to remain faithful to Yahweh in the city

Dt 13:13-19   A legal instruction concerning an apostate city

Dt 19:1-13   A legal instruction concerning the use of cities as asylums

Dt 4:41-43   A supplement on cities of refuge

Dt 20:10-20   A legal instruction concerning the siege of cities

Dt 21:1-9   A legal instruction concerning a *corpus delicti* discovered outside the jurisdiction of any particular city

Dt 21:18-21   A legal instruction concerning an incorrigible son from an urban family

Dt 22:13-21   A legal instruction concerning charges of premarital promiscuity against a woman from an urban family

Dt 22:23-27   A legal instruction concerning the rape of a fiancee from an urban family

Dt 25:5-10   A legal instruction concerning the obligations of a brother-in-law to a sonless widow from an urban family.

Few books in the Hebrew Bible are as important for the theology of Israel as Deuteronomy.[45]

12

Initially, Deuteronomy introduced the *Deuteronomist's History*, found today in Deuteronomy, Joshua, Judges, 1 Samuel, 2 Samuel, 1 Kings and 2 Kings. According to Noth, this ambitious work uses the principles set down in Deuteronomy to evaluate the rulers of Israel from Joshua (1200 BCE) to Zedekiah (587 BCE).[46] What the anonymous authors of both Deuteronomy and the Deuteronomist's History have in common is a strong conviction that the *uniqueness* of Yahweh should be reflected in the worship of a *united* Israel at a *single* sanctuary. This is not the only tenet of Deuteronomy, but it is an important one. This is not the only relationship between Deuteronomy and the Deuteronomist's History, but it is a strong one.[47]

For Noth, the survey in the Deuteronomist's History diagnoses the exile as Yahweh's punishment of Israel for the sins of her rulers. Von Rad took a different point of view.[48] For him, the intention of the Deuteronomist was not to explain punishment, but rather to encourage repentence. Yahweh had made unconditional promises to David--promises which had never been revoked.[49]

> . . . the Lord will make you a house. When your days are fulfilled and you will lie down with your fathers, I will raise up your offspring after you, who shall come forth from your body, and I will establish his kingdom. He shall build a house for my name, and I will establish the throne of his kingdom forever I will be his father, and he shall be my son. When he commits iniquity, I will chasten him with the rod of men, with the stripes of the sons of men; but I will not take my steadfast love from him, as I took it from Saul, whom I put away from before you. And your house and your kingdom shall be made sure for ever before me; your throne shall be established forever. (2 S 7:11-16)

The sins of Israel were never permanent, the punishment--even as disastrous as the destruction of Jerusalem and the exile in Babylon--was never terminal. There was always hope, as the note on the release of David's successor, Jehoiachin, from his maximum security prison in Babylon at the end of the History was intended to show.[50] Repentence will reverse the suffering of the exile just as repentence

13

reversed every previous suffering of Israel, as the survey provided by the Deuteronomist has shown.

Wolff, like von Rad, also argues that the Deuteronomist's survey encourages Israel to repent and be saved as she has done so many times in the past.[51] However, repentance will not restore the Davidic monarchy. Wolff considers the Deuteronomist much more reserved about the consequences of repentence than does von Rad. According to Wolff, the Deuteronomist simply contends that the destruction of Jerusalem and the exile are not Yahweh's last word. So long as the history of Israel remains open-ended there is hope. However, according to Wolff, the Deuteronomist does not specify what Yahweh's last word to Israel will be.[52]

Noth, von Rad and Wolff all assume that the major work on the Deuteronomist's History was done after the destruction of Jerusalem.[53] Cross disagrees, claiming that this theory leaves too many unanswered questions.[54] For Cross, the setting of the history is the hope-filled time of Josiah's reform. The judgment studied by Noth and characterized by the do-evil formula (*la'ăśôt hārâ'*) is counterbalanced by the salvation studied by von Rad and characterized by the do-good formula (*la'ăśôt hayyaśār*). Judgment is pronounced on all the kings of Israel and most of the kings of Judah. Salvation is promised only to David, Hezekiah and Josiah. The intention of the history was to encourage Judah to submit to the program of austerity promoted by Josiah's government, on the promise that it would save her from judgment.[55] According to Cross, the history was edited after the destruction of Jerusalem, and the exile. Manassah was charged with sealing the fate of Judah, a fate which the piety of Josiah only postponed. Jerusalem's destruction is soberly noted without any theological reflection. Thus the element of hope is not removed, it is simply *muted*.[56]

Since the literary tradition connected with the Deuteronomic reform was extremely dynamic, it is possible that Noth, von Rad, Wolff and Cross are discussing different stages in the development of the Deuteronomist's History and not conflicting interpretations of the same stage. Thus the finality of the judgment described by Noth might reflect an edition of the History closer in time to the actual destruction of Jerusalem, while the encouraging intention suggested by von Rad an edition made during the exile.

Eventually, Deuteronomy came to close the
Pentateuch, explaining how the traditions of Genesis,
Exodus, Leviticus and Numbers are not trapped in the
time of Abraham, Isaac, Jacob and Moses, but are re-
sumed generation after generation.[57]

Deuteronomy also chaperoned the editors of the
prophets to guarantee their support of Deuteronomy, or
at least the Deuteronomist. For example, the prose
material in Je 26--29 and 34--35 has more in common
with the Deuteronomist's History than with the other
parts of Jeremiah.[58] But the influence of Deuteronomy
is not limited to the Hebrew Bible alone. Deuteronomy
is one of the most quoted books in the New Testament.[59]

Thus with the focus of the canon on Deuteronomy
the urban traditions of Deuteronomy are the key to
Israel's theology of the city, and yet they remain un-
studied. Halligan has studied the city in the
literature of the Yahwist; Sklba and Frick have
studied the city in the literature of the prophets.[60]
Therefore, *Deuteronomy and City Life* continues this
research with its study of the city texts in Dt 4:41--
26:19.

Only one criterion was used to select the texts
for this study, viz., the explicit mention of the city.
Each text contains the word *city ('îr)*. There are
other words for *city* in the Hebrew Bible, but *'îr* is
the most common and occurs throughout the Hebrew
Bible.[61] There was no attempt to separate texts which
discuss the city directly, such as Dt 13:13-19 from
texts like Dt 22:23-27 which do not. Nonetheless,
this criterion does separate city texts from centralization texts in Deuteronomy, because passages de-
manding centralization do not use the word *city*, but
simply limit worship to the *place (māqôm) which Yahweh
chooses*.[62] Although in the rest of the Deuteronomist's
History, *the place* may be *a city* and *the city* may be
Jerusalem, Deuteronomy itself never makes that identification.[63] 2 Kings 23:25-27 is a good example of how
the later segments of the History clarify the intentional vagueness of the place-formula in
Deuteronomy by identifying the city as Jerusalem.

Before him [Josiah] there was no king like
him, who turned to the Lord with all his

15

heart and with all his soul and with all his
might, according to all the law of Moses;
nor did any like him arise after him. Still
the Lord did not turn from the fierceness
of his great wrath, by which his anger was
kindled against Judah, because of all the
provocations with which Manasseh had pro-
voked him. And the Lord said, "I will remove Judah also out of my sight, as I have
removed Israel, and I will cast off this
city which I have chosen, Jerusalem, and
the house of which I said, My name shall be
there."[64]

In fact, Deuteronomy 12 contrasts *within your gates* an
urbanization formula--with *in the place which the Lord
your God chooses*--a centralization formula.[65]

However, you may slaughter and eat flesh
within any of your towns (*urbanization
formula*), as much as you desire, according
to the blessing of the Lord your God which
he had given you; the unclean and the clean
· may eat of it, as of the gazelle and as of
the hart. Only you shall not eat the blood;
you shall pour it out upon the earth like
water. You may not eat within your towns
(*urbanization formula*) the tithe of your
grain or of your wine or of your oil, or
the firstlings of your herd or of your
flock, or any of your votive offerings
which you vow, or your freewill offerings,
or the offering that you present; but you
shall eat them before the Lord your God
in the place which the Lord your God will
choose (*centralization formula*) . . . .
(Dt 12:15-18).[66]

These two formulas indicate two different
physical environments, and therefore the theology of
the *place (māqôm)* and the theology of the *city ('îr)*
are not the same. The *māqôm* theology concerns the institution of *sacred place*. The *sanctuary* may be inside the city proper or outside the city, for example,
on a hilltop. The *māqôm* formula specifies the ark
sanctuary, which, in fact, was erected in a number of
particular cities: Gilgal, Bethel, Shechem, Shiloh
and Jerusalem. But the formula does not sanctify the
city as an institution. By using the word *place*, it
avoids saying: *the city which Yahweh chooses*, and

thus carefully side-steps the Mesopotamian conclusion
that the city was divine![67]

Carmichael explains the use of *place*, rather than
city, or *Jerusalem* in Deuteronomy by understanding
place as *standing* or *position*.[68] There is no precedent
for the use of *māqôm* in this metaphorical sense in the
Hebrew Bible. Furthermore, Deuteronomy considers
Yahweh the landlord of Canaan, and his *place* if
Deuteronomy has considered it, would not be limited to
Jerusalem, but would have needed to extend throughout
the land!

Distinguishing the *māqôm* theology from the city
theology of Deuteronomy does not deny the validity of
the *māqôm* theology. As Nicholson has pointed out,
efforts to regard the *māqôm* texts as nothing more than
a demand that all shrines be authentic, or as secondary
interpolations have failed.[69]

Furthermore, distinguishing the *māqôm* theology
from the city theology does not deny the importance of
the capital city of Jerusalem in Deuteronomy.
Jerusalem was not only the liturgical center of the
nation, but the administrative and judicial center as
well. Jerusalem played a unique role in the society
of Israel, and the *māqôm* texts address that uniqueness.
The city texts, on the other hand, are more general.
They focus on the city, not the capital city. The
theology of the *māqôm* texts is limited to the city of
Jerusalem, while the theology of the city texts applies
to Jerusalem as well as the other urban centers in
Israel.

These city texts are not simply an afterthought.
They are part of the fundamental orientation of the
Deuteronomic reform.[70] Because these ten city texts
contain no internal contradictions, use a common
vocabulary and style, and prefer second person singular
forms, both Hölscher and von Rad include them in their
reconstructions of the earliest fixed form of
Deuteronomy (the *Ur-Deuteronomium*).[71]

The presence of the city text, not only in the
legal section of Deuteronomy (chapters 12-26), but in
the other chapters as well, also accents the fundamental orientation of Deuteronomy toward the city.
City texts were so integral to the nature of
Deuteronomy that no stage of the reform could omit them
and remain true to the orientation of the movement.

17

Deuteronomy's concern with the city is not surprising. Significant urban events flank the Deuteronomic reform. In 722 BCE, Samaria, the capital city of Israel, was destroyed by the Assyrian army, while in 701 BCE, Jerusalem, the capital city of Judah, was delivered from the Assyrian army. The contrast between the fates of Samaria and Jerusalem suggested a uniquely religious role for the city in the reform. When the Babylonians destroyed Jerusalem in 587 BCE, the reform's theology of city was soberly re-evaluated. Furthermore, the reform celebrated David, a successful urban administrator and theologian.[72]

Texts from the time of the Deuteronomic reform, like those in Jos 15 & 19, clearly reflect a society in which the basic unit is not the family or the clan or the tribe, but the city.[73] Following the urban strategy of David, its hero, the reform developed and preserved national unity by means of cities, through which it regulated the public and private lives of all Judah's citizens, regardless to what segment of society they belonged.

· The use which the reform made of the city does not mean that it created a social monolith composed only of urbanites. Not even the severe leveling policies of the monarchy were able to turn the alliance of tent and village and city peoples, which made up ancient Israel, into an exclusively urban culture. Yet for Deuteronomy, Israel is educated, civilized, and cosmopolitan.[74] Without a doubt, Deuteronomy is an outspoken critique of the quality of the civilization in which Israel lives, but Deuteronomy assumes that it is in civilization and not in the desert that Israel will find a home and serve her god.

The method it uses

With the method of the Form Critical Project from the Institute of Antiquity and Christianity at the Claremont Graduate School, Claremont, CA., *Deuteronomy and City Life* studies traditions which retribalized cities brought to early Israel.[75] *Retribalized cities* are significant walled settlements together with their adjacent walled and unwalled sister settlements and their farms, forests and pastures which make a thoroughly Yahwist way of life possible. *Deuteronomy and City Life* is not an archeological, a sociological

or an historical study of the city. Kenyon has done
archeological studies.[76] Mumford, Loewensten and Frick
have done sociological studies.[77] Hammond has done an
historical study.[78]

A study of literary traditions of retribalized
cities is not primarily sociological, but it does re-
veal something of the social institution of the city
as well as the psychological mind set (*Geistes-
beschäftigung*) of the citizen.[79] This close connection
between institutions and literary genres which Gunkel
established for form criticism is very sociological,
i.e., literature gives insight into concrete expressions of human life in a particular community.[80]
However, Jolles softened the connection between institutions and literary genres, and argued instead that
literary forms tell more about the human mind, than
about human institutions.[81] Thus the results of form
criticism can be sociological and psychological.

As an institution, the city has six characteristics.[82] In a city, people *physically live close together.*[83] In a city, people are *directed by a single
government.* In a city, people *make their homes in a
unified complex of buildings, surrounded by a wall.*[84]
In a city, *most people are not farmers.* This does not
mean that cities discriminated against farmers or that
farmers did not live in the cities, but simply that
less than 50% of a city's population raised food for
the entire population.[85] Even cities with specialized
industries like the winemaking in Gibeon or the
textile dying in Debir had farmers and herders to feed
them. And even though they made their livings outside
the walls of the cities proper, farmers and herders
enjoyed the protection, as well as the other social
and economic benefits of urban life. In more peaceful
times, the wealthy might build villas in the country
(Is 5:8), but not even farmers and herders made
permanent homes outside the walls for more than short
periods of time during the harvest and shearing
seasons.[86]

In a city *the size of the territory which is
economically, militarily or religiously controlled is
larger than necessary for survival.*[87] An urban
economy is not a subsistence economy, it is affluent.
In order to provide the luxuries demanded by the
citizens, surplus food is needed to sell or trade for
non-staples. Importing exotic items from far away
places requires trade routes, which need to be

protected. Therefore, more land than is necessary for raising food is acquired so that trade routes may be established and protected.

And finally, in a city, *the politics and the commerce and the worship all use writing.* Writing made elaborate legal systems, and fixed liturgies, and schools with libraries possible. The first known written documents deal with the administration of cities.[88] The association between writing and the cities is so close that Childe considers writing *the* essential characteristic of an urban society.[89] For example, despite the size of Jericho's population in 7800 BCE, and the specialization of its people in one trade or the other, and the organization necessary to build its massive walls and tower, its irrigation canals and farms, Childe still criticizes Kenyon's identification of the site as a *city* because she has no evidence of writing at Jericho.[90]

According to Childe, three developments in Mesopotamia, between 8000-3200 BCE led to the invention of the city.[91] First, changes in climate made it impossible for humans to survive unless they worked in groups to find shelter and obtain food. Second, such cooperation allowed various people to specialize in one task, knowing they could exchange their product or service with other members of the group for necessities. Third, inventions like the plow and the wheel, made the struggle for survival less time consuming.

When the city did appear, it flourished at a number of sites in Mesopotamia between the latitudes of Eridu (30° north) and Uruk/Erech (32° north) and was quickly exported to Canaan in the west and the Indus Valley in the east.

A city had appeared at Jericho around 7800 BCE, but soon vanished, and Canaan remained without cities until almost 3000 BCE.[92] From 3000 BCE onward, however, the city was a stable part of the ecology of Canaan, even though the ethnic make-up of the population there continued to change. All continued to use the city because of the harmony it created between humanity and the environment in Canaan.

Not all cities in Canaan are identical. The cities mentioned in the Execration Texts and the Amarna Tablets are administrative centers. Many of the early cities such as Ugarit, Harran, Megiddo, Hazor and Hebron were religious communities under the direction of temple and palace personnel. But in general from 2350 BCE on, religion became less important in founding cities, as the Akkadians began using cities as military bases and centers of trade. Byblos, Ugarit, Sidon, Tyre, Alalakh, Hamath, Damascus, and Jericho, for example, were all brisk trading centers.

According to Gottwald, the city as the hub of Canaan's feudal economy was established by the Hyksos invaders during the 18th century BCE.[93] These chariot-warriors used the cities as fortresses and centers for the industry necessary to manufacture and maintain their novel horse drawn battle wagons. Because the Hyksos were military specialists, they needed the natives to farm and graze for them. Thus, they developed a social system in which only Hyksos warriors (maryannu) were eligible to become landowners (ḫazannu). Native peasants (ḫupshu) had to work the land, pay taxes and render other services to their ḫazannu.

Descriptions of the precise relationship between the hupshu and the ḫazannu are often contradictory. Albright calls the ḫupshu -- serfs.[94] However, Mendelsohn calls the ḫupshu -- free proletarians.[95] He uses the coloni, who were tied tenant farmers in the Roman empire as an example of the relationship he has in mind. Heltzer and Klengel, on the other hand, call the ḫupshu -- clients of the king, i.e., of the ḫazannu.[96] As clients, they rendered not only military, but craft, trade and professional services as well.

When Canaan came under Egypt's sphere of influence, and Egyptian governors (rabiṣu) were stationed in Canaan, the ḫazannu continued to collect the taxes and direct the labor. Not even during the zenith of Egyptian power in Canaan from 1490-1436 BCE was this feudal economy disrupted. Between 1200-1000 BCE, the Egyptians replaced their rabiṣu with Philistine colonists. Yet, although the Philistines settled down and made Canaan their home, they did not alter the feudal economy.[97]

Gottwald identifies at least two important forms of dissent which preceded Israel: the 'apiru and the Shosu.[98] The 'apiru were peasants uprooted or cast out of society.[99] They supported themselves as

21

mercenaries, seldom working as farmers or herders like other peasants, but completely dependent on the cities who hired them. As infantry-for-hire, the *'apiru* commanded more respect in urban society than their *ḥupshu* comrades, and they enjoyed much greater freedom. The Shosu were peasants who specialized in herding, returning to the cities to farm only during the dry season. As a mobile part of the economy whose assets were fluid, the Shosu were subject to less control and fewer taxes than other peasants. However, without the cities to which they could return, and to whom they could sell their flocks, they would starve. Neither the *'apiru* nor the Shosu constituted an alternative to the city in Canaan. Although geographically they spent a good deal of time away from the city, both were integral parts of urban life.[100]

Eventually, it was at the geographical extremes of Canaan that the strongest and most successful effort to free the cities from feudalism developed. Early Israel was an integral part of this movement, not against the cities, but against feudalism.[101] The base of this movement against the feudal system in Canaan was the extended family (*bêt 'āb*).[102] The quality of life here was simple, but it was totally self-governing. Extraordinary needs for survival and defense of the extended family were provided through alliances with other extended families. These protective associations (*mišpāḥôt*) made the walls and warrior classes of feudalism unnecessary. According to Gottwald, this movement, which he calls *retribalization*, took place in Canaan during 1350-1225 BCE affecting every level of society.[103] Traditions from every sector of Canaanite culture were reunited. The sharp divisions of feudalism were gone.

Feudal and retribalized cities share five institutional characteristics. In both communities, people live physically close to one another in a unified complex of buildings surrounded by a wall under the direction of a single government. Most are not farmers, and the politics, commerce and worship of both feudal and retribalized cities use writing.

However, the social system of the feudal city is dramatically different from that of the retribalized city. The feudal system supports a surplus economy in which the size of the territory economically, militarily or religiously controlled is larger than necessary for survival. The retribalized city, on the other hand, is a simple, self-governing subsistence economy. Hulst's observation that the Hebrew Bible mentions the kings of Canaanite cities, but the only Israelites who exercise urban authority are the rulers, elders and men of the city, reflects this distinction.[104]

The retribalized city is not an innovation, but a reform returning urban life to the more democratic style common in the early cities of Mesopotamia.[105] Retribalization reacted strongly against the unfortunately brutal development of feudalism in urban life, and appealed to the more ancient and benign instincts of the city. It is these humane, democratic and god-fearing traditions which appear in the city texts in Deuteronomy. Unfortunately, retribalization was only temporarily successful. From 1000-843 BCE, David and Solomon and Omri and Ahab, among others, systematically reestablished urban feudalism in both Judah and Israel.

The city texts in Deuteronomy consider the retribalized city a model community in which Yahwists should be proud to live. Having centralized the worship of Yahweh in Jerusalem, Josiah seemed at first to have deprived the cities of Judah of all claim to being authentic Yahwist communities. The city texts, by appealing to the ancient traditions of the retribalized cities which entered early Israel, stress that liturgy is not the only, or even the most important characteristic of the Yahwist community. In fact, an over-emphasis on liturgy led the cities of Judah to ignore the more fundamental urban institution in which faithfulness to Yahweh is reflected, viz., the municipal court. The prophets repeatedly drew attention to this oversight.

Deuteronomy and City Life describes Israel as an *urban culture*.[106] During the time of the ancestors, and the time of the exodus, and the time of the exile, Israel was, in fact, without land, but not without the promise of land. Israel was at times migrant, and itinerant, and pastoral, but she was not nomadic, because she was always going somewhere. The history and the life and the hope of Israel as a culture centers on Yahweh's promise to lead her into a land where she may be secure, and the core of this land with which the destiny of ancient Israel is so closely tied is the city!

23

The position it takes

Deuteronomy and City Life argues that the ten
texts in Dt 4:41--26:19 which contain the word *city*
('ir) in Hebrew developed from a segment of early
Israel which was both thoroughly urban, and thoroughly Yahwist. The Israelites who promoted these traditions encountered Yahweh in the city, and fulfilled
their obligations to Yahweh through the ordinary
institutions of city life. Although these texts are
not an urban decalogue, they emphasize the same
Yahwist values as the classic decalogues of Dt 5 and
Ex 20: Yahweh (Dt 6:10-19); worship (Dt 13:13-19);
family (Dt 21:18-21 and Dt 22:13-27); humanity
(Dt 20:10-20 and Dt 21:1-9); and neighbor (Dt 25:5-
10).[107]

This urban tradition makes no claim to be the
exclusive interpretation of Israel's identity as the
people of Yahweh. It neither affirms, nor denies the
validity of encounters with Yahweh in the deserts of
Sinai, or the towns and villages of the Shephelah.
The traditions simply regards its experience of
Yahweh as authentic, and does not consider the traditions of the desert or of the town and village to
have any priority or prestige in the formation of
Israel's religious identity.

For this tradition, the city is an *inheritance*
(nahalâ) from Yahweh: *every man to his land.*[108]
In the city, liturgical obligations are fulfilled and
the observance of the *tôrâ* is possible. Through the
city, Yahweh cares for the defenseless: defendants
charged with unwitnessed murders; victims in unsolved crimes; parents of incorrigible children;
wives accused of promiscuity; women victims of
sexual assault, and widows without heirs.

[1]Instead of *Old Testament*, the scriptures of
Ancient Israel will be identified here as the *Hebrew
Bible*, since the primary language in which these
writings were preserved was Hebrew. However,
Christianity's contact with these writings was through
the Septuagint or Greek version.

[2]New Catholic Encyclopedia, s.v. "Marcion," by
A. A. Stephenson.

[3]Gerhard F. Hasel, Old Testament Theology:
Basic Issues in the Current Debate, revised ed.
(Grand Rapids, MI.: William B. Eerdmans Publishing
Company, 1975, p. 120. See Adolf von Harnack, Marcion:
Das Evangelium vom fremdem Gott (Darmstadt:
Wissenschaftliche Buchgessellschaft, 1960: Friedrich
Delitzsch, Die grosse Täuschung, 2 vols. (Stuttgart:
Deutsche Verlags Anstalt, 1920-21); Emanuel Hirsch,
Das Alte Testament und die Predigt des Evangeliums
(Tübingen: Mohr, 1936); Rudolf Bultmann, "Prophecy
and Fulfillment," in Essays on Old Testament
Hermeneutics, ed. Claus Westermann, trans. James Luther
Mays (Richmond, VA.: John Knox Press, 1960), pp. 50-
75; Friedrich Baumgärtel, "The Hermeneutical Problem
of the Old Testament," in Essays, ed. Westermann, pp.
134-59; Franz Hesse, Das Alte Testament als Buch der
Kirche (Gütersloh: G. Mohn, 1966).

[4]Bultmann, "Prophecy," pp. 72-3.

[5]Georg Fohrer, Theologische Grundstrukturen des
Alten Testaments (Berlin: DeGruyter, 1972) and John
L. McKenzie, A Theology of the Old Testament (New
York: Doubleday and Company, 1974) are theologies
based on this assumption.

[6]Theological Dictionary of the New Testament,
s.v. "   by Herman
Strathmann.

[7]See Nu 21:25; 31:10; Jos 11:12; 2 K 3:19, etc.
All citations from the Bible are the Revised
Standard Version.

[8]TDNT, "πολις ." Cf. Phil 3:20 where *politeuma* is translated *commonwealth* in RSV.

[9]Ibid.

[10]Walther Eichrodt, Theology of the Old Testament, vol. 1, trans. J. A. Baker (Philadelphia: The Westminster Press, 1961), p. 26. Brevard S. Childs, The Book of Exodus, a critical theological commentary (Philadelphia: The Westminster Press, 1974) uses the NT to interpret Exodus.

[11]Theologisches Handwörterbuch zum Alten Testament, s.v. '*ir* by A. R. Hulst. Theologische Wörterbuch zum Alten Testament follows the same format, although as of 1981, the article on '*ir* remained unpublished.

[12]H. J. Dreyer, "The Roots QR, 'R, GR and S/TR = 'Stone, Wall, City, etc." in De Fructu Oris Sui: essays in honor of Adrianus van Selms, pp. 17-25, ed. I. H. Eybers, F. C. Fensham, C. J. Labuschagne, W. C. van Wyk and A. H. van Zyl, vol. 9: Pretoria Orienta Series (Leiden: Brill, 1971) argues that the letters *qọp (Q)* and *ayin (')* are interchangeable, and thus '*îr* may mean *what is protected by a wall [qîr]*. THAT, "'*îr*" questions Dreyer's theory, because Dt 3:5 contrasts *cities fortified with high walls* with *unwalled villages*. Thus '*ir* can mean a walled or an unwalled settlement.

[13]See Ez 38:11; Lv 25:29, 31.

[14]L. M. Muntingh, "The City which has foundations: Hebrews 11:8-10 in light of the Mari texts," in De Fructu Oris Sui, p. 108; see 1 S 15:5; 30:29.

[15]Judges 19 describes a repulsive sin in connection with Gibeah, which it says has a city square (Ju 19:15, 17), even though Tell el Ful, a site identified with Gibeah, shows only a very small village at the archeological level for 1200-1150 BCE. See Paul Lapp, "Tel el-Ful," BA 28 (1965):2-10; L. Sinclair, "An Archaeological Study of Gibeah: Tel el-Ful," AASOR 34-5 (1954-6):1-52. The narrative also contrasts *Gibeah which belongs to Benjamin* in Ju 19:14

with *this city of the Jebusites* characterized as *the city of foreigners* in Ju 19:11-12.

[16]See Am 4:1ff; Mi 6:9ff; Is 3:16ff; 5:8ff; Hb 2:12.

[17]G. Wallis, "Die Stadt in den Überlieferungen der Genesis," ZAW 78 (1966):148.

[18]Claus Westermann, Genesis, Vol. 1: Biblischer Kommentar (Neukirchen: Erziehungsverein, 1966), p. 444.

[19]See Jos 24:1-28.

[20]Dt 28:49 + 52-3.

[21]Dictionary of Biblical Theology, 2nd ed., s.v. "City," by Pierre Grelot. The original edition did not contain an article on *City* although articles on *Jerusalem* and *Babylon* gave the term some treatment.

[22]Gn 4:17.

[23]Gn 10:10 ff.

[24]Dictionary, s.v. "City."

[25]Ibid.

[26]Ac 3:12-23.

[27]Interpreter's Dictionary of the Bible, supplementary volume, s.v. "Typology," by Elizabeth Achtemeier.

[28]*Zion theology* is distinct from *Zionism*, a movement beginning at the end of the nineteenth century to establish an exclusively Jewish state. *Zionism* saw the emergence of the State of Israel in 1948 as the attainment of its goal. The two words, however, are not always distinguished.

[29] 2 S 5:16-19.

[30] Ps 48.

[31] See McKenzie, Theology, p. 27.

[32] The wording: *A mighty fortress is our God* is Martin Luther's translation of Ps 46:12, *a high spot for us*.

[33] Eichrodt, Theology, p. 469. See Lorenz Dürr, Ursprung und Ausbau der israelitsch-jüdischen Heilandserwartung (Berlin: C. A. Schwetscke & Sohn, 1925), pp. 116ff for a collection of statements about shepherds in ancient oriental royal writings.

[34] The terms *migration* and *settlement* allow for the definition of the ancestors as *village pastoralists* instead of *camel* or *ass nomads*; for only a part of the Hebrew community having *gone down* to Egypt, and later to rejoin other Hebrews who have no Egyptian experience; for the non-violent occupation by Palestine by the Hebrews; or for the Hebrews as revolutionaries within the Canaanite city state system, rather than defining them as invaders sweeping into Palestine from east Jordan. There has been so much rethinking of the pre-monarchial period that the terms *patriarchal, desert* and *conquest* no longer identify a period of history so much as a particular interpretation of that period, hence some new neutral terms without such limited definitions are necessary. Therefore, *Deuteronomy and City Life* uses the following terms to identify the periods discussed in the Hebrew Bible:

EPOCH	PRIMEVAL		Gn 1-11, etc.
MIGRATION	2,100 BCE-- 1,250 BCE	Middle & Late Bronze	Era of Ancestors
	1,250 BCE-- 1,200 BCE	Iron	Era of Moses
SETTLEMENT	1,200 BCE-- 1,000 BCE		Era of Joshua & judges

MONARCHY	1,000 BCE--922 BCE		United Kingdom
	922 BCE--722 BCE		Divided Kingdoms
	722 BCE--587 BCE		Kingdom of Judah
EXILE	587 BCE--537 BCE		Babylonian cap-
			tivity
POST-EXILE	537 BCE-- 70 BCE		Reconstruction

[35]Johannes Pedersen, Israel its Life and Culture, vol. 3, trans. A. Møller and A. I. Fausbøll (London: Cumberlege, 1946-7), p. 65.

[36]Klaus Koch, The Growth of the Biblical Tradition: the form critical method, trans. by S. M. Cupitt. Scribner Studies in Biblical Interpretation (New York: Charles Scribner's Sons, 1969), pp. 111-31.

[37]John Martin Halligan, "A Critique of the City in the Yahwist Corpus" (Ph.D. dissertation, University of Notre Dame, 1975); Frank Smith Frick, The City in Ancient Israel. SBL Dissertation Series, No. 36 (Missoula, MT.: Scholars Press, 1977), pp. 205-209.

[38]Sydney E. Ahlstrom, A Religious History of the American People, vol. 1 (Garden City, N.J.: Doubleday and Company, 1975), p. 668.

[39]Richard J. Neuhaus, Christian Faith and Public Policy (Minneapolis, MN.: Augsburg Publishing, 1977).

[40]National Federation of Priests' Councils. Hear the Cry of Jerusalem: a national urban pastoral statement. (Chicago: National Federation of Priests' Councils, 1979).

[41]David E. Anderson, "Theologians clash over Bible's stance on cities," Los Angeles Times, 21 January 1978.

[42]Harvey Cox, The Secular City: secularization and urbanization in theological perspective (New York: The Macmillan Company, 1965).

[43]Keith D. Martin, Perspectives on an Urban Theology (Washington, D.C.: Center for Theology and Public Policy, 1977), p. 4.

29

[44]Jacques Ellul, The Meaning of the City, trans. Dennis Pardee (Grand Rapids, MI.: William B. Eerdmans Publishing Company, 1970).

[45]Ronald E. Clements, Old Testament Theology: a fresh approach (Atlanta, GA.: John Knox Press, 1978), p. 110. See also, James A. Sanders, Torah and Canon, 2nd ed. (Philadelphia: Fortress Press, 1974).

[46]Martin Noth. Uberlieferungsgeschichtliche Studien, vol. 1: Die samelnden und bearbeitenden Geschichtswerke im Alten Testament (Tübingen: Max Niemeyer Verlag, 1943).

[47]Ibid., pp. 108-109.

[48]Gerhard von Rad, Studies in Deuteronomy, trans. David Stalker (Chicago: H. Regnery Co., 1953) and Old Testament Theology, trans. David Stalker (New York: Harper and Row Publishers, 1962).

[49]Like many scholars since Kuenen and Wellhausen, von Rad assumes there are at least two editions of the Deuteronomist's History, one before the destruction of Judah together with the monarchy, and one after. (See Abraham Kuenen, Historisch-kritisch Onderzoek naar het ontstaan en de verzameling van de boeken des Ouden Verbonds [Leiden: Brill, 1861-65] and Julius Wellhausen, Prolegomena to the History of Israel, trans. M. Menzies and M. Black [New York: World Publishing, Times Mirror, 1957; reprint ed., Gloucester, MA.: Peter Smith, 1973]). Since von Rad bases this analysis of the Deuteronomist's History on the pre-exilic edition, he considers passages with references to the destruction of the monarchy and the exile, like 1 K 9:6-9 and 2 K 20:17-18, secondary to that edition.

[50]2 K 25:27-30.

[51]Hans Walter Wolff, "The Kerygma of the Deuteronomic Historical Work," in The Vitality of the Old Testament Traditions, ed. Walter Brueggemann and Hans Walter Wolff (Atlanta, GA.: John Knox Press, 1975), pp. 83-100.

[52]Ibid., p. 99.

[53]Noth and von Rad consider the Deuteronomist's History written in Babylon for the exiles; Wolff, on the other hand, considers it written in Palestine for the Hebrew caretakers. See Ibid., p. 84.

[54]Frank Moore Cross, Canaanite Myth and Hebrew Epic: Essays in the History of the Religion of Israel (Cambridge, MA.: Harvard University Press, 1973), pp. 274-90.

[55]Ibid., p. 284.

[56]Ibid., p. 288.

[57]Brevard S. Childs, Introduction to the Old Testament as Scripture (Philadelphia: Fortress Press, 1979), p. 222.

[58]Interpreter's Dictionary of the Bible, supplementary vol., s.v. "Deuteronomic History, The," by David Noel Freedman.

[59]Elizabeth Achtmeier, Deuteronomy, Jeremiah, Proclamation Commentaries (Philadelphia, PA.: Fortress Press, 1978), p. 9. See also Pierre Buis, "Le Deutéronome dans le nouveau testament," in Le Deutéronome, Verbum Salutis, Ancien Testament, Vol. 4 (Paris: Beauchesne, 1969), pp. 476-81.

[60]Halligan, "Critique"; Richard J. Sklba, The Faithful City, Herald Biblical Booklets (Chicago: Franciscan Herald Press, 1976); and Frank Smith Frick, The City in Ancient Israel, SBL Dissertation Series, no. 36 (Chico, CA.: Scholars, Press, 1977).

[61]Frick, City, pp. 25-78 contains a study of the terms for *city* in the Hebrew Bible.

[62]See Gottfried Seitz, "Die maqôm Formel," in Redaktionsgeschichtliche Studien zum Deuteronomium (Stuttgart: Kohlhammer, 1971), pp. 212-222; and Frick, City, p. 45.

[63]Gustaf Adolf Danell, Studies in the name _Israel_ in the Old Testament (Uppsala, Appelbergs, boktryckeri-a.-b., 1946) considers the original _place which Yahweh chooses_, to be Shechem and the intention of the original document on which Deuteronomy is based was to discredit Jerusalem as a holy place and promote Shechem. So far, no one has verified this rivalry between Shechem and Jerusalem. In the city-text, Dt 21:18-21, _māqôm_ and _'îr_ are used as synonyms, but not in reference to Jerusalem. . . . _his father and mother shall take hold of him and bring him out to the elders of his city ('îrô) at the gate of the place where he lives (meqomô)._ (Dt 21:19)

[64]See John 11:48 "If we let him go on thus, every one will believe in him, and the Romans will come and destroy both our holy place (τον τοπον) and our nation."

[65]S. R. Driver, A Critical and Exegetical Commentary on Deuteronomy, The International Critical Commentary (Edinburgh: T. & T. Clark, 1895), p. 144 considers _gates_ and _cities_ synonyms in Deuteronomy. However, Calum M. Carmichael, The Laws of Deuteronomy (Ithaca, NY.: Cornell University Press, 1974), pp. 261-2 distinguishes the two. Gate-texts, e.g., Dt. 17:2-7 deal with matters pertaining to the internal affairs of a single urban community. City texts, Dt 13:13-19, deal with matters which pertain to Israel as a whole, which is made up of many urban communities. See also, Childs, Introduction, pp. 205-206.

[66]See Childs, Introduction, pp. 205-206.

[67]Henri Frankfort, The Birth of Civilization in the Near East (Bloomington, IN.: Indiana University Press, 1951), pp. 52-53.

[68]Carmichael, Laws, p. 129n.

[69]E. W. Nicholson, Deuteronomy and Tradition (Philadelphia: Fortress Press, 1967), p. 55.

[70]Roland de Vaux, Ancient Israel: Its Life and Institutions, trans. John McHugh (New York: McGraw

Hill Book Company, Inc., 1961), p. 68.

[71]Gustav Hölscher, "Komposition and Ursprung des Deuteronomiumn," ZAW 40 (1922):191; and Gerhard von Rad, "Das Gottesvolk im Deuteronomium," in Gesammelte Studien zum Alten Testament, vol. 2., ed. Rudolf Smend (München: Chr. Kaiser Verlag, 1973), p. 4.

[72]Dictionary of the Bible, s.v. "Jerusalem" by John L. McKenzie. Cf. A. Malamat, "Aspects of the foreign policies of David and Solomon," JNES 22 (1963): 1-17.

[73]Albrecht Alt, "Judas Gaue unter Josia," in Kleine Schriften zur Geschichte des Volkes Israel, vol. 2 (München: Beck, 1968), p. 284. See William Foxwell Albright, "The List of Levitic Cities," in American Academy for Jewish Research Louis Ginzburg Jubilee Volume (Philadelphia: Jewish Publication Society of America, 1945), pp. 49-73; and Frick, City, p. 115.

[74]Otto Bächli, Israel und die Völker: eine Studie zum Deuteronomium, ATANT, vol. 41 (Zurich: Zwingli Verlag, 1962), pp. 182-183.

[75]Five members of the Project report on its method and progress in Interpretation 27 (1973): 387-468. Co-editor of the Project, Gene M. Tucker, has an introduction: Form Criticism of the Old Testament, Guides to Biblical Scholarship, ed. J. Coert Rylaarsdam (Philadelphia: Fortress Press, 1971). Descriptions of form criticism appear in Interpreter's Dictionary of the Bible, supplementary vol., s.v. "Form Criticism, O.T.," by Gene M. Tucker; John H. Hayes, ed., Old Testament Form Criticism (San Antonio: Trinity University Press, 1974); Hermann Barth and Odil Hannes Steck, Exegese des Alten Testaments: Leitfaden der Methodik, 2nd ed. (Neukirchen-Vluyn: Neukirchener Verlag, 1971); Koch, Growth; and James Muilenberg, "The Gains of Form Criticism in Old Testament Studies," The Expository Times 71 (1960): 229-33. Applications of the method to biblical literature include: Wolfgang Richter, Recht und Ethos: Versuch seiner Ortung des Weisheitlichen Mahnspruches (München: Kösel Verlag, 1966); Georg Fohrer, Studien zur alttestamentlichen

Prophetie (Berlin: A. Topelmann, 1967); and Ernard
Gerstenberger, Wesen und Herkunft des apodiktischen
Rechts (Neukirchen-Vluyn: Neukirchener Verlag, 1965).

[76]Kathleen Kenyon, Digging up Jerusalem (New
York: Praeger, 1974), Royal Cities of the Old Testa-
ment (New York: Schocken Books, 1971), and Digging
up Jericho (New York: Praeger, 1957). See also,
James A. Sanders, ed., Near Eastern Archeology in the
Twentieth Century: essays in honor of Nelson Glueck
(Garden City, NY.: Doubleday & Co., 1970).

[77]Lewis Mumford, The City in History: its
origins, its transformations and prospects (New York:
Harcourt, Brace and World, 1961); Susan Fleiss
Loewensten, "The Urban Experiment in the Old Testament" (Ph.D. dissertation, Syracuse University, 1971),
and Frick, City.

[78]Mason Hammond, The City in the Ancient World
(Cambridge, MA.: Harvard University Press, 1972).

[79]Rolf P. Knierim, "Old Testament Form Criticism Reconsidered," Interpretation 27 (1973):436.

[80]Herman Gunkel, Genesis, 3rd ed. (Göttingen:
Vandenhoeck & Ruprecht, 1969).

[81]Andre Jolles, Einfache Formen, Legende, Sage,
Mythe, Rätsel, Spruch, Kasus, Memorabile, Märchen,
Witz (Halle: M. Niemeyer Verlag, 1930). Cf. Knierim,
"Criticism," pp. 441-2.

[82]Hammond, City, pp. 1-91, and Frick, City, pp.
171-250 study the city as an institution in the
ancient Near East.

[83]Yigael Yadin, The Art of Warfare in Biblical
Lands in the Light of Archeological Discovery (London:
Weidenfeld and Nicolson, 1963), pp. 18-19.

[84]Frick, City, p. 81; see A. Leo Oppenheim,
Ancient Mesopotamia: Portrait of a Dead
Civilization (Chicago: University of Chicago Press,
1977), p. 127.

[85]Gideon Sjoberg, The Preindustrial City: Past and Present (Glencoe, IL.: The Free Press, 1960), and Frick, City.

[86]Is 5:8.

[87]Hammond, City, p. 6.

[88]Frick, City, pp. 192 & 197.

[89]V. Gordon Childe, "Civilization, Cities and Towns," Antiquity 31 (1957):36-8.

[90]Kathleen Kenyon, Archeology in the Holy Land (New York: Frederick A. Praeger, 1960).

[91]V. Gordon Childe, What Happened in History?, rev. ed. (New York: Penguin Books, 1954).

[92]Kenyon, Cities, p. 6.

[93]Norman K. Gottwald, Tribes of Yahweh (Mary-knoll, NY.: Orbis Books, 1979), pp. 389 ff. Gottwald uses the term *feudal* advisedly when describing the economy of Canaan. There are at least three differences between feudalism in Canaan during the Amarna Age and feudalism in Western Europe during the Middle Ages. In Canaan the economic relationships between nobles and serfs is very poorly defined; in Europe it is very clearly defined. In Canaan feudalism develops while authority is being centralized and foreign trade is increasing; in Europe feudalism develops while centralized authority is disappearing and foreign trade is at an ebb. See Norman K. Gottwald, "Early Israel and 'The Asiatic Mode of Production' in Canaan," in SBL Seminar Papers, vol. 1, ed. Paul J. Achtmeier [Chico, CA.: Scholars Press, 1976], p. 145.)

[94]William Foxwell Albright, "Canaanite *hapsi* and Hebrew *hofsi*, JPOS, 6 (1926): 107, and "New Canaanite Historical and Mythological Data," BASOR, 63 (1936):29.

[95]Isaac Mendelsohn, "The Canaanite Term for *Free Proletarian*," BASOR, 83 (1941):36-9, and "New Light on the HUPSHU," BASOR, 139 (1955):9-11.

[96]Michael Heltzer, "Problems of the Social History of Syria in the Late Bronze Age," in La Siria nel Tardo Bronzo, ed. M. Liverani (Rome: Orientis Antiqui Collectio), pp. 31-46, and Horst Klengel, "Probleme einer politischen Geschichte des spätbronzeitlichen Syrien," in La Siria nel Tardo Bronzo, ed. M. Liverani (Rome: Orientis Antiqui Collectio), pp. 15-30.

[97]Gottwald, Tribes, p. 413. Giogio Buccellati, Cities and Nations of Ancient Egypt: An Essay on Political Institutions with special reference to the Israelite Kingdom, Studi Semetici, no. 26 (Rome: Instituto di Studi del Vinino Oriente, University of Rome, 1967), pp. 65-6.

[98]Gottwald, Tribes, pp. 389-488.

[99]M. B. Rowton, "Dimorphic Structure and the Problem of the *'Apiru- 'Ibrim*," JNES 35 (1976):13-20.

[100]Giorgio Buccellati, "*'Apiru AND Munnabtutu*-- The stateless of the first cosmopolitan age," JNES 36 (1977):147. See also: J. Bottero, "Le probleme des Habiru," Cahiers de la Societe Asiatique (1954): 192-8; M. Liverani, "L'estradizione dei rifugati in AT," RSO (1964):111-15.

[101]John M. Halligan, "The Role of the Peasant in the Amarna Period," in SBL Seminar Papers, vol. 1, ed. Paul J. Achtmeier (Chico, CA.: Scholars Press, 1976), p. 164.

[102]Gottwald, Tribes, p. 292.

[103]Ibid., pp. 589-90.

[104]THAT, s.v. *'ir*.

[105]Gottwald, Tribes, pp. 580-1.

[106]Walter Brueggemann, The Land: Place as gift, promise, and challenge in Biblical faith. Overtures to Biblical Theology, ed. Walter Brueggemann and John R. Donahue (Philadelphia: Fortress Press, 1977), pp. 5-6.

CHAPTER II

REVIEW OF SCHOLARSHIP

Until recently, four basic concepts controlled the interpretation of Deuteronomy: covenant, amphictyony, law and liturgy. Although each was developed from models found in city life, they are generally considered characteristic of Israel as a semi-nomadic, a non-urban people! The idealization of nomadic life as the only possible setting for the living of a truly Israelite life creates an unnecessary prejudice against considering any segment of early Israel an urban people. Therefore, the nomadic ideal and the urban aspects of covenant, amphictyony, law and liturgy need to be reviewed.

The Nomadic Ideal

The Theory

Alt calls 'the earliest level of piety in the Hebrew Bible the *god of the fathers religion*.[1] Two of his three characteristics for this religion imply a theology of the city. For Alt, the gods of the fathers do not have proper names of their own, but have names indicating a relationship to some individual human being, such as *the mighty one of Jacob* (Is 49:26) or *the fear of* . . . *Isaac* (Gn 31:53). Furthermore, the relationship of the gods of the fathers to a group of people is a more important characteristic than the god's relationship to a particular shrine or any other geographic feature. And finally, Alt considers the gods of the fathers religion characteristic of *tribes still living outside the sphere of ancient civilization*.

Now, if these ancient Hebrews believed in gods who were *not* connected with permanent shrines or cities, where religion, trade and other social events took place, then this religion was clearly *a-city* if not *anti-city*. And *if* these Hebrews lived *outside* the pale of civilization, then they were not influenced by the values of the city cultures of the ancient Near East. This *nomadic ideal* contains at least two assumptions:

39

1) every human society evolves through a fixed series of life-styles, viz., hunter, nomad, sedentary villager, then city dweller, and 2) hostility between nomadic and sedentary groups is inevitable.

Inspired by the journals of amateur anthropologists like Doughty, the nomadic idea was generally popular in the 19th century.[2] Budde studied the ideal and applied it to the Hebrew Bible.[3] Flight canonized it as the essence of Biblical religion.[4] There are still scholars who use the nomadic ideal to interpret the culture of Abraham, Moses and Joshua. For example, Schmidt devotes 81 of the 267 pages in his text to the *nomadische Vorzeit*.[5] Bronner even identifies Je 35:6-7 as five commandments, which she says are half a decalogue used by the Rechabites.[6] According to Bonner these first five commandments ordered the worship of Yahweh and prohibited the worship of Baal, the offering of wine or meal, and the building of temples.

Bronner looks for a Rechabite decalogue because she considers that genre an explicit statement of the fundamental values of early Israel; an Israel she assumes is exclusively nomadic; an Israel she considers Jeremiah to be recommending to the men of Judah and the citizens of Jerusalem. But Bronner's reconstruction is weak.[7] The directives *Worship only Yahweh* and *Do not worship Baal* are found neither in 2 K 10 nor Je 35—both critical texts for the Rechabite theory. Therefore, Bronner's first and second commandments have no textual basis. Even if they did, Bronner should count them as one and not two directives. The two are parallel, one stating positively what the other states negatively. One is a command, the other a prohibition. The remaining three directives appear only in Je 35:6-7. Bronner's exegesis makes no effort to relate these two verses form critically to Je 35:1-5 + 8ff which are integral to the unit. Finally, the Rechabites in Ne 3:14 are involved in rebuilding the city of Jerusalem

> Malchijah the son of Rechab, ruler of the district of Beth-haccerem repaired the Dung Gate; he rebuilt it and set its doors, its bolts, and its bars. (Ne 3:14)

Therefore, they have either abandoned Bronner's fifth commandment: *Build no Temple for me!* or the Rechabites in Je 35 were never very anti-urban in the first place.

The Rechabites have been considered the Puritans of ancient Israel, and their existence has been used to argue that, first and foremost, ancient Israel was nomadic, ascetic and non-urban.[8] But the presence of the Rechabites during the siege of Jerusalem is not, in itself, an argument that throughout its history segments of Israel's population remained fiercely nomadic out of loyalty to their origins and religious idealism. Their life style need not be nomadic, but only itinerant; and the purpose of their itinerant life style need not be religious, but only economic.[9] If these Rechabites are metal workers originally associated with the chariot industry they needed to move from city to city in order to find customers and from place to place in order to obtain ore and fuel. Metal workers generally camped outside the city because their industry was a noisy, dirty and hot one. But they also protected the secrets of metal work by living alone and staying sober.

But even if the Rechabites are a nomadic, ascetic and anti-urban segment of Israelite society, Jeremiah is not commending the Rechabites for any of these traits. At a time when most of Israel took houses and farms and vineyards for granted, the Rechabites are eccentric. These amenities are not despised, but considered as gifts given to Israel by Yahweh (Dt 6:10-19)! And even if the Rechabites were metal workers, their trade had long since ceased to be an itinerant and secret art. The monarchy would certainly have nationalized the bronze and iron industry to outfit its professional army. In Jeremiah's time, the military no longer depended on tinkers like the Rechabites, but built forges served by resident smiths in every city where the army was garrisoned. Thus metal working itself was now an urban art.

For Jeremiah, it is ironic that even eccentrics like the Rechabites know how to obey, while the men of Judah and the citizens of Jerusalem do not. The incongruity is clearly drawn. The Rechabites are only one small sect in Israel; the men of Judah and the citizens of Jerusalem are powerful, educated and cosmopolitan. The Rechabites are committed only to their ancestor Jonadab, Rechab's son; the men of Judah and the citizens of Jerusalem have a commitment to Yahweh. The relevance of the Rechabites' commitment for the faith of Israel is questionable: being nomadic, or itinerant or non-drinking, or anti-urban are not the essentials of Yahwism. On the other hand, the

commitment of the men of Judah and the citizens of
Jerusalem to free the slaves touches the very heart of
Yahwism, which is the exodus itself. To be a Yahwist
was to be a slave set free! Reneging on a commitment
to free slaves was the worst kind of apostasy.

A Critique

Not all Israel's ancestors are nomads

Hahn was an early critic of the nomadic ideal, but
only the more recent work of Mendenhall, Luke, Talmon,
Gottwald, Zuber, Frick and others has seriously cross-
examined the usefulness of the ideal in Biblical
studies.[10]

The settlement is a migration

In their reconstruction of the settlement period
of Israel (1200-1000 BCE), Alt and Noth both reduced
the dichotomy between Israel and the city.[11] Prior to
this reconstruction, the Albright, Wright, Bright
school saw the conflict between Israel and the city as
a duel to the death. The archeological evidence of
Albright is the strongest continuing argument for
accepting the Deuteronomic historian (Jos--2 K) at his
word, when he says in Joshua that the Hebrews swept
like a fury across Canaan, leaving the cities smolder-
ing in their wake. In the Late Bronze period (1570-
1200 BCE), the archeological sites in Canaan all show a
level of destruction, followed by a very poor period
of occupation. All this took place *prior* to the in-
vasions of the Sea Peoples (1200-1188 BCE), who were
the ancestors of the Biblical Philistines. Therefore,
in the opinion of Albright and his school, it was the
Israelites who destroyed these Late Bronze period cities
and towns like Hazor and Lachish.[12]

Noth, however, allowed the influence of the city
states to remain. According to Noth, the various
nomadic clans gradually slipped in among the city
states and little by little gained control of Canaan.
It was not a question of destroying the city, but of
absorbing it.[13]

The settlement is a revolt

For Mendenhall, Yahwism rejected the divine right of the kings who dominated 13th century cities in Palestine.[14] Because the king of the city was the delegate of the gods, any opposition to him was not simply a political offense; the opposition was a religious crime which threatened the entire process of fertility and peace.

The citizens of Palestine and Syria suffered greatly under this kind of city government. The kings were foreigners and ruthlessly selfish. The climate for revolt grew. The people drifted away from the tracts of land they were sharecropping for the king, and began to clear new land far away from the power of the kings. These communities were composed of people without any status in the feudal system which dominated the society of their day. Their common bond was not a common ancestor, nor a common race, nor a common language, but a common rejection of the right of feudal kings to exclusive ownership of the land; and the common consensus that Yahweh was the only landlord (*ḫazannu*) in Canaan. Arguing that social change, rather than migration better explains the origins of Yahwism, Mendenhall clearly allows for the presence of urban people in early and democratic Israel.[15]

The camel is not domesticated

By the 1950's, archeologists were satisfied that prior to the settlement the camel, which made life in deep desert regions possible, was still undomesticated.[16] The Assyrians considered Tiglath-Pileser I (ca. 1100 BCE) responsible for domesticating the camel, however Ju 6:5 indicates that camel nomadism on a large scale existed among the Midianites somewhat earlier. Neither of these examples, nor any of the other references to camel riding, however, coincide with the appearance of Israel in Canaan. Israel develops too early to be connected with either the domestication of the camel or travel much beyond the pasturelands used by the cities of Canaan.

Settlers become nomads, not *vice versa*

The most significant discovery in support of Mendenhall's thesis has been made by sociologists and

43

anthropologists who continue to find examples, both in ancient and modern cultures, that nomads do not move *in* and become settlers, but that settlers tend to move *out* and become nomads![17] Not all those who abandoned urban life became nomads. Some moved to more forti- fied or more fertile cities; others were simply refugees who would return to urban life.[18]

The invasion theory of the settlement proposed by Albright, and the immigration theory of the settlement proposed by Noth both assume Israel moved into the cities of Canaan and settled down, while only the revolution theory of the settlement proposed by Mendenhall assumes Israel was formed by at least some elements of the indigenous, urban culture of Palestine, whose revolution moved them into positions of power over the cities where they established a new social order.[19]

Immigrants to Canaan come from the north, not the south

According to Kempinski, some urbanization came to Canaan as the result of Egypt's interest in the rich farmlands there. But immigration to Canaan from the south was meager.[20] The kind of immigration into Canaan outlined by the exodus literature in the Hebrew Bible has no parallel.[21] Time after time, new populations appear in Palestine, but enter from the north. Abraham conforms to this pattern as he migrates to Palestine with his family from Mesopotamia in the north (Gn 12); Jacob, too, moves to Palestine from Syria in the north (Gn 31-33), and the north was the civilization of cities.[22] This northern connection increases the possibility that at least some segments of early Israel came from urban cultures.

Abraham's urban image

Albright and Gordon both picture Abraham as the governor of an urban league: a merchant prince in the service of the great cities of Syria and Mesopotamia.[23] Muntingh does not find enough Biblical evidence to call Abraham a professional merchant. Muntingh con- siders him a rancher who has pasture rights some distance from his village home, and to which he seasonally drives his flocks and herds. Nonetheless, Abraham is still not a nomad.[24]

44

Until the libraries of Ebla were discovered at
Tell Mardikh, Syria during 1974-75, the cities named
as Abraham's allies in Gn 14 were completely unknown, and hence this picture of Abraham presented as
an urbanite was questionable.[25] Now, however, these
same cities appear on the tax rolls of Ebla making
their existence more certain, and the image of
Abraham the urbanite more credible. Thus the urbanization of Israel's ancestors continues.[26]

The city and the country are complementary

In pre-industrial cultures

Mendenhall's research made it unnecessary to
automatically assume the Israelites were once nomads.
But even some scholars who do *not* consider Israel's
ancestors to be nomads, use the nomadic ideal. For
example, van Seters draws a sharp contrast between
sedentary and nomadic ways of life in order to argue
that Israel's ancestors show far too many sedentary
characteristics to be nomads.[27] Nonetheless, even
for these scholars, the city and the country were
still considered enemies. They continued opposing the
people, the values, the religions, the industries
and the life styles of the city and country,
especially in ancient Israel.

Sjoberg, a sociologist, questioned this
assumption.[28] Such a dichotomy between city and
country was possible, according to him, only in the
post-industrial era, i.e., after the late 18th century
CE! Earlier the city and country were part of a
single economic, social and religious unit. In pre-
industrial times farmers lived in the city and went
to the farms only for work. Cities depended upon the
farms to provide them with goods to maintain themselves and to provide a surplus on which an urban
culture could be built. Cities protected the farmers'
crops, offered farmers homes and markets for their
harvests, and the benefits of other skills, such as
metal work, pottery making, cloth weaving, etc., which
farmers themselves, as specialists, no longer had time
to practice. According to Sjoberg, there may have
been divisions in pre-industrial cities between rich
and poor, between powerful and weak, between military
and civilian, between governing and governed, but
there was no conflict between the citizen and the

farmer.

In ancient Israel

Frick tested Sjoberg's sociological theory with the Biblical data on the cities of ancient Israel.[29] According to Frick, Biblical farmers and citizens were part of a unified social structure. The city in ancient Israel emerged as the result of social reorganization. When a class of people appeared who through their ability, strength, and cunning could get surplus crops and cattle away from farmers and herders, urbanization began.

In Mari

Archeologists like Kupper, studying Mari, a Semitic culture which flourished west of Canaan from 2600-1757 BCE, also questioned the city-country dichotomy.[30] At Mari, the nomadic segments of the society were related politically to the settled segments of society, but they did not settle down and become villagers like their kinsmen. When hostility existed between the nomadic and the settled segments of Mari culture, it was the result of political competition and not some radical hostility between city and country. This particular kind of movement is not *nomadism* in the strict sense of the word, but *transhumanence,* i.e., migration in search of pastures as the seasons change.[31] Rowton distinguishes transhumanence which he calls *enclosed nomadism,* from *external nomadism.*[32]

Conclusions

Such research has made one Biblical scholar after the other wonder if the Israel who survived in the desert only through miracles, and who clung so tenaciously to the promise of a homeland in which to settle down, could be anything but a refugee.[33] The assumption that city dwellers were once nomads or that city dwellers and nomads are ancient enemies is no longer necessary in Biblical studies.[34] The city provides not only *an experience of Yahweh,* but a *language* with which to express the significance of that experience, and *a model of the community* in which

Israel responded to that experience. Israel's posi-
give experience of Yahweh in the desert was not
compromised by a negative experience of Yahweh in the
city. It was Israel's positive experience of Yahweh
in the city which was highlighted by her experience
of Yahweh in the desert.[35]

Baly demonstrates this collateral function of the
desert for the faith of Israel in his discussion of
"The Geography of Monotheism."[36] Nineteenth century
scholars were convinced that the uniform vastness of
the desert was the incentive for Israel's belief in
one god. Baly, however, points out that most desert
dwellers are polytheists.[37] Monotheism, according to
Baly, have never developed in desert cultures;
monotheism always develops in cities! It is not the
desert alone, but the stark contrast between Israel's
city and desert experiences which prepared Israel for
monotheism. Societies limited to one environment--
whether desert or urban--worship the elements and
cycles of that environment to stay alive and maintain
order. Because she survived in both environments, it
was clear to Israel that nature was not a key to her
existence.[38]

The Urban Alternative

Genres for Deuteronomy

Covenant

According to von Rad, writing in 1938, Dt 25:5b-
9 outlines Gn-Ex-Lv-Nu-Dt-Jos.[39] Von Rad identified
this brief summary of the things Yahweh had done for[48]
Israel as a *creed*. Because Dt 26:5-9 does not
mention the Sinai traditions, von Rad argued that the
exodus traditions in this creed and the Sinai traditions developed separately. The exodus traditions
developed at the shrine in Gilgal; the Sinai traditions at Shechem. Only during the time of the
monarchy in Israel (1000-587 BCE) were the two traditions joined to form the canonical sequence in the
Hebrew Bible.

Von Rad's double-tradition theory is frequently
questioned.[41] However, his argument that both traditions followed a common pattern has been more

favorably received. This pattern in the exodus and
Sinai traditions also intrigued Mendenhall. He
suggested that Israel inherited the pattern from the
Hittites, who were an Indo-European and not a Semitic
people like Israel, and who flourished in contemporary
Turkey from 1570-1200 BCE. Mendenhall argued that the
pattern followed in Ex 19--24 and the pattern
followed in the treaties which Hittites made with
their urban colonies (*suzerainty treaties*) were related. Korošec did the initial studies cataloging
the elements of these Hittite treaties, and
Mendenhall accepted his results.[42] This classic
analysis includes six parts. The Hittite king introduces himself to his new colony using a litany of
titles which he has won. This component of the treaty
is the *titulary*. The king then reminds the colony of
all the ways in which he has enriched its economy and
guaranteed its security. This component is the
history. Then the king imposes obligations on the
colony. Korošec called this component the *stipulations*. The *document clause,* which follows the
stipulations, requires the treaty be written down,
filed in a sanctuary, and read publicly in the colony
from time to time. The *God list* records the names of
the gods by whom the king and the representatives of
the colony swore when they ratified the treaty, and
finally there is a section of *blessings and curses*.
The blessings itemize the rewards the colony will receive for fulfilling the treaty, and the curses indicate the penalties which the colony will incur for
violating the treaty.[43]

What Mendenhall's study proposed was that von
Rad's creed is not an independent literary pattern
with a particular setting all its own. The creed was
originally only the titulary and history (elements
#1, 2) of the covenant pattern. Sinai traditions
originally were elements #3, 4, 5, 6. Exodus and
Sinai traditions were subdivisions of one genre.
According to Wright, they were separated from one
another during the monarchy![44]

McCarthy studied 3,000 Ancient Near Eastern
treaties, among which are the Hittite treaties between
equals, between sovereigns and vassals as well as
Syrian and Assyrian treaties. He concludes that while
there are variations in details, such as the ter-
minology used in the treaties, and the function of
the various elements in the form, there was a common
treaty form used throughout the Ancient Near East.
He identifies Dt 5--28 as a *covenant,* which is

supported by the technical language in Dt 28:1-2 + 15.

> And if you obey the voice of the Lord your
> God, being careful to do all his command-
> ments which I command you this day, the
> Lord your God will set you high above all
> the nations of the earth. And all these
> blessings shall come upon you and overtake
> you, if you obey the voice of the Lord
> your God [*this blessing (#6) is a reward
> for obeying the covenant*]. . . . But if
> you will not obey the voice of the Lord
> your God or be careful to do all his
> commandments and his statutes which I
> command you this day, then all these
> curses shall come upon you and overtake
> you [*this curse (#6) is a punishment for
> disobeying the covenant*].

However, historical contacts between the
Hittites and the Israelites are hard to establish.
McCarthy also questions the credentials of Ex 19--24
as a treaty, since some important elements of the
Hittite genre are missing.[45]

Since its appearance in the 1950's, contemporary
covenant studies have enthusiastically pursued a
variety of questions. For example, Baltzar did a
careful form critical analysis of the covenant genre,
and was convinced that Deuteronomy as a whole, as
well as particular parts of it such as Dt 1:1--4:40
(41-43) and 28:69--30:20 were modeled according to the
Ancient Near Eastern treaty form.[46] In some places
only fragments of the full covenant form remain, such
as the history, or the blessings and curses. Kline
followed Baltzar's argument that every treaty was
initially recorded (Dt 31:9) and then a duplicate of
that record made and read periodically to suggest
that the stones in Dt 4:13 were the original record
of Israel's vassal treaty with Yahweh, and
Deuteronomy the duplicate read periodically to the
people.[47] Weinfeld considers Deuteronomy a creative
piece of nostalgia designed by the scribes of
Hezekiah's and Josiah's courts. These 8th and 7th
century sages used the Assyrian treaties of their time
as patterns into which they worked the covenant
motifs of ancient Israel.[48]

What is interesting about this discussion of the
covenant genre is that, although the Hittite empire
was an urban culture, and although the covenant genre

is an urban instrument, Israel is assumed to be a completely nomadic or semi-nomadic culture. There is no attempt to explain why such a completely nomadic or semi-nomadic culture describes her fundamental relationship with Yahweh in such urban terms.

Law

Alt is another scholar, publishing in the 1930's, who used urban models in his research.[49] Alt studied two genres: he called one *case law*; and the other *apodictic law*. The form of case law is clear and distinct: a situation is described and a sentence is imposed. For example: *If a man is found lying with the wife of another man* [=situation] *both of them shall die* [=sentence]. . . . (Dt 22:22) The form of apodictic law, however, is far from uniform. For example, Alt catalogued each of the following forms as apodictic law. *Whoever strikes a man so that he dies shall be put to death* (Ex 21:12). *Cursed be he who dishonors his father or his mother* (Dt 27:16). *You shall do no injustice in judgment* (Lv 19:15).[50]

By over-identifying genre with grammatical form, Alt committed himself to radically different settings for each, despite the fact that case law and apodictic law occur side by side in the Hebrew Bible, and even meld in a single text.[51] *But if a man willfully attacks another to kill him treacherously* [=case law], *you shall take him from my altar that he may die* [=apodictic law] (Ex 21:14). According to Alt, case law originated as an instrument of the settled and highly developed culture of Palestine.[52] More than once, subsequent scholarship has verified that case law was common to the urban cultures of the Ancient Near East.[53] On the basis of texts like Dt 27:15-26, Alt argued that apodictic law originated in a liturgy celebrating the alliance between Yahweh and Israel.

> And Moses charged the people the same day, saying, 'When you have passed over the Jordan, these shall stand upon Mount Gerizim to bless the people: Simeon, Levi, Judah, Issachar, Joseph, and Benjamin. And these shall stand upon Mount Ebal for the curse: Reuben, Gad, Asher, Zebulun, Dan, and Naphthali. And the Levites shall declare to all the men of Israel with a loud voice: "Cursed be the man who makes

a graven or molten image, an abomination
to the Lord, a thing made by the hands of
a craftsman, and sets it up in secret."
And all the people shall answer and say,
"Amen." . . .' (Dt 27:11-15).

According to Alt, apodictic law is authentically
Israelite in content and uniquely liturgical in form.

Alt's penchant for assigning distinct settings
for each grammatical form is reinforced by his conviction that early Israel was a completely non-urban
society. Therefore, municipal traditions like case
law were not authentically Israelite, but were
adapted to the Yahwist faith. Alt's analysis of the
origins of law in Israel reflects the nomadic ideal
which assumes that Israel stood against its urban
environment instead of being part of its urban environment. This dichotomy between city and desert,
secular and sacred in ancient Israel is unnecessary
and artificial, even though it appears not only in
Alt, but in the studies of Albright and Wright and
others as well.[54]

Yet similarities between Israel and other forms
of Canaanite culture such as Ur in Lebanon and Ebla
in Syria are thoroughly revising definitions of
Israel's uniqueness. Israel may not have been a
logical evolution in Canaanite culture; Israel may
have been a radical reaction to the direction the
culture was taking, but that reaction took place
within the culture, and not outside that culture.
Therefore, Israel could easily continue aspects of the
culture of Canaan, such as the city, to which Israel
had no objections. Limiting membership in Israel to
the rural or nomadic elements of Canaanite society,
as Alt does, is an oversimplification. Without a
categorical commitment to identifying a radically
different setting for each grammatical form, and to
the nomadic ideal, it is unnecessary to assume that
case law arose in the city, while apodictic law arose
in the desert. Since they are so closely related in
the Hebrew Bible, it is possible that the urban
setting which has been so clearly demonstrated for
case law, is also applicable to apodictic law.

According to Gerstenberger, apodictic law was
used in the public worship of Israel, as Alt suggests,
but probably originated elsewhere. Gerstenberger
himself sets apodictic law in the teaching traditions
of the extended family (*Sippenethos*).[55] Because many

assume the city destroys family life, *the* family
setting in Israel is considered to be the *tribal*
family setting, and *the tribal* family setting is
nomadic, not urban.[56] However, it is possible to
accept Gerstenberger's argument that the prohibition
originated in the family, without arguing that it
originated in the nomadic family rather than in the
urban family.[57] According to Frick, it is only
scholars of *industrial cities* in the 18th century
Western nations, such as Wirth, who argue that urbanization dissolves the primary bonds which unite
people through family ties and replaces these bonds
with such secondary relationships as profession,
place of residence and economic status.[58] Frick argues that during the monarchy, both land and politics
were dominated not by individuals but by large and
tightly-knit families. The credentials of these
families were established primarily by a record of
stability and excellence within the Hebrew community,
preserved in the genealogies. The centrality of the
family during this period, according to Frick, is emphasized by two well-attested institutions: the inheritance (*naḥălâ*) and the Levirate law.

According to Frick, the inheritance was a tract
of land which could have been surveyed only during the
period of the monarchy and was inherited only by a
family. This inheritance was not passed on simply to
an individual whose ability or strength or cunning
may have set him above his peers. According to Frick,
the Levirate law, requiring the next male of kin to
have intercourse with a sonless widow until a male
heir was born, is likewise based on a strong respect
for family integrity. The male heir was necessary to
keep the inheritance intact. Frick's conclusions
coincide completely with the sociological obser-
vations of Sjoberg.[59]

McKay not only considers the city the setting of
the prohibitive and case law; he considers them both
to be genres which developed primarily in the
municipal court. The use of the prohibitive in
liturgy, as Alt has suggested, and in the family, as
Gerstenberger has suggested, is secondary. McKay
draws these conclusions from his study of Ex 23:1-3+
6-8, which he considers a decalogue of prohibitives
used to inform both judges officially appointed to the
municipal courts, and elders of the city temporarily
deputized to serve the court either as judges or
witnesses.[60]

Therefore, without the prejudice of the nomadic ideal, there is no need to assume that setting apodictic law in the extended family means setting apodictic law in an extended nomadic family. Apodictic law can still reflect Israel's uniquely religious heritage in an urban setting, viz., the extended *urban* family. Therefore, both casuistic and apodictic genres can have urban settings in authentically Yahwist communities, and there is no need to assume they appear together in the Hebrew Bible for the purpose of adapting Israel's nomadic way of life to a foreign urban culture.

Parenesis

In 1907, Klostermann pioneered the identification Deuteronomy as *preached law*, a genre with a liturgical setting.[61] This identification of Deuteronomy as *preached law*--not the kind used in a court, but quoted in a sermon--became standard. Von Rad was most responsible for promoting *preaching* as the genre best describing this unique literature in Deuteronomy. From his initial essay in 1929 until the appearance of his commentary in 1965, von Rad continued to refine this definition.[62] Parenesis was considered interchangeable with preaching as a description of Deuteronomy.

However, in 1978, Tiffany carefully reviewed the studies of both Deuteronomy and parenesis, pointing out that seventy years of active scholarship on these two closely-related problems produced neither a clear definition of parenesis nor any agreement on the genre to which Deuteronomy belongs.[63] Tiffany considers *preaching*, *sermon* and *parenesis* to be varieties of *rhetoric*. Preaching and parenesis have many different settings, while sermon always has a cultic setting.[64] *Sermon* and *preaching* have a variety of intentions. When the intention is to present the essentials of the faith the genre is *kerygma*.[65] When the intention is to proclaim promises and demands which Yahweh makes on Israel, his people, the genre is *paraclesis*. When the intention is to teach norms of conduct which have already been promulgated, the genre is *instruction*. When the intention is to encourage compliance with the law, the genre is *parenesis*. Therefore, Tiffany concludes, *parenesis* is only one of the many elements of *preaching* or *sermon*; one is not identical with the other.

53

Rather than describing Deuteronomy as *preached law*, Tiffany prefers *preaching about the law*.[66] As *preaching*, Deuteronomy may or may not have a setting in the cult. As *preaching*, Deuteronomy may intend to present the essentials of the faith; proclaim promises and demands which Yahweh makes on Israel, his people; teach norms of conduct; or encourage compliance with these norms. Only when Deuteronomy intends to encourage, advise or counsel its audience to follow a particular norm of conduct is it *parenesis*.

The settings in which Tiffany considers parenesis to be operating in Deuteronomy--king, priest, parent--are primarily urban settings, not nomadic or semi-nomadic settings. Likewise, the laws, which the parenesis in Deuteronomy assumes, have developed primarily in urban, and not nomadic or semi-nomadic settings. And, finally, the use of parenesis reflects a clear preference for persuasion, rather than coercion to achieve cooperation. *Parenesis* shows a respect for individuality, while recognizing the importance of harmony. Each segment of the community must cooperate in order for the community itself to survive.[67] The importance of harmony and cooperation in a fixed community are clearly urban virtues. There is little to be gained from the use of force, or breaking up the community and moving on in different directions. Without the prospect of new resources, or new frontiers, the urban community must take advantage of the resources at hand. *Parenesis* was an important means of attaining that end.

Settings for Deuteronomy

Liturgy

In 1878, Wellhausen found no unified social structure monitoring *all* Israel during the pre-monarchial period (1200-1000 BCE).[68] Since there are Biblical traditions older than the monarchy, interested not just in particular families or cities, but Israel as a whole, Alt wanted to know how these traditions developed without some unified social structure.[69] In 1930, Alt's student, Noth, proposed that the social structure integrating the traditions of sub-groups in Israel was an *amphictyony*.[70] The traditions of the amphictyony include a strong respect for covenant law; the practice of holy war; and

the use of charismatic leadership, rather than
monarchy, as a preferred form of government.

The primary examples of amphictyonies are the
urban leagues which developed among the Greek and
Italian city states.[71] Therefore, the amphictyony is
an urban institution. Nonetheless, Noth considers the
Israel which used this urban institution a semi-nomadic
people, who would only become urbanized under the
monarchy. In fact, Buccellati rejects Noth's comparison between the social structure of ancient Israel
and the Greek Amphictyonies, precisely because these
urban leagues require the settled conditions of an
urban culture.[72]

The Biblical examples of the traditions connected
with the amphictyony show a close connection with city
life. For example, covenants--as was argued above--
are the legal instruments of urban empires. Many of
the stipulations which these Biblical covenants impose
are to be adjudicated at the city gates! In addition,
Noth's primary example of the Biblical amphictyony
engaged in holy war involves cities (Ju 19--20)! And
finally, it is the city of Shechem, which in Ju 9 shows
a clear preference for charismatic leadership over
the monarchy of Abimelek. Even Noth's association of
the amphictyony with the ancient city of Shechem, on
the basis of Dt 27 and Jos 8:30, should argue that the
amphictyony was an urban institution.[73] The other
centers of the amphictyony--Bethel, Shiloh and Gilgal--
are also cities, whose municipal courts continue to be
important even in the time of Samuel.[74] Therefore,
Noth's theory would be far easier to understand if at
least some of the corporate members of early Israel
were urban. Then Israel could have developed
amphictyonies on the basis of the previous experience
which these segments of the population had enjoyed in
the urban leagues in Canaan!

The particular social institution within the
amphictyony, which most scholars consider responsible
for traditions like those preserved in Deuteronomy is
liturgy. Mowinckel and Gunkel originally focused
attention on the importance of public worship in
Biblical interpretation.[75]

Mowinckel in 1921-24 used the new year's festival
celebrated for the Babylonian god--Marduk, as a model
for his theory that Yahweh was annually enthroned in
Israel.[76] This enthronement festival was the axis of

Israel's liturgical year. According to Hooke, the
theology of the festival was parallel to dying-and-
rising celebrations held annually by most Ancient Near
Eastern peoples. The earth and the god responsible
for life on the earth died each year, and were brought
back to life through a ritual marriage. The king--as
the divine deputy--played a prominent role in this
ceremony.[77] Because this ceremony was the major feast
of the entire year, his part in the liturgy was considered the king's most important function.[78]
Eventually, according to Engnell, the king's role as
the divine deputy was replaced by the theology of the
king as divine.[79] The *suffering servant* in Is 52-3 is
an example of how Israel adapted this theology to her
culture.

> Behold my servant shall prosper,
>   he shall be exalted and lifted up
>   and shall be very high . . . .
>
> He was oppressed, and he was afflicted . . . .
>
> Yet it was the will of the Lord to bruise him
>   . . . .
>
>   because he poured out his soul to death
>   and was numbered with the transgressors;
> yet he bore the sins of many
>   and made intercession for the transgressors.
>   (Is 52:13 + 53:7,12b)

The servant's death and resurrection saves Israel.
Engnell considers many of the references to the king
as *messiah*, indications of Israel's practice of the
theology of divine kingship, and her faith in the
ability of the king to save the people.

A liturgical setting need not imply a rural or
anti-urban setting, although that assumption is frequently made. Wellhausen's scholarship influenced
this assumption. In 1878, he chronologically
arranged the sources of Gn-Ex-Lv-Nu-Dt according to a
principle of liturgical evolution. According to
Wellhausen, liturgy in Israel developed from a fasci-
nation with nature through a very laity-oriented
series of ethical and moral customs to a very ritual
religion watched over by the hierarchy.[80] The more
abstract or separated from nature the religious practices reflected in the source, the later the time of
their development. It is easy to infer from

Wellhausen's principle that early worship, because it is nature worship is rural or anti-urban worship. However, as Sjoberg and Frick have shown, cities in antiquity were agriculturally based. Urban worship was extremely concerned with good crops and herds.

The Canaanites in the Hebrew Bible are clearly urban people, yet their worship is preoccupied with nature. Israel was not trying to counteract the natural religion of the Canaanites. The tension between Israel and Canaan had to do with the kind of nature religion which would best guarantee Palestine's fertility.[81] The distinction between Israel and Canaan is not whether to worship in the desert and country or in cities. In fact, cities were a favorite place for all segments of the population to pray, regardless of their lifestyle. Cities and sanctuaries were partners in the Ancient Near East.[82] Even the sanctuary built outside the city, was connected to the city by a sacred road, and was considered an integral part of urban life.[83]

West Semitic mythology reinforced this connection between the city and the liturgy because it regarded cities as the wives of various gods.[83] The understanding developed from the tradition--unique to the West Semitic culture to which Israel belonged--which considered cities as women. Even when no male consort is mentioned in any written sources, Phoenician coins always depict cities as women, and the title *mistress* is used interchangeably for goddesses and cities. Many cities carried the feminine form of the god-husband's name, e.g., *ba'ălâ* (Jos 15:9); *aštarôt* (Jos 9:10). This *Mr.* (the god) and *Mrs.* (the city) pattern developed from the Ancient Near Eastern custom of considering gods and goddesses as married. From the West Semitic cultures, the city-as-a-woman tradition influenced the cultures of the east Semitic family like Assyria, and cultures, like Greece, to the west. Such an intimate relationship between the city and the god made public worship an essential part of urban life.

References to prominent cities as *mothers*, and the towns within their spheres of influence as *daughters* in the Hebrew Bible illustrate Israel's use of the city-as-a-woman tradition.[84] Jerusalem is a *woman*, and heresy is *adultery*. The prophets also use the tradition to describe the cruel and unusual violence which Israel is to suffer for her sins. She was not simply to be beaten by an equal, but battered

57

by her husband.[85]

Since the city-as-a-woman tradition presumed close contact between liturgy and the city, Israel during the monarchy certainly did not consider her worship rural or anti-urban. In the pre-monarchy as well, the city and the liturgy were complementary. Studying 1 S 20:1-42, Pedersen concludes that the city was as important a liturgical community as one's extended family.[86]

In 1 S 9, the urban liturgy consists in a meal presided over by Samuel, and during which Saul is designated king. In Ju 9:27, the harvest is brought to the city where a celebration is held and Abimilech is rejected as king. The city of Shiloh celebrated its wine harvest with a circle dance (Ju 21:21), and the city of Mizpah observed a feminist moratorium in honor of Jephthah's daughter (Ju 11:39). As a rule, citizens were bound to attend only the celebrations of their own city, however some cities were centers of pilgrimage as 1 S 1-2, Am 4-5, Ho 13, and 1 K 19 indicate.

Furthermore, two very ancient cities--Bethel (Gn 12:8; 13:3-4) and Shechem (Gn 12:6-7; 33:18-20; Jos 24)--are sites where Yahweh directs Abraham to establish liturgies! Bethel was a city founded around 2000 BCE, at least a century before Abraham, and Shechem was already a city in 4000 BCE.[87] Abraham's worship at such venerable metropolitan centers commemorates their hospitality and holiness, not their hostility to his own way of life. Therefore, it is unlikely that Abraham's worship was considered rural or anti-urban.

The definitive association of Deuteronomy with liturgy was made in 1938 by von Rad. He argued the liturgical character of Deuteronomy with three kinds of evidence.

First, Deuteronomy uses the formula *today (hayyôm)* to create a liturgical present. Von Rad refers to the *immediacy (Anliegen)* of the event; *resolute synchronism (diese entschlossene Gleichzeitigkeit)*; and *emphatic contemporaneity for all succeeding generations of what occurred at Sinai (diese betonte Gleichzeitigkeit des Sinaigeschehens für alle nachfolgenden Generationen)* to describe the characteristic.[88] More so than any other book in the

Hebrew Bible, Deuteronomy upholds the ability of believers to take part in the saving events of the past
and can therefore radically change their future.[89]
Von Rad concludes that only liturgically can the past
and the future be telescoped into a single moment.

Second, both Exodus and Deuteronomy assume that
Yahweh will not speak directly with Israel, but
through a liturgical minister. Von Rad considers
this characteristic an explanation (etiology) of the
prophet's function in the public worship of Israel,
viz., to speak for Yahweh. Von Rad concludes that
vicarious experience of Yahweh is always liturgical.

Finally, adopting the research of Klostermann,
von Rad considers Dt 1--11 to be parenesis: a genre
which accompanies the recitation of history and introduces the proclamation of law in Israel.[90] Von Rad
concludes that such recitation and proclamation occur
exclusively in liturgy.

Both Mowinckel and von Rad associate this
liturgical setting for Ex 19--24 and Dt with cities.
Mowinckel located the liturgy with Jerusalem, but
according to von Rad, he used too many texts not connected with the Sinai tradition to support his conclusion.[91] Von Rad, on the other hand, limits himself to texts from the Sinai tradition, such as Jos
8, 24; Dt 11, 27, and argues that Shechem, and not
Jerusalem is the site of this celebration. Von Rad
substantiates his conclusion by combining elements
from the liturgy described in Jos 8 with those in
Jos 24 arriving at the same pattern used in Ex 19--
24 and Dt.

A liturgical setting for Deuteronomy is
attractive because in liturgy more than one
specialized interest in Israel is acknowledged and
absorbed. Since Deuteronomy has access to traditions
from Israel's entire walk of life, a liturgy in which
parents, teachers, priests, lawyers, prophets and
kings were expected to participate is a likely
setting. Even if Deuteronomy developed within a
particular segment of Hebrew culture, or a particular
social institution, it would still have passed
through a long period of repetition, oral and
written, and would have benefitted by the work of a
variety of anonymous contributors.

Baltzar has argued that the document found in
the temple (2 K 22) was the text of a covenant and not

the work of an individual or any circle acting in a purely private capacity.[92] In the early 19th century, DeWette had argued that Deuteronomy was instant literature, hurriedly written and hidden by temple personnel in the area being renovated by king Josiah.[93] This pious fraud was a well-meaning effort to influence the king and endorse his reform. Albright discarded DeWette's theory since literature throughout the Ancient Near East is never the work of a single artist or composed impulsively on a moment's notice.[94] Ancient literature is developed and preserved by the institutions of a culture.[95]

Baltzar wanted to determine the theoretical elements of the covenant form in order to appreciate the particular variations of the form in the structures of individual covenant texts. He presumes that the general characteristics of covenant texts are identical. He also argues that, like the Hittite treaties, the Old Testament covenant was written down.

> And Moses *wrote (wayyiktob)* this law, and
> gave it to the priests the sons of Levi,
> who carried the ark of the covenant of
> the Lord, and to all the elders of Israel.
> And Moses commanded them, . . . you shall
> read this law before all Israel in their
> hearing. (Dt 31:9)

A duplicate of the official copy was periodically read to the people. Baltzar is convinced that the Old Testament was aware of the covenant form, and that Deuteronomy as a whole and various parts of it were modeled according to the Ancient Near Eastern treaty, e.g., Dt 1:1--4:40 (41-43); 28:69--30:20 and in some places only fragments of the full covenant form, i.e., the pre-history, the curses and blessings etc., are present.

However, Wright, studying Gn-Ex-Lv-Nm, questions liturgy's *creative* role in the development of the community literature of Israel: . . . *does cult ever really create historical tradition, or does it only reshape, reformulate, supplement, while even adding aetiological details to something already in existence?*[96] Is the liturgy of Israel simply an archive which catalogues and stores the literature developed by other institutions?

This function of liturgy as curator, rather than

as creator of traditions in Israel is implicit in Lohfink's identification of the final form of Deuteronomy, not as *narrative*, not as *law code* as Wellhausen did, nor *ritual* as von Rad, nor *covenant document* as McCarthy, but rather as *archive*. For Lohfink, an archive is a collection of documents placed one beside the other, each with its title to indicate the contents. Lohfink admits that it is a prosaic and common form, but suggests that Deuteronomy in its final form presents itself as an archive--a collection of what Moses uttered during the last days of his life.[97]

Wright disagreed with European scholars who assigned so many of the genres in the Hebrew Bible a liturgical setting.[98] Wright did not deny that much of the literature in the Hebrew Bible was used in the liturgy, but that was not its original setting. According to Wright the liturgy had no interest in the detail found in legends like Gn 12-50 and Ex 1--15 or the heroics in Ju 3--16. Wright's critique of the liturgy as a creative setting exempts Deuteronomy, but he certainly could have included it. Just as Wright asked what interest the liturgy has in the story-teller's detail in narratives from Gn, Ex, Lv, Nm, he could also have asked what interest the liturgy has, for example, in the sophisticated distinctions and complicated procedures set down in the ten city texts. Did the liturgy create these traditions, or was the liturgy transformed and shaped by these traditions which it borrowed from some other creative urban institution?[99] The liturgy, no doubt, is a factor in Deuteronomy, as it is a factor in much of the literature in the Hebrew Bible. Liturgy was a setting which borrowed a genre like Deuteronomy more often than the setting which developed the genre in the first place.[100] Liturgy does not set the tone for life; life sets the tone for liturgy. The liturgy celebrates the accomplishments of the daily life of its congregation, and motivates that congregation to new objectives, not within the liturgy itself, but in daily life. As Bächli argues, liturgy does not develop as an island, but is simply one means used by the king along with preaching, law and power, to protect Israel from contamination.[101]

Monarchy

According to Bächli, Deuteronomy wants Israel quarantined (*die Abwehrung*) from other nations.

Through the proper use of the urban institutions of *preaching, law, liturgy* and *government,* the king--as spokesman for the property owners (*'am hā'areṣ*)-- sponsors the reform. Bächli is much too specific in limiting Israel's hostility toward outsiders to the period of Josiah, when the Edomites, Moabites, and Ammonites were harassing her. As community literature, Deuteronomy draws on attitudes aged more than one generation. Therefore, Bächli's analysis of the thoroughly urban orientation of Deuteronomy and its traditions should not be restricted to the 7th century BCE. Israel considered herself an urban people long before.

The significance of the king and of Jerusalem in the development of Deuteronomy are outstanding among Bächli's conclusions. The monarchy is not an after-thought in Israel's development; it is integral to her structure as the people of Yahweh. Deuteronomy 17:14-20 does not restrict the king, it protects his honor as the steward and the proclaimer of the law, designated by Yahweh. *You may indeed set as king over you him whom the Lord your God will choose* (Dt 17:15) assumes the king is designated by Yahweh, although even in Judah, the property owners frequently influenced his selection. According to Bächli, Alt limited Deuteronomy to a northern setting because he considered Israel the only Hebrew state with a monarch chosen by the people.[102] Bächli considers this limitation unnecessary.

Deuteronomy assumes the king is the keeper and the proclaimer of the law.

And when he sits on the throne of this king-dom, he shall write for himself in a book, a copy of this law, from that which is in the charge of the Levitical priests; and it shall be with him, and he shall read in it all the days of his life that he may learn to fear the Lord his God, by keeping all the words of this law and these statutes . . . . (Dt 17:18-19)

The king is not, according to Bächli, being assigned the personal piety of Torah reading, but the liturgical responsibility of reading the law aloud for the good of the entire community.[103] This is precisely the function which Deuteronomy's hero Josiah performs.

And the king went up to the house of the
Lord, and with him all the men of Judah
and all the inhabitants of Jerusalem, and
the priests and the prophets, all the
people, both small and great; and he read
in their hearing all the words of the book
of the covenant which had been found in
the house of the Lord.   (2 K 23:2)

Bächli validates his emphasis on the king with
the Deuteronomic historian's evaluation of the entire
histories of Israel and Judah solely on the basis of
the king's performance in liturgical matters.

As advocates of urban life, the kings could certainly have promoted the cosmopolitan description of
Israel assumed in Deuteronomy.[104] According to
Bächli, Deuteronomy does not idealize Israel's time
in the desert. Civilization is not a heresy, it is
Israel's heritage from Yahweh. There is no back-to-
the-desert movement in Deuteronomy. Israel becomes
the people of Yahweh not by returning to the desert,
but by joyfully accepting the gift of the land with
its farms and pastures and settlements and cities.[105]
Deuteronomy does not even isolate Israel's time in the
desert and treat it as a separate tradition.
Deuteronomy simply regards Israel's desert period as
one phase of the exodus![106]

As the chief of state (*der höchste Staatsbeamte*),
the king would have access to the required traditions.
To account for the presence of teaching, liturgical,
legal and military material in Deuteronomy, Bächli
argues that in Israel, only the king qualifies as
master teacher, high priest, chief justice and supreme
commander. However, Bächli's position that Dt 17:14-
20 has a positive and not a negative attitude toward
the king, that it protects (*Vorsichtmassnahmen*) the
king rather than restricts him, is maverick.
Immunizing the king was important in the royal
theology of Assyria.[107] However, the courtiers who
served David and Solomon were administrators, not
doctors and wizards.[108] A court of administrators
rather than spiritualists was common in Babylon, where
the palace and temple were separated and the king
exercised only civil authority. In Assyria, Syria,
Asia Minor and Palestine, however, the king was considered a divine deputy who performed many liturgical
services. Therefore in these cultures, the temple
and the palace were connected. In Israel, the

monarchy follows neither the pattern of the Babylonians, nor the Assyrians faithfully. By contrast with
her relationship to the monarchy, Israel's relationship to the city is far more consistent.[109]

Furthermore, few critics find support in the
vocabulary and syntax of Dt 17:18-19 for Bächli's
theory that the most important part of the text is
the king's proclamation of the law.[110] The king is
not only being assigned the liturgical responsibility
of proclaiming the law, but some personal obligation
to the Torah as well. Yahweh imposes the same obligation on Joshua.

This book of the law shall not depart out of
your mouth, but you shall meditate on it
day and night, that you may be careful to
do according to all that is written in it;
for then you shall make your way prosperous,
and then you shall have good success.
(Jos 1:8)

Bächli's suggestion that the reserve with which
Deuteronomy treats the monarchy stems from the un-
timely death of King Josiah, which disillusions the
royal hopes of the reform does not adequately explain
the difficulty. The suggestion places too much importance on the singular event, and too little importance on the theological assessment of a slowly
developing tradition about the role of the king.

Finally, Deuteronomy is concerned with the rights
of the poor: the widow, the orphan, the alien, the
defendant in an unwitnessed murder (Dt 19:1-13), the
victim without an avenger (Dt 21:1-9), the parents
of an incorrigible child (Dt 21:18-21), a slandered
wife, and other women victims of sexual violence
(Dt 22:13-21 + 23-7), and a widow without an heir
(Dt 25:5-10). Since royal policies often were responsible for the sufferings of such people, it is
unlikely that the kings would have sponsored legislation to protect the very people deprived by the
policies of their governments, since such protection
would have spelled the end to monarchy! Theologically,
the king may have been considered the protector of
the poor, but practically he was not their messiah.[111]

Neither Bächli's method which studies the intention of a text without studying its form, nor his
conclusions concerning the importance of the nations
of Edom, Moab and Ammon and the role of the king in

the formation of Deuteronomy, can be applauded. However, his appreciation for the solidly urban orientation of Deuteronomy is remarkable. Although Bächli himself would consider Israel's urban identity a novelty in the 7th century BCE, other research shows that as a whole Deuteronomy's sources are venerable. It is unlikely that Deuteronomy's urban tradition constitutes an exception.

Prophecy

According to Nicholson, the prophets inherited the traditions of the amphictyony, and were the mentors of the Deuteronomic reform.[112] Furthermore, the emphasis, which both Hosea and Deuteronomy place on the Sinai covenant and the way in which both describe that relationship between Yahweh and Israel as *love* strengthens this prophetic connection. However, as Claburn emphasizes, prophecy is a clearly independent phenomenon in Israel, and is by no means identical with the *collective behavior* of the Deuteronomic reform.[113]

According to Claburn, the liturgy (and presumably *any* institution) in ancient Israel combine traditions far too old and far too complicated for scholars to separate accurately. The efforts of tradition-historians and form critics are hopelessly hypothetical. Furthermore, the liturgy of any culture preserves its normative values. However, Deuteronomy is a radical break with the normative values of Israel. Finally, a liturgical setting for Deuteronomy accounts only for *institutional* behavior in Israel, which all societies reflect *collective* behavior as well.[114] Therefore, Claburn argues that the language and literature of Deuteronomy reflect a spontaneous revolt in Israel (*collective* behavior) and not a ritual--aged, developed, modified and expanded through the years (*institutional* behavior.[115]

Claburn concludes that under the pressure of urbanization and class struggles in Israel during the reign of Josiah (640-609 BCE), the prophets led a revolt against the city dwellers, parodied as *Canaanites.* Farmers from the heartland of Israel welded themselves into a fiercely loyal community governed by the laws of Deuteronomy. While the movement struggled to completely overhaul the social world of its time, it nonetheless clung nostalgically to past traditions with which it justified the

65

demands it imposed.

This sociological model is at least as helpful to Claburn, in explaining the characteristics of Deuteronomy as the form critical models of von Rad, Mendenhall and Noth.

The concise summaries of Yahweh's efforts on Israel's behalf (e.g., Dt 26:5-9), which von Rad calls *creeds*, Claburn calls *slogans*. The narratives in the Abraham, Isaac and Jacob cycles did not develop from these creeds; on the contrary, these slogans sum up the narratives.[116] The pattern in Deuteronomy which von Rad and Mendenhall call *covenant*, Claburn considers the *typical stages* of any social movement. Such movements 1) summarize the historical events which led to the crisis; 2) present their reform programs; 3) promise rewards to the obedient and punishment to the disobedient; 4) appeal to disenfranchised segments of society; and 5) identify their enemies.[117] The first three characteristics are identical with the *historical prologue, series of apodictic laws,* and *blessings and curses* elements of the covenant genre.

Deuteronomy's binding power, which Noth identified as the *amphictyony*, Claburn considers the *social movements* common in the ancient world.[117] Finally, the persuasive speech in Deuteronomy, which Klostermann, Koehler and von Rad called *parenesis,* Claburn calls *propaganda.*[119] Like parenesis, propaganda addresses its audience directly with a simple and repetitive syntax. Both emphasize *remembering* and *doing.* The genres are categorical: there is no *both . . . and,* no gray; everything is *either . . . or,* black or white. Each issue is carefully selected and each case carefully argued to eliminate alternatives. Emotional language and oversimplification strengthen the distortion. *Distortion, selecting the issues, case making, emotional languages* and *oversimplification of issues* are all technical terms in sociology.[120]

Thus, for Claburn, the *creed, covenant, amphictyony* and *parenesis* of the traditions-historians are better explained by the *slogans, stages, social movements* and *propaganda* of the sociologists, and the setting of Deuteronomy is not the institutional behavior of ritual, but the collective behavior of revolt.

However, Claburn's theory that Deuteronomy reflects an uprising of the prophets against the city does not account for the carefully established process of appeals in texts like Dt 21:18-21, where parents, then judges, then all adult males must be consulted before the defendant can be sentenced. Claburn's theory that Deuteronomy oversimplifies the issue does not account for the sophisticated distinctions made in texts like Dt 19:1-13 where murder and manslaughter are carefully separated. Nor does Claburn's theory that Dt 26:5-11 *sums* up rather than *inspires* the ancestral cycles, explain why the Sinai material is missing from Dt 26:5-11. Even if Dt 26:5-11 was *over-simplifying*, some mention of this bulk of legal material would be expected. Therefore, von Rad concluded that Dt 26:5-11 draws on earlier traditions than the ancestral cycles. Had Dt 26:5-11 developed after the ancestral cycles, it would have contained the Sinai material.

Also, Claburn's social movement would destroy Israel's court system, and yet texts like Dt 19:1-13, 21:1-9; 21:18-21, 22:13-21; 22:23-7 and 25:5-10 all uphold this urban institution. While it is possible to associate the persuasive speech patterns in Deuteronomy with the propaganda of social movements, the same genre, as Weinfeld as shown, is used by scribes in support of the institutional status quo. There is no question that the prophets were *anti-monarchial*, but that does not mean that the prophets were *anti-city*, or *anti-institutional*.[121] Nonetheless, the prophets are generally considered responsible for canonizing the fear of the city in ancient Israel. Despite strong individual differences in their personal lives and ministeries, an urban paranoia was considered to dominate their preaching. Cities epitomized the wickedness permeating Israel.[122] It seemed as if the prophets looked at the desert as the only fit place for the people of Yahweh to live.

However, according to Riemann, the prophets were not announcing a joyful return to the desert, but rather, that as the result of her unfaithfulness, Israel would be reduced to a desert![123] The desert is not glorified; it is portrayed as a punishment for an urban people. The city, as well as the army, the monarchy, learning, foreign policy, etc. were all temptations to over-confidence. For example, the cooking song in Ez 24:1-14, which compares the city to a pot, indicts Israel for having succumbed to just such over-confidence.[124]

> Therefore, thus says the Lord God: Woe to
> the bloody city! I also will make the pile
> great. Heap on the logs, kindle the fire,
> boil well the flesh, and empty out the
> broth, and let the bones be burned up.
> Then set it empty upon the coals that it
> may become hot, and its copper may burn,
> that its filthiness may be melted in it,
> its rust consumed. In vain I have wearied
> myself; its thick rust does not go out of it
> by fire. (Ez 24:6, 11-12)

Those who flee to the security of the city will find
themselves trapped. Only in Yahweh can Israel be
secure. Human arrogance and not the city was the
reason for Israel's condemnation, because such a
sense of overconfidence leads to social corruption,
so ingrained that the city cannot even be scoured
clean, but can only be melted, slag and all.

This prophetic condemnation of over-confidence
is not identical with a condemnation of city life. In
fact, the association of Israel with city life was so
permanent that even when Jerusalem was destroyed in
587 BCE, less than 400 years after it became an
Israelite city, there was no call for Israel to abandon the city. Lamentations show how difficult it was
for the Jews to come to terms with the loss of their
city, and the destruction of their temple. There is
little rejoicing that, at last, Babylon had freed the
people of Yahweh from the corrupting influence of the
city!

Even the development of Judaism--a religion without a city--did not prevent Jerusalem's deportees
from returning to their native land obsessed with a
single idea: to rebuild the city! Haggai and
Zechariah promised that *only* with the rebuilding of
the city would prosperity and peace return to the
land. By rebuilding the city, Nehemiah gave the Jews
a renewed sense of security and self-worth.

Wisdom

Weinfeld's rejection of the liturgy as
Deuteronomy's setting is considerably different from
Claburn's.[126] For Weinfeld, the key text in

68

identifying the setting of Deuteronomy is Je 8:8.

> How can you say, 'We are *wise*, and the *law* of the Lord is with us'? But behold, the false pen of the *scribes* has made it into a lie.

With this foundation, Weinfeld proposes the syllogism: if *scribes care for Torah*, and if *Torah is Deuteronomy*, then . . . *the scribes of the Shaphan family were the leading components of this literary school.*[127]

> And Hilikiah the high priest said to Shaphan *the secretary* 'I have found the book *of the law* in the house of the Lord'. And Hilikiah gave the book to Shaphan, and he read it. And Shaphan the secretary came to the king, and reported to the king . . . . And Shaphan read it before the king . . . .
>
> And when the king heard the words of the book of the law . . . the king commanded Hilikiah the priest, and Ahikam the son of Shaphan and Achbor the son of Micaiah and Shaphan the secretary . . . 'Go, inquire of the Lord . . . concerning the words of this book . . . .
>
> So Hilikiah the priest, and Ahikam, and Achbor, and Shaphan . . . went to Huldah the prophetess . . . and they talked with her. (2 K 22:8-14)

The king in this passage is Josiah (640-609 BCE). Because Deuteronomy endorses his reforms and those of his grandfather, Hezekiah, DeWette identified the book of the law discovered here with Deuteronomy.[128] Thus, Weinfeld can associate the scribes with the most active period of the reform. But with the authority of Pr 25:1. *These also are proverbs of Solomon which the men of Hezekiah king of Judah copied.* Weinfeld extends the influence of the scribes even to the early period of the reform under Hezekiah (715-687 BCE).

Weinfeld then compares the technical vocabulary of Deuteronomy with wisdom, the genre customarily associated with scribes.[129] However, the most striking similarity for Weinfeld appears in the efforts of both wisdom and Deuteronomy to demythologize and

secularize Israelite life.[130] Weinfeld studies this
trend in Deuteronomy's treatment of Yahweh's
presence, holy days, ritual purity, the court system,
fear of Yahweh, etc. For him, Deuteronomy represents
a moral rearmament, seeking to control the influence
of liturgy in Israel by substituting ethical, moral
humanism as a motivation for national life. He
associates the movement with the epitome of urban
bureaucracy: the scribes who served as cabinet
officers to the kings of Judah.

Unlike the theory of Claburn, Weinfeld's theory
does provide for the gradual and institution development of Deuteronomy, and an urban setting for the tradition. First, Weinfeld's major premise: *scribes
care for Torah,* converts the general indictment for
disobedience in Je 8:8 into a technical identification of scribes with the Torah, and oversimplifies
the evidence. Scribes are only one of the many
custodians of Torah in the Hebrew Bible. In Je 18:18,
priests care for Torah:

> Then they said, "Come, let us make plots
> against Jeremiah, for law shall not perish
> from the priest, nor counsel from the wise,
> nor the word from the prophet. Come let us
> smite him with the tongue, and let us not
> heed any of his words.

In Is 8:16-20, *prophets* care for Torah:

> The record is to be folded and the sealed
> instruction kept among my disciples. For
> I will trust in the Lord, who is hiding
> his face from the house of Jacob; yes, I
> will wait for him. Look at me and the
> children whom the Lord has given me: we
> are signs and portents in Israel from the
> Lord of hosts who dwells on Mount Zion.
> And when they say to you, 'Inquire of
> mediums and fortune-tellers (who chirp and
> mutter!); should not a people inquire of
> their gods, apply to the dead on behalf
> of the living?'--then this document will
> furnish its instruction.

In Dt 33:8-10, *Levites* care for the Torah:

> And of Levi he said, "Give to Levi thy
> Thummim, and thy Urim to the godly one,

70

whom thou didst test at Massah, with whom
thou didst strive at the waters of Meribah;
who said of his father and mother, 'I
regard them not'; he disowned his brothers,
and ignored his children. For they observed thy word and kept thy covenant.
They shall teach Jacob thy ordinances and
Israel thy law.

In Pr 3:1-2, *parents* or *sages* care for Torah:

My son, do not forget my teaching, but let
your heart keep my commandments, for the
length of days and years of life and
abundant welfare will they give you.[131]

And in Is 2:3, *the king* provides Torah for his
people:

. . . and many peoples shall come and say:
'Come, let us go up to the mountain of the
Lord, to the house of the God of Jacob;
that he may teach us his ways and that we
may walk in his paths.' For out of Zion
shall go forth the law and the word of
the Lord from Jerusalem.

Therefore, it is impossible to limit Torah to one
particular setting. The genre of the priest may be
liturgical_law (da'at); genre of the sage may be
counsel (māsăl); the genre of the prophet may be *word
(dābār)*; and the genre of the king may be *decree
(miswâ)*, but all must obey *The Torah (tôrâ)*.[132]

Second, Weinfeld's minor premise: *Torah is
Deuteronomy*, focuses only on one of the many possible
definitions of this genre. It is true that in
Deuteronomy and some post-exilic literature, *Torah*
means *law* or *law code*, but even Lindars is careful to
refine that definition to avoid making *Torah* and
Deuteronomy exclusive synonyms for one another.[133]

But *Torah* cannot be restricted to *Deuteronomy*,
law or *law code*. Begrich, for example, traces the
development in Torah's meaning from *priestly oracle*
to *religious instruction*.[134] As a priestly oracle,
Torah requires 1) a question of ritual purity, 2) put
to a priest, 3) in a cultic setting. Haggai uses this
rite of questions and answers to pronounce a judgment
on Israel.

71

On the twenty-fourth day of the ninth month,
in the second year of Darius, the word of
the Lord came by Haggai the prophet, "Thus
says the Lord of hosts: Ask the priests to
decide this question, 'If one carries holy
flesh in the skirt of his garment, and
touches with his skirt bread, or pottage,
or wine, or oil, or any kind of food, does
it become holy?'" The priests answered
"No." Then said Haggai, "If one who is
unclean by contact with a dead body touches
any of these, does it become unclean?" The
priests answered, "It does become unclean."
Then Haggai said, "So is it with this
people . . . ." (Hg 2:10-14)

Ritual purity was not the only subject of the
priests' *Torah*. Priests also dealt with homicide,
legal rights, assault and battery, in fact, any case
appealed from the municipal courts!

If any case arises requiring decision
between one kind of homicide and another,
one kind of legal right and another, or
one kind of assault and another, any case
within your towns which is too difficult
for you, then you shall arise and go up
to the place which the Lord your God will
choose, and coming to the Levitical priests
and to the judge who is in office in those
days, you shall consult them, and they
shall declare to you the decision. Then
you shall do according to what they declare
to you from the place which the Lord will
choose; and you shall be careful to do
according to all that they direct you;
according to the instructions which they
give you, and according to the decision
which they pronounce to you, you shall do;
you shall not turn aside from the verdict
which they declare to you, either to the
right hand or to the left . . . .
(Dt 17:8-13)

Hosea also expands the subject of the Torah.[135] In
Hosea, *Torah* always means more than *individual
instructions* given by a priest. It means *Yahweh's
will* or *everything Israel knows about Yahweh* as the
result of her covenant with him.[136] Thus *law* is only
part of the genre *torah*.[137] As an umbrella genre
Torah is basically a *story* which contains what later

Judaism calls *halakah* or rules of conduct, commandments, statutes and ordinances; and *haggadah* or more
general religious teachings.[138]

Furthermore, Je 8:8 need not refer to the scribes'
failure as teachers, but simply as copyists, whose
sloppy work is intentional and destructive. Jeremiah
believes a good text is the basis of a good
theology. Without a decent text it is no wonder the
moral fiber of the land is rotting. Although
Weinfeld cites Is 5:21, 29:14, Pr 25:1, 2 S 8:17,
Ps 45:2 as evidence that a scribal movement as early
as Hezekiah's time saw the didactic importance of
setting down teachings in writing, the passages could
simply refer to the institution of copyists, not
sages! Although Weinfeld goes to great lengths to
demonstrate that the scribes of the Jerusalem court
were patrons of Jeremiah, he does not explain why in
Je 8:8 Jeremiah criticizes the very people who de-[139]
fended and supported him and the reform of Josiah.
Sages in the royal courts of the Ancient Near East
were humanists, encouraging literacy, cosmopolitan
virtues, syncreticism, and would have been very much
at home with Deuteronomy's concern for the poor, for
women, for the weak and for nature. Likewise, sages
relied on exhortation, rather than authority, for
motivating their disciples--also a characteristic of
Deuteronomy. However, it is difficult to see what
these universal humanists would have in common with
the isolationist and sectarian theology of
Deuteronomy. It was only during the much later
period of Ben Sira that such explicit nationalism
could be identified with wisdom.

The association of Jeremiah with the reform of
Josiah is still questionable. However, assuming the
prophet did support the reform in light of a general
renaissance of religious traditions throughout the
Ancient Near East, he would more likely criticize the
sages for their pluralism, humanism, syncretism,
which threatened to destroy Israel.[140] Such attitudes, promoted by David, Solomon, Omri, Ahab
Manasseh, Amon and others were outright contradictions of the theology of Deuteronomy. How such
sages would be the custodians of such a tradition is
hard to understand.

Finally, Deuteronomy in its canonical form
appears at a time when Judah and Israel for 400 years
have been influenced by the wisdom of the Ancient
Near East. It was a systematic policy of the monarchy

73

from David onward to support the arts through the presence of sages at the courts. That traces of such learning appear in the literature of the monarchy argues only that the influence of the wisdom tradition was effective, not that the sages were the setting in which that literature developed.

Conclusions

In most assessments of Deuteronomy, the city is a factor. Yet no one seriously considers the significance of that factor or where that factor originates. The research of Bächli, Weinfeld and Claburn on Deuteronomy show how frequently the city factor is present and not pursued.[141]

In their studies, Claburn and Weinfeld concentrate on literary patterns in Deuteronomy, which Claburn considers characteristic of a social movement in rural Judah, and Weinfeld considers typical of a renaissance movement in metropolitan Jerusalem! Bächli also situates Deuteronomy in the city of Jerusalem, but he is not interested in the genre used, but in why Deuteronomy was written.

Claburn associates Deuteronomy with the farmers of Judah, while Weinfeld and Bächli link it to the palace. However, Weinfeld nominates the scribes of the royal court because of their access to the cosmopolitan wisdom traditions throughout the Ancient Near East, while Bächli singles out the king because of the control which he has over the social institutions of Israel's uniquely Yahwist culture at home.

Claburn and Bächli both consider the Israel in Deuteronomy under pressure, Claburn from the ill effects of the cities, Bächli from the nations. Claburn returns to the nomadic ideal as support for his social movement hypothesis: Bächli leans heavily on the Israel-against-its-environment positions of Albright and Wright. Claburn sees the city as an enemy, Weinfeld and Bächli see it as a friend.

Alt, Noth, von Rad--among others--assume that Deuteronomic concepts such as *covenant, amphictyony, law* and *liturgy* are properties of Israel as a non-urban culture.[142] Yet there is an alternative. *Covenants,* in Mesopotamia, are treaties between great metropolitan empires and their urban colonies.

Amphictyonies, in Greece and Italy, are urban leagues established to provide each city with fit liturgy and adequate defense. *Law,* throughout the Ancient Near East, is an instrument by which cities protect and govern their citizens. And *liturgy,* in Syro-Palestine, is the expression of a city's relationship with her god-husband, who guarantees the fertility of her land. How could so many features of city life be so helpful or so important to Israel unless even *early* Israel encountered Yahweh in the city, and had a profound respect for the sacred significance of ordinary urban institutions.

FOOTNOTES - CHAPTER II

[1]Albrecht Alt, "The God of the Fathers," in Old Testament History and Religion, trans. R. A. Wilson (Garden City, NY.: Doubleday and Company, Inc., 1968), p. 40. Italics added.

[2]C. M. Doughty, Travels in Arabia Deserts (Boston: J. Cape, 1888; reprint ed., Leiden: Brill, 1979).

[3]Karl Budde, "Nomadic Ideal in the Old Testament," New World 4 (1895):726-45.

[4]John W. Flight, "Nomadic Idea and Ideal in the OT," JBL 42 (1923):158 ff.

[5]Werner H. Schmidt, Alttestamentlicher Glaube in seiner Geschichte, Neukirchener Studienbücher, no. 6 (Neukirchen-Vluyn: Neukirchener Verlag, 1975).

[6]Leah Bronner, "The Rechabites, a sect in Biblical Times," in De Fructu Oris Sui: essays in honor of Adrianus van Selms, ed. I. H. Eybers, F. C. Fensham, C. J. Labuschagne, W. C. van Wyk and A. H. van Zyl (Leiden: Brill, 1971), p. 12.

[7]Jon D. Levenson, "On the Promise to be Recha- bites," CBQ 38 (1976):508. Levenson assigns the promise made to the Rechabites to the genre: covenant of grant identified and described by Moshe Weinfeld, "The Covenant of Grant in the Old Testament and in the Ancient Near East," JAOS 90 (1970):184-203; and Ronald E. Clements, Abraham and David: Genesis XV and its Meaning for Israelite Tradition (Naperville, IL.: Alec R. Allenson, Inc., 1967). The covenant of grant is a reward for past loyalty; the treaty covenant identified and described by George E. Mendenhall, "Ancient Oriental and Biblical Law," in Biblical Archeologist Reader, vol. 3, Edward F. Campbell, Jr. and David Noel Freedman (Garden City, NY.: Doubleday & Company, Inc., 1970), pp. 3-24 is a guarantee of future loyalty. See also Shemaryahu Talmon, "The 'Desert Motif' in the Bible and Qumran Literature," in Biblical Motifs, ed. A. Altmann (Cambridge, MA.: Harvard University Press, 1966), pp.

31-63; and W. Rudolph, Jeremia, 3rd ed. (Tübingen: J. C. B. Mohr-Paul Siebeck, 1968), pp. 225-9.

[8]For a brief description of this classic theory, see de Vaux, Israel, pp. 14-15; based on studies such as Antonin Causse, Du groupe ethnique à la communauté religieuse. Etudes d'histoire et de philosophie religieuse (Paris: F. Alcan, 1937), and Samuel Nyström, Beduinentum und Jahwismus. Eine soziologisch-religionsgeschichtliche Untersuchung zum Alten Testament (Lund: C. W. K. Gleerup, 1946).

[9]Interpreter's Dictionary of the Bible, supplementary vol. s.v. "Rechabites," by Frank S. Frick. Frick's theory first appeared in "The Rechabites Reconsidered," JBL 90 (1971):379-87.

[10]Edøuard Hahn, Von der Hacke zum Pflug (Leipzig: Quelle & Meyer, 1914); George E. Mendenhall, "The Hebrew Conquest of Palestine," in Biblical Archeologist Reader, vol. 3, ed. Edward F. Campbell, Jr. and David Noel Freedman (Garden City, NY.: Doubleday & Company, 1970), pp. 76-99; John T. Luke, "Pastoralism and Politics in the Mari Period: A Reexamination of the Character and Political Significance of the Major West Semitic Tribal Groups on the Middle Euphrates, ca. 1828-1758 BC" (Ph.D. dissertation, University of Michigan, 1965); Talmon, "Motif"; Interpreter's Dictionary of the Bible, supplementary vol., s.v. "Nomadism," by Norman K. Gottwald and Gottwald, Tribes; Beat Zuber, Vier Studien zu den Ursprüngen Israels: Die Sinaifrage und Probleme der Volks-und Traditionsbildung (Gottingen: Vandenhoeck and Ruprecht, 1976).

[11]Albrecht Alt, Kleine Schriften zur Geschichte des Volkes Israel, 2 vols. (München: C. H. Beck, 1968), and Martin Noth, The History of Israel, 2nd ed. (New York: Harper & Row, 1960).

[12]Paul Lapp. "The Conquest of Palestine in the Light of Archeology," Concordia Theological Monthly 38 (1967):298-9.

[13]Noth, History, p. 149n.

[14]Mendenhall, "Conquest," p. 110. This same theory has been proposed by Jan Dus, "Moses or Joshua? On the Problem of the Founder of the Israelite Religion," in The Bible and Liberation: Political and Social Hermeneutics, ed. Norman K. Gottwold and Antoinette C. Wire (Berkeley, CA.: Radical Religion, 1975), pp. 26-41. Unlike Mendenhall, however, Dus argues that none of the members of ancient Israel came from outside Canaan. Mendenhall does not completely rule out the influence of a segment of ancient Israel having had an Egyptian experience, which contributed significantly to the understanding of Yahweh as a liberating god.

[15]See Ernest Pulgram, "Linear B, Greek, and the Greeks," Glotta 38 (1960):171-81, who, according to Mendenhall, . . . vigorously attacked this migration theory in a work that should be required for anyone dealing with ancient theory. (George E. Mendenhall, "Migration theories v Culture Change as an Explanation for Early Israel," in SBL Seminar Papers, vol. 1, ed. Paul J. Achtmeier. [Chico, CA.: Scholars Press, 1976], pp. 131-43.)

[16]R. Walz, "Zum Problem des Zeitpunktes der Domestifikation der altweltlichen Cameliden," Zeitschrift der Deutschen Morgenländischen Gesellschaft 100 (1951):29-51; W. G. Lambert, "The Domesticated Camel in the Second Millenium--Evidence from Alalath and Ugarit," BASOR 160 (1960):42 ff; William Foxwell Albright, Yahweh and the gods of Canaan: an historical analysis of two contrasting faiths (Garden City, NY.: Doubleday & Company, 1968; reprint ed., Winona Lake, IN.: Eisenbrauns, 1978); M. A. Littauer and J. H. Crouwel, Wheeled Vehicles and Ridden Animals in the Ancient Near East (Leiden: Brill, 1979). Interpreter's Dictionary of the Bible, s.v. "Camel" by J. A. Thompson.

[17]Oppenheim, Mesopotamia, pp. 82-3.

[18]Aharon Kempinski, The Rise of an Urban Culture: the urbanization of Palestine in the early bronze age, 3000-2150 BC. Israel Ethnographic Studies, vol. 4, ed. Heda Jason (Jerusalem: Israel Ethnographic Society, 1978), pp. 15-16.

[19] John Bright, *A History of Israel*, 2nd ed. (Philadelphia: Westminster Press, 1972), p. 133n. ". . . whatever the size of the group coming from the desert may have been (and it may have been larger than Mendenhall *seems* to suggest), its crucial role in what took place must receive full stress . . ." Yohanan Aharoni, *The Land of the Bible: a historical geography*, trans. A. F. Rainey (London: Burns and Oates, 1968) and Aharon Kempinski, "Israelite Conquest or Settlement? New Light from Tell Mosos," *BAR* 2 (1976):25-30 continue the analysis of archeology's contribution to the settlement question. Frick, *City*, pp. 186-200 summarizes and critiques the three current explanations of the Hebrew settlement of Palestine, viz., invasion (Albright), immigration (Noth), revolution (Mendenhall).

[20] Kempinski, *Rise*, pp. 7, 30.

[21] Mendenhall, "Migration," pp. 141-2.

[22] Oppenheim, *Mesopotamia*, pp. 110-11.

[23] William Foxwell Albright, "Abraham the Hebrew: a New Archeological Interpretation," *BASOR* 163 (1961): 36-54. Cyrus Gordon, "Abraham and the Merchants of Ura," *JNES* 12 (1958):28-31.

[24] Muntingh, "City," pp. 119-20.

[25] See J. A. Emerton, "Some False Clues in the Study of Genesis XIV," *VT* 21 (1971):24-47, and "The Riddle of Genesis XIV," *VT* 21 (1971):403-39.

[26] Giovanni Pettinato, "The Royal Archives of Tell Mardikh-Ebla," *BA* 39 (1976):44-52.

[27] John van Seters, *Abraham in History and Tradition* (New Haven, CT.: Yale University Press, 1975), p. 9.

[28] Sjoberg, *Pre-industrial City*.

[29] Frick, *City*.

[30]Jean R. Kupper, Les nomades en Mesopotamie au temps des rois de Mari (Paris: Musée national du Louvre, 1957).

[31]Luke, "Pastoralism," pp. 72-5; 277-9 argues that the movements of the three major West Semitic tribal groups are best explained in terms of tribal seasonal migration into pastureland, and not as evidence for nomadic invasion or infiltration from the desert or steppe.

[32]M. B. Rowton, "Autonomy and Nomadism in Western Asia," Orientalia NS 42 (1973):249. The terms *excluded nomads* and *enclosed nomads* were coined by Owen Lattimore, Studies in Frontier History (New York: Oxford University Press, 1962), p. 487.

[33]Talmon, "Motif," pp. 42-3.

[34]This would not be the first time the application of categories developed in Western cultures has detoured Biblical scholarship. Wellhausen in the later 19th century was similarly criticized for assuming Israel evolved according to the philosophical pattern of Hegel (1770-1831). Western categories can be used only with great reservation in interpreting the Hebrew Bible. They can never be assumed, but always must be carefully demonstrated to apply. See J. Alberto Soggin, Introduction to the Old Testament (Philadelphia: Westminster Press, 1976), pp. 85-7.

[35]Talmon, "Motif," p. 37. Wandering and tents were also symbols of war. Cf. 1 K 12:16: *To your tents, oh Israel!*

[36]Denis Baly, "The Geography of Monotheism," in Translating & Understanding the Old Testament: essays in honor of Herbert Gordon May, ed. Harry Thomas, Frank and William L. Reed (New York: Abingdon Press, 1970), pp. 253-78.

[37]Baly, "Geography," p. 255.

[38]In all, Baly identifies five contributions of

the desert experience of Israel to her preparation for
monotheism. Ibid., pp. 268-72.

[39]Gerhard von Rad, "The Problems of the Hexateuch,"
in The Problem of the Hexateuch and other essays,
trans. E. W. Trueman Dicken (New York: McGraw Hill
Book Company, 1966), pp. 1-78.

[40]Handbook of Biblical Criticism, s.v. "Credo,"
by Richard N. Soulen. Brueggemann calls this genre
primal narrative. See Walter Brueggemann, The Bible
Makes Sense (Winona, MN.: St. Mary's College Press,
1978), pp. 45-60.

[41]E. W. Nicholson, Exodus and Sinai in History and
Tradition (Richmond, VA.: The John Knox Press, 1973),
pp. 23-25 surveys criticism of von Rad and his mentors:
Wellhausen and Gressmann.

[42]Viktor Korošec, Hethitische Staatsverträge: ein
Beitrag zu ihrer juristischen Wertung, Leipziger
rechtswissenschaftliche Studien, no. 60 (Leipzig: T.
Weicher, 1931).

[43]Dennis J. McCarthy, Treaty and Covenant, a study
in form in the Ancient Oriental Documents and in the
Old Testament, rev. ed., Analecta Biblica, vol 21A
(Rome: Biblical Institute, 1978), pp. 51-2.

[44]G. Ernest Wright, "Cult and History," Interpretation 16 (1962):17.

[45]Dennis J. McCarthy, Old Testament Covenant: a
survey of current opinions (Richmond, VA.: The John
Knox Press, 1972), p. 57.

[46]Klaus Baltzar, The Covenant Formulary in the Old
Testament, Jewish and early Christian writings, trans.
David E. Green (Philadelphia: Fortress Press, 1971).

[47]Meredith G. Kline, Treaty of the Great King:
the covenant structure of Deuteronomy (Grand Rapids,
MI.: William B. Eerdmans Publishing Company, 1963).

[48]Moshe Weinfeld, Deuteronomy and the Deuteronomic

School (Oxford: The Clarendon Press, 1972).

[49]Albrecht Alt, "The Origins of Israelite Law," in Essays on Old Testament History and Religion, trans. R. A. Wilson (Garden City, NY.: Doubleday and Company, Inc., 1967; Anchor Books, 1968), pp. 107-171. See Sigrid Loersch, Das Deuteronomium und seine Deutungungen. Stuttgarter Bibelstudien, no. 22 (Stuttgart: Verlag Katholisches Bibelwerk, 1967), pp. 71-4.

[50]See W. Malcolm Clark, "Law," in Old Testament Form Criticism, ed. John H. Hayes (San Antonio, TX.: Trinity University Press, 1974), pp. 105-16.

[51]Erhard Gerstenberger, "Zur alttestamentlichen Weisheit," Verkundigung und Forschung 14 (1969):28-44 makes the same criticism of Richter, Recht.

[52]Alt, "Origins," p. 116. See T. and D. Thomson, "Some Legal Problems in the Book of Ruth," VT 18 (1968):79-100, who accepts Alt's setting for case law as the municipal court, but considers the idea that the courts could directly apply this law an oversimplification.

[53]For example, David Daube, Studies in Biblical Law (Cambridge: The University Press, 1947) has argued that case law was developed for the specific purpose of trying cases in the gate court; and Gerhard Liedke, Gestalt und Bezeichnung alttestamentlicher Rechtssätze, WMANT, no. 39 (Neukirchen-Vluyn: Neukirchener Verlag, 1971) that abstract case laws like those in the Hebrew Bible developed from the court records of actual decisions.

[54]G. Ernest Wright, The Old Testament Against its Environment (Chicago: H. Regnery, 1950), and William Foxwell Albright, From the Stone Age to Christianity: monotheism and the historical process, 2nd ed. (Baltimore, MD.: The Johns Hopkins Press, 1940; Doubleday Anchor Books, 1957).

[55]See Gerstenberger, Wesen.

[56]See Eberhard von Waldow, "Social Responsibility and Social Structure in Early Israel," CBQ 32

(1970):184-5.

[57]Frick, City, pp. 115-16. Cf. pp. 104-11.

[58]Louis Wirth, "Urbanism as a Way of Life," in Cities and Society: The Revised Reader in Urban Sociology, ed. Paul K. Hatt and Albert J. Reiss (Glencoe, IL.: Free Press, 1957), pp. 46-63.

[59]Frick, City, p. 106. Sjoberg, City, p. 159.

[60]J. W. McKay, "A Decalogue for the Administration of Justice at the City Gate," VT 21 (1971):325.

[61]August Klostermann, Der Pentateuch: Beiträge zu seinem Verständnis und seiner Enstehungsgeschichte, vol. 2 (Leipzig: A. Deichert, 1907), p. 344.

[62]Von Rad, Das Gottesvolk and Deuteronomy, p. 19. See Ronald M. Hals, "Is There a Genre of Preached Law?" SBL Seminar Papers, vol. 1, ed. Paul J. Achtemeier (Chico, CA.: Scholars Press, 1973), pp. 1-12.

[63]Frederick Clark Tiffany, "Parenesis and Deuteronomy 5-11 (Deut. 4:45; 5:2-11:29): a form critical study" (Ph.D. dissertation, Claremont University, 1978), pp. 3-12.

[64]Tiffany, "Parenesis," pp. 22-23.

[65]Cross, Myth, p. 277n. "Incidentally, the importation of the term kerygma into the form criticism of the Hebrew Bible [for example, H. W. Wolff, "Das Kerygma des deuteronomistischen Geschichtswerkes," ZAW 73 (1961):171-86] is to be deplored as an inelegant and presumptuous anachronism."

[66]Tiffany, "Parenesis," pp. 10-11.

[67]Von Rad, Theology, p. 37.

[68]Wellhausen, Prologmena.

[69]Alt, "Formation," pp. 222-309.

[70]Martin Noth, Das System der Zwölf Stämme Israels (Stuttgart: Kohlhammer, 1930). See also Loersch, Deuteronomium, pp. 86-7. Nicholson, Exodus, p. 14. So, also, Nicholson, Deuteronomy, pp. 58-82. It should be noted that in Ezekiel the term Israel has other connotations than these mentioned by Nicholson. "Ezek's prophetic mission is to warn the 'house of Israel' of coming ruin (3:16-21). This term as used in the book refers to Judah--except where it means the N kingdom as distinguished from the S (e.g., 4:4-5)-- and is limited to the people in Palestine (cf. esp. 22:17-22). When the exiles are included it is charged to the 'whole house of Israel' (11:15; 37:11)." (The Interpreter's One-Volume Commentary on the Bible, s.v. "Ezekiel," by William Hugh Brownlee.)

[71]Paulys, Real Encyclopäedie der Klassichen Altertumswissenschaft, s.v. "Amphictyonia," by F. Cauer.

[72]Buccellati does not consider the possibility that early Israel used the amphictyony as a social structure, precisely because it was a settled and urban culture. Buccellati, Cities. See McCarthy, Covenant, p. 64 and John Hayes and J. Maxwell Miller, eds., Israelite and Judean History (Philadelphia: The Westminster Press, 1977), pp. 354-6.

[73]Dictionary of the Bible, s.v. "Shechem," by John L. McKenzie.

[74]Nicholson, Deuteronomy, p. 62.

[75]Hans Joachim Kraus, Geschichte der historisch-kritischen Erforschung des Alten Testaments (Neukirchen: Neukirchener Verlag, 1969), p. 460.

[76]Sigmund Mowinckel, The Psalms in Israel's Worship, vol. 1 (New York: Abingdon Press, 1962), pp. 106-92.

[77]Samuel Henry Hooke, ed., Myth and Ritual: Essays on Myth and Ritual of the Hebrews in relation

to the Cultural Pattern of Ancient East. (London: Oxford University Press, 1933). In his third volume, Hooke *does not* argue as strongly that in the liturgy, the king was a stand-in for the god, who was humiliated and then elevated to symbolize the connection between his death and resurrection and the dying and rising cycle of nature. See Hayes and Miller, History, p. 373.

[78]J. de Fraine, L'aspect religieux de la royaute israelite. L'institution monarchique dans l'Ancien Testament et dans les textes mesopotamiens (Rome: Pontifical Biblical Institute, 1954); Martin Noth, "Gott, König, Volk im Alten Testament (Eine methodologische Auseinandersetzung mit einer gegenwartigen Forschungsrichtung)," ZTK 47 (1950):157-91; and K. -H. Bernhardt, Das Problem der altorientalischen Königsideologie in Alten Testament (Leiden: Brill, 1961) consider the king's role in liturgy very insignificant. A. R. Johnson, Sacral Kingship in Ancient Israel (Cardiff: University of Wales Press, 1967) does not consider the king's role in liturgy to be as important as Hooke and Engnell, nor as unimportant as de Fraine, Noth and Bernhardt.

[79]Ivan Engnell, Studies in Divine Kingship in the Ancient Near East (Uppsala: Almquist & Wiksells Bokt, 1943).

[80]Wellhausen, Prolegomena.

[81]Von Rad, Theology, vol. 1, pp. 25-26.

[82]Die Religion in Geschichte und Gegenwart, 3rd ed., s.v. "Stadkult," by F. C. Grant and W. von Soden. Oppenheim, Mesopotamia, p. 115.

[83]Aloysius Fitzgerald, "The Mythological Background for the presentation of Jerusalem as a queen and false worship as adultery in the Old Testament," CBQ 34 (1972):403-16.

[84]Jos 15:45, 47; Nu 21:25; 32:42; Ju 1:27, for example.

[85]Fitzgerald, "Background," pp. 415-16.

[86]Pedersen, Israel, vol. 4, p. 380.

[87]Interpreter's Dictionary of the Bible, s.v. "Bethel," by J. L. Kelso and "Shechem," by W. L. Reed and L. E. Toombs.

[88]Von Rad, "Problem," pp. 28-9 and "Das form-geschichtliche Problem des Hexateuch," Gesammelte Studien zum Alten Testament, vol. 2, ed. Rudolf Smend (München: Chr. Kaiser Verlag, 1961), pp. 36-7.

[89]Von Rad, Studies, pp. 70-71. Among Christians, this theology of the liturgical present appears as anamnesis. See, for example, Gregory Dix, The Shape of the Liturgy (London: Dacre Press, 1945), p. 243.

[90]Klostermann, Pentateuch, p. 348. Tiffany "Parenesis," pp. 11-12 considers these definitions of parenesis only in terms of other genres, such as history or law, misleading.

[91]Mowinckel, Psalms, vol. 1, p. 175.

[92]Baltzar, Formulary, pp. 89-93.

[93]W. M. L. DeWette, Dissertatio critica que Deuteronomium a prioribus Pentateuchi libris diversum alius suisdam recentioris opus esse monstratus (Jena, 1805).

[94]Albright, Stone Age, p. 319.

[95]Childs, Introduction, p. 209.

[96]Wright, "Cult," p. 14.

[97]Norbert Lohfink, "Lectures in Deuteronomy," Rome, 1968 (Mimeographed). See also, Interpreter's Dictionary of the Bible, supplementary vol., s.v. "Deuteronomy," by Norbert Lohfink.

[98]Wright, "Cult," pp. 13-14.

[99]Gottwald, Tribes, p. 14.

[100]R. Lapointe, "La valeur linguistique du Sitz im Leben," Biblica 52 (1971):469-87.

[101]Bächli, Israel, p. 192.

[102]Albrecht Alt, "Die Heimat des Deuteronomium," in Kleine Schriften zur Geschichte des Volkes Israel, vol. 2 (München: Beck, 1968), pp. 250-75. See F. Dummermuth, "Zur deuteronomischen Kulttheologie und ihren Voraussetzungen," ZAW 70 (1958):59-98. Actually Alt has other reasons for assigning Deuteronomy a northern setting, and he is aware that David, too, was an *elected* monarch!

[103]Bächli, Israel, p. 90. The command: *meditate on it* (the Torah) *day and night* appears in Jos 1:8 and in Ps 1:2. However, in both places, the verb is *hāgâ*, and not *qārā'* as in Dt 17:19 and 2 K 23:2.

[104]Oppenheim, Mesopotamia, p. 98.

[105]Bächli, Israel, pp. 163-4.

[106]Ibid., pp. 213-14.

[107]Oppenheim, Mesopotamia, p. 100.

[108]Hayes and Miller, History, pp. 356-9.

[109]R. A. F. MacKenzie, "The City and Israelite Religion," CBQ 25 (1963):60.

[110]W. L. Moran, Review of Israel und die Völker, by Otto Bächli, in Biblica 44 (1963):377.

[111]See Keith W. Whitelam, The Just King: Monarchial Judicial Authority in Ancient Israel (Sheffield, England: Journal for the Study of Old Testament Press, 1979).

[112]Nicholson, Deuteronomy, p. 69.

[113]William E. Claburn, "Deuteronomy and Collective Behavior" (Ph.D. dissertation, Princeton University, 1968), p. 99.

[114]Claburn, "Deuteronomy"; Gottwald, Tribes and Frick, City also use the social sciences in Biblical interpretation.

[115]Von Rad, Deuteronomy, pp. 11-30; Walter Brueggemann, "A Form Critical Study of the Cultic Material in Deuteronomy: an analysis of the nature of the cultic encounter in the Mosaic tradition" (Th.D. dissertation, Union Theological Seminary, 1961), p. 25 and Weinfeld, Deuteronomy, p. 125 are among the scholars assuming an institutional paradigm.

[116]Claburn, "Deuteronomy," p. 3. See Brevard S. Childs, "Deuteronomic Formulae of the Exodus Traditions," in Hebräische Wortforschung, ed. Benedict Hartmann et al. (Leiden: Brill, 1967), p. 39.

[117]Ralph H. Turner and Lewis M. Killian, Collective Behavior (Englewood Cliffs, NJ.: Prentice-Hall, 1957), p. 332. See Claburn, "Deuteronomy," pp. 4-6.

[118]Claburn, "Deuteronomy," p. 5. See A. R. Burn, The Pelican History of Greece (Baltimore: Penguin Books, 1966), pp. 97-98. J. P. Mahaffy, Social Life in Greece from Homer to Menander (London: Macmillan, 1888), pp. 83 ff; and A. Andrews, The Greek Tyrants (London: Hutchinson's University Library, 1956).

[119]Klostermann, Pentateuch; Ludwig Koehler, Die hebräische Rechtsgemeinde (Zürich: Jahresbericht der Universitat Zürich, 1930), and von Rad, Deuteronomy.

[120]Aage Bentzen, Die Josianische Reform and Ihre Voraussetzungen (Copenhagen: P. Haase & Sohne Verlag, 1926), pp. 34, 37, 100. See Claburn, "Deuteronomy," pp. 9-17 + 23. Bentzen also identifies this persuasive speech in Deuteronomy as *propaganda*, but, according to Claburn, Bentzen did not exploit his insight. Bentzen associated the genre with the Levites, however, and

not as Claburn does with the prophets. Von Rad also
proposed the Levites were Deuteronomy's curators, but
on the basis of their association with the genre
parenesis!

[121]Von Rad, Theology, vol. 2, p. 28.

[122]Albright, Stone Age, p. 312. See also, Sklba,
City.

[123]Paul A. Riemann, "Desert and Return to Desert
in the Pre-exilic Prophets" (Ph.D. dissertation,
Harvard University, 1964).

[124]William Hugh Brownlee, "Ezekiel's Copper
Caldron and Blood on the Rock (Chapter 24:1-14) in
For Me to Live: Essays in Honor of James Leon Kelso,
ed. Robert A. Coughenour (Cleveland, OH.: Dillon/
Liederbach Books, 1972), pp. 21-43.

[125]Weinfeld, Deuteronomy.

[126]Deuteronomy has been equated with the Torah
in such works as John Skinner, Prophecy and Religion
(Cambridge: The University Press, 1922), p. 103.

[127]DeWette, Dissertatio.

[128]Weinfeld, Deuteronomy, pp. 320-370 gives over
two hundred examples of Deuteronomic formulas.

[129]Weinfeld, Deuteronomy, pp. 188-9.

[130]See also, John 10:34, where Ps 82:6 is called
Torah: *Jesus answered them, "Is it not written in
your law (εν νομων υμων)* , 'I said, you are gods?'
(Ps 82:6).

[131]See Je 18:18 where *law, word,* and *counsel* are
specifically mentioned. However *law* translates *tôrâ*
and not *da'at.*

[132]For example Dt 4:44-5. See Barnabas Lindars,
"Torah in Deuteronomy," in Festschrift for D. W.

Thomas (New York: Cambridge University Press, 1968), p. 131.

[133]For example, Dt 4:44-5. See Barnabas Lindars, "Torah in Deuteronomy," p. 128.

[134]J. Begrich, "Die Priesterliche Tora," in Gesammelte Studien (München: Kaiser Verlag, 1964), pp. 232-60. Cf. "Das Priesterliche Heilsorakel," ibid., pp. 217-31.

[135]Hans Walter Wolff, Hosea (Philadelphia: Fortress Press, 1974), pp. 78-80 + 138.

[136]This tradition appears, for example, in Ho 4:6, 8:12, Dt 1:5, 17:19, 31:9 ff, Ps 1.

[137]James A. Sanders, "Adaptable for Life." The nature and function of Canon," in Magnalia Dei: The Mighty Acts of God, Essays on the Bible and Archaelogy in Memory of G. Ernest Wright, ed. F. M. Cross, W. E. Lemke and P. D. Miller (Garden City, NY.: Doubleday and Co., 1976), pp. 531-60.

[138]See Interpreter's Dictionary of the Bible, supplementary vol., s.v. "Torah," by James A. Sanders. See also: C. H. Dodd, The Bible and the Greeks (London: Hodder and Stoughton, 1935), pp. 25-41; Theological Dictionary of the New Testament, s.v. "νομος," by W. Gutbrod; George F. Moore, Judaism in the First Centuries of The Christian Era, vol. 1 (Cambridge: Harvard University Press, 1950-54), pp. 235-80; Gunnar Östborn, Tora in the Old Testament: a semantic study (Lund: Ohlsson, 1945), pp. 60-64; Sanders, Torah and E. Würthwein, "Der Sinn des Gesetzes im AT," ZThK 55 (1958):255-70.

[139]Weinfeld, Deuteronomy, 158 ff.

[140]Albright, Stone Age, p. 315.

[141]Bächli, Israel; Weinfeld, Deuteronomy; and Claburn, "Deuteronomy."

[142]Alt, "Origins," Noth, System and von Rad, Deuteronomy.

CHAPTER III

THE CITY TEXTS

Deuteronomy 6:10-19

Genre[1]

Structure analysis

Parenesis to remain faithful to Yahweh in the city	Dt 6:10-19
I. Protasis (kî temporal clause)	10-11
A. Conditions satisfied by Yahweh	10-11a
1. Condition proper	10a α
2. Qualifications of *the land*	10a β-11a
a. Oath formula	10a β-δ
1) Oath formula proper	10a β γ
a) Basic formula	10a β
b) Qualifications of *your fathers*	10a γ
2) Land grant formula	10a δ
b. Catalogue	10-11a
1) Entry	10b
a) Entry proper *(Cities)*	10b α
b) Qualifications	10b β
(1) *great and godly*	10b β 1-2
(2) *which you did not build*	10b β 3-5
2) Entry	11a α
a) Entry proper *(Barns)*	11a α 1
b) Qualifications	11a α 2-6
(1) *full of all good things*	11a α 2-4
(2) *which you did not fill*	11a α 5-6
3) Entry	11a β
a) Entry proper *(Cisterns)*	11a β 1
b) Qualification	11a β 2-4
4) Entry	11a γ
a) Entry proper *(Vineyards & trees)*	11a γ 1-2
b) Qualification	11a γ 3-5

91

                    (1) Formula proper   Dt 6:19a
                    (2) Qualification
                        (oath formula)   19b

Dt 6:10-19:   Parenesis

        Deuteronomy 6:10-19 appeals for compliance with
the obligation that Israel serve Yahweh alone. This
stipulation appears, for example, in the Decalogue
(Dt 5:6-10) and *Hear, O Israel: The Lord our God is
one Lord; and you shall love the Lord your God with all
your heart, and with all your soul, and with all your
might* (Dt 6:4). Deuteronomy 6:10-19 specifies this
obligation with six directives:

        1) ...take heed lest you forget the
                Lord   (Dt 6:12)
        2) You shall fear the Lord your
                God....   (Dt 6:13)
        3) You shall not go after other
                gods...   (Dt 6:14)
        4) You shall not put the Lord your
                God to the test....   (Dt 6:16)
        5) You shall diligently keep the
                commandments of the Lord....   (Dt 6:17)
        6) And you shall do what is right
                in the sight of the Lord....   (Dt 6:18)

        This text motivates its audience with gratitude
*(who brought you out of the land of Egypt, out of the
house of bondage* in Dt 6:12), fear *(lest the anger of
the Lord your God be kindled against you, and he
destroy you from off the face of the earth* in Dt 6:15),
and materialism *(that it may go well with you, and
that you may go in and take possession of the good
land* in Dt 6:18). These subjective appeals urge the
audience personally to will to be faithful to Yahweh,
and to Yahweh alone, thus averting punishment (Dt
6:15a).

        The silent audience is addressed some 37x with
second person forms (30x in the singular; 7 x in the
plural). This one-way, direct address character of
the unit is indicative of *rhetoric*, the umbrella genre
to which Dt 6:10-19 belongs. This particular kind of
rhetoric is *parenesis*: an arrangement of commands
(Dt 6:13, 17-18a), prohibitions (Dt 6:14, 16), and
admonitions (Dt 6:12), which are qualified by

                            93

motivations (Dt 6:15, 18b-19).

The logic of Dt 6:10-19 is simple: Yahweh is blessing you with abundance; use that abundance to strengthen your faith not to weaken it.

The impact of Dt 6:10-19 is strongest in the repeated use of *which you did not (āser lō')* in Dt 6:10-11. Craigie can even scan the lines for a regular poetic stress.

Great and good cities	which you did not build (3+3)
And houses filled with every good thing	which you did not fill (3+3)
And hewn cisterns,	which you did not hew (3+3)
Vineyard and olive trees	which you did not plant (2+3)
Then you shall eat	and you shall be satisfied (1+1)[2]

Repetition drives home the argument that gratitude is a duty.

The author also employs the technique of presenting both the negative and positive sides of the argument, basically saying the same thing twice. The positive-negative technique is a literary cousin of repetition. The negative argument is made in Dt 6:12-15, the positive in Dt 6:16-19.

...lest you forget...	...you shall not...test
...you shall fear...	...you shall keep...
...you shall serve...	
...you shall swear...	
...you shall not go...	

The conditions set forth in Dt 6:10-11 must be fulfilled before the parenesis in Dt 6:12-19 makes any sense. This protasis-apodosis structure convinced Liedke that the unit is a case law similar to those introduced by *and when (wehāyâ kî')* in the Qumran material.[3] However, as Merendino points out, *and when* is characteristic, not of case law, but parenesis.[4] Furthermore, the *when (kî)* clause in Dt 6:10-11 is not a *case*, but rather a *temporal condition*.[5] Yahweh will grant Israel cities; Israel will enjoy them. *When* those two conditions are satisfied, *then* Israel must

94

conscientiously serve Yahweh alone.

Without the provisional element in Dt 6:10-11, Dt 6:10-19 would be what Tiffany calls *paraclesis...a speech of exhortation directed to those who have already received....*[6] However, even if the Moabite perspective in Dt 6:10a is only a literary fiction, the assumption is still made that the unit is addressed not to those who inhabit cities, but to whose who will, and is thus *parenesis*.

Dt 6:10b-11: Catalogue

Deuteronomy 6:10b-11 is the only section of the parenesis with vocabulary that is not Deuteronomic. The remaining portions of the unit use cliches familiar throughout the book. Weinfeld identifies eleven separate examples.[7]

...take heed lest you forget the Lord	Dt 6:12a
...the house of bondage	12b
...you shall serve the Lord	13
You shall not go after other gods	14
...the gods of the peoples who are round about you	14
...and he destroy you from off the face of the earth	15
...the commandments...and his testimonies and his statutes	17
And you shall do what is right and good in the sight of the Lord	18a
...you may go in and take possession of the land	18b
...the good land	18b
...that it may go well with you	18b

There are four physical objects in Dt 6:10b-11: 1) cities; 2) barns; 3) cisterns; and 4) vineyards and olive trees, and four possible collection-genres to which the passage may belong: *catalogue, list, series,* or *register.* Knierim distinguishes these genres from one another on the basis of the relationship of the objects to one another, the order of the objects in the collection, and the purpose of the collection.[8]

95

Although he uses the word *die Aufzählung,* rather than *die Liste,* von Rad describes Dt 6:10b-11 as a *list.*[9] But, according to Knierim, the objects in a list are not related to one another, and therefore Dt 6:10b-11a is not merely a list. Each object is a characteristic of *the land (hā'āres)* mentioned in Dt 6:10a.

Furthermore, Dt 6:10b-11a is not a *register.* A register is compiled explicitly for the purpose of collecting taxes. Deuteronomy 6:10b-11a, on the other hand, is a legal document which inventories the property which Yahweh, as testator, bequeaths to Israel, his beneficiary.[10] Such documents appear frequently in Ancient Near Eastern treaties as Baltzer and Nougayrol have shown.[11]

Moreover, Deuteronomy 6:10b-11a is not a *series.* In a series, the elements always occur in the same traditional or logical sequence. The lack of traditional or logical sequence in Dt 6:10b-11a can be seen by contrasting it with Dt 8:7-10.

There are six different objects in the two catalogues: 1) cities, 2) water, 3) crops, 4) trees and vineyards, 5) bread and 6) natural minerals. Only three appear in both catalogues. The sequence in Dt 6 is 1) crops, 2) water, 3) trees and vineyards, while the sequence in Dt 8 is 1) water, 2) crops, 3) trees and vineyards.

Furthermore, in Dt 8, *vines* is mentioned with the cash crops: *wheat and barley, ...vines and fig trees and pomegranates.* This element in Dt 8 occurs at the same place in the structure as *barns* in Dt 6. However, in Dt 6 *vineyards* joins *olive trees.* These two kinds of orchards or gardens are linked to form a single element and balanced in Dt 8 with *olive trees and honey.*

Style is not the only difference between the two units. Deuteronomy 6 enumerates the assets of Canaan resulting from human productivity, while Dt 8 itemizes the natural resources with which Yahweh himself has blessed the land. The land itself is the primary value in Dt 8, while the improvement which human beings have made to the land is the primary value in Dt 6. Thus Dt 8 refers to Canaan as *the good land* (7a, 10b), while in Dt 6 it is the cities (10b) and the crops (11b) which are *good.*[12]

However, the repetition of *land* in Dt 8 and *which you did not...* in Dt 6, indicates that the objects are arranged to reflect a concern for places-to-live, i.e., *cities;* things-to-eat, i.e., *barns full of goods;* water-to-drink, i.e., *cisterns;* and raw-materials-to-manufacture, i.e., *vines and olive trees.* All four are critical for a stable urban economy. Thus the genre of Dt 6:10b-11a is not *list, register* or *series;* Dt 6:10b-11a is a *catalogue:* an enumeration of items according to a particular system of classification.[13]

Deuteronomy 8:7-10 is not the only parallel of this kind of catalogue describing the land. Je 2:13, Ne 9:25-26, and Dt 28:1-4, and 2 C 26:9-10 also have such descriptions. Jeremiah 2:13 considers cisterns the product of apostasy. They are monuments to Israel's futile attempt to insure herself against drought. Deuteronomy 6:10-19, on the other hand, considers cisterns gifts from Yahweh. For Jeremiah, urbanization is a transgression, whereas for Deuteronomy, urbanization is a temptation. Nehemiah 9:25-26 is part of a confession of penitential prayer with close ties to the tradition on which Dt 6:10-19 is based. Its order in the catalogue, cities, barns, cisterns, vineyards and olive groves, is identical to that of Dt 6:10-19. In Dt 28:1-6, as in Dt 6:10-19, cities appear first in the catalogue. Other than that, the objects in the two units are completely different.

> And if you obey the voice of the Lord your
> God, being careful to do all his command-
> ments which I command you this day, the
> Lord your God will set you high above all
> the nations of the earth. And all these
> blessings shall come upon you and overtake
> you, if you obey the voice of the Lord your
> God. Blessed shall you be in the city, and
> blessed shall you be in the field. Blessed
> shall be the fruit of your body, and the
> fruit of your ground, and the fruit of your
> beasts, the increase of your cattle, and the
> young of your flock. Blessed shall be your
> basket and your kneading-trough. Blessed
> shall you be when you come in, and blessed
> shall you be when you go out (Dt 28:1-6).

The presence of the city in the collection of objects connected with fertility emphasizes the centrality of the city in the economy of Israel. 2 Chronicles 26:9-10 arranges the accomplishments of Uzziah, king

97

of Judah from 783-742 BCE, in the same order as
Dt 6:10-19, viz., cities, cisterns and vineyards. This
text and Ne 9:25-26 are directly dependent on Dt 6:10-
19.

Dt 6:11b: Conditions

Like Dt 6:10a, Dt 6:11b only presents a question
of time-when, and not possibility. Israel will enjoy
the benefits of an urban land. The formula *you eat and
are full* appears frequently.[14] Technically, there are
not two conditions but one, since the formula is a
hendiadys in which two independent words connected by
and are used instead of a condition and a qualification.
The sense is *you will eat your fill*.

Dt 6:12-19: Parenesis proper

The motivations which appear in Dt 6:15 and Dt
6:18b-19 divide Dt 6:12-19 into two parts.[15] The resulting subdivisions are Dt 6:12-15 and Dt 6:16-19.
Each subdivision is a parenesis also consisting of two
parts: directives and motivations. The dominant
character of Dt 6:12-15 as an attempt to persuade the
audience *not to do* something is indicated by the
admonition in Dt 6:12 and the prohibition in Dt 6:14.
The character of Dt 6:16-19 as an attempt to persuade
the audience *to do* something is indicated by the
commands in Dt 6:17-18a.[16]

In order to create a parenesis which generally
requires both a negative and a positive element, the
admonition in Dt 6:12 and the prohibition in Dt 6:14
are paired with a command in Dt 6:13. Likewise, the
commands in Dt 6:17-18a are paired with a prohibition
in Dt 6:16.

This analysis of Dt 6:12-19 questions Seitz'
position that Dt 6:15 is the crux of the unit.[17] The
greatest difficulty with *chiasm* as a literary pattern
continues to be defining the genre. Soulen describes
chiasm as *the inverted sequence or cross-over of
parallel words or ideas in a bicolon (distich),
sentence or larger literary unit.*[18] Apart from the
characteristic that *chiasm* or *an inverted sequence or
cross-over of parallels,* the rest of the definition
is too broad to use in analyzing any text. Seitz, for
example, builds his chiasm for Dt 6:10-19 not only
with words (*šāmar* in Dt 6:12 & 17), but on ideas
(*good land* in Dt 10-11 & 18), genre (prohibitions in

98

Dt 6:14 & 16) and number (plurals in Dt 6:14 & 16) as well. It is questionable whether such a variety of principles can be used to form a single sequence, or whether only one principle, such as genre, should be used, especially in longer units such as Dt 6:10-19. Without establishing some guidelines for what constitutes a parallel, the number of chiasms in any text is uncontrolled. Therefore, although Dt 6:10-19 is a coherent unit as Seitz argues, Dt 6:15 is not the focal point around which the remaining elements of the structure are arranged.

Lohfink, on the basis of parallels in Dt and elsewhere, divides Dt 6:12-19 after Dt 6:16.[19] However, Lohfink does not take the motivations in Dt 6:15 and Dt 6:18b-19 into account. He attaches Dt 6:15 to the prohibition in Dt 6:14 and considers Dt 6:17-19 a cluster of cliches separate from his text. He gives no formal reasons for not including the commands in Dt 6:17-18a in the commands which are supposed to make up his apodosis. Separating Dt 6:17-19 from the rest of the unit simply on the grounds that its vocabulary is stereotyped is unreasonable. Most of the language in the entire unit is stereotyped.[20] Separating Dt 6:17-19 from the rest of the unit on the grounds that it is introduced by a grammatical construction using the infinitive and finite form of the verb *keep, observe (šāmar)* is also unreasonable. This infinitive absolute is not the irrefutable sign of a new unit. For example, the command: *Observe the sabbath day* (Dt 5:12) is introduced by the same grammatical construction, and yet the verse does not begin a new unit.[21] Therefore, Dt 6:17-19 should be analyzed as an integral part of Dt 6:10-17 and not separated from it.

Finally, Tiffany separates Dt 6:12-13 from Dt 6:14-15 on the basis of content. Deuteronomy 6:12-13 deals with fidelity; Dt 6:14-19 with obedience.[22] Content is one key to the structure of this text, but the distinction between *fidelity* and *obedience* is not clear enough. It would be hard to show that the characteristics of *fidelity* are consistently *not forgetting Yahweh* and *fearing the Lord, serving him, and swearing by his name,* while *obedience* is recognized as *not walking after other gods, not putting Yahweh to the test, diligently keeping the commandments, and doing what is right and good.*

Also in his structure, Tiffany considers the

motivations in Dt 6:15 & 18b-19 applicable only to the
directive which immediately precedes each. Thus Dt
6:15 is a motivation only for Dt 6:14; Dt 6:18b-19 is a
motivation only for Dt 6:18a. Allowing the motivations
to affect not only the directive immediately preceding,
but the three directives immediately preceding,
strengthens the persuasive character of the entire unit,
by toning down the emphatic nature of the commands and
prohibitions. Furthermore, there is nothing in the
definition of a motivation limiting its use to the
directive closest to it in the text.[23]

Dt 6:12: Admonition

Generally, an admonition has two parts: 1) a
directive with the verb in the imperative mood; and
2) a motivation. Deuteronomy 12:23 is an example of
the standard admonition.

DIRECTIVE: *Only be sure that you do not eat
the blood...*

MOTIVATION: *...for the blood is life...*

Deuteronomy 6:12, however, is an admonition consisting
only of a directive. Therefore, the construction
Be careful lest... (hiššāmer lekā pen) is used
instead of the imperative form of the verb, or the
negative particle (*lō'*) plus the imperfect. The
construction is a counsel or warning against fault or
oversight and not an order to restrain or stop. This
is, in fact, how both von Rad and Seitz describe the
genre of Dt 6:12--a warning.[24] The same construction
appears in Dt 8:11; 12:13,19,30; 15:9 in the singular;
and Dt 4:23; 11:16 in the plural, as well as Gn 24:6,
31:24; Ex 34:12.

According to Lohfink, the construction *be careful
lest* introduces not only *parenesis,* the umbrella genre
to which both *admonition* and *exhortation* belong, but
order and *instruction* as well.[25] Tiffany, however,
considers Dt 6:12 an *admonition,* not on the basis of
the construction *be careful lest,* but on the basis of
its intention to remove any obstacles the audience
might have to remaining faithful to Yahweh.[26]
Exhortation and admonitions are generally distinguished
from commands and prohibitions by this characteristic
of seeking to persuade the listener rather than to
compel the listener. Commands and prohibitions use
imperative verb forms, and make no effort to remove the

subjective obstacles to compliance which the listener might have. Motivations are completely missing. Especially in Deuteronomy, motivations recall past history, as Dt 6:12 does by referring to the exodus; and as Dt 6:16 does by referring to Massah; and as Dt 6:17 does by referring to the covenant. However, here in Dt 6:12-15, the primary motivation affecting the directive in Dt 6:12 is found in Dt 6:15. It employs fear more than history. Therefore, three characteristics identify Dt 6:12 as an *admonition*, rather than a *prohibition:* 1) the construction *be careful lest*; 2) the motivations in Dt 6:15; and 3) the intention of the text.

Dt 6:13: Command

The genre of Dt 6:13 is *command;* a direct commission, based upon authority such as custom, law, decree. It is expressed by an imperative form of the verb, or forms with an imperative function. Of the six directives contained in this parenesis in Dt 6:12-19, Dt 6:13,14,16,17,18a are compulsive.[27]

There are at least three reasons why these commands and prohibitions do not transform the entire unit from parenesis into the compulsive genre order. First, as a genre, parenesis customarily ,combines directives which are compulsive (command and prohibition) with those that are persuasive (exhortation and admonition), so the presence of compulsive directives here in Dt 6:12-19 along with persuasive directives is not irregular. Second, the presence of persuasive directives in the same unit with command and prohibition greatly modifies their influence on the unit as a whole. Third, the general motivations in both Dt 6:15 and 18b-19 apply to the command in 13 and the prohibition in 16, respectively. Therefore, although both lack their own special motivation clauses, the persuasive character of the general motivations does soften the compulsive impact of the forms in Dt 6:13,16.

Dt 6:13β -b: Secondary commands

Deuteronomy 6:13 is a coherent unit of three commands. Deuteronomy 6:13aβ is primary, because it could stand alone, independent of the surrounding material, and be completely intelligible: *You shall fear the Lord your God....* This primary command in Dt 6:13a also occurs alone in Dt 6:2.

Deuteronomy 6:13a β-b is secondary, not only because it follows *You shall fear the Lord your God...,* but because it uses pronominal suffixes (*him* and *his name*) which makes no sense without the antecedent (*Lord*) in Dt 6:13a α. Neither of these secondary commands could stand independently and be intelligible. Hence both are qualifications of the primary command in Dt 6:13a α.

Dt 6:15a: Motivation

The motivation in Dt 6:15a is a credential (*eine Bekenntnisformel*), which Yahweh uses to describe himself.

> ...you shall not bow down to them or serve them; for I the Lord your God am a jealous God visiting the iniquity of the fathers upon the children to the third and the fourth generation of those who hate me. (Dt 5:9)

Here, this formula is distinct from Dt 6:15b, mainly on traditio-historical grounds.[28] The distinction between Dt 6:15a and Dt 6:15b is also indicated by the particles which introduce each motivation. Deuteronomy 6:15a is introduced by *for (kî)* while Dt 6:15b is introduced by *lest (pen)*.

Dt 6:15b β: Extermination formula

Independent of its use here in Dt 6:10-19, the extermination formula in Dt 6:15a has a tradition-history in which *pĕnê hā'adāmâ* means *the face of the earth*. However, Deuteronomy favors reading *hā'adāmâ* as *the land of Canaan* in particular, and not *the planet earth* in general. Furthermore, here in Dt 6:10-19, the *face* indicates the human improvements catalogued in Dt 6:10b-11a, viz., cities, barns, cisterns, vinehard and olive trees, and not natural resources as it does elsewhere (e.g., Dt 8:7-10).[29]

Dt 6:17: Comand

Like the admonition in Dt 6:12, Dt 6:17 consists only of a directive, and uses the verb *You shall diligently keep (sāmôr tišmerûn)*. However, Dt 6:12 is an *admonition,* while Dt 6:17 is an *order,* not a standard parenesis as Lohfink suggests.[30] The distinction between the two is based on syntax and the ideological matrix of the verb *keep*.

102

Deuteronomy 6:17 uses the infinitive absolute with the finite form of the verb: a construction which is standard for the genre *order*.[31] In addition, behavior such as *loving* and *remembering*, which in Western culture are considered only subjective attitudes which cannot be ordered, are observable and public responsibilities in ancient Israel.[32]

Dt 6:19b: Oath formula

Deuteronomy 6:19b uses the verb *promised*, rather than *swore*. However, the genre of this clause is the *oath formula* common in Deuteronomy, and not the *messenger formula:* ... *thus says the Lord* common in prophecy.   This oath formula is often connected with the land grant formula to stress that the land is a gift from Yahweh to Israel.   In view of Dt 6:10-19, however, it is impossible to argue, as Plöger does, that it is Yahweh who gives Israel the land.   Moses never gives Israel the land, but only its cities (Dt 3:9) and its estates or inheritances (Dt 3:20).[33] It may be true that Moses never gives Israel the land, but here in Dt 6:10-19, it is clearly Yahweh and not Moses who gives Israel the cities, barns, cisterns, orchards and vineyards.

Setting[34]

The institutional or societal matrix of Dt 6:10-19 is the Jerusalem court, where priests exercising a caretaker role over the Judean monarchy were preparing the way for complete independence from Assyria, whose power in Canaan was declining.   These priests are influential not only with the king, but with the people of Jerusalem and the pilgrims from the outlying cities of Judah.   However, their authority is not official. Therefore, they employ parenesis, rather than law to promote their ideals.

Weinfeld has argued that sages rather than priests are the custodians of these traditions.[35]   Both were present in Jerusalem society.   However, here in Dt 6:10-19, although there is a wisdom vocabulary, the theology of blessing as a free gift, rather than a deserved reward is not sapiential.[36]   Likewise, it was the priests rather than the sages who had an historical connection with the covenant liturgies of ancient Israel, and Dt 6:10-19 makes use of elements from the covenant genre, such as the history in Dt 6:10-11 and the stipulations in Dt 6:12-19. Nicholson can only point to the motivation in Dt 6:18b-19 as characteristic of the militant piety of the prophets, who threatened Israel with exile.[37] However, the genre parenesis is not characteristic of the prophets who preferred oracles of judgment or verdicts.

The cultural, epochal or historical matrix of Dt 6:10-19 is the reign of Josiah (640-609 BCE), not Hezekiah (716-687 BCE) nor Manasseh (687-642 BCE), nor the Exile (587-538 BCE). Both Josiah and Hezekiah are considered to be kings like David. Both did *what was right in the eyes of the Lord* (cf Dt 6:18) and *walked in all the ways of David* (cf 2 K 22:2b). However, only in Josiah's time is there an historical expansion of the kingdom; Hezekiah did not expand his kingdom, but in fact followed such nationalistic policies that Assyria reduced the size of his kingdom. Therefore, passages like Dt 6:10-19, built on the condition of imminent expansion (*And when the Lord your God brings you....*) are a more likely form of encouragement for the armies of Josiah poised on the eve of a new campaign, than words addressed to Hezekiah or to the persecuted Yahwists under Manassah, or, for that matter, to the exiles in Babylon.

The key to the expansion formula in Dt 6:10a is the verb *bring (bô'): And when the Lord your God brings you into the land....* The verb does appear with Yahweh as the subject in the exilic literature of Ez 33-48 and Is 40-55. Yahweh *brings* Cyrus (e.g., Is 43:5), the exiles home (e.g., Is 49:22), enemies against Israel (e.g., Ez 38:16) and Ezekiel to one section of the temple after the other (Ez 40-46). The greatest similarity between the use of *bring* in the expansion formula in Deuteronomy and its use in the exilic literature appears in constructions like Ez 34:13: *And I will bring them out from the peoples, and gather them from the countries and will bring them into their own land.* But in Ezekiel, the destination is not simply *the land* or *the land which he swore to your fathers to give you,* but *their own land* or *the land of Israel.* Also, Ez 33--48 and Is 40--55 never describe this destination as a land of cities, and silos and cisterns and vineyards. Only in Deuteronomy is the land already developed. Exilic literature celebrates the liberation of Israel, more than her expansion, and the land into which she is brought needs to be restored.

Deuteronomy 6:10-19 certainly criticizes policies like those pursued by Manassah. However, even a brief comparison of the language and content of the parenesis in Dt 6:10-19 and the description of the reign of Manassah in 2 K 21:1-18 reveals only the vocabulary of the Deuteronomic Historian and the points of comparison by which he weighed all the kings of Israel and Judah. There is nothing unique or compelling in the passages that would suggest the speaker in Dt 6:10-19 was delivering veiled warnings to the Yahwists of Manassah's time, which would keep them faithful to the reform of Hezekiah. Furthermore, persecution threatened these Yahwist reformers (2 K 21:16), and it is unlikely that a command like Dt 6:13 would have been veiled enough to avoid reprisals.

The intellectual, ideological and theological matrix of Dt 6:10-19 is not just the Deuteronomic reform of the 7th century BCE. The values which Dt 6:10-19 promotes, and the policies which it opposes, were also relevant in the 12th and 10th centuries BCE.

Deuteronomy 6:10-19 clearly states that cities, cisterns, barns, vineyards and orchards are given to Israel by Yahweh. Feudal kings were notorious builders. They remodeled temples, fortified cities, built garrisons to house and supply their mercenaries, and to provision their courts. The language of Dt 6:10-11 referring to *great and goodly cities* (language used in Judges to describe the fortifications of the Canaanite cities), and foodstuffs and water certainly applies to these elaborate efforts of the Israelite monarchy to create just such an empire of plenty. Such efforts placed heavy burdens on the common people. So, Dt 6:10-19 recalls that it is Yahweh alone who provides. The promethean efforts of the royal building programs were sacrilegious because they encouraged the builder to look at his plenty and feel secure. But in the early monarchy as well, there were strong objections from segments of ancient Israel for whom the suffering caused by feudal kings in Canaan was still vivid. Among those which have been studied are Shechem, Gibeon, Shiloh and Hebron.

In 1976, Knierim proposed a 10th century BCE setting for the early decalogue.[38] The genre was used by the priests of Shechem in an effort to counteract the expanding power of the king. This carefully anti-monarchial reform of the priests was a forerunner

to the role of the prophetic movement as the king's
loyal opposition. Like Knierim, Wolff also sees a
similarity between the priests and the early
prophets.[39] Since the cities of Canaan would have
suffered most under the feudalism of pre-Israelite
kings, it is not surprising that the urban segments of
Israel would have been the most vocal opponents of the
Israelite kings. Shechem was just such a segment.

Blenkinsopp has studied the covenant by which the
metropolitan communities of both Shechem and Gilgal
joined ancient Israel.[40] According to Blenkinsopp,
Jos 9 recalls a disparity treaty which took place at
Gilgal between an urban league and Israel. The urban
league was a tetrapolis consisting of Gibeon,
Chephirah, Beeroth and Kiriath-jearim (Jos 9:17). The
treaty established peace between the Hurrians, who were
citizens of the league, and the Israelites from
Benjamin/Joseph. The Gibeonites were to serve as cult
personnel for the central sanctuary. This level of the
text is not the least hostile toward the incorporation
of the urban league into Israel.

Although Shechem is never named in Deuteronomy,
scholars like Mendenhall and Lewy have argued that the
covenant ceremony described in Jos 24 and the covenant
ceremony described in Dt 27 are parallel and hence
should both be set in Shechem.[41] Blenkinsopp sees
enough similarity between this covenant ceremony and
the treaty with the Gibeonite league to argue that
Shechem too was an early corporate member of Israel.[42]
The resistance which an urban league like that
connected with Shechem would have toward monarchy can
be seen in the failure of Abimelek and his family to
establish an hereditary kingship. Therefore, it is
likely that the same resistance would be shown to the
hereditary kingship which David and his family
established. These urban leagues were among the
staunchest custodians of the traditions of equality on
which ancient Israel was based.

Flanagan has suggested that it was precisely to
overcome such opposition to the monarchy that David
moved his government from Hebron to Jerusalem.
Flanagan studies the traditions connected with the
cities of Hebron and Shiloh and concludes that because
of their strong support of non-monarchial principles,
the great tradition developed by David in Jerusalem
systematically downplays the contribution of these two
urban centers to early Israel.[43] Together with the

urban leagues of Gibeon and Shechem, there was the
urban community of Shiloh which, as a corporate
member of early Israel, was a center of opposition to
the attempts of David and his family to reestablish an
hereditary monarchy on feudal principles in Canaan.
All three are northern communities and possible
settings for the kind of traditions represented by
Dt 6:10-19--traditions which respect urban life as a
gift of Yahweh, and not the king.

There is also an urban league which joined early
Israel at Hebron in the south.[44] There was an early
community of Yahweh worshippers here at Hebron. Caleb,
not Joshua, is the hero of the Hebron traditions,
which eventually gave birth to the Priestly Tradition
(P). This community was consistently anti-monarchic
and stubbornly opposed David's efforts to turn Israel
into a kingdom.

The significance of urban centers like Shechem,
Gibeon, Shiloh and Hebron for the theology on which
early Israel was built is not simply their opposition
to hereditary monarchy and its feudal form of government. These urban communities brought into early
Israel a profound respect for the city and its
institutions as Yahweh's gift. Thus they provide the
intellectual, ideological and theological matrix for
traditions found in Dt 6:10-19.

Prior to its present setting in the Hebrew canon,
Dt 6:10-19 enjoyed at least two other literary
settings. Tiffany considers Dt 4:45 + 5:12--11:29 an
independent composition which he calls a *memorandum*.[45]
The composition applies early traditions to situations
occurring throughout the turbulent reign of Josiah in
Judah. Appealing to the authority of Moses, the
memorandum attempts to influence royal policies.
Tiffany is able to argue the independence of Dt 5--11
from Dt 12--26, since his definition of parenesis does
not assume the prior existence of law. Since the 19th
century, Dt 5--11 had been considered a secondary
development of Dt 12--26.[46] Tiffany's research has now
made that assumption unnecessary.

Julius Wellhausen considered Dt 5--11 a duplicate
of Dt 1--4.[47] Both were introductions to the legal
material in Dt 12--26. Originally, according to
Wellhausen, there were separate legal sections to go
with each introduction, but these had been combined
and their introductions placed one in the front of the

other. Martin Noth, however, argued that the legal
material in Dt 12--26 had only one introduction: Dt
5--11. Deuteronomy 1--4, on the other hand, introduced
the entire Deuteronomist's History: Dt 5--26 + 28,
Jos, Ju, 1S, 2S, 1K and 2K.[48] Lohfink accepted Noth's
analysis of Dt 5--26 as a single unit.[49] According to
Lohfink, Dt 5--11 is the *tôrâ (Hauptgebot)*, which Dt
12--28 studies in detail. Deuteronomy 5--28 is one of
the four speeches of Moses, each introduced by its own
title (Dt 1:1, 4:44, 29:1 and 33:1) which make up the
archive of Deuteronomy. Lohfink calls Dt 5--11 *the law
or the teachings of Moses (tôrâ)* in contrast to the
speech (debārim) in Dt 1--4, the *ritual (dibrê habberît)*
in Dt 29--32, and the *blessing (berākâ)* in Dt 33.[50]
Finally, Childs suggests that Dt 5--11 capitalizes on
the issue raised in Dt 1--4, viz., *what do we do
now?*[51] For Israel, history is never *just* a memory.
History is always told for the practical purpose of
resolving a present crisis. According to Dt 1--4,
Israel had rebelled against Yahweh by refusing his
gift of the cities, a gift which Moses pleaded with
Israel to accept and enjoy. Dt 5--11 then explains
how this can be done. In Dt 1--4, Moses performed the
historical role assigned to him in Exodus, leading the
people to salvation in times past. In Dt 5--11, Moses
is the continuing mediator between Yahweh and Israel
for all time. By reviewing the history of Israel,
Dt 5--11 encourages the present Israel to accept the
land and its cities with confidence as well as
caution.

Intention

     The intention of Dt 6:10-19 is to clear away
whatever will keep a prosperous and urban Israel from
remembering Yahweh. For Dt 6:10-19 success and surplus are the gifts of Yahweh, and the response expected from Israel is fidelity, not forgetfulness.
Fidelity is possible only when the Israel who now lives
in the cities of a good land remembers she once lived
in the land of Egypt; when the Israel who now enjoys
houses full of all kinds of good things remembers how
she once suffered in the house of slaves. The only
role which Israel had in this sudden success was eating
and drinking her fill. The very length of the
passage describing what Yahweh has done (Dt 6:10-11a)--
in contrast to the short formula describing Israel's
contribution (Dt 6:11b)--emphasizes the disparity.

This parenesis does not condemn cities, cisterns, barns, vineyards and olive trees as intrinsically evil. They are all gifts of Yahweh to his people, and therefore the sign of his affection and care. Human improvements on the face of the land, the development of the natural resources of Canaan is not sacrilege, it is stewardship. The significance of Dt 6:10-19 for the urban tradition in Deuteronomy is that it defines the land promised to Abraham, Isaac and Jacob as an urban land.[52]

It is significant that the assets of the promised land which Deuteronomy 5--11 celebrates are urban assets. Canaan is a civilized land in which there are large dairy herds and successful bee colonies, fields of cash crops, olive orchards and vineyards.[53] The affluence of this economy allows it to produce not only food for its people, but fodder for its livestock.

... he will give the rain for your land in its season, the early rain and the later rain, that you may gather in your grain and your wine and your oil. And he will give grass in your fields for your cattle, and you shall eat and be full (Dt 11:14-15).

Nothing is wild; everything is cultivated. Not even the animals will need to forage for food.

This assessment of Canaan corresponds to the overall theology of Dt 5--11, where the desert is a place of infidelity and rebellion, full of unpleasant memories.

Take heed ... lest ... you forget the Lord your God, who led you through the great and terrible wilderness, with its fiery serpents and scorpions and thirsty ground where there was no water, ... (Dt 8:15).

The desert in Dt 5--11 is a proving ground.

And you shall remember all the ways which the Lord your God has led you these forty years in the wilderness, that he might humble you, testing you to know what was in your heart, whether you would keep his commandments, or not. And he humbled you and let your hunger.... Know then in your heart that, as a man disciplines his son, the Lord your God disciplines you (Dt 8:2-5).

In Dt 5--11 the gift of the cities is on a par with
the exodus. It is one of Yahweh's mighty acts.

> If you say in your heart, 'These nations are
> greater than I; how can I dispossess them?'
> you shall not be afraid of them, but you
> shall remember what the Lord your God did to
> Pharoah and to all Egypt, the great trials
> which your eyes saw, the signs and the
> wonders, the mighty hand, and the outstretched
> arm, by which the Lord your God brought you
> out; so will the Lord your God do to all the
> peoples of whom you are afraid (Dt 7:17-19).

Like Yahweh himself the cities are *great (gādōl)*
goodly (tōb).[54] *Great* acts are those connected with
the saving power of Yahweh; *good* acts are connected
with his creating power.[55] The city is no rival for
Yahweh. It is his possession. But just as the city
is not a divine competitor in Dt 5--11, it is also not
a human achievement.

> Beware let you say in your heart, 'My power
> and the might of my hand have gotten me
> this wealth.' You shall remember the Lord
> your God, for it is he who gives you power
> to get wealth; that he may confirm his
> covenant which he swore to your fathers, as
> at this day (Dt 8:17).

But Dt 6:10-19 is not an unqualified endorsement
of city life, which exposes all but the most observant
Israelites to greed and materialism. Only strict
observance of the commandments, testimonies and
statutes of the Deuteronomic code can deliver urban
Israel from the same fate which her predecessors met.
Israel has now reached the same heights of
civilization and technology as the feudal states in
Canaan before her. If Israel remembers the source of
her success in Yahweh, she will enjoy the destiny of
things going well with her; if she does not, she will
be destroyed.

The responsibilities of urban Israel are primarily judicial: *Swear by his name* Dt 6:13b).
Integrity in the municipal court is the primary service which Israel is to render in the city. The experience of Yahweh in the municipal court was critical

for Israel. Through the municipal court, Israel--the defenseless had been defended, and through that deliverance encountered Yahweh, her savior. Therefore, the quality of justice in Israel had to be maintained if subsequent generations were to know Yahweh, and the service *par excellence* which every Israelite was expected to render to Yahweh was as a witness or a judge in the municipal court. In Dt 5:11+20, it is of the utmost importance that witnesses and judges be impartial and take their oaths sincerely. If the word of a witness or judge in the muncipal court was not trustworthy, the word of Yahweh as the just prosecutor and judge would be compromised.

> For the Lord your God is God of gods and Lord of lords, the great, the mighty, and the terrible God who is not partial and takes no bribe. He executes justice for the fatherless and the widow, and loves the sojourner, giving him food and clothing. Love the sojourner therefore for you were sojourners in the land of Egypt. You shall fear the Lord your God; you shall serve him and cleave to him, and by his name you shall swear. He is your praise,... (Dt 10:17-21).

Yahweh exercises his ownership of the land in deeding it to Israel who enjoy the legal, not the military or even moral right to it. This legal right remains in force, according to Dt 6:17, so long as the terms of the agreement are met: *the commandments of the Lord your God, and his testimonies and his statutes....* These are all legal terms. Furthermore, Yahweh established this arrangement through legal means, binding himself by an oath (Dt 6:10,18). The municipal court is the forum where Yahweh and Israel are presumed to meet and where their relationship is authorized. The ancestors in 6:10-19 are the beneficiaries of this legal instrument, and are bound to use only Yahweh's name in legal processes (Dt 6:13b). The grounds on which the cities are placed in Israel's care are legal, not military. Israel did not conquer the city. That was the virtue of the Assyrians. Israel did not invent the city. That was the virtue of the Mesopotamians. Israel acquired a right to cities by reason of legal inheritance, and that right was established not by intelligence, or by power, but by the court.

In the Deuteronomic reform, Dt 6:10-19 addressed

111

primarily the outlying cities of Judah. It emphasized
the purely civil blessings which Yahweh had conferred
on them. The interest of the monarchy in appropriating
Yahweh worship and centralizing it in Jerusalem would
leave the outlying cities with a sense of worthless-
ness. Deuteronomy 6:10-19 is careful to acknowledge
the diversity of Yahweh's blessings, far beyond
liturgy. For later generations, texts like Dt 6:10-19
would explain why, in fact, Israel lost the cities and
their blessings. By continuing to worship Yahweh outside Jerusalem, the cities of Israel forfeited their
privileged status as Yahweh's heirs, and thus were
dispossessed.

Deuteronomy 13:13-19

Genre

Structure analysis

LEGAL INSTRUCTION concerning an	
apostate city	Dt 13:13-19
I. Protasis (sign: *kî*)	13-14
A. Protasis proper	13a
B. Specifications	13a βγδ-14
1. Specification of *cities*	13a βγ
a. Land grant formula	13a β
b. Dwelling formula	13a γ
2. Specification of rumor	
(sign: *lē'mor*)	13a δ-14
a. Allegation: revolt	13a α-14aα
b. Allegation: sedition	14a β-b
1. Allegation proper	14a β
2. Citation (sign:	
lē'mor)	14a γ-b
II. Apodosis (sign: *we-*	15-19
A. Apodosis proper	15-18
1. Preliminaries	15
a. Inquest requirement	15a
1) ...*then you shall*	
inquire	15a α
2) ...*and make search*	15a β
3) ...*and ask diligently*	15a γ
b. Findings requirement	15b
1) Declaratory formula	15b α
2) Findings proper	15b β

```
2. Basic apodosis              Dt 13:16-18
   a. Double command                16-17b α
      1) Command proper             16a-b β
         a) ...put...to the
            sword                   16a
         b) ...destroy....          16b αβ
      2) Qualifications             16b γ-17b α
         a) Interpretation of
            inhabitants of the city 16b γ
            (1) Interpretation
                proper              16b γ 1-2
            (2) Marker: lepî hāreb  16b γ 3-4
         b) Explanation of it...
            all who are in it       17a-b α
            (1) Chiastic ritual     17a
                (a) all its spoil +
                    Verb            17a α
                (b) Verb + all its
                    spoil           17a β
            (2) Qualifications      17a γ+b α
                (a) ...a whole burnt
                    offering        17a γ
                (b) ...a heap forever 17b α
   b. Double prohibition            17b β-18b δ
      1) Prohibition proper         17b β-18a
         a) ...shall not be built   17b β
         b) None...shall cleave...  18a
      2) Double motivation
         (sign: lema'an)            18b
         a) Motivation              18b α
         b) Motivation              18b β-ε
            (1) ...the Lord...show
                mercy...            18b β
            (2) ...and have
                compassion          18b γ
            (3) ...and multiply you 18b δε
                (a) Formula proper  18b δ
                (b) Qualification
                    (Oath formula)  18b ε
B. Parenesis (sign: kî)             19
   1. Exhortation                   19a α
   2. Qualifications                19a β-b
      a. Observe formula            19a β
         1) Formula proper          19a β 1-4
         2) Qualifications          19a β 5-8
            a) Promulgation formula 19a β 5-7
            b) Today formula        19a β 8
      b. Righteousness formula      19b
```

113

Dt 13:13-19:   Legal instruction

Some scholars tag Dt 13:13-19 as *law*. L'Hour, for example, argues that the passage is *purge law*.[56] This genre has four characteristics: its form is casuistic; its content is behavior punishable by death; its setting is urban; and the vocabulary of the purge and midst formula is fixed.[57]   Ostensibly, L'Hour considers the purge law a *case law*, with the purge and midst formulas added for motivation. Actually, L'Hour changes Alt's definition of case law considerably, as his pattern for the purge law shows.

> If a man *is found* stealing one of his brethren, the people of Israel, and if he treats him as a slave or sells him, then that thief shall die; *so you shall purge the evil from the midst of you.*   Dt 24:7, italics added)

L'Hour's pattern assumes a process of discovery. The defendant *is found* stealing. The classic case law reads simply: *If anyone steals . . . .!*   This process is important enough for Dt 13:13-19 to carefully explain each step.

> . . . then you shall inquire and make search and ask diligently; and behold, if it be true and certain that such an abominable thing has been done among you . . . .   (Dt 13:14)

L'Hour's pattern also includes both second and third person forms. A *man* is found stealing *one* of *his*, etc. But, *you* shall purge . . . from the midst of *you!* Although the mixture of forms with different persons and numbers in legal material has been of continuing interest to scholars, Alt limited case law to third person forms.[58]   For Alt, only Dt 24:7a is casuistic: *If a man . . . steal[s]. . . of his brethren . . . then that thief shall die!* By itself, Dt 24:7b is apodictic: *. . . purge the evil from the midst of you!* The question is: what genre combines these two forms? Neither Alt nor L'Hour answered that question, though both discussed the intention of the genre in very similar terms. For Alt, the technique of combining casuistic and apodictic laws helped Israel adapt its semi-nomadic culture to city life. For L'Hour purge laws highlighted the most Yahwist aspects of city life.[59] Both intentions differ from

114

the intention of law. Law sets limits on human behavior, whereas this combination of casuistic and
apodictic forms makes adaptations and urges compliance.

     There are other problems with considering
Dt 13:13-19 a law. First, only portions of two verses
even remotely resemble Alt's case law structure.

> If . . . certain . . . fellows . . . saying
> 'Let us go and serve other gods,' . . .
> then you shall surely put the inhabitants
> of that city to the sword . . . . (Dt 13:14-
> 16)

Second, in Alt's structure the grammatical subject of
the verb in the protasis is identical with the
grammatical subject of the verb in the apodosis. Here
in Dt 13:14-16, the *certain fellows* who preach
apostasy are not the same as *the inhabitants of that
city* who are executed! If the strict case law pattern
were present in Dt 13:13-19, it would read: *If anyone says 'Let us go and serve other gods,' he shall be
put to death*. And, finally, there is the problem of
the third person forms (*certain fellows*) in the
protasis, and second person forms (*you shall . . .
put . . . to the sword*) in the apodosis.

     L'Hour is aware that Dt 13:13-19 has only distant
connections with purge laws since it includes *you
hear* in the protasis and is missing the purge and
midst formulas altogether. Therefore, he relies
heavily on Dt 17:2-7 for his own reconstruction and
analysis.[60] Seitz also identifies all three units in
Dt 13 as case law (*Gesetze*) but then admits they share
few characteristics of the genre.[61] Therefore, Dt
13:13-19 is not law.

     For Weinfeld, Dt 13:13-19 is a *covenant stipu-
lation* prohibiting sedition, solicitation or conspiracy
of any kind.[62] Although there are no parallels in the
Hebrew Bible for the specific list of temptations to
apostasy in Dt 13, Weinfeld cites ANE parallels from
14th century, 8th century and 7th century BCE
treaties.[63] These parallels not only prohibit sedition,
they use the same language as Dt 13:13-19. The 8th
century example at Sefire orders the city to be *put to
the sword*. The 7th century example warns against
prophets, just as Dt 13:2-6, and against family members
just as Dt 13:7-12. Those solicited are obligated to
report the rebel.

Weinfeld stresses that the idolatry has already occurred, whereas Dt 13 says only that the solicitation has occurred. Weinfeld stresses that the idolatry is secret, whereas only in Dt 13:7-12 is the solicitation secret. The prophets and the dreamers in Dt 13:2-6 and the conspirators in Dt 13:13-19 are public. Weinfeld stresses that the knowledge spreads by rumor and must be substantiated by investigation. That is true only in Dt 13:13-19. In the other two instances in Dt 13, the crime is obvious and the punishment should be immediate. There is no need for an inquest. Weinfeld emphasizes that the obligation of those solicited is to report to the sovereign; in Dt 13, however, those solicited are not expected to report but to punish. The problem with Weinfeld's analysis is that he considers all three subdivisions in Dt 13 identical, whereas they are only compatible because they seek to restrict conspiracy in any form. They do not provide a uniform code of law to deal with conspiracy wherever it is found.

Although McCarthy considers Weinfeld's comparisons with other ANE treaties *less than convincing*, the comparisons are helpful to show that the consideration in Dt 13:13-19 is theological, not tactical.[64] In the 13th century example, conspiracy is forbidden by *a man* or *a city*. It does not matter how important the individual is: . . . *whether he is a prince, a great noble . . . an official of the palace or any other man . . . *.[65] Likewise in the 8th century example, it does not matter the source of the information, action must be taken. In Dt 13:13-19, the concern is that the information be verified through a legal process. The Sefire treaty is not so specific. It simply says the individual is to be denounced. In Dt 13, the city is the largest social unit, and the most important social unit in the experience of the audience. It is contrasted with the prophets, dreamers and family members mentioned in the companion texts.

Deuteronomy 13:13-19 is *legal instruction*. The land and its cities are the gift of Yahweh to those who are faithful to him. The laws of Deuteronomy express the conditions necessary for taking possession of the land and for continuing to live in the land.[66]

116

Deuteronomy 13:13-19 assumes that the city belongs only
to those faithful to Yahweh, regardless of their military capability. Those who reject Yahweh are helpless,
just as those who accept Yahweh are indomitable. Because the cities were not Israel's by reason of her
military prowess or her cultural ingenuity, but only by
reason of Yahweh's undeserved goodness to her,
Dt 13:13-19 does not even consider the tactical ramifications of its instruction. Theologically there are
not any! Deuteronomy 13:13-19 instructs those faithful to Yahweh on the importance of confronting anyone
at all who rejects Yahweh.

A better label for the genre of Dt 13:13-19 than
law or *covenant* is *rhetoric*. In one way or the other,
the suggestion appears in the commentators. Junker,
for example, considers Dt 13:2-5 and 13:6-12 *model
sermons (Predigt-beispiels)* and Dt 13:13-19 a *model
speech (rhetorisches Beispiel)*.[67] In his discussion of
the larger and complex units into which Deuteronomy
has converted the laws in Exodus, von Rad calls them
interpretations, sermons, instructions, preaching.[68]
Rhetoric is the umbrella genre to which sub-genres
such as *sermon, preaching, speech, instruction,
paraclesis, kerygma, parenesis* and others belong.
Tiffany suggests an initial distinction be made between
sermon/preaching and *speech*. *Sermon/preaching* enjoys a
liturgical setting, *speech* does not.[69]

The contrast between *law* and *rhetoric* can be seen
by setting a clear example of *case law* (Ex 22:20)
alongside Dt 13:13-19 and its companion piece,
Dt 17:2-5. All three concern apostasy, yet the
passages from Deuteronomy are much more concerned with
teaching the norms of conduct which have already been
promulgated. In neither unit in Deuteronomy is the
law cited in its standard form, but both presume the
existence of a law prohibiting worship of other gods
than Yahweh. Both passages in Deuteronomy consider
special circumstances: the crime, for example, is not
a matter of fact but of hearsay. Both passages
identify particular classes of defendants: they are
residents of the cities and towns given to Israel by
Yahweh. Both passages detail the executions which the
Exodus law demands.

Merendino considers Dt 13:13-19 a *war sermon.*[70]
According to Merendino, there is no way Dt 13:13-19 can
be addressed to a single individual, a family or even a
municipal court. Unlike such passages as Dt 17:2-7;
19:15-20; 21:18-21 and 22:13-21, where the municipal
court has jurisdiction over an individual, only all
Israel has jurisdiction when the defendant is an entire
city as in Dt 13:13-19.

However, Dt 13:13-19 applies the theology of holy
war on far too limited a scale to be a formal war
sermon. In holy war, for example, Israel, under the
leadership of a warlord designated by Yahweh, defended
herself against her enemies.[71] Sometimes the war involved all the corporate members of Israel; sometimes
it did not. All or part of the war prizes were sacrificed to Yahweh as his commission for the victory.
Deuteronomy 13:13-19 does not technically envision a
holy war. The discernment process before the battle
in 1 S 28:6; 30:7 and 2 S 5:19 becomes a juridical
process in Dt 13:15.[72] The attack is not accompanied
by trumpets nor the sound of Yahweh's voice as in Ju
3:27 and 6:3. There is no consecration of the warriors
of Israel as in 1 S 21:6 and 2 S 11:11. There is no
mention of Yahweh terrorizing the city under attack as
in Ju 4:15, 1 S 7:10 and Jos 10:10. There is no conscious reduction of the warriors needed for battle to
clearly indicate that the victory belongs to Yahweh and
not to Israel as in Ju 7:2 ff and 1 S 14:6. The sacrifice after the battle includes more offerings than required in any other holy war text.

Deuteronomy 13:13-19 belongs to a particular sub-
genre of rhetoric called *legal instruction,* or, as von
Rad describes it, *preaching about the law (. . .*
Deuteronomium . . . hier wird über die Gebote
gepredigt).[73] *Legal instruction* does not promulgate
law, but it clearly assumes its existence.

According to Patrick, the Ur-genre on which both
law and legal instruction develop is a *verdict or*
court decision.[74] However, law is more than an
anthology of court decisions. Court decisions address
very specific situations; law enunciates the underly-
ing principles on which the decisions are based.
Therefore, although, as a literary phenomenon, law may
follow court decisions, logically the verdict rests on
the law. Thus the first two steps in the evolution of
legal instruction as a genre are *verdict* and *law.*

What motivated the literary expression of law,
according to Patrick, was the ajudication of difficult
cases, where the grounds for the verdict were not
obvious. In such circumstances, the court would introduce or expand its verdict with a presentation of
law, so that the justice of its decisions would be
clear. Sometimes, the law was a statement of the
primary rights which citizens of Israel enjoyed;
sometimes the law was a statement of the remedial
rights which entitled a citizen to relief, compensation
or retaliation for the violation of his or her primary rights. Remedial law was much more clear cut
than primary law, which the courts found difficult to
administer. Therefore, the court appealed to the
conscience of the parties and threatened them with
the punishment of Yahweh if they did not comply with
the remedy prescribed.[72] *Legal instruction* is one of
the genres which appeared during this secondary
development of law as Patrick has described it.

Not only does a legal instruction like Dt 13:13-
19 assume the existence of laws like Ex 22:20, but it
has an interest in the ramifications of that law.
Although legal instruction is authoritative, it is
not constraining, preferring parenesis to punishment
as a motivation for obedience. According to
Carmichael, legal instruction can pick up a theme introduced earlier in a work and refine or enlarge
it.[73]

Dt 13:13-14: Protasis

The particle *if (kî)* and the imperfectly inflected verb *you hear (tišm'a)* identify Dt 13:13-14
as the premise on which Dt 13:15-19 depends.
Deuteronomy 13:13-14 is grammatically dependent on
Dt 13:15-19, even though logically the condition in
Dt 13:13-14 must be fulfilled *before* Dt 13:15-19 can
take effect. This protasis modifies the concern with
insurgency and sedition dealt with in Dt 13:13a - 14,
and turns the attention of the text to the rumor or
report of insurgency and sedition. The sophistication of the protasis can be seen not only in its
concern for hearsay as well as witnessed crimes, but
in the emphasis on the city as Israel's inheritance
from Yahweh. Therefore, the crime is not one of
rebellion against the king, but of default by
tenants against their landlord: a more ancient and
sacred relationship.[74]

The protasis underlines its concern with the city by drawing the phrase *in one of your cities* away from the verb *have gone out* and putting it in a more emphatic position at the beginning of the unit.[75] The expected position of the phrase would be: *If you hear that certain base fellows in one of your cities, which the Lord your God gives you to dwell there* . . . . The text also stresses that the apostate cities are *Israelite cities* by modifying *your cities* with both the land grant and the dwelling formulas. There is no question as far as Dt 13:13-19 is concerned: Yahweh gave the cities to Israel and he wants Israel to live in these cities.[76]

Dt 13:13aδ-14: Specification of rumor

Deuteronomy 13:13-14 is framed by the infinitives *saying (le'mor)* in Dt 13:13a and Dt 13:14. The verb *have gone out (yāṣû')* introduces a narrative sequence of verbs: *have drawn away (wayyadîhû); you shall inquire (wedāraštā); make search (wehāqartā); ask diligently (wešā'altā)*. Hebrew forms such chains using two verbal conjugations to complement one another. Here the imperfectly inflected verb introduces the chain and the perfectly inflected verbs are each connected to it with the conjunction *and (waw)*. As the anchor verb for the chain in Dt 13:14-15, *have gone out* could stand alone in the protasis with all the remaining verbs in the chain to be found in the apodosis (see Dt 21:1-9). However, *have gone out* is not independent. Likewise, the entire chain together with its anchor verb could make up the case, while an entirely different syntax (such as the intensive *you shall surely put* . . . *to the sward)* would introduce the apodosis, but it does not. The consecutive chain in Dt 13:14-15 begins in the protasis, in which the anchor verb *have gone out* and one member of the chain *(have drawn away)* occur and ends in the consequence in which the members *you shall inquire, make search* and *ask diligently* occur. This disregard which the structure of the consecutive chain has for the protasis-apodosis rhythm indicates that chain develops after the protasis-apodosis and overlooks the protasis-apodosis rhythm in order to make its own contribution to the text.

Merendino considers . . . *certain base fellows have gone out among you and have drawn away the inhabitants of the city* . . . . as the protasis from an original case law on which Dt 13:13-19 is based.[77]

If such a case law did exist, it would violate a
number of the canons which characterize the genre.
Case law deals with individuals, not with institutions. But even if case law did consider the city
as a defendant, the protasis of such a hypothetical
law should state the crimes of the city and its
inhabitants because it is the city and its inhabitants
who are punished in Merendino's apodosis. But
Merendino's case law combines the crime of one group
with the punishment for another. Technically,
Merendino needs two case laws: *If the inhabitants of
a city say: 'Let us go and serve other gods!,'
those inhabitants shall sure die.* *If certain base
fellows have drawn away the inhabitants of the city,
those base fellows shall surely die.* Finally the
you-form in Merendino's hypothesis is atypical.

Dt 13:14aγ -b: Citation

The call: *Let us go and serve other gods* is a
direct violation of the prohibition *You shall have no
other gods before me* found, for example, in Dt 5:6.
Each unit in Dt 13 (13:2-6; 7-12; 13-19) contains
this same phrase (cf. Dt 13:3,7,14). Von Rad argues
that this citation is the link between the three
sections of Dt 13.[78]

Dt 13:15-19: Apodosis

The apodosis details the requirements to be met
when the conditions in the protasis are fulfilled.
In classic examples of case law, the apodosis is a
succinct description of the punishment which the
defendant must undergo, e.g., *you shall surely put the
inhabitants of that city to the sword* in Dt 13:16a.
However, the apodosis in this unit has a very complex
structure, quite unlike the simple statements of
punishment found in Exodus 20:22--23:19.

Dt 13:15: Preliminaries

Customarily case law dealt with matters witnessed by at least two persons. However, in Dt
13:13-19, the allegations are made only through rumor
or report. Therefore, before a formal court process
can be initiated, the validity of the hearsay
evidence must be established.

Deuteronomy 17:2-7, which is closely related to
this text also prescribes a preliminary

investigation.[79] Leviticus 19:20 also demands an inquiry be held before the consequences stipulated in the apodosis are applied. Whether this investigation was mandatory only in certain kinds of crime or became necessary only during a certain period of history, or whether all trials presumed a preliminary investigation although only a few texts specifically mention it, is unclear. The three terms used here in Dt 13:13-19 to describe the preliminaries are not exclusively legal terms, nonetheless--as Buis has done--they should be translated as technical terms.[80] *You shall inquire* here in Dt 13:15, as well as Dt 17:4 and 19:18 it indicates a systematic examination of the evidence prior to the actual trial, hence an *investigation* or *pre-trial hearing*. *And make search* occurs nowhere else in Deuteronomy. Interestingly enough in Jb 28:20-27, this verb is used in the same context as here in Dt 13:13-19, viz., *verifying a rumor*. The difference between Yahweh on the one hand, and Abaddon and Death on the other, is: Abaddon and Death are content with rumor, Yahweh verifies it!

> Abbadon and Death say, 'We have heard a rumor of it with our ears'. God understands the way to it, and he knows its place. For he looks to the ends of the earth, and sees everything under the heavens. When he gave to the wind its weight, and meted out the waters by measure; when he made a decree for the rain, and a way for the lightning of the thunder; then he saw it and declared it; he established it, and searched it out. (Jb 28:20-27)

Here in Dt 13:13-19, the term refers to a carefully detailed and formal study of the evidence in court designed to uncover any pertinent information necessary to rule in the matter in question. Here, *and make search* has the connotations of Jb 29:16 and Pr 28:11, which assume a kind of examination carried out by a defense attorney for the purpose of exposing the weaknesses of the case against his client. *And ask diligently* like *you shall inquire* appears in Dt 17:4 and 19:18, both of which are passages containing the purge-formula. The term refers to a series of questions designed to check or discredit the answers to previous questions.[81]

Dt 13:15b: Findings Requirement

Deuteronomy 13:15b presents the findings of the inquest. The jury announces: *It is true.* In 1 K 10:6, Sheba concludes her audience with Solomon using the same formula. *And she said to the king: 'The report was true which I heard . . . '.* Since Sheba had heard of Solomon in her own land, and went to a great deal of trouble to verify the reports which had come to her of his wisdom, this formula is probably standard in announcing the results of any effort to verify hearsay evidence. The similarity between the requirements of Dt 13:13-19 and the Solomon and Sheba narrative in 1 K 10:1-13, implies that both wisdom and foolishness are to be investigated completely before taking any action.[82]

Dt 13:16-18: Basic Apodosis

Four asyndetic directives form the core of this apodosis: *You shall surely put the inhabitants of that city to the sword* (Dt 13:16a); *Destroying it utterly all who are in it* (Dt 13:16baβ); *It shall not be built again* (Dt 13:17b); *None of the devoted things shall cleave to your hand* (Dt 13:18a). The first two are commands, the second two are prohibitions. Command is customarily composed of one positive and one negative directive as it is here, although pairs of positive and negative directives are not unusual.

The use of the absolute infinitive *surely (hakē)* with the imperfect second person form of the finite verb *you shall put (takeh)* in Dt 13:16a is the standard construction for the command. This suggests Dt 13:16a is probably the oldest portion of the text. It is also completely independent of the three interlocking directives which follow.[83]

The *Hip'īl* imperative in Dt 13:16b is acceptable as a construction for a command. However, it occurs less frequently and is a weaker expression than the absolute infinitive and the finite form of the imperfect verb in the second person. This fact and the fact that both grammatical objects of the imperative are explained by the prohibitions suggests that Dt 13:16b, 17b, 18a are expansions of Dt 13:16a. *Destroying it (It shall not be built again) utterly, all who are in it (None of the devoted things shall cleave to your hand) . . . .*

The *Ni'pal* imperfect third person form of the
verb, *it shall be built* and *shall cleave* are unusual
constructions for the prohibition. *It shall not be
built again* is found as a prediction against Tyre
(Ez 26:14). In Jb 22:23 Eliphaz argues that if Job
will repent, El Shaddai will *rebuild* him, whereas, in
Jb 12:14 Job has argued that if El tears down, *no one
can rebuild* (See Ps 69:35-6). Thus the prohibitions
here in Dt 17:16b carry overtones of a divine
judgment having been pronounced. The building and
razing of cities in Canaan is divine not human work.
In the original command in Dt 13:16a only the inhabitants of the city were to be slain. This in fact is
the judgment on the cities of Sihon.

> And the Lord our God gave him [Sihon] over
> to us; and we defeated him and his sons and
> all his people. And we captured all his
> cities at that time and utterly destroyed
> every city, men, women and children; we
> left none remaining; only the cattle we
> took as spoil for ourselves, with the booty
> of the cities which we captured (Dt 2:33-35).

With the addition of Dt 13:16b, 17b and 18a, buildings,
beasts, and booty are *herem* as well. This is the only
case in Deuteronomy where such a total sacrifice is
demanded.[84] Before the battle the soldiers would take
an oath to sacrifice all or only a portion of the
spoil to Yahweh after the victory. In Dt 20:16 and
1 S 15:3, the soldiers vow to sacrifice everything to
Yahweh; in Dt 2:34 and Dt 3:6 they sacrificed the city
and its citizens; in Dt 20:10 they sacrificed the
enemy soldiers. Here in Dt 13:16-18 everything must
be sacrificed.

Dt 13:17a-bα: Explanation

    Deuteronomy 13:17b might be a *taboo order* with *It
shall be a heap forever* as the *command* and *You shall
not rebuild it* as the *prohibition*. These two
directives occur together nowhere else in the Hebrew
Bible, and *shall be* is a very weak verb to be used in
a command. These two reasons and the more convincing
unity of Dt 13:16ab αβ + 18a, described above,
suggest that Dt 13:17b is not a sub-section of the
text. Rather, Dt 13:17b α is parallel to Dt 13:17a γ
identifying the category of sacrifice to which this
herem belongs, and Dt 13:17b β with its *lō'* and the
Nip'al third person imperfect construction is parallel

to Dt 13:18a forming a negative directive.

Both Steuernagle and Merendino point out that
. . . *burn the city and all its spoil with fire, as a whole burnt offering to the Lord* . . . (Dt 13:17) does not classify *ḥerem* as a sacrifice.[85] Although *kālîl* is used as a technical term for sacrifice, Deuteronomy nowhere considers sacrifice a means of atoning for sin.[86]

Dt 13:17a: Ritual

The sentence *You shall gather all its spoil into the midst of its open square* in Dt 13:17a may be a third command parallel to *you shall surely put the inhabitants of that city to the sword, destroying it utterly* in 16, or simply an explanation of . . . *it* . . . *and all who are in it* . . . in 16b. Given the change from the imperative to imperfect verb forms and the use of *and (wāw)* it is better to describe Dt 13:17a as an explanation rather than as a command. The integrity of the ritual

all its spoil, collect in the square

then, burn the city and all its spoil

is strengthened by chiasm, which repeats the phrase *all its spoil* at the beginning of the first line and the end of the second.

Dt 13:18b: Motivation

That the Lord may turn from the fierceness of his anger (Dt 13:18b): is not grammatically a negative construction. It is negative, however, insofar as in this portion of Dt 13:18b Yahweh takes something away, while in the remaining portions of the verse, Yahweh gives Israel something. This anger formula occurs in Ex 32:12; Nu 25:4; Jos 7:26; Je 4:8 etc. . . . In each instance, the text describes Yahweh's reaction to Israel's worship of other gods, or her neglect of the interdict. Here the formula is independent of the three remaining motivations, which are positive.[87]

Although it would be tempting to read *and have compassion* and *multiply you* as a qualification of *the Lord . . . show mercy . . .*, it is better to leave each of the elements as independent and equal parts of the motivation. They do not occur together anywhere else in the Hebrew Bible, where some idea of their relationship might be gathered.

As Mayes and Seitz both emphasize, these three motivations are inconsistent with the punitive expedition called for in Dt 13:16-18a.[88] Since Deuteronomy nowhere promises to increase the population of Israel, Merendino considers this motivation to have been added by the Deuteronomic Historian.[89]

Setting

The institutional or societal setting of Dt 13:13-19 is the Jerusalem court where the most avid proponents of the Deuteronomic reform had determined that liturgical centralization was the key to maintaining the independence of Judah from the Ancient Near Eastern super-powers in both Egypt and Mesopotamia. Only under the auspices of the king and the watchful eye of the priests could the liturgy achieve the kind of national solidarity envisioned by the reform.

Liturgy, as a means of building a national coalition, had been used by kings since David.[90] As an important arm of the state, the priests were responsible to the king for the tradition developed and preserved in liturgy. The proscription of dissidents, as Weinfeld has pointed out, is a common theme of covenants, a genre with which priests are commonly associated.[91] Finally, only priests and kings escape indictment in Dt 13. The sweeping criticism of prophets--true and false (Dt 13:2)--in Dt 13:1-6, and the omission of any criticism of the king at all in Dt 13, suggests that the setting of this text is not prophetic. The aristocrats of Judah's leading families would not have waived their privilege of immunity from prosecution for themselves or their family members, as Dt 13:7-12 requires. And finally the elders who presided over the municipal courts did not consider it within their jurisdiction to investigate and punish the citizens of cities other than their own.

The cultural, epochal or historical setting of Dt 13:13-19 is late in the era of the Deuteronomic reform, at a time when the fate of Judah was already sealed. Deuteronomy 13:13-19 is an instruction, not

an order, therefore the priests do not have to or do
not choose to exercise their powers of enforcement.
This deference to persuasion is even more significant
when the theoretical nature of the text is taken into
consideration.[92] At the beginning of the reform, and
certainly during the height of its effectiveness in
Judah, the reformers were both powerful and pragmatic.
Therefore, Dt 13:13-19 is part of a reflection made by
the reformers after their influence in Jerusalem and
Judah has started to decline.

Finally, Dt 13 assumes the existence of Dt 12,
portions of which are set only in the height of the
Deuteronomic reform.[93] Deuteronomy 12 and Dt 13 both
have three sections, each dealing with the danger of
worshiping Yahweh improperly. The repetition of the
observe, command and do good and evil formulas in
Dt 12:28 and Dt 13:19 emphasizes the connection
between the two chapters.

Be careful to heed all these words which I command you, that it may go well with you and with your children after you for ever, when you do what is good and right in the sight of the Lord your God. (Dt 12:28)	. . . if you obey the voice of the Lord your God, keeping all his commandments which I command you this day, and doing what is right in the sight of the Lord your God. (Dt 13:19)

Deuteronomy 12 reflects several different stages
of the reform which developed rapidly under the reign
of Josiah. At the height of the reform, not only was
worship centralized in Jerusalem, but all the outlying
shrines were ordered destroyed. This development is
reflected in Dt 12:2-7. Deuteronomy 13:13-19
addresses the failure of cities to follow just such a
radical demand, and likewise the failure of the elders
of the cities to prosecute the dissidents.

The intellectual, ideological and theological
setting of Dt 13:13-19 is also late in the Deuteronomic
reform. The setting of Dt 13:13-19 is urban. Like
the rest of Dt 12--26, Dt 13:13-19 is addressed to an
Israel who will live not in the desert, but in a land
of cities. Nowhere is the desert celebrated as the
cradle of Yahwism nor a novitiate for Israel. The
desert is neither held up, nor put down. Indeed,
throughout Dt 12--26, there is not one reference to
the wilderness.

Yahweh is frequently identified as the God of the exodus, but without mention of the wilderness.[94]

> But that prophet or that dreamer of dreams
> shall be put to death, because he has
> taught rebellion against the Lord your God,
> who brought you out of the land of Egypt
> and redeemed you out of the house of
> bondage, to make you leave the way in which
> the Lord your God commanded you to walk.
> So you shall purge the evil from the midst
> of you (Dt 13:5).

Because of von Rad's use of Dt 26:5-10 in analyzing the first six books of the Hebrew Bible, the desert was considered the setting in which all the significant relationships between Israel and Yahweh set forth in Deuteronomy and elsewhere in the Torah took place.[95] However, von Rad himself does not argue that every tenet in the creed is of equal value for understanding the faith of Israel. To stress the importance of *wandering* for an understanding of Israel is to distort the analysis. In fact, Noth identifies only two major tenets: the deliverance from Egypt and the settlement in Canaan.[96] Wandering only supports these two themes. By explaining the presence of Hebrews in Egypt, and the superiority of Israel's settled and urban condition over her condition as a homeless people.

It is also possible that here in Dt 26:5-10, wandering simply refers to the migration of some Hebrew communities to Egypt during a crop failure, as the words *went down to Egypt* indicate. Certainly an urban people from Palestine would be more vulnerable to crop failure than would a nomadic people. And also an urban people would be more easily settled in Egypt for as long a period of time as Exodus envisions, a period during which the Egyptians used them to build cities! Finally, exaggerating the wandering trait of Israel upgrades her ancestral traditions as historical records at the expense of their theological value. Israel's ancestral traditions stressed her unity as a people regardless of the many differences among her corporate members. Even if some of the corporate members of Israel belonged to nomadic traditions of one sort or another, there is no reason to assume that this nomadic tradition was dominant for ancient Israel.[97] Even assuming that *wandering Aramean* identifies the ancestors of Israel with the Amorite (!)

128

migrations in 2000-1800 BCE is questionable. If there are bonds between the ancestors of Israel and the Arameans, they need to occur during the peak of Israel's urbanization under David and Solomon![98] If David took over the Aramaean kingdom of Hadadezer, then the Aramaean connection in this literature was an important political tool for consolidating the acquisition.[99] David was extremely sensitive to the potential of literary traditions in governing an empire containing as many ethnic and political components as Israel.[100]

In Dt 12--26, Israel is clearly a people in transition, but there is no reason to assume that the passage is from a rural, nomadic, non-urban way of life to an urban way of life. Israel's passage is from renter to resident; from margin to main stream; from outcast to owner--but both the first and the last state are urban conditions. This is the context in which the creed should be understood.

> A wandering Aramean was my father; he went down into Egypt and sojourned there, few in number; and there he became a nation, great, mighty, and populous. And the Egyptians treated us harshly, and afflicted us, and laid upon us hard bondate. Then we cried to the Lord the God of our fathers, and the Lord heard our voice, and saw our affliction, our toil, and our oppression, and the Lord brought us out of Egypt with a mighty hand and an outstretched arm, with great terror, and with signs and wonders, and he brought us into this place and gave us this land, a land flowing with milk and honey. And behold, now I bring the first of the fruit of the ground, which thou, O Lord, has given me (Dt 26:5-10).

As an instruction, Dt 13:13-19 considers the city--not the tribe--the largest social unit in Israel. The victims of sedition, the conspirators and the convicts in Dt 13:13-19 are all citizens, not nomads or villagers. Like the rest of Dt 12--26, Dt 13:13-19 assumes that Israel lives in cities, and that the culture of Israel is an urban culture.

> If you hear *in one of your cities, which the Lord your God gives to you to dwell*

there, that certain base fellows have gone
out among you and have drawn away the inhabitants of the city . . . (Dt 13:13,
italics added).

Deuteronomy 13:13-19 contrasts the city with other
social units: the family in Dt 13:7-12 and the congregation in Dt 13:1-6. The city in Dt 19:1-13 is the
public defender and the judge. The city in Dt 20:10-
20 is the delegation through which society in Palestine
negotiates. In Dt 21:1-9 the city is the party
responsible for law and order, and the agent by which
harmony is to be restored. In Dt 21:18-21, the city
is the guardian of the Hebrew family.

Deuteronomy 12:17 and Dt 13:26 assume grain and
wine and oil--the products of an urban economy.
Dt 12:17, 21 mention flocks and herds. Dt 13:22-29
prescribes that taxes be paid on crops; and 13:25
assumes the use of money. Standing crops presume
stability and a time of peace; money requires a
central form of government. Dt 16:9-12 legislates for
the harvest, and 16:13-17 addresses a culture with
the technology to construct both a threshing floor and
a wine press.

There is no condemnation of these aspects of city
life. The city appears without polemic. Deuteronomy
12--26 speaks to an urban people with no apology for
the technology of civilization. Deuteronomy 12--26
does not argue that Israel should accept the ways of
city life, but assumes Israel will make permanent
homes in the cities (Dt 12:20-21). Deuteronomy 12--26
assumes the city is Israel's teacher and her home
and seeks to fashion that urban culture according to
authentically Yahwist customs, rules and practices.

Buis considers Ju 19--20 the model used by
Dt 13:13-19.[101] Although he doubts such punitive expeditions were ever again carried out on such a grand
scale, the history of Israel is familiar with smaller
reprisals.

And when Moses saw that the people had
broken loose . . . then Moses stood in the
gate of the camp, and said, 'Who is on
the Lord's side? Come to me.' And all
the sons of Levi gathered themselves together to him. And he said to them, 'Thus
says the Lord God of Israel, "Put every

man his sword on his side, and go to and
fro from gate to gate throughout the camp,
and slay every man his brother, and every
man his companion, and every man his
neighbor."' And the sons of Levi did
according to the word of Moses; and there
fell of the people that day about three
thousand men (Ex 32:25-28).[102]

The most likely time for such interventions, according
to Buis, would be during the divided monarchies, whose
kings had the military capability for attacking and
destroying cities. Deuteronomy 13:13-19 does not
mention the king.

The literary setting of Dt 13:13-19 before it
reached canonical status is connected exclusively with
Dt 12--26. Dt 12--26 is not simply a *law book*. This
genre collects customs, practices and rules in no
particular order. The law book is not promulgated by
an authority, but assembled by librarians. The
function of the law book is to provide an historical
record. Dt 12--26 is a *law code* similar to Ex 20:22--
23:33; Lv 17--26 and Ex 25:31; 34:29--Lv 16 + Nm. The
code is a systematic arrangement of customs, practices
and rules, usually promulgated by the king. The law
code fixes the norms for administering justice during
his reign. Both the law book and the law code bring
together literature from a variety of settings. Although the code reinterprets the literature, the book
does not.[103]

The setting of Dt 13:13-19 is judicial. Not only
is the instruction about a legal instrument, it prescribes a legal remedy. Finally, the setting of
Dt 13:13-19 is Yahwist. It assumes that Yahweh is an
urban landlord in Dt 13:13; and that the city is a
fitting sacrifice in Dt 13:17. But most important it
considers the city a community committed to the worship
of Yahweh, and the urban institution of the municipal
court the means through which such worship is
guaranteed.

Weinfeld has suggested that Dt 13 is modeled on
the stipulations in covenants establishing urban
leagues.[104] Although his best examples are dated in
the same century as the Deuteronomic reform, there are
·older parallels. Deuteronomy 13:13-19 may have inherited the concept that cities allied with one
another are responsible for the behavior of one

another. In fact, Judges 19-20 tells the story of how
the cities of Benjamin (Ju 20:14) were punished by all
Israel for murdering a guest in Gibeah. However,
there is nothing in the text of Dt 13:13-19 itself
which suggests antiquity.

In Mesopotamia, kings issued law codes at regular
intervals during their reigns.[105] In this way they
fulfilled their obligation to care for the city
through responsible administration of the municipal
courts. Eulogies acknowledged such urban renewal.[106]

To celebrate the promulgation of legal codes,
Mesopotamian kings often granted amnesty for various
debts.[107] The Moabite perspective in Deuteronomy may
reflect this tradition of amnesty. Returning Israel
to the beginning of her national existence, in effect,
pardons all the debts she has incurred to Yahweh
during the 600 years between Joshua and Josiah.

No convincing principle of organization has been
suggested for Dt 12--26. Eissfeldt, for example,
considers it a new edition of Ex 20:22-23:33.[108] Von
Rad also considers the arrangement of the material in
Dt 12--26 traditional.[109] Deuteronomy, as a whole--
according to von Rad--reflects the order of worship
followed in the covenant festival at Shechem and preserved in Ex 19--21. Therefore, Dt 12--26:15 is a
proclamation of the law and Dt 26:16-19 is a commitment ceremony. Although the description of the arrange-
men as traditional and connected in some way with
patterns followed in covenants is appealing, analyzing
the logic of the arrangement can be frustrating, as
McCarthy has pointed out.[110] Horst divided Dt 12--18
from Dt 19--26 and argued that the basic privileges of
Yahweh as Israel's Lord form the outline for Dt
12--28.[111] These privileges were the decalogue from
which three successive editions of Deuteronomy were
developed. In the last edition, the concern for the
centralization of worship was added. Merendino, on
the other hand, considers Dt 12--28 to contain the
guidelines for Israel's relationship with Yahweh,
while Dt 19--26 monitors the relationship of one individual Israelite with another.[112] Finally, Schulz
has argued that it is the ten directives of the
decalogue in Dt 5 which form the outline according to
which the material in Dt 12--26 has been organized.[113]

Yet despite their differences, these interpretations all consider the instructions concerning Israel's

exclusive relationship to Yahweh the most important
part of Dt 12--26. Deuteronomy 13:13-19 holds a significant position at the beginning of those
instructions as well as the emphatic position at the
end of a series of three instructions (Dt 13:2-6;
7-12; 13-19) on temptations to break off this relationship and follow other gods (Dt 13:3, 7, 14).
Deuteronomy 13:13-19 uses this prominent literary
setting to stress that the responsibility for protecting this relationship between Israel and Yahweh primarily belongs to the cities. If the cities and
families and prophets are faithful, Israel will be
faithful.

                         Intention

        The intention of Dt 13:13-19 is to explain why
the Deuteronomic reform failed to save Judah from
destruction. According to Dt 12, the key to the reform was liturgical centralization. Without strict
adherence to this principle, everything else was
meaningless. As successful as the reform may have
been in other areas, prophets and aristocratic
families and the venerable old cities of early Israel
stubbornly refused to accept liturgical centralization
completely. Although they are not mentioned in
Dt 13:13-19 the elders of the city, whose responsibility
it was to *inquire and make search and ask diligently
and behold if it is true* had failed to prosecute those
who did not cooperate with the centralization
policy.

        The dissidents in Dt 13:13 are *certain base
fellows,* who like their counterparts in Dt 13:2 and
Dt 13:7 are portrayed as apostates. Worshipping
Yahweh anywhere but Jerusalem was like worshipping
other gods which you have not known (Dt 13:14).

        Most commentaries assume *other gods* (Dt 13:3, 7,
14) means only gods other than Yahweh, the God of
Israel. Therefore, they consider the intention of
Dt 13:1-19 is solely to warn Israel against
paganism.[114] According to Je and Ez, paganism did
plague Judah to the very end of her existence as a
nation.

        Therefore, son of man, speak to the house
of Israel and say to them, Thus says the

Lord God: in this again your fathers
blasphemed me, by dealing treacherously
with me. For when I had brought them
into the land which I swore to give them,
then wherever they saw any high hill or
any leafy tree, there they offered their
sacrifices and presented the provocation
of their offering; there they sent up
their soothing odors, and there they
poured out their drink offerings . . . .
Wherefore, say to the house of Israel,
Thus says the Lord God: Will you defile
yourselves after the manner of your
fathers and go astray after their de-
testable things? When you offer your
gifts and sacrifice your sons by fire,
you defile yourselves with all your idols
to this day. And shall I be inquired of
by you, O house of Israel? As I live,
says the Lord God, I will not be inquired
of by you (Ez 20:27-31).[115]

Therefore, at any number of points in its tradition
history, Dt 13:1-19 may have been used to warn against
paganism.

But as Dt 12 now stands in Deuteronomy in
particular and the Deuteronomist's History in general,
translating *other gods* exclusively as *foreign gods*
is too literal. The Deuteronomic reform was concerned,
not only with outright paganism, but also with
illicit forms of Yahweh worship as well. The in-
tegration of these two concerns appears in Dt 12:1-31
which introduces the legal instructions in Dt 13.[116]
Deuteronomy 12:2-7, for example, condemns decentralized
Yahwist sanctuaries with anti-pagan zeal.

You shall surely destroy all the places
where the nations whom you shall dispossess served their gods, upon the high
mountains and upon the hills and under
every green tree you shall tear down
their altars, and dash in pieces their
pillars, and burn their Asherim with fire;
you shall hew down the graven images of
their gods, and destroy their name out of
that place. You shall not do so to the
Lord your God. But you shall seek the
place which the Lord your God will choose
out of all your tribes . . . (Dt 12:2-5).

Having welded these two concerns so tightly together
in Dt 12:1-31, there is no reason for Deuteronomy
suddenly to drop one of them completely in Dt 13:1-9.
Therefore, in Dt 13:1-19, *elohîm ahērîm* needs not only
the connotation of *foreign gods*, but also of
additional sanctuaries to fulfill the intention of the
instruction.

Restricting the intention of Dt 13:1-19 to an
instruction on paganism also overlooks the connection
which these initial units in Dt 12--26 have with the
Deuteronomist's History for whom both paganism and
centralization were important concerns. Deuteronomy
13:1-19 is part of the Deuteronomist's tradition that
the rivals of centralization were prophets, families
and cities. For example, 1 K 12:25--13:32 records how
Jeroboam was designated king by Ahijah, the prophet of
Shiloh, and established a Yahwist sanctuary in the
city of Bethel. The sanctuary was authentic enough to
receive the endorsement of at least one local prophet.
Both the city of Bethel and its prophet are condemned
by Josiah in 2 K 23:4-25. Likewise, the Deuteronomist
explains Solomon's tolerance for sanctuaries outside
Jerusalem as the result of the influence of his wives.

> Now King Solomon loved many foreign women;
> the daughter of Pharaoh, and Moabite,
> Ammonite, Edomite, Sidonian, and Hittite
> women, from the nations concerning which
> the Lord had said to the people of Israel,
> 'You shall not enter into marriage with
> them, neither shall they with you, for
> surely they will turn away your heart
> after other gods'; Solomon clung to these
> in love. He had several hundred wives,
> princesses, and three hundred concubines;
> and his wives turned away his heart. For
> when Solomon was old his wives turned away
> his heart after other gods; and his heart
> was not wholly true to the Lord his God
> . . . (1 K 11:1-4).

Josiah also met and destroyed these rivals, just as he
had met his rivals from the cities and among the
prophets (2 K 23:13).

The use of *'elōhîm* as synechdoche for
sanctuaries appears in at least three laws from the
Covenant Code, viz., Ez 21:2-6; 22:7-8, 9.

When you buy a Hebrew slave, he shall serve
six years, and in the seventh he shall go
out free, for nothing. If he comes in
single, he shall go out single; if he comes
in married, then his wife shall go out with
him. If his master gives him a wife and
she bears him sons or daughters, the wife
and her children shall be her master's and
he shall go out alone. But if the slave
plainly says, 'I love my master, my wife,
and my children; I will not go out free,'
then his master shall bring him to God
['elōhîm] and he shall bring him to the
door or the doorpost; and his master shall
bore his ear through with an awl; and he
shall serve him for live (Ex 21:2-6).

Exodus 21:6 directs the slave owner to take the slave
to the nearest sanctuary *(his master shall bring him
to God)* and there pierce his slave's ears. The
passage uses *'elōhîm* to mean *sanctuary*.[117]

  The common way to say *pagan gods* is *'elōhî nēkar
hā'āreṣ* (Dt 31:16), not *'elōhîm 'aḥerîm* (Dt 13:3,7,
14).[118] The use of *'aḥer* as a relative adjective
meaning *additional* is far more common than its use as
a euphemism for *pagan*.[119] Here in Dt 13:1-19, the
sense antecedent to which *'aḥerîm* refers is *the place
which the Lord your God will choose* (Dt 12:5, 11, 14,
18).

  Therefore, this instruction charges the prophets,
the aristocrats and the cities with having opposed
centralization, and announces the judgment of Yahweh
on Judah because of them: *it shall be a heap forever,
it shall not be built again* (Dt 13:17b). Paganism
was the initial concern of the Deuteronomic reform, but
ultimately it focused all its attention on centralization. Against paganism the reform was successful; against decentralized forms of Yahwism, supported
by prophets, aristocrats and cities, it was not.
Deuteronomy 13:1-19 acknowledges this failure and
indicts its rivals not only for their historic involvement in paganism, but their stubborn support of
decentralized worship of Yahweh as well. Since they
did not obey the command of the reformers who
announced a new day to Judah (Dt 13:19a), they face
the anger of Yahweh and forfeit his mercy, his compassion, his blessing of population.

The reformers' despair appears in the manner in
which they describe the destruction in Dt 13:13-19. It
is absolute, there are no survivors, therefore, the
passage was certainly complete before 587 BCE, since
some did, in fact, escape death and even deportation.
But they are not mentioned. The reformers' hope
appears in the simple fact that they took time to make
one last appeal to those who stood in their way.

Deuteronomy 19:1-13

Genre

Structure analysis

```
LEGAL INSTRUCTION concerning
 use of cities as asylums        Dt 19:1-13
 I. Command                          1-3
    A. Circumstantial intro-
       duction (sign:  kî)            1
    B. Command proper                2-3
       1. Primary command            2
       2. Secondary commands         3
          a. You shall prepare the
             roads                   3a α
          b. ...and divide into
             three parts...          3a βγ-b
             1) Basic command        3a β
             2) Qualifications       3a γ-b
                a) Inheritance formula 3a γ
                b) Purpose clause    3b
 II. Qualifications                 4-13
    A. Title                         4a
    B. Homicide provision           4b-13
       1. Conditions for granting
          asylum                    4b-10
          a. General principles
             (sign:  'ašer)         4b (cf 11)
             1) No advertance        4b α
             2) No malice of fore-
                thought              4b β
          b. Specific example
             (sign:  wa'ašer)       5-6
             1) Protasis             5a
                a) ...a man goes...
                   to cut wood...    5a α
```

137

138

<u>Dt 19:1-13:   Instruction</u>

The basic components of Dt 19:1-13 are a *command*
to establish cities of refuge (Dt 19:1-3) and *qualifications* distinguishing accidental death and murder
(Dt 19:4-13). The position of the qualifications
following the directive as well as adverbs of place
such as *there* in Dt 19:4 & 12 and *to one of these
cities* in Dt 19:5 & 11, whose antecedents occur only
in the directive, subordinate them to the directive.
They detail the due process which city government must
grant refugees. This combination of *directives* with
limitations and *parenesis*, e.g., Dt 19:13, identifies
Dt 19:1-3 as an *instruction* on the order *You shall not
kill* (Dt 5:17). Horst in 1930 was the first to
suggest that Dt 12--18 contains concrete applications
of the Decalogue (*das Privilegrecht Yahwehs*).[120]
The three layers of text in Dt 12 suggest that these
applications had been edited three times. If Dt
19:1-13 is an application of Dt 5:20 then Horst's
unit would have to be extended beyond Dt 18.

An order always addresses its audience directly:
. . .*you shall not kill, you shall not steal.* . . .
Instruction switches from one form of address to the
other. Dt 19:1-3 + 7-10 + 13 uses second person forms,
while Dt 19:4-6 + 11-12 uses third person forms. This
combination of verb forms of *different persons* which
is characteristic of instruction should not be confused with the study of sources in Deuteronomy using
verb forms of different numbers.

Order is unmediated; the legislator and the en-
forcer are the same. Instruction is mediated. In Dt
19:1-13 there are at least two officials mentioned,
viz., the avenger of blood and the elders of the city.
These officials are assumed to be traditional; their
jurisdiction does not depend on royal appointment.
The list of officials established by David on the
basis of Canaanite and Egyptians parallels indicates
the kinds of appointed officials with which the kings
tried to replace the traditional urban officials.[121]

The audience of instruction is seldom professional. *The traditional material is often expanded, explained in very non-legal and laity-
oriented ways.*[122] For example, Dt 19:1-13 explains the
effect of bloodshed in terms of the damage it does to
the landlord-tenant relationship between Yahweh and
Israel. This comparison is popular, not professional.

An order binds absolutely. Death is the implicit penalty for disobedience; instruction binds only with logic and motivation. Here in Dt 19:1-13 contamination is the explicit penalty, not death.

An order determines basics. For example, in Dt 5:17 murder is forbidden.[123] Instruction, on the other hand, spells out implications. For example, Dt 19:4-13 explains that the summary execution of a person involved in an accidental death is a form of murder. Hence, an order is short and to the point; instruction is long and drawn out.

Dt 19:1: Circumstantial introduction

Even though Dt 19:1 is a subordinate clause introduced by *when (kî)*, it is not the protasis of a case law, but a circumstantial introduction. There are a number of examples of texts like Dt 19:1-13 which combine second and third person forms and imitate case law in the protasis, for example Dt 12:20; 14:24; 15:7; 18:6; 20:10; 23:10; 26:1.[124] The purpose of this kind of introduction for Seitz is to combine centralization laws with case laws.[125]

Dt 19:2: Command

Setting apart is a common verb in Lv and Nm and is parallel in meaning to *qados* meaning *to set apart, to declare holy, to consecrate to Yahweh.*[126] The use of *bdl* here in Dt 19:2 for setting apart cities of refuge indicates that at least the city of refuge is a worthy reflection of Yahweh to whom it is consecrated. *Setting apart* also shares some of the theological characteristics of *bhr* meaning *to choose.*[127] For example, *by being chosen, the place becomes holy. It is the free action of Yahweh which gives a place its special character.*[128] The critical element for determining the holiness of the city is that it is chosen by Yahweh. There is no innate holiness in the city. Yahweh chooses the city, and the choice makes the city holy.

The primary command is specified by two secondary commands. Both explain how the cities of refuge are to be established so that everyone involved in a killing may have easy access to them. Steuernagel has suggested that the secondary command *You shall prepare the roads* is concerned not so much with building roads or marking roads, but with locating the cities in some

141

central position.[129]

Dt 19:4-13: Qualifications

There are two qualifications distinguishing the killer who is eligible for asylum from the killer who is not. The verdicts: *may save his life* in Dt 19:4a, 6 and *may die* in Dt 19:12 mark the contrast. This distinction between accidental death and murder appears in Ex 21:12-14 and is common in the Ancient Near East. However, the distinction between accidental death and murder in the Ancient Near East and in English Common Law are not the same.[130] But there is no indication that Israel considers these distinctions important enough to assign them specific vocabulary.[131]

Dt 19:4a: Title

According to Ex 34:28 and Dt 4:13; 10:4, *provision (dābār)* is a technical term for the directives of a decalogue. On the other hand in Ex 2:15 *thing (dābār)* refers to the act of murder itself, and not the provision for the murderer. The knowledge of the murder of the Egyptian overseer *(dābār)* causes Moses to flee. As it appears here, this same title occurs in Dt 15:2 and in the Siloam inscription as well.[132]

The word *killer (hārōsēah)* has been generally considered a technical term designating anyone liable to blood vengeance.[133] The *manslayer* has killed his personal enemy, and in the process threatened the harmony of his community. According to Stamm, these two characteristics distinguish *rāsah* from other verbs of killing, such as *hārag* and *hēmît.*[134] Harmony can be restored only if the offender is granted the due process of a trial before the community.[135]

Dt 19:4b: General principles

Though Dt 19:14b distinguishes *unintentionally* from *without having been at enmity with him in the past:* the second phase may be a gloss introduced by *when someone (wehû')* to explain the meaning of the technical term: *unintentionally.*[136] According to Horst, these distinctions are the earliest indication that Israelite Law separated objective and subjective responsibility.[137] These general principles are introduced in a protasis composed of the relative pronoun and the imperfect verb form. This particular construction consciously imitates the protasis-apodosis

142

pattern of case law.[138]

The word *neighbor* here in Dt 19:4 is a technical term by which the citizens of Israel's urban communities referred to themselves. In general, Deuteronomy refers to the citizens of Israel in Josiah's time as *brothers*.[139]

Dt 19:6: Opinion

The *avenger (gō'ēl)* has the responsibility of killing the victim's assailant. In the Ancient Near East, full citizens had an executor or second with power of attorney to handle their responsibilities whenever they were unable to do so. Since a murder victim could not retaliate, his avenger would do so in his place.[140]

When the avenger sought a life on behalf of his client he is called an *avenger of blood (gō'ēl haddām)*. Phillips, however, argues that there is no reason to modify *avenger* with the phrase *of blood*.[141] According to Phillips, *avenger* already carries the connotation *of blood*, and hence would be redundant. Furthermore, Phillips points out there are no examples in the Hebrew Bible in which one Israelite takes vengeance on another. In Israel, blood belongs to Yahweh, not to the family of the victim.

The verdict: *this man did not deserve to die* is a formula which appears in Je 26:11 as well as here in Dt 19:6. Like the formula *innocent blood*, it refers to the state of declared innocence, i.e., a person whom the court has officially ruled is not guilty. Liedke considers both this verdict in Dt 19:6 and the verdicts in Dt 21:22; Je 26:11, 16; 1 S 27:11 to be official legal language.[142]

Although Boecker considers Dt 19:6b *a popular explanation (eine Freispruchserklarung)*, the language is not popular but official.[143] Therefore Dt 19:6b is an *opinion*: the official explanation of the verdict by the court itself.

Dt 19:8a: Expansion formula

And if the Lord your god enlarges your border appears in Dt 19 as a development affecting the institution of asylum, and in Dt 12:20 where the effect of centralization on the slaughter of animals is

143

discussed. The only other cases in the Hebrew Bible
using the *Hip'il* of *enlarge (rāhab)* are an etymology for
Rehobath in Gn 26:22; Ex 34:24 in the Sinai pericope
(Ex 19--24 + 32--34), and Moses' blessing for Gad in
Dt 33:20. In each case, Yahweh causes the growth.

The concept of imminent expansion may be political
or theological. Units containing the formula may have
developed during a particular historical period in
which territorial expansion took place, or may simply
reflect a theology that obedience to Yahweh leads to
growth. Political expansion occurred a number of
times during the history of Israel.

David (1000-970 BCE)

Stinging from the defeat handed her by the
Philistines, Israel under David committed all her resources to military and political expansion. Some of
this expansion was necessary for her national defense,
but in many cases the expansion was necessary simply
because the bureaucracy of the empire had been
designed to promote expansion.[144]

According to Ju 1:28, David incorporated the
cities of Palestine into his empire, and according to
district lists from Solomon's time the cities were
fully integrated into the economy. Blood vengeance
continues between cities during David's time. The
city of Gibeon took revenge on Saul's family and the
city of Beeroth took revenge on Saul's son, Ish-Baal.
Therefore, the expansion formula, and perhaps a
passage like Dt 19:1-13 may reflect the events of this
period of political expansion.

Solomon (970-930 BCE)

Solomon continued to expand Israel toward the
Mediterranean Sea. He also divided his empire into
twelve administrative districts, and constructed
various kinds of cities: cities for stores, cities
for chariots, cities for cavalry. In addition,
Solomon was connected with the court system in Israel,
and was celebrated as the incarnation of the Ancient
Near Eastern idea of the *just king*.[145] Perhaps
Solomon's inaugural vision at Gibeon called for the
institution of cities for asylum.

Asa of Judah (908-868 BCE)

Baasha (906-883 BCE) of Israel invaded Judah when Asa was king and captured Ramah only about six miles north of Jerusalem. With this city in his possession, Baasha controlled two important roads leading to Jerusalem. To get Baasha out of Judean territory, Asa persuaded Baasha's ally, Ben Hadad of Aram, to betray Israel. The Aramean armies marched on Abelbeth Maacah, Ijon, Dan and the territory of Nepthali, forcing Baasha to transfer his army out of Judah in order to counterattack. The armies of Judah then reoccupied Ramah and pushed almost three miles across their border with Israel and captured Mizpah. Asa secured this buffer zone with outposts at Mizpah and Geba. Perhaps the formula *and if the Lord your God enlarges your border* reflects the excitement which the invasion of Israel produced in Judah.

Jeroboam II (786-46 BCE)

Jeroboam II recaptured all the territory along the traditional northern border claimed by David. This frontier extended from the tip of the Dead Sea to the southern end of the valley between the Lebanon and anti-Lebanon mountain ranges. Since kings in both Israel and Judah were complemented with the characteristics of David, it is uncertain whether Jeroboam II of Israel actually made any territorial acquisitions. If there was expansion connected with Jeroboam II's reign, then perhaps this is the political setting for the expansion formula.

Ahaz of Judah (735-716 BCE)

During the reign of Ahaz, Israel and Aram formed an alliance against Judah and invaded her in 734-33 BCE.[146] Ahaz appealed to Assyria for help, and Assyria responded by dispatching her armies across the borders of both Israel and Aram. The invaders withdrew, and the armies of Judah, in hot pursuit, crossed the border of Israel and annexed part of her territory.

Hezekiah of Judah (715-686 BCE)

Hezekiah invaded Philistia and recaptured territory which Ahaz (735-716 BCE) had been unable to maintain.

145

Josiah of Judah (640-609 BCE)

According to Cross and Freedman, Josiah took advantage of a decline in Assyria power in Palestine and
liberated portions of Israel *irredenta* as far north as
Bethel.[147] The Assyrian empire, according to Cross
and Freedman, began to weaken after the death of
Asshur-ban-apal (669-633 BCE). At the death of his
successor, Asshur-etel-ilani (633-629 BCE), Josiah
annexed the provinces into which Assyria had divided
the kingdom of Israel in 721 BCE. Cross and Freedman
use the text of 2 C 34 and the chronology of
Dubberstein to establish this correlation between the
decline of Assyria and the rise of nationalism in
Judah under Josiah. On the basis of references in
Ezra and Nehemiah to Jews from *Ekron*--a traditionally
Philistine city to the east of Judah--Alt argues that
Josiah also annexed Philistine territory from the
Assyrians.[148] From a battle report of Sennacharib, the
Assyrian emperor in 701 BCE, Alt determines that the
Philistines were contained in a limited area around
the city of Ashkelon. Ekron and all the other
Philistine cities north and south of Ashkelon were
annexed by the Assyrians. According to Alt, Josiah
annexed these lands, consolidated them as a Judean
province after Assyrian influence waned.

Any of these periods of political expansion might
offer a setting for the expansion formula, but at least
three factors argue that the formula reflects a
theological, rather than a political, development in
Israel. First, the expansion formula is used
editorially in the Sinai pericope.[149] The traditions
from which the covenant-on-Sinai narrative in Ex 19--
24 + 32--34 is drawn contain two different descriptions of covenant making: one in the E tradition,
one in the J tradition. To preserve both accounts, one
covenant ceremony is described before the expansion of
Israel into Canaan, the other ceremony described as
that to be celebrated after the expansion.

Second, Deuteronomy modifies this promise of expansion with the condition that Israel obey the
command, etc. This argues that the expansion, in fact,
never took place. For example, the Deuteronomic
Historian explained things which never happened, e.g.,
the deliverance of Jerusalem from the Babylonians, on
the grounds that Israel's disobedience made fulfillment of the promise impossible.

Finally, increase is regarded as a blessing in Deuteronomy. For example, Jacobs identifies a *life-motif* with a fixed series of blessings, viz., life, well-being, length of days, many descendants, and blessing.[150] The expansion envisioned in Dt 12 and 19 is related to this increase-theology reflected in the life-motif.

Dt 19:9a: Qualifications

There are three qualifications to the promise of Yahweh to enlarge the territory of Israel. Yahweh will fulfill his promise--which without Dt 19:9a is not even a promise, but simply a fact--*only* if Israel heeds Yahweh's voice, loves Yahweh, and walks in Yahweh's path. The three conditions are impossible for Israel.[151]

Dt 19:10: Blood formula

The judicial as well as the liturgical character of the formula: *you shall not shed innocent blood* appears in Je, where the formula indicates killings connected with child sacrifice or mistrial. Therefore, according to Je, Judah was destroyed for not only illegal forms of worship, but the miscarriage of justice as well. Judah was expected to fulfill her obligations to Yahweh with correct worship and justice for all in the municipal court.

Dt 19:11-13: Conditions for denying asylum

Deuteronomy 19:11-13 is generally considered a part of Dt 19:1-13. Hempel considered Dt 19:11-13 the oldest section of the text.[152] Steuernagel joined it to Dt 19:4-7 as an original unit to which Dt 19:3a and 9a were added.[153] Von Rad called Dt 19:11-13 a *specification with a warning,* following the *principal case (Grundsatz)* in Dt 19:1-3 and the legal interpretation in Dt 19:4-7.[154] Von Rad considered Dt 19:8-9 additions to the text and Dt 19:10 a *parenetic rendition of an apodictic prohibition.* For L'Hour, Dt 19:11-13 is a purge law, and constitutes the second level of the text as found in Deuteronomy.[155]

Dt 19:11a: Protasis

The specific example in Dt 19:11 describes the assailant's attack on the victim by using vocabulary

147

that is characteristic of the priests in Israel.[156]

Dt 19:13:   Parenesis

Deuteronomy 19:13 concludes only Dt 19:11-12 and not Dt 19:1-12. The focus of this conclusion and that in Dt 19:7-10 is innocent blood. The formula: *your eye shall not pity him* in Dt 19:13a refers only to the defendant in Dt 19:11-12 and not to both defendants. It allows the court no discretion, but imposes a mandatory penalty.

Setting

Deuteronomy 19:1-13 developed from the legal institutions of the city. The legal basis, the legal consciousness, and the legal style of Dt 19:1-13 all point to a legal setting.

The legal basis of Dt 19:1-3 is the apodictic law: *you shall set apart three cities for you . . . so that any manslayer can flee to them.* The legal bases of Dt 19:4-13 are the two casuistic laws: *if anyone kills his neighbor unintentionally . . . he may save his life; . . . but if any man hates his neighbor . . . and wounds him mortally so that he dies . . . then . . . he may die.*

Legal institutions have a vested interest in murder, guilt, innocence, immunity, due process, extradition and execution, all mentioned in Dt 19:1-13. Although developed by prophets like Jeremiah, Hosea and Isaiah, the formula *to shed innocent blood* (Dt 19:10, 13) means to deprive an individual of due process in the courts. Only a legal institution would have so conscientiously preserved all the legal nuances in Dt 19:4-13.

The only prophetic element in Dt 19:1-13, according to Nicholson, is the warlike spirit of the circumstantial introduction in Dt 19:1.[157] *When the Lord your God cuts off the nations whose land the Lord your God gives you, and you dispossess them . . . .* The only liturgical reference in Dt 19:1-13 is the exhortation: *provided you are careful to keep all this commandment which I command you this day, loving the Lord your God and by walking ever in his ways . . . (Dt 19:9).* These formulas, however, occur

148

throughout Deuteronomy. They have no particular connection with the setting of Dt 19:1-13, but
characterize the redaction of Deuteronomy as a
covenant document.

The city in Dt 19:1-13 is an asylum not because
the temple is there, or because it is *the place which
Yahweh chooses* but because in the city due process is
possible. While the substitution of cities of refuge
for local sanctuaries, discontinued after Josiah centralized worship in Jerusalem, *may* have been necessary,
Dt 19:1-13 does not offer that rationale.

The city is *the* point of reference throughout Dt
19:1-13. For Dt 19:1-13, asylum is not in Midian as it
was for Moses (Ex 2:15); nor in Ziph as it was for
David (1 S 23:15); nor at the altar of Yahweh as it was
in the covenant code (Ex 21:12-14), for Adonijah (1 K
1:50) and for Joab (1 K 2:28). Here asylum is the
city. For Dt 19:1-13, authority does not rest in the
king, or the priests, or the Levites, or the avenger
of blood, or the tribal council, or parents. Here
authority is in the elders of the city, who have
jurisdiction over the defendant, authority to request
extradition, and the right to authorize execution.
Everyone in authority in Dt 19:1-13 is a city dweller,
so it is not a question of urbanites turning over a
nomad to the avenger of blood, because the nomad does
not qualify for urban justice. It is the elders of one
city who request extradition from the elders of
another city.

The term *elders* occurs throughout the Hebrew Bible.
It is also significant that the second largest category
of specified elders are those *of the city.*[158] There is
a precedent in Dt 19:1-13 for the procedure which Jehu
follows in 2 K 10:1-5 with the elders of the city of
Samaria.

> Now Ahab had seventy sons in Samaria. So
> Jehu wrote letters, and sent them to Samaria
> *to the rulers of the city, to the elders,*
> and to the guardians of the sons of Ahab,
> saying, 'Now, then, as soon as this letter
> comes to you, seeing your master's sons are
> with you, and there are with you chariots
> and horses, fortified cities also, and
> weapons, select the best and fittest of your
> master's sons and set him on his father's
> throne, and fight for your master's house.

But they were exceedingly afraid, and said,
'Behold, the two kings could not stand before
him: how then can we stand?' So he who was
over the palace, and *he who was over the city,
together with the elders* and the guardians,
sent to Jehu, saying, 'We are your servants,
and we will do all that you bid us. We will
not make anyone king . . . (2 K 10:1-5).

For Dt 19:1-13, the promise of a home is not fulfilled simply *in the land which Yahweh is giving you.*
Here the home is the city (Dt 19:1). Cities and
houses and territory, according to Dt 19:1-13, are
part of Yahweh's promised gift. Deuteronomic formulas
are used with these pre-Deuteronomic terms to clearly
indicate that they are all part of the promised land.

Pre-Deuteronomic terminology	Deuteronomic terminology
Dt 19:1	whose land the Lord your God gives
1	and dwell
in their cities and houses	
2 cities	in the land which the Lord your God as he swore to your fathers
8 territory	

In Dt 19:1, the significant verb is *dwell.*
Customarily, Israel *dwells in the land* in fulfillment
of the promise of Yahweh to the ancestors. Here Israel
dwells in cities and houses! This expression, however,
appears only in Deuteronomy, not in Gn, Ex, Lv or Nm.
In Gn 4:16, Cain *dwells* in the land of Nod. In Gn
13:7, 12, the Canaanites are *dwelling* in the land. It
is interesting that both Canaanites and Hebrews *dwell
in the land,* and that Cain and the Canaanites dwell in
the *land* and not in cities. The assumption that the
Hebrews live in the country and that the Canaanites
live in the cities, or that Hebrews have more claim
to the land than the Canaanites is not verified by the
use of this indicator. Furthermore, in Gn 13:12 Lot
dwells in the cities of the plain, which indicates that
the verb is not more characteristic of farmers than of
citizens.

The cultural, epochal or historical matrix of

150

Dt 19:1-13 as it stands in the canonical text is the
Deuteronomic reform at a time when the priests in
Jerusalem were centralizing all worship of Yahweh in
that city. The enthusiasm with which the reform had
been received in Jerusalem allowed it to dominate
national life. To consolidate the gains they were
making, the priests began institutionalizing the goals
of the reform. Thus, after the renovation of the
Jerusalem temple, they incorporated many earlier traditions into their own literature. The most drastic
changes were made in Dt 12--18. In the following
chapters, many older traditions and customs and institutions were also oriented toward the reform, but left
virtually intact. The cities of refuge are one
example.

However, the institutional or societal matrix of
Dt 19:1-13 is not the reform, but rather treaties
through which ancient urban leagues in Canaan were
established. Cities of refuge were an important means
of preventing individual acts of violence from rup-
turing the more important relationships between the
corporate members of an urban league. When various
urban communities like those at Hebron, Shiloh,
Shechem and Gibeon entered Israel, they brought with
them this institutional tradition. Shechem and Hebron
are both mentioned by name in the list of urban
asylums in Jos 20.

> So they set apart Kedesh in Galilee in the
> hill country of Nepthali, and Shechem in the
> hill country of Ephraim, and Kiriath arba
> (that is, Hebron) in the hill country of
> Judah. And beyond the Jordan east of Jericho,
> they appointed Beser in the wilderness on
> the tableland, from the tribe of Reuben,
> and Ramoth in Gilead, from the tribe of Gad,
> and Golan in Bashan, from the tribe of
> Manasseh (Jos 20:7-8).

But the Deuteronomic reform was not the only
cultural, epochal or historical matrix of this text.
Texts like Dt 19:1-13 were also an important part of a
legal struggle which went on between the kings of
Israel and the elders of the ancient cities, whose
legal prerogatives had been challenged by the kings.
In 1961, Knierim argued that the reign of Jehoshaphat
of Judah (876-52 BCE) was the climax of this judicial
struggle between the kings and the elders. The description of Jehoshaphat's judicial reform in 2 C 19:3-8

is an important text for Knierim's argument.[159] Because of the reform's similarity with Josiah's (640-609 BCE), Galling and Junge refused to accept the Chronicles' report.[160] Knierim, however, argued that Chronicles had no reason to credit Jehoshaphat in the 9th century with the reform of Josiah in the 7th century. There is no evidence that Chronicles' account of Jehoshaphat's judicial reform is directly taken from Deuteronomy's account of Josiah's reform, and therefore both Jehoshaphat and Josiah could have reformed the courts of Judah. Chronicles is interested in systems that organize national life. Jehoshaphat's reform is a good example of the kind of system Chronicles admires, and perhaps the reason only Chronicles preserved a report of it.

Knierim's study of Ex 18 led him to look for a judicial reform during the monarchy, since only judges who were not part of either the traditional municipal court structure or religious courts at the shrines would need the kind of justification Ex 18 provides. The passage is not concerned with Moses' responsibilities as a judge, but the Mosaic prerogatives of other judges. The genre of Ex 18 is not *report* or *legend*. Exodus 18 is an *etiology*.[161] Knierim argued that only royal judges needed such a defense. The right of these civil servants, stationed by the king in royal cities, to exercise judicial tasks was questionable since they were not prophets, priests, or elders, but simply *able men*.

> Moses chose able men out of all Israel, and made them heads over the people, rulers of thousands, of hundreds, of fifties, and of tens. And they judged the people at all times; hard cases they brought to Moses, but any small matter they decided themselves (Ex 18:25-6).

Knierim isolated texts in Micah, Isaiah and Deuteronomy to show that the heads of Hebrew households were as responsible as the priests and the prophets and the judges for the public judicial process.[162]

Micah, active around the fall of Samaria in 722 BCE, condemns the *rulers of the house of Israel* for rendering judgments for a bribe, the priests for giving decisions for a salary, and prophets who divine for money.[163] Isaiah, a contemporary of Micah, considers the delinquency of the *princes* in carrying out their

judicial responsibilities *the* cause of Jerusalem's
decline. Isaiah goes on to associate the restoration
of Jerusalem with the appointment of new leading
citizens to be judges and lawyers

> Therefore the Lord says,
>   the Lord of hosts, the Mighty One of Israel;
> 'Ah, I will vent my wrath on my enemies
>   and avenge myself on my foes.
> I will turn my hand against you
>   and will smelt away your dross as with lye
> And remove all your alloy.
> And I will restore your judges as at the first
> And your counselors as at the beginning.
>   Afterward you shall be called
> The city of righteousness,
>   The faithful city (Is 1:24-6).

Assuming that the *rulers* and the *princes* are
neither priests, nor prophets nor elders but simply
able men like those Moses appoints as judges in Ex 18,
Knierim concluded that the connection between the heads
of families and the public judicial process was significant by at least 722 BCE, at which time it was already corrupt. According to Knierim, Ex 18 attempted
to defend royal judges from the damage which their lack
of credentials in the judicial establishment and their
own corruption causes. Exodus 18 does this by stressing the Mosaic origin of their office.

The unifying figure in Ex 18 is Jethro, a non-Jew.
Jews preserved Jethro-traditions to explain the strong
ties between Jews and certain families--like Jethro's--
in Midian, Israel's ancient enemy. To confirm Jethro's
membership in the people of Yahweh, Ex 18 stresses his
liturgical and judicial connections with Israel.
Knierim emphasized, however, that Jethro does not introduce Israel to Yahweh, nor to the court system;
Israel's worship of Yahweh and Moses' office as a
judge are assumed. Jethro listens to the accounts of
Yahweh's actions on Israel's behalf and responds with
a profession of faith (Ex 18:9-11) and a communion
service (Ex 18:12). But Jethro's response is not
merely liturgical, since he also advises Moses how to
expedite the Israelite judicial process. Neither a
Yahwist faith nor the judicial system originate in
Midian, but both are shared by Israel and Midian.

While the liturgical portion of the chapter (Ex

153

18:1-12) is older than the judicial portion (Ex 18:13-27), the judicial reform is the main interest of the entire chapter. Junge applied this etiology to the military drafting policies of Josiah because the text mentions commissioning *officers over groups of thousands, of hundreds, of fifties and of tens* (Ex 18:21, 25).[164] Knierim, on the other hand, pointed out 1) the military is never *explicitly* mentioned; 2) Ex 18:21,25 may have been *added* to the etiology at a later time; and 3) even if Ex 18:21,25 are original, Moses wants the courts to supervise the military, and not for the military to take over the courts in order to draft soldiers, as Junge proposes!

Knierim's research demonstrates the thoroughly Israelite character of the court system. The courts are not a foreign element. They are venerable, authentic, Mosaic. Furthermore, Exodus 18 considers the court as important a setting for encountering Yahweh as the liturgy. A democratic and accessible court system is a natural response to faith in Yahweh. In the court, Israel not only experiences Yahweh, but serves him. Knierim assumes a close connection between the city and the court, which makes it unlikely that Israel would so thoroughly embrace the court and yet reject the city. Jehoshaphat and Josiah certainly respect the connection between city and court in their reforms, by locating the royal courts in the royal cities. Judicial reform and urban renewal are partners in the culture of ancient Israel.

L'Hour and Macholz are among the scholars who have made use of Knierim's suggestions in their own research on the development of the judicial system.[165] Both agree that the reign of Jehoshaphat was a time of important judicial developments. L'Hour accepted the description of the nature of those developments proposed by Knierim; Macholz did not.

In 1963, L'Hour argued that some group in Judah--which he does not identify--was so encouraged by Jehoshaphat's political efforts to unify Judah that it initiated a corresponding theological effort. The group's project established parallels between the case law traditions of the municipal courts and the apodictic laws of Israel.

This identification of Yahwism with city life remains in a criminal code (*une législation criminelle*) made up of purge (*bi'artā*) laws, which L'Hour

154

reconstructs from Dt 12--26. Through the municipal
court each citizen was accountable for the fulfillment
of the terms of the covenant with Yahweh. Thus the
encounter with Yahweh in daily life reflected in the
liturgy took place in the muncipal court. Deuteronomy
expanded this insight. L'Hour's reconstruction includes most of the texts which *Deuteronomy and City
Life* studies.[166]

L'Hour used four characteristics to pick out elements of the code. Each element has case law
structure, deals with crimes punishable by death, regards the city as the basic community in Israel, and
uses the formula: *thus you shall purge the evil from
your midst.* Each characteristic emphasizes the
identity between city life and Israelite life. In case
law structure, the protasis or conditional clause
contains the evidence: *If anyone does thus and so . .
. .* The apodosis or main clause stipulates the
sentence: *. . . then the individual shall be . . . .*
L'Hour accepts Alt's arguments that case law is
typically urban law, which is found in cities throughout the Ancient Near East.[167] Therefore, the case law
genre of the components of the code requires a city
setting. A *criminal* offense is serious and public and
falls under the jurisdiction of the entire community.
Although case law occasionally dealt with criminal
offenses, Alt considered apodictic law the *proper*
genre for such matters in Israel. These apodictic
laws are unconditional directives prohibiting (*Worship
no other god!*) or commanding (*Observe the sabbath!*)
behavior which would distinguish Israelites. Apodictic
law monitored the essentials of Yahwism. L'Hour argues
that the code uses the Decalogue in Dt 5:6-21 to
select municipal case laws   dealing with behavior
Israel considered indicative of her special relationship with Yahweh. In this way, the code demonstrates
the compatibility of Israelite life with urban life.[168]
Each law component of the code was notarized as
authentically Yahwist by the formula: *thus you shall
purge the evil from your midst.* By adding this
formula, Israel changed non-Yahwist ordinances into
critical Yahwist legislation. The formula is a
primitive exhortation as the emotional connotations of
the words *purge* and *evil* indicate. The non-liturgical
character of the formula, according to L'Hour, can
be seen by contrasting it with an excommunication
formula from the holiness code (Lv 17--26) and the
priests' tradition (P): *he shall be cut off from
among his people.*

CHART

City texts and L'Hour's *Législation criminelle*

City texts	*Une législation criminelle*
Dt 6:10-19	
	Dt 13:2-6
	Dt 13:7-12
Dt 13:13-19----------------------	Dt 13:13-19
	Dt 17:2-7
Dt 19:1-13----------------------	Dt 19:11-13
Dt 20:10-20	
Dt 21:1-9----------------------	Dt 21:1-9
Dt 21:18-21----------------------	Dt 21:18-21
Dt 22:13-21----------------------	Dt 22:13-17
	Dt 22:22
	Dt 22:23-27
	Dt 22:28-29
	Dt 24:1-4
	Dt 24:7
Dt 25:5-10----------------------	Dt 25:5-10

Von Rad considers both the purge formula and the excommunication formula to have a liturgical setting.[169] L'Hour does not.

The contrast reveals four differences. The purge formula authorizes the execution of the defendant; the excommunication formula ostracizes, but does not execute. The purge formula follows the verdict; the excommunication formula is the verdict. The purge formula orders the entire city to carry out the verdict of the court; the excommunication formula is enforced only by liturgical officials.[170]

In the code the city is the nuclear community in which Israel lives. Adjudication takes place *at the gate of the city*. The defendant is always tried in his or her own city.[171] *City judges and city officials* (Dt 16:18) or *city elders* (Dt 22:17) hear the cases. They turn their verdict over to *the men of the city* (Dt 22:21) who must carry out the sentence. The city is a democracy in which all live subject to the terms of the covenant with Yahweh. The authority of the municipal court in this urban structure is not artificially established. It is the natural development of parental responsibility (Dt 21:18-21). The good of the family and the good of the city are identical.[172]

The setting for the code is not the royal court. The king could hardly have used *Israel* without any allusion to the civil war which had divided the Hebrews into the separate kingdoms of Israel and Judah. In the code, *Israel* is not the *northern* kingdom or even the *united* kingdoms; it is the *ideal* kingdom. It is also unlikely that a criminal code developed by the monarchy would not mention the king, or that such a code would seek only to inspire obedience, and not to command it. Therefore, according to L'Hour, the code did not federalize the courts: that *political* effort was the work of the king. The criminal code was a *theological* effort to give meaning to the federalized court system which the king had created and which Deuteronomy describes.

If any case arises requiring decision between one kind of homicide and another, one kind of legal right and another, or one kind of assault and another, any case within your towns which is too difficult for you, then you shall arise and go up to the place which

157

CHART

Comparison of Israelite apodictic law and
Municipal case law

Mutual interests	Israelite apodictic law	Municipal case law
Other gods	Dt 5:6-15	Dt 13:2-6
		Dt 13:7-12
		Dt 13:13-19
		Dt 17:2-7
Parental respect	Dt 5:16	Dt 21:18-21
Killing	Dt 5:17	Dt 19:11-13
		Dt 21:1-9
Adultery	Dt 5:18	Dt 22:13-21
		Dt 22:22
		Dt 22:23-27
		Dt 22:28-29
		Dt 24:1-4
		Dt 25:5-10
Stealing	Dt 5:19	Dt 24:7
False witness	Dt 5:20	Dt 19:16-19

the Lord your God will choose, and coming to
the Levitical priests, and to the judge who
is in office in those days, you shall consult
them, and they shall declare to you the
decision. Then you shall do according to
what they declare to you from that place
which the Lord will choose; and you shall be
careful to do according to all that they
direct you; according to the instructions
which they give you, and according to the
decision which they pronounce to you, you
shall do; you shall not turn aside from the
verdict which they declare to you, either
to the right hand or to the left. The man
who acts presumptuously, by not obeying the
priest who stands to minister there before
the Lord your God, or the judge, that man
shall die; so you shall purge the evil from
Israel. And all the people shall hear,
and fear, and not act presumptuously again
(Dt 17:8-13).

The municipal court is the place where concrete applications of the covenant are made, and where Israelites fulfill their obligations to Yahweh, and in which
Israel had a profound and enduring experience of
Yahweh. Just who made such an appeal through this
criminal code--judges, citizens, prophets, priests,
elders, Levites, parents--L'Hour does not say.

In 1969, Merendino accepted at least the conclusions of L'Hour's research which identified a
legal genre in Deuteronomy with four characteristics:
1) case law structure; 2) criminal law content;
3) common sociology which considered the city as the
basic community; and 4) the formula *you shall purge*.
Merendino included these purge laws among the
sources of Deuteronomy. However, he described fewer
texts than L'Hour as purge laws and argued that not
just one but two codes made up of purge laws were
eventually absorbed by the Deuteronomic tradition.[173]

Furthermore, Merendino questions the specifically
urban purpose which L'Hour had ascribed to the purge
laws, viz., to adapt Yahwism to the city culture of
the monarchy. According to Merendino, these codes of
purge laws in Dt 19--24 are among the oldest sources
in Deuteronomy.[174] Originally, these laws reflected
a wisdom tradition from a patriarchal society in which

all relationships took place within the narrow confines
of the family and the community. Now, however, the
concluding purge formula contains a judicial emphasis.
Traditio-historically, Merendino connects these purge
laws with the amphictyony in Judges.

Nonetheless, the laws do have an urban connection
at one point in their development. According to
Merendino, the laws were adapted to a number of city
ordinances (*Bestimmungen burgerlichen Rechts*) dealing
with asylum and the principle of talion (Dt 19:2-13,
15-21); war brides (Dt 21:10-14); legal heirs (Dt
21:15-23b) and sexual intercourse (Dt 22:13-29). This
edition of the purge laws also included a series of
humanitarian laws (*Humanitätsbestimmungen*) in Dt 23:
16--24:18. This development of a code of purge laws
occurred prior to the end of the 8th century BCE.
During the time of King Hezekiah (715-687 BCE), the
now enlarged code was joined with other sources to
form the *pre*-Deuteronomic tradition, and the purge
laws from Dt 13 & 17 were added during the time of
King Josiah (640-609 BCE).

Clark criticized Merendino's defense for this
complicated process.[175] Merendino's critical arguments assume: 1) the shortest form of the text is
original; 2) the original text contains no repe-
titions; 3) the original text always contains a
statement of the basic legal principle in question;
4) the original text has a clearly recognizable
rhythm; and 5) the original text frequently contains
a chiasm. None of these principles is as absolute as
Merendino makes them in his effort to reconstruct
the history of the text.

L'Hour and Merendino also assume that apodictic
law is older than case law in the development of
legal genre, at least for Israel. Alt developed this
theory in 1934 by identifying apodictic law with the
Yahweh worship of Israel and case law with the
municipal courts of Canaan.[176] Apodictic law laid
down the fundamental principles of Israel's life, and
case law made the concrete applications. Therefore
the purge laws, which are casuistic, are assumed to
be applications of the Decalogue, which is apodictic.
However, research on legal genre during the last 50
years has failed to confirm Alt's assumption that
apodictic law and case law are related as principle
and application. In fact, what Alt identified as
apodictic *law*, Gerstenberger has argued is really

160

CHART

Comparison of L'Hour's *Législation criminelle*
with Merendino's list of purge laws

L'Hour's list of purge laws	Merendino's list of purge laws	Deuteronomic additions	Pre- deuteronomic code
13:2-6	13:2-6	13:2-6	
13:7-12			
13:13-19			
17:2-7	17:2-7	17:2-7	
19:11-13	19:11-13		19:11-13
21:1-9			
21:18-21	21:18-21		21:18-21
	22:20-21		
22:22	22:22		22:22
22:23-27	22:23-25		
24:1-4			
24:7	24:7		24:7
25:5-10			

apodictic *wisdom*, and thus not a legal genre at
all.[177]

Finally, none of L'Hour's characteristics for the
purge laws, with the exception of the purge formula,
is clear and distinct enough to separate these laws
from any number of others in Deuteronomy, and the use
of the formula as a critical characteristic is therefore questionable.[178] Furthermore, in his study,
Lohfink has indicated that some formulas occur at
complete random; some are connected with the content
of the pericope to which they are attached and whose
sole purpose is to emphasize that content; some are
unique in Deuteronomy and appear only in one text or
another; and finally, some can be explained only as
portions of texts and traditions which Deuteronomy
absorbed and which remain to indicate the portions of
the canonical text to which these sources have been
assigned.[179] Although L'Hour and Merendino assume
the purge formula is used to indicate the portions of
Deuteronomy absorbed from the criminal code, the
formula could occur completely at random, or be used
in any of the other fashions Lohfink observes.

Formulas occur throughout Dt 12--26. Each has a
complicated theological history. When two or more
formulas are used together, it is not clear what elements of the theology of each formula are being emphasized, adjusted or denied. At least a dozen
formulas occur separately or in combinations in the
city-texts studied here. Formulas are difficult to
use in analyzing the theology or the setting of a
unit. Whether L'Hour and Merendino can defend their
theory that elements of Deuteronomy containing the
purge formula originally made up a criminal code law
is questionable. There are too many possible uses for
the formula in Deuteronomy, and neither L'Hour nor
Merendino make any effort to establish the use of the
purge formula as a source clue, both simply presume it.

Merendino also attempts to establish the coherence of the purge laws by matching them with a
similar code from Ex 21:12-16. Even though
Merendino rearranges his material to fit his theory
by placing Ex 21:16 after Ex 21:17, he still does
not make a good match.[180] Deuteronomy 19:11-13 should
not be analyzed as an independent unit, but as a sub-
unit of 19:1-13. Furthermore, Dt 19:11-13 deals with
a man who *hates* his neighbor, *ambushes* his neighbor,
kills his neighbor. Exodus 21:12 deals with a man

who *strikes* his neighbor a mortal blow. There are obvious differences, beyond just a development of moral consciousness. Exodus 21:12 deals with accidental death, a concern of Dt 19:4-10, not 19:11-13! Deuteronomy 19:11-13 deals with murder. Deuteronomy 21:18 addresses the parents; Ex 21:15 addresses the child. The subject is the same in both, viz., the relationship of parents and children.

Deuteronomy 22:22, as Merendino admits, does not appear in the series from Exodus 21. However, Merendino claims it is parallel to the law on bestiality in Ex 22:18. *Whoever lies with a beast shall be put to death.* But nowhere else are adultery and bestiality considered together. Adultery is a matter of justice, i.e., violating the property of another male. Bestiality is a matter of religion, i.e., participating in rites in which a sacred man or woman has intercourse with an animal, commonly used as the symbol of the deity. Deuteronomy 24:7 concerns selling Hebrew slaves to others; Ex 21:16 concerns selling or using Hebrew slaves, or perhaps simply not having sold the slave at the time of apprehension. The two laws are similar, but distinct.

Merendino's argument that these laws have the same number of stress syllables is difficult to defend since the mechanics of such a rhythm in Hebrew is questionable here. Finally, the fact that there is only one common word in the vocabulary of the two series argues strongly that the laws in Deuteronomy and Exodus are not related in the fixed literary or even oral traditions of either.

Finally, Merendino argues for the unity of the purge laws as a code on the basis of the traditional relationships which the laws protect. The purge laws, like the laws in Ex 21, and like the Decalogue in Ex 20, deal with three fundamental relationships which every Israelite is committed to protect: the relationship between members of the same family; the relationship between the individual and the community; the relationship between the individual and material property. The *evil* which the formula seeks to purge is any serious disorder in these relationships. The concept of what constituted a disorder was refined as time went on, according to Merendino. In Ex 21, one's parents could not be physically abused, while in Deuteronomy verbal abuse of one's parents was disorder enough. In Ex 21, adultery was forbidden, while in

163

CHART

Une législation criminelle and the Covenant Code

But if any man hates his
neighbor and lies in
wait for him, and attacks
him, and wounds him
mortally so that he
dies, and the man flees
into one of these
cities (Dt 19:11).

Whoever strikes a man so
that he dies shall be
put to death (Ex 21:12).

If a man has a stubborn
and rebellious son, who
will not obey the voice
of his father or the
voice of his mother
and, though they chas-
tise him, will not give
heed to them (Dt 21:18).

Whoever strikes his
father or his mother
shall be put to death
(Ex 21:15).

Whoever curses his father
or his mother shall be
put to death (Ex 21:17).

If a man is found lying
with the wife of another
man, both of them shall
die, the man who lay
with the woman, and the
woman; so you shall
purge the evil from
Israel (Dt 22:22)

If a man is found steal-
ing one of his brethren,
the people of Israel and
if he treats him as a
slave or sells him then
that thief shall die; so
you shall purge the evil
from the midst of you
(Dt 24:7).

Whoever steals a man,
whether he sells him or
is found in possession
of him shall be put to
death (Ex 21:16).

Deuteronomy homosexuality and bestiality were equally
serious disorders.

Horst (1930) was the first to suggest that the
Decalogue in Dt 5 was basically a statement of
Yahweh's legitimate expectations from Israel
(*Privilegrecht Jahwes*). Deuteronomy 12--18, according
to Horst, then detailed these expectations.[181]
Lohfink pursued this same theory in his study of
Dt 5--11.[182] Therefore, L'Hour's suggestion followed
by Merendino that the criminal code and the Decalogue
have the same value structure is not surprising.
There is no doubt that Dt 12--26 contains many
practical applications of the Decalogue in Dt 5. However, it is questionable whether the origin of the
canonical set of values (family, community,
property) is the Israelite amphictyony in particular,
and not simply Ancient Near Eastern city life in
general.

L'Hour and Merendino have demonstrated that in
Deuteronomy there is a pre-Deuteronomic tradition
which considers the city as the nuclear community in
Israel. The criminal code and other laws such as the
city-texts in this study, are part of this tradition.
There is no need to separate these laws into a unique
literary source. It is sufficient that the same
values reflected in the Decalogue are reflected in
laws with an urban perspective. Since the Decalogue
is a reflection of an authentically-Israelite
theology, then there does not need to be a conflict
between that theology and the urban culture reflected
by laws like those of the purge formula and the city
texts. There is a tradition in Deuteronomy which is
both authentically Israelite and authentically urban.

If L'Hour and Merendino had not been so committed
to the nomadic ideal and had not assumed that Israel
was originally a completely non-urban people and
hostile to the city, they could have studied the
criminal code as a reflection of Israel's theology.
While the code itself may have developed during the
monarchy to endorse the judicial reforms of the king,
it represents a pre-monarchial tradition. In this
tradition, the city is an acceptable form of
community, whose life style is a model for the people
of Yahweh. Although L'Hour argued that the intention
of this code was to adapt a semi-nomadic people to an
urban way of life, there is no reason why it could not
have been used to federate Yahwist cities into a

Yahwist nation.

While L'Hour proceeded to investigate the ramifications of his cultural, epochal, and historical
matrix for texts like Dt 19:1-13, Macholz did not.
L'Hour is interested in the intellectual, ideological
and theological matrix which produced this literature
he called the purge laws. Macholz, on the other hand,
is interested strictly in the institutional or
societal matrix which produced texts like Dt 19:1-13.

Macholz agrees with Knierim's emphasis on the
reign of Jehoshaphat at a period during which the
monarchy increased its involvement in legal questions
in Israel. However, for Macholz, the gate courts
presided over by the elders of the cities and the
royal courts in the military garrisons were complementary, not competitive. There were a variety of
judicial systems in Israel throughout her history,
not simply one monolithic complex of jurisdictions.
Gate courts and royal courts were among them. The
gate courts handled matters which dealt with daily
life in the cities of Canaan. The monarchy, on the
other hand, established courts to deal with the
particular circumstances created by life in a national
state governed by a king created. These matters
according to Macholz included crimes such as high
treason, exemptions from military service, in-
subordination and other breaches of martial law. The
royal courts also had jurisdiction over members of
the king's bureaucracy and foreigners living in the
land.[183] The central court established by
Jehoshaphat is only a court of information (*Rechts-
findungs-Behörde*), thus not really a court at all,
but a kind of fact-finding institution. The interest
of the kings in the municipal courts in Israel stems
from the strongly democratic traditions of urban
justice, traditions at odds with the manner in which
monarchs dispensed justice. As an institution which
contributed much to the daily life of the people, the
kings needed control of the courts in order to guarantee the uniform enforcement of their policies.

The municipal court is part of the urban heritage
of the Ancient Near East.[184] The municipal court was
an institution whose very presence questioned the
divine right style of monarchy, which non-Canaanite
invaders brought into the land, and to which Hebrew
monarchies returned. As a more ancient institution
than the monarchy, the municipal court enjoyed

166

prerogatives that even the king could not ignore. Although by 2800-2525 BCE, government in Mesopotamia was already autocratic, courts remained democratic. According to Jacobsen, the courts preserved a primitive democracy which existed in Mesopotamian society as a whole at one time.[185] The divine democracy in which Mesopotamian gods lived also reflected this primitive democracy. Since the attributes of the gods were all anthropomorphic, their democracy was no doubt modeled on the human social structures of the early communities in Mesopotamia.

Jirku maintains that this tradition of judicial democracy was also practiced in Palestine during the 13th century BCE.[186] He cites as an illustration the story of WEN-AMUN of Egypt.[187] A crewman stole some gold from WEN-AMUN and jumped ship in Dor. WEN-AMUN asks the king of Dor to extradite the thief, which his host agrees to do. The king of Dor, however, does not post a bond with WEN-AMUN during the extradition process, although had the thief been from Dor, her king would have been obliged to do so. The host community is responsible if foreign guests are robbed by its citizens during their visit.

Another example which Jirku cites concerns Hittite merchants at Ugarit.[188] While on business in Apsuna, several employees of the merchant Talimu were murdered. Not only the murderers, but also the citizens of the place where the murders were committed are fined. In Dor, the host community merely posts a bond until a conviction is made. In Ugarit (Apsuna), the host community and the convicts both are liable for restitution, as the reciprocity between King Ini-Teschub of Carchemish and Ugarit shows.[189]

Texts like Dt 19:1-13 are part of a tradition in which the ancient cities of Canaan cooperated to ensure that murder would not disrupt the peace. The cities of refuge were established on principles consistent with the practice of the municipal courts which were committed to an extremely democratic way of administering justice. The ancient cities brought these traditions of asylum with them when they became corporate members of early Israel.

When the monarchy appeared in Israel, urban traditions like Dt 19:1-13 again became important because of the emphasis which they placed on the prerogatives of the cities and the authority of the elders. Such

texts acted as a restraint on the kings' efforts to
consolidate all forms of power in Israel under their
own control. According to Knierim, one urban center
of resistance to the monarchy was Shechem. In his
work on the Decalogue, Knierim focused on a reform by
the priests of Shechem in the early days of the
divided monarchy prior to the time when prophets
assumed the role of loyal opposition to sovereigns in
both Israel and Judah.[190]

This non-monarchial setting which Knierim proposed for the Decalogue bears some interesting similarities to and differences with the non-monarchial
setting L'Hour proposed for the criminal code.[191]
Both Knierim and L'Hour are proposing *non-monarchial*
settings for these pre-Deuteronomic traditions;
neither discusses the setting of Deuteronomy as a
whole. For L'Hour, however, the setting is *pro-
monarchial*, for Knierim it is not. Neither regard
their sources as architects of centralization, power
brokers in the community at large, or representatives
of the state.[192] Nonetheless, both L'Hour and Knierim
agree that their sources are reacting to the kings'
efforts at federalization.

Finally, for L'Hour the city is a theological
model, while for Knierim it is a practical reality.[193]
While L'Hour describes the setting of the purge laws
only in generalities, Knierim fixes detail after
detail to make the setting of the Decalogue as concrete
as possible. He argues that the Decalogue was a
familiar part of *public assemblies at Shechem* in which
adult males from *all over Israel* were taught how to
preserve their faith in Yahweh while living *in a
pluralist society* during the *10th and 9th centuries.*

The decalogues in Lv 18:7-16, Ex 23:1-3, 6-9,
10-19, Pss 50, 81, Ho 4:1-3 and Je 7:1-15 assume
public worship, rather than private religious
instruction as a setting. There is no reason to presume the decalogues in Dt 5 and Ex 20 did not share
that association with public assemblies. The
Decalogue prohibits images and conspicuously avoids
mention of the monarchy or any other state institution. The state shrines at Dan and Bethel would
certainly have made some reference to their royal
patrons, and, considering the Canaanite calf-pedestals
in their sanctuaries, would certainly have found the
prohibition of images in poor taste. The only remaining sanctuary of significance is Shechem.

168

Only adults would be cautioned to avoid adultery, a topic too mature for the religious instruction of children before the age of puberty. And although second person grammatical forms used in the Decalogue can refer to men or women, Lv 18:7-16 interprets the prohibition of adultery as addressed *only* to men. Furthermore, Ex 23:14-17 and Ex 34:18-23 require only the men to make regular pilgrimages. Thus the Decalogue is directly addressed only to men. And since commanding Israel as a nation to *honor your father and mother* is awkward and unlikely the Decalogue speaks to these adult males as individuals, rather than as a corporate person. If these men were all from the same city, the Decalogue would address more specific issues in more concrete detail. However, faced with representatives from all Israel, its directives remain necessarily general.

The Decalogue is neither militant nor missionary: it seeks neither to destroy non-believers nor convert them. Thus according to Knierim, the Decalogue developed when those who worshipped Yahweh and those who did not had to live together in a single society. The final authorization of every text in Deuteronomy is the Sinai theophany, whose centerpiece is the Decalogue. Only if the Decalogue originated before the rest of Deuteronomy could it have acquired the respect and influence in the community which Deuteronomy presumes. Thus the setting of the Decalogue is not only ecumenical, it is early.[194]

Resistance to the hereditary monarchy in Israel was systematically reduced by absorbing the opponents' traditions into the great tradition of the monarchy in Jerusalem. Such was the fate of texts, like Dt 19:1-13, which now stand as elements of the royal policy of organization and centralization.

Intention

As indicated by the blood formulas which conclude both the conditions for granting asylum and the conditions for denying asylum, the intention of Dt 19:1-13 is to broaden the definition to culpable killing to include both murder and the execution of individuals connected with accidental death. Both contaminate the land and destroy its prosperity. Like the imposters who pretend to be prophets, but are only fortune

tellers, soothsayers, charmers, diviners, and casters
of spells (Dt 18:9-22) and like the imposters who pretend to be landowners, but are really only thieves
(Dt 19:14), the avengers who pretend to purify the land,
are often the very ones who spoil it. However, this
taboo can be avoided and the community's responsibility
for bloodshed can be fulfilled through the correct use
of the city and its judicial institutions.

The directive guarantees every killer asylum by
designating three cities, establishing three regions,
and improving the roads to each city. No refugee is
to be denied the opportunity for asylum because
facilities are inadequate. However, the adequacy of
the cities may not rest only on their availability,
but on their religious legitimacy as well. The number
three is mentioned twice (Dt 19:2,3); and the
directive consists of three commands: *set apart* (Dt
19:2), *prepare* (Dt 19:3), and *divide* (Dt 19:3). The
number three is the correct number because of some
inherent power it releases. Additional cities are
authorized (Dt 19:9-10) but only in three's. If three
were not a magic number, additional cities would be
authorized on a needs basis.

The number three also occurs in Dt 19:6 as part
of the idiom for *previously,* which literally means
for the past three days. The number three occurs in
other sections of Deuteronomy as well, e.g., Dt 14:28
*at the end of every third year, you shall bring all
your tithes of your produce . . . . and . . . three
times a year, then every male among you shall appear
before the Lord . . . .*

The number three may be an exact or simply an
approximate number in Hebrew. It is the most frequently used cultic number after seven, and indicates
integrity or completeness, i.e., beginning + middle +
end. The number three can also indicate the
universe, i.e., heaven + earth + sheol, or family,
i.e., father + mother + child.[195]

However, the magical quality of the number three
is modified in the final form of the text, where a
very practical reason is given for the multiple
number of cities (Dt 19:6): *should the distance be
too great.* This concern appears in Dt 14:24 as well:
*If, however, the journey is too much for you . . .
because the place which the Lord your God chooses for
the abode of his name is too far for you . . . .*

170

The connection between this concern for distance and the *maqom* theology is the basis for arguing that cities of refuge were established when worship of Yahweh was centralized in Jerusalem.[196]

Centralization of worship affected such practices as the butchering of animals (Dt 12), but there is no mention of centralization in Dt 19:1-13. To presume that cities of refuge were necessary now that high places dedicated to Yahweh were eliminated is an argument from silence. Furthermore, the centralization laws contrast *the place* with *the gates*. The focus of Dt 19:1-13 is not *the* gates, but *the city* mentioned in Dt 19:1,2,5,7,9,11. Then, too, sanctuary was still available at the altar, even while the cities of refuge were in existence (1 K 1:50; 1 K 2:28; Ne 6:10), so it is not likely that the concept of sanctuary in a city replaced the concept of sanctuary at the altar.[197]

The preoccupation with the magical quality of numbers and the liturgical accuracy of religious institutions are both characteristic of P.[198] Since both Dt 19:1-13 and 4:41-43 are concerned with cities of refuge, it would be more difficult to establish Dt 19:1-13 as a P tradition than to argue that the similarities are shared with a common parent tradition. As it stands, Dt 19:1-13 is concerned with the legitimacy of cities of refuge, and not the establishment of cities of refuge.[199] The existence of cities of refuge is assumed by Dt 19. The sequence in Dt 19:1-3 is the key to the emphasis which is to be placed on the various interests in the directive. The mention of the number three comes before the mention of the purpose of the cities. Also Dt 19:1-3 mentions that the number of the cities is to be three twice! Therefore, the concept of a refuge for killers developed first; then the use of cities as refuges; then the need for cities used as refuges to be established in three's. The concern of both subdivisions is *the killer* (Dt 19:3,4). One subdivision guarantees the killer's right to asylum (Dt 19:4b); the other limits the right. The second subdivision makes two points, each concluded by the bloodshed formula (Dt 19:10,13). Unjust punishment (Dt 19:4-9) and unjust murder (Dt 19:10-13) both violate the community's responsibility for bloodshed, established in the Decalogue (Dt 5:17). Cities and city government will keep the community faithful.

A very sophisticated legal consciousness guided the development of these limitations. Several indications appear in the text. First, the limitations, in general agreement with the directive in Dt 19:1-3, acknowledge that any killer might claim asylum, however, such a claim did not prevent extradition and execution (Dt 19:12). This subtle but significant revision of the directive in Dt 19:1-3 is accomplished by the use of the title: *This is the provision for the manslayer* at the beginning of Dt 19:4. Thus the law reading: *whoever flees ('aser) there may save his life* becomes *this kind of killer who ('aser) flees there may save his life*. The *'aser* changes from an independent pronoun (*whoever*) to a relative pronoun (*who*).[200] Second, Dt 19:5a emphasizes that the defendant did not know, nor did he have reason to know that his actions were potentially lethal. He goes into the forest *to cut wood*, not to murder his neighbor. His actions are not reckless. He is using his axe *to cut down a tree* not in foolishness, or to kill his neighbor.[201] His intentions are non-culpable. No Hebrew should be executed for wishing to chop wood or to fell a tree. Third, the defendant lacked complicity in the death of his neighbor. The *axe head*, not the woodcutter, is the subject of the verb *strikes (nāsal)* in Dt 19:5a. It is the axe head which *comes loose* or *flies off*, not the woodcutter who *aims* or *throws* the axehead. It is also the axe head which *hits*, literally *finds* the neighbor by accident. The example in Dt 19:5 could win a judgment of homicide due to the accidental and non-culpable nature of the circumstances even in a contemporary court of law. Fourth, the example in Dt 19:6 established the concurrence between the *mens rea* of the defendant and the *actus reus* (Dt 19:11), in order clearly to convict him of premeditated murder. Thus, although the defendant surmounts the ordeal of flight to the city of refuge and claims immunity from prosecution, he is summarily extradited and executed. Innocent blood shed is innocent blood shed, regardless in whose name.

This intention has remained consistent throughout the history of the text. Cities establishing treaties with one another recognized the need to control violence in order to keep the peace. Those cities who entered Israel continued to recognize that value because of their faith in Yahweh as the one who defends the defenseless. During the power struggle between monarchists and non-monarchists in Israel, the prerogatives of the cities as sanctuaries and their elders as judges militated against the consolidation of power in the king alone. And, finally, the Deuteronomic reform made use of Dt 19:1-13 as a means to centralize the liturgy without totally upsetting the balance of power and the public order throughout Judah. Cities of refuge were to continue to function.

Deuteronomy 4:41-3

Genre

Structure analysis

Supplement on Cities of Refuge	Dt 4:41-3
I. Historical introduction (*'āz*)	41a α
II. Notice	41a β-43
A. Notice proper	41a β
B. Qualifications	41b-43
1. Specification of *beyond the Jordan*	41b
2. Specification of *set apart*	42
a. Specification proper	42a α
b. Citation (sign: *'ašer*)	42a β-b
1) Protasis	42a β-δ
a) Protasis proper	42a β
b) Mitigating circum-stances	42a γδ
(1) No advertance	42a γ
(2) No malice of forethought	42a δ
2) Apodosis	42b
3. Gazetteer	43
a. Bezer	43a
1) Identification	43a α
2) Jurisdiction	43a β
b. Ramoth	43b αβ
1) Identification	43b α
2) Jurisdiction	43b β
c. Golan	43b γδ
1) Identification	43b γ
2) Jurisdiction	43b δ

Dt 4:41-43: Supplement

The literary form of Dt 4:41-3 is frequently
contrasted with the literary form of Dt 4:1-40, i.e.,
sermon, and Dt 4:44-49, i.e., *narrative introduction*.
The sermon in Dt 4:1--40 addresses its audience
directly using second person forms. Persuasive style
is characteristic of this literary pattern. Moses
appeals to Israel to remain faithful to the imageless
worship of Yahweh which she learned on Sinai. There
was no Yahweh visible during the theophany on Sinai,
therefore, Moses argues, there would be no Yahweh
visible in Israel's liturgy.

Dt 4:44-9 is a narrative introduction. It provides information. The introduction describes the
time, *when they came out of Egypt* (Dt 4:45); the
place, *beyond the Jordan in the valley opposite Beth
Peor, in the land of Sihon* (Dt 4:45) where Moses delivered the sermon. In the narrative introduction,
there is an artist, and not simply an archivist, at
work. The information draws the audience into the excitement of the event. Details of the narrative are
chosen for their connotations as well as for their
information. For example, the time here is not long
after the coming out of Egypt, when the people were
electric with the presence of Yahweh; the place is
beyond the Jordan near Beth Peor, with its alluring
and frightening memories of sacrilege and excess; the
enemy is Sihon, the mighty warrior whose face had been
rubbed in his own disdain for Israel when his fearful
kingdom collapsed before them; the speaker is Moses,
aging ancestor of the people. There is suspense and
the characters have personality.

Von Rad calls Dt 4:41-3 a *notice*, a simple and
undramatic prose statement of the facts.[202] Notice
provides information without extras: WHEN? WHAT?
WHO? WHERE? WHY? The genre contains no tension, no
development of character, no interest in colorful
details. The intention of notice is documentation
and it is related to report and account.[203] However,
only Dt 4:1aβ-3 technically corresponds to von Rad's
definition of notice. The historical introduction
then absorbs the notice into a somewhat different
genre: *supplement*. The supplement is attached to an
existing passage in order to make an addition or a
correction. Here in Dt 4:41-3, the supplement has
all the features of the notice, but dates the information it provides by attaching it as a rider to

Dt 4:44--5:1.

Dt 4:41aα: Historical introduction

        The particle *then* in Dt 4:41a functions as an
historical introduction.[204] For Carmichael, who sees
Dt 4:41-43 as an outline for Dt 19:1-13, this introduction fulfills the same function as the expansion
formula in Dt 19:1.[205]

Dt 4:42αβ-b: Citation

        The clause *that the manslayer might flee there*
in Dt 4:42a is repeated in Dt 4:42, viz., *that by
fleeing to one of these cities he might save his life.*
The repetition frames the case law cited in Dt 4:42.
The case law in Dt 4:42 is self contained because it
can be removed from the notice without destroying its
integrity.

        that the manslayer might flee there, who
        kills his neighbor unintentionally, without
        being at enmity with him in time past, and
        that by fleeing to one of these cities he
        might save his life (Dt 4:42).

The subdivision is subordinate to the rest of the
passage because the reference *to one of these cities*
is ambiguous without the explanation given in Dt 4:41.

Dt 4:43:   Gazetteer

        A gazetteer is an important part of the notice.
Both of the notices in Ju 1:16-17 name cities, i.e.,
the city of the palms; Zephath; Hormah; and locate
the sites geographically, i.e., *which lies in the
Negeb near Arad.* A *gazetteer* is a geographic list
naming and locating cities. Lists follow some logical
principle of organization. Here, Dt 4:43 puts the
southernmost city at the head of the list and the
northernmost city at the bottom. The arrangement reflects the route of march which Deuteronomy describes
the Hebrews taking into East Jordan.

        The phrases *for the Reubenites; for the Gadites;
for the Manassites;* restrict the jurisdiction of the
cities to particular classes of people.[206]

Setting

The ideological matrix of Dt 4:41-3 is urban. The city is an inheritance given to Israel. Moses himself is executor of that will. The city is a place of refuge, where those without witnesses to call to their defense may find justice. The city is the official unit into which Israel as a people is divided. The ideological matrix of Dt 4:41-3 is judicial. Jurisdiction is granted. Due process is established. Murder and manslaughter are distinguished. Verdicts are rendered. The literary forms on which Dt 4:41-3 draws are legal forms: statute, restriction, case law, notice. The ideological matrix of Dt 4:41-3 is Yahwist. Moses, the architect of Israel, is honored as the founder of the cities. Cain may have invented the city as a social institution, but it was Moses who authorized the use of the city in Israel.

The use of the city as an administrative center was common during the monarchy in Israel.[207] However Dt 4:41-43 does not mention the king. It is Moses, not the monarch, who establishes the legal institution of asylum. In fact, the monarchy was notorious for violating the privileges of asylum. For example in 1 K 2:28-45, Solomon ordered Benaiah to assassinate Joab, even though Joab had claimed asylum at the altar! Therefore, asylum need not be part of a royal policy, but is promoted, instead, by a judicial reform seeking to contain the king's power. This reform considered the king and the city as distinct institutions. Rejecting the authority of the king, the reform appealed to the traditions of the city; traditions associated, according to Dt 4:41-3, with the ancestral period of Israel herself.

The union of the Deuteronomist's history and the Torah is generally considered the setting of Dt 4:41-3.[208] According to this theory, if Dt 4:41-3 developed before the Deuteronomist's History and Gn-- Nm were joined then Dt 19, which provides for the designation of cities of refuge, would have mentioned Dt 4:41-3.

The language of Dt 4:41-3 is not from P; as Driver points out according to the P tradition in Nm 35:10-14, it was Joshua and not Moses who designated the cities of refuge on both sides of the Jordan.[209] To identify the formation of the canon as the cultural, epochal or historical matrix of Dt 4:41-3 assumes that the intention of the passage is to coordinate the traditions in Js 20:1-9 and Nm 35:9-15 with Dt 19. If, however, the intention of Dt 4:41-3 is to extend the legislation in Dt 5:2 ff from Israel in east Jordan to all Israel, then this supplement could appear much earlier in the development of Deuteronomy. For example, according to Noth, the Deuteronomist inherited only chapters 5--26+28 of Deuteronomy. To introduce this material, the Deuteronomist composed a short and highly interpreted history of Israel found in Dt 1--3. This introduction was then expanded by the sermon in Dt 4.[210] Deuteronomy 4:41-3 may have already been in place in the Deuteronomy which the Deuteronomist inherited.[211]

Intention

Generally, scholars consider Dt 4:41-3 an effort to organize the conflicting information in the Hebrew Bible on the cities of refuge. Only two scholars have suggested that Dt 4:41-3 serves a critical purpose in the structure of Deuteronomy: Driver and Carmichael.[212] For Driver, Dt 4:41-3 serves as an editorial boundary *designed to separate the intro-ductory discourse (1:6--4:40) from c. 5 ff . . . .*[213] For Carmichael, the intention of the text is more complex. Carmichael argues that the introductory material in Dt 1--11 and the legal material in Dt 12--26 follow the same outline. He calls this characteristic *D's revision principle.*[214] Therefore the treatment of the prophet in Dt 4:1-40 and the treatment of cities of refuge in Dt 4:41-3 serve as an outline for the treatment of the prophet in Dt 18:15-22 and the treatment of cities of refuge in Dt 19:1-13. For neither Driver nor Carmichael could the genre of Dt 4:41-3 be *supplement*, since its intention is to make corrections or additions to an existing passage. For both Driver and Carmichael, Dt 4:41-3 is an essential element in the original structure.[215]

There are problems with such a position. Why the author of Dt 4:41-3 was so concerned about the varying traditions on the cities of refuge, and not any number of other discrepancies, is not clear. And if it is the intention of Dt 4:41-3 to clarify the situation, why insert it here instead of at some more logical place in the text, such as Dt 3:12b-13a or

Dt 3:14-17?[216]

> When we took possession of this land at
> that time, I gave to the Reubenites and the
> Gadites the territory beginning at Aroer,
> which is on the edge of the valley of the
> Arnon, and half the hill country of Gilead
> with its cities; the rest of Gilead and all
> Bashan, the kingdom of Og, that is all the
> region of Argob, I gave to the half-tribe
> of Manasses (Dt 3:12-13).

Even as it stands, Dt 4:41-3 does not definitively
resolve the question of just how many cities of
refuge there are, and whether those in East Jordan
were established by Moses or Joshua, which were the
things in question in the first place!

The reason for the location of Dt 4:41-3 here,
instead of some more logical point in the narrative,
is that the notice *Then Moses set apart three
cities* . . . was already part of the introduction to
the law in Dt 4:44--5:1 when the addition was made.
As Mittmann has pointed out, there are formal
connections between the two passages.[217] Both use
third person, rather than second person forms. Both
use the phrases *beyond the Jordan* (Dt 4:41+46,+47),
which they both describe as *in the east*. According to
Mittmann, both texts have been expanded. The
original unit would have read:

> Then Moses set apart three cities in the east
> beyond the Jordan . . . . This is the law
> which Moses set before the children of
> Israel . . . beyond the Jordan . . . . And
> Moses summoned all Israel and said to them
> . . . (Dt 4:41+44+5:1).

Deuteronomy frequently expands superscriptions
like Dt 4:44--5:1; Deuteronomy 28:28, 69 and 33:1 have
all been supplemented.[218] The intention of the
original introduction was to indicate that Moses
designated three cities in east Jordan, and then
promulgated the laws by which these cities were to be
governed. Therefore, Dt 1:6--3:29 + 4:41--28:68 was
originally addressed to an urban league living in
east Jordan. In order to transfer this literature to
Israel living in west Jordan, the supplement in Dt
4:41-3 was added to the superscription in Dt 4:44--
5:1. Thus the cities designated are no longer

corporate members of an urban league in east Jordan, but simply cities of refuge. Their designation is not the occasion on which Dt 1:6--3:29 + 4:41--28:68 was promulgated, but is simply an isolated notice which seems to attend to some *unfinished business* left hanging from the preceding chapters.[219] The puzzle which Dt 4:41-3 resolves is how to extend the material originally connected with Israel in east Jordan to all Israel.

Once Dt 4:41-3 is added to the text it shares in the theology of the desert and the city found, not so much in Dt 12--26, but in Dt 1--4. These chapters contain Moses' testimony that, among other things, Israel, by refusing to accept Canaan and its cities had rebelled against Yahweh. Likewise, Moses pleads that a new Israel take possession of the land and its cities. Both contain very positive attitudes toward the city.

In Dt 1--4, the desert is not idealized: it is a passing phase, a place in which Israel had been marooned, a means of punishment. In Dt 1:6-8, Yahweh orders Israel out of the desert and into the land of Canaan. *You have stayed long enough at this mountain . . . .* The desert was a rest stop, but it was not Israel's home. In Dt 1:29-36, Moses reminds Israel that she was completely helpless in the desert. *. . . in the wilderness, where you have seen how the Lord your God bore you, as a man bears his son, in all the way that you went until you came to this place.* The desert was a good place to die, but an impossible place to live. Finally, Yahweh orders Israel back into the desert as a punishment and Moses explains that Israel's stay in the desert was not her initiation as the people of Yahweh, but her sentence for mutiny.

> And the Lord heard your words, and was angered, and he swore, 'Not one of these men of this evil generation shall see the good land . . . turn, and journey into the wilderness . . . .' So you remained at Kadesh many days, the days that you remained there (Dt 1:34+40+46).[220]

According to Dt 1:26-38, Israel was punished in the desert because she questioned Yahweh's jurisdiction over the cities of Canaan. Yahweh gives the cities to Israel as an inheritance, and she questions his ability to make good his promise. How

179

could the city which the Yahwist tradition had discarded as the invention of Cain (Gn 4:17) and had
criticized as the achievement of a vain and bragging
humanity (Gn 11) now be the possession of Yahweh?

> The people are greater and taller than we;
> the cities are great and fortified up to the
> heaven; and moreover we have seen the sons
> of the Anakim there (Dt 1:28).

Israel frequently found it difficult to expose herself
to a future laid down by Yahweh and to subject herself
to his care. There was always the temptation to
protect herself through foreign policy and military
spending, and, as she does here in Dt 1:26-8, to
analyze things in terms of her own capability. However, Israel will possess the cities of Hesbon and
Bashan, not because she is a military power, but because she is Yahweh's legal heir.

Yahweh delivers the cities to Israel. The exiles
in the Babylonian concentration camps to whom Dt 1--4
is addressed were people from a civilized and highly
urban culture. Nabuchadnezzar in 587 BCE had left the
poor as caretakers in Palestine. Few if any had been
considered worth deporting to the suburbs of his own
royal city. As urban refugees, the exiles no doubt
looked with some justifiable pride on the ability of
their ancestors to conquer the Canaanite cities
fortified to the skies (Dt 1:28). They also found
it incredible that the pagan armies of Babylon had
conquered the holy city of Jerusalem. Dt 1--4 explains that victory is not the result of military
power, but of Yahweh's will.

The formula . . . *the Lord has delivered them up*
appears in Dt 2:36; 3:2 and 3:19, as well as Jos 6:2,
8:1, 10:8 emphasizing that Yahweh is master of the
cities, and he deeds them to whomever he wills. Just
as he gave Hesbon and Bashan to the Israelites, he has
now given Jerusalem to the Babylonians. The Hebrews
will be victorious only if they can trust in this
deliverance formula: *which the Lord our God gives us*.
More than 130x, Deuteronomy reminds Israel that it is
Yahweh who gives, and not Israel who conquers!
Yahweh gives blessings and curses, life, mercy and
prosperity. Yahweh gives sons and daughters, and good
things like bread, clothes, meat, flocks, fodder and
rain. Yahweh gives a prophet, the tablets of the law,
the commandments, statutes, decrees. Yahweh gives

death, doom, an iron yoke, diseases, dust, stumbling and the stigma of innocent blood. But first and foremost, Yahweh gives Israel the land (64x) and its cities (10x) as a resting place, and guarantees the power and superiority of Israel over feudal kings like Sihon and Og and anyone else who would reduce Israel to slavery again. Yahweh puts fear and dread into the nations which are unable to keep Israel from plundering them.

But these are promises which give Israel a clear legal right to Canaan; the question is--will she have the faith to exercise that right?[221] Thus the city became a test of faith, par excellence. Since nothing in the land invoked greater fear, nothing required greater courage. The cities were the key to the promise. If these ancestors of the urban exiles in Babylon are to be remembered, it must not be for their military prowess, but for their living faith.

There is some contrast in Dt 1--4 between the deliverance formula found in Dt 2:36; 3:2+19 and Dt 2:36 and 3:4. The expression: *There was not a city too high for us* reflects the Yahwist tradition that the city is a human accomplishment, and not a divine possession. The expression stands out from the surrounding text. It uses the word *qiryâ* for city, while the surrounding text prefers *'îr*. *Qiryâ* is a poetic word, suggesting the expression was a refrain from a poetic tradition celebrating the ancestors of Israel. Deuteronomy 1--4 contrasts this *boasting formula* with the deliverance formula. The boasting formula repeats the tragedy of Babel, and leads to the destruction of Jerusalem.[222]

The deliverance formula is part of a tradition recognizing the gift of the cities as just one more example of the power of Yahweh. Just as the deliverance of the slaves from the power of Pharoah was considered to be a classic reversal in which the weak overcome the strong, the conquest of the walled cities of Canaan, also reflects this same understanding of a god who delights in such reversals. Slaves are not only set free by Yahweh, but are made victorious over the most feared builders of cities as well. The overwhelming power of Yahweh is emphasized by his ability to accomplish such mighty deeds with such little people.

Inheritance is a popular concept in the Hebrew

Bible.[223] In some passages, the whole land is considered Israel's inheritance, e.g., Ex 32:13, Nm 16:14; 34:2; Dt 4:21, 38; 12:10; 15:4, 19:10; 20:16, 21:23; 24:4; 25:19; 26:1; 1 K 8:36; Je 3:19; Ez 35:15, 36:12. In other passages only the portions assigned to each protective association or tribe (mišpāḥâ) are considered an inheritance, e.g., Gn 48:6; Nm 26:52-6; 32:18; 33:54; 34:14; 36:2; Jos 13:7; 14:2, 19:49. However, here in Dt 1--4 the inheritance of Israel is the cities.

Considering inheritance (naḥalâ) part of a nomadic culture has made it easy to ignore the city as the inheritance of Israel. However, Forshey indicates that the inheritance is not a nomadic phenomenon, but an urban one.[224] Inheritance is a technical term for a bonus which commanding officers paid their soldiers. Victorious commanders divided enemy lands and distributed them to soldiers for conduct above and beyond the call of duty. Such an institution assumes a settled and urban economy capable of surveying lands and assigning titles.

Frick also assumes the city is the setting for the inheritance.[225] For Frick, the inheritance is not the possession of an individual, but of a family. Only a urban society recording landowning and carefully tracing genealogies could guarantee the safe transfer of the inheritance from one generation to the next. The importance of the family for this urban institution questions the assumption that urbanization hurt the Hebrew family. On the contrary, according to Frick, the city needed the family!

If the city is Israel's inheritance from Yahweh, then the city is not a rival of Yahweh, nor should Israel fear the city. In the Yahwist tradition in Gn 11, the city is a threat to Yahweh.

> And the Lord came down to see the city and
> the tower, which the sons of men had built.
> And the Lord said, 'Behold, they are one
> people, and they have all one language;
> and this is only the beginning of what
> they will do; and nothing that they propose
> to do will now be impossible for them.
> Come, let us go down, and there confuse
> their language, that they may not under-
> stand one another's speech. So the Lord
> scattered them abroad from there over the

face of all the earth, and they left off
building the city (Gn 11:5-8).

However, what Yahweh can give as a gift is no threat
to his supremacy. The city has been tamed.

Initially, the city throws Israel into panic.
This same fear which the cities of Canaan incite in
Israel, the city of Jerusalem will incite in her
enemies. In Ps 48, for example, a coalition of kings
attack Jerusalem, but are routed. The psalm celebrates the terrifying quality of Jerusalem in
language similar to that used by Dt 1--4 to describe
the cities of Canaan. It is the fear of one con-
fronted with God. It is the fear of one about to die.
But Yahweh's gift should not threaten his people.
Therefore, Dt 1:29 prohibits fear of the city: *Do not
be in dread or fear of them.*

It is not the fortification of the cities which
should attract the attention of Israel, according to
Dt 1--4; it is their municipal courts, for which
Moses establishes judges in Dt 1:9-18, and empowers
them to try murder cases in Dt 4:41-3. It is in the
municipal court that Yahweh is revealed, and not in
the walls and gates and battle towers. It is in the
municipal court that the presence of Yahweh is to be
immortalized, and not in the ceremonies and rituals
of public worship. The administration of law in the
municipal court is Israel's urban theophany. And,
therefore, in support of such a tradition, Dt 4:41-3
argues that the designation of cities for such purposes is a legitimate, humanitarian and Mosaic
process.

Deuteronomy 20:10-20

Genre

Structure analysis

Dt 20:10-20: Legal instruction

Deuteronomy 20:10-20 is neither apodictic law, i.
e., command or prohibition, nor casuistic law. Yet
many critics describe it as war laws.[226] Altogether in
Deuteronomy von Rad blocks off six war laws (Dt 20:1-9;
20:10-20; 21:10-14; 23:10-15; 24:5 and 25:17-19), as
well as a number of war sermons (Dt 7:16-26; 9:1-6;

11:18-25; 31:1-6).[227] He refers to Dt 20:19-20 as *a rule to protect fruit-growing and an ordinance.*[228] As the structure analysis shows, Dt 20:10-20 contains at least two kinds of law, viz., commands (Dt 20:10b, 14a+b , 15a, 17a, 20aβ+b and prohibitions (Dt 20:16b, 19aβ+). However, neither of these is the controlling genre of the present text.

In classic patterns of case law, the major case dominating the section is introduced by *when (kî)*, the remaining laws which reflect some derivation of the major case or some variation in the circumstances are introduced by *but ('im)*.[229] This genre makes use not only of third person forms, but third and second person forms together.[230]

> If any harm follows, then you shall give
> life for life, eye for eye, tooth for tooth,
> hand for hand, foot for foot, burn for
> burn, wound for wound, stripe for stripe
> (Ex 21:23).

Therefore, scholars like Mayes have implied that Dt 20:10-20 is case law.[231]

However, neither the *when-but (kî-'im)* constructions, nor the protasis-apodosis style is unique to case law. Here in Dt 20:10a, the *when (kî)* clause is a circumstantial introduction, not the protasis of a case law. It describes the conditions under which a city is to be given the opportunity to join Israel, not the crime for which punishment will be specified. Then, too, Dt 20:11-20 is not the apodosis of a case law imposing a penalty, but a statement of the results of a suit for peace. Cities willing to join Israel are to be enjoyed as a gift of Yahweh. Cities unwilling to join Israel are to be sacrificed to Yahweh. Were Dt 20:10-20 a case law, and the protasis-apodosis used as a criterion for locating the case and the consequence, the results would be nonsense: *Anyone who goes to war against a city shall be punished by being required to sue that same city for peace!*

Inevitably, even those who refer to all of Dt 12 --26 as laws are careful to specify the analogous way in which they are using the term. Carmichael is a good example. He devotes an entire chapter to the peculiar characteristics of law as a genre in Deuteronomy.[232] Critics use a variety of terms to

186

categorize the peculiarities of the genre in Dt
20:10-20. Von Rad refers to it as part of a *sermon;*
Craigie calls it a *detailed instruction;* and Buis, *une
predication.*[233]

Dt 20:10b: Command

Legal instruction assumes the existence of laws
which are known to its audience. Deuteronomy 20:10-
20, for example, assumes a law compelling its audience
to seek peace before laying siege to a city. This
expectation that nations declare war before attacking
is reflected in Dt 20:10b, which is a command. In
Dt 20:10a, the army approaches *for (lamed) war* and in
Dt 20:10b sues *for (lamed) peace.* The *lamed* specifies
the aim of the verbs in both parts of the instruction
proper, and creates an artistic balance which
integrates the law into the instruction.

Dt 20:16-17: Order

Deuteronomy 20:10-20 also assumes a law requiring
its audience to annihilate its enemies. This order
dovetails prohibitions and commands to increase the
emphasis it places on destroying the enemy.

A   But in the cities of these peoples. . . .

B   you shall save alive nothing that breathes,

B' but you shall utterly destroy. . .

A' the Hittites and the Amorites, the Canaanites
    and the Perizzites, the Hivites and the
    Jebusites. . . (Dt 20:16-17).

Dt 20:14a-17b: Formulas

Legal instruction expands laws. For example,
Dt 20:14a the land grant formula: *which the Lord your
God has given you* expands the command: *but the women
and the little ones, the cattle, and everything else
in the city, all its spoil, you shall take as booty
for yourselves* in Dt 20:14a+bα. In the same way, the
land grant formula and the inheritance formula in
Dt 20:16a expand the prohibition: *you shall save
alive nothing that breathes* in Dt 20:16b. Finally,
the command formula: *as the Lord your God has
commanded you* in Dt 20:17b expands the command:

187

you shall utterly destroy them in Dt 20:17a.

Dt 20:11-20: Results

Legal instruction explains laws. Explanation plays a large role in Dt 20:10-20. For example, Dt 20:11-20 explains the two possible reactions to an ultimatum: acceptance and rejection. Each possibility is carefully detailed. Both protasis in Dt 20:11a and Dt 20:12-13a spell out circumstances under which the laws assumed by the apodosis in both Dt 20:11b and Dt 20:13b-20 are pertinent.

Dt 20:12-13a: Protasis

For the law assumed in Dt 20:13b-20 to take effect, four conditions must be met. The land grant formula: *and when the Lord your God gives it into your hand* in Dt 20:13a could be subordinated to Dt 20:12b, or coordinated with Dt 20:12b. If the formula is subordinate to Dt 20:12b, then there would be only two conditions to be met: *it makes no peace . . . makes war against you. You shall besiege it* would become part of the apodosis.

However, it seems best to coordinate Dt 20:12b and 13a. The land grant formula is not a secondary qualification of *you shall put all its males to the sword* (Dt 20:13b). It is joined to the rest of the sequence with a *then (waw)* and is a full stipulation on its own. The principle of organization in this series of four is the sequence of events as they take place chronologically, i.e., ultimatum rejected, war declared, siege begun, city delivered. At that point, the consequence requires *you shall put all its males to the sword*.

Dt 20:19a β-b: Double prohibition

War, peace, siege, interdict and *booty* are all technical terms which the instruction explains. *Siege,* for example, is the sanction applied against cities refusing to join Israel. It is not a wholesale destruction of the orchard industry or the standing timber of a city as was common. Ancient Egyptian and Mesopotamian battle reports often brag of a general's ability against the trees of his enemy. For example, Pharoah Thut-mose (1490-1436 BCE) campaigned in the Euphrates Valley and claimed to have

188

destroyed its economy by mowing down its grain fields
and felling both lumber and fruit trees.[234] Likewise,
the Assyrian Ashurnasirpal II (883-859 BCE) celebrated
his victories in Charchemesh (Syria) boasting about
his ability to harvest the timber in the Amanus
mountains.[235] At Medinet Habu, there is a scene de-
picting the Egyptians under Ramses III attacking
Tunip.[236] In the foreground Egyptian troops use
wooden ladders to scale the city walls, while in the
background others are cutting down trees.[237]

Habakkuk shares Deuteronomy's disgust for total
wars which devastate natural resources such as lumber-
producing trees and wild life:

The violence done to [the forests of]
Lebanon will overwhelm you; the destruction
of the beasts will terrify you, for the
blood of men and violence to the earth,
to cities and all who dwell therein
(Hb 2:17).

Dt 20:20: Triple command

Like *but (raq)* in Dt 20:14,16, the *only (raq)*
here in Dt 20:20 indicates that the content of the
verse limits what has been said in the previous
material. Thus the prohibition against felling trees
belonging to a city under siege applies only to fruit
trees. Commercial trees producing lumber only may be
cut down and used to build the siege stockade.
Technically, the use of *only (raq)* indicates that
Dt 20:20 is subordinate to Dt 20:19, and not coordinated with it.

Dt 20:19a: Motivations

Legal instruction encourages its audience to obey
the laws under discussion. To accomplish this, it
employs various forms of parenesis. The motivations
in Dt 20:19 are good examples of how the legal
instruction appeals to the subjective will of its
audience to urge compliance with the limits set by
the prohibitions in Dt 20:19a.

Deuteronomy 20:19b is a proverb introduced by the
particle *ki*. The didactic character of 19b, necessary
to distinguish it from a simple wisdom saying is its
interrogative style. To understand the verse

189

as a rhetorical question, it is necessary to follow the Greek and Syriac text traditions.[238] One could argue in agreement or disagreement with the question: *Are the trees in the field men that they should be besieged by you?* In the process of resolving that argument, learning takes place, which is precisely what the proverb wants to happen.

The parenesis in Dt 20:19aγ and Dt 20:19b are even more creative efforts at persuasion. Neither contains vocabulary or opinions commonly found in Deuteronomy. The parenesis in Dt 20:19aγ is practical. Its advice is the kind offered by such sayings as: *Don't bite the hand that feeds you; Don't kill the goose that lays the golden egg.* Deuteronomy 20:19a is straightforward and shows no sign of being a wisdom saying or a proverb: . . . *for you may eat of them.* These parenesis anticipate the difficulties which may arise for the audience and prevent them from complete adherence to the interpretation being offered.

Legal instruction also combines second and third person forms for particular stylistic reasons. For example, the change in language in Dt 20:13a emphasizes the theology of the unit. The three stipulations in Dt 20:12 use the second person forms to describe the actions of Israel. Deuteronomy 20:13a uses the third person forms to point out that Yahweh is giving the city to Israel. The courage, tactics and military capability of Israel have no role in the victory. This passage repeats the message of Dt 20:1 with which the chapter begins.[239]

Setting

The key to the setting of Dt 20:10-20 appears in Dt 20:15: *Thus you shall do to all the cities which are very far from you, which are not cities of the nations here.* This distinction appears in Js 9, where the Gibeonites obtain a treaty with Israel by arguing that they are not from cities in Canaan, but from very far away.

On the basis of at least seven different similarities between Dt 20:10-20 and Js 9, Blenkinsopp concludes *that this chapter, in common with others in Jos, has undergone editing on the part of the D-group.*[240] Telling pieces of evidence that

190

Dt 20:10-20 enjoys its ultimate setting in the
Deuteronomic History are the list of nations in
Dt 20:17 and the second person plural explanation, so
characteristic of the History. But the Deuteronomic
Historian has not composed Dt 20:10-20 like one of the
many speeches through which the theology of the History
is presented. In fact, the passage occurs after
Dt 20:1 in which the Deuteronomic Historian's own
material declines remarkably.

The passage was also part of the Deuteronomy of
Josiah's reform. According to von Rad, this was where
Dt 20:10-20 originated.[241] He argues that only after
Israel had a king did she fight wars of expansion in
far away places with sophisticated siege techniques.
Furthermore, only at a time when the wars themselves
were forgotten could the decision to spare or destroy
a city be said to rest on so simple a principle.

. . .that they may not teach you to do according to all their abominable practices which
they have done in the service of their gods,
and so to sin against the Lord, your God
(Dt 20:18).

However, Stolz has shown that the strategy of ultimatum
followed by action was common throughout the Ancient
Near East.[242] Whether or not Israel was able to use
this combination of diplomacy and tactics before the
reign of David, there is no reason to assume that
Israel was unaware of it. The intention of Dt 20:10-
20 is not to issue a regulation governing the use of
newly-acquired military capabilities, but to emphasize
that with faith in Yahweh, even Israel was capable of
taking cities in the finest military style.[243] In
fact, it is this precise theology which allows Israel
to remember Joshua, long before the monarchy, as
negotiating with cities in precisely the manner
Dt 20:10-20 describes![244]

When Adonizedek king of Jerusalem heard how
Joshua had taken Ai, and had utterly destroyed
it, doing to Ai and its king as he had done
to Jericho and its king [See Dt 20:12-14]
and how the inhabitants of Gibeon had made
peace with Israel and were among them [Dt 20:
10-11], he feared greatly, because Gibeon
was a great city, like one of the royal
cities, and because it was greater than Ai,
and all its men were mighty (Js 10:1-2).

191

Moses himself negotiates before taking any action
against Sihon in East Jordan.[245]

> So I sent messengers from the wilderness
> Kedemoth to Sihon the king of Hesbon,
> with words of peace [Dt 20:10]
> ....
> But Sihon the king of Hesbon would not let
> us pass by him [Dt 20:12]..............
> And the Lord our God gave him over to us;
> and we defeated him and his sons and all his
> people. And we captured all his cities at
> that time and utterly destroyed every city,
> men, women, and children; we left none re-
> maining; only the cattle we took as spoil
> for ourselves, with the booty of the cities
> we captured. [Dt 20:13-14]...............
> (Dt 2:26--3:11).

Therefore, there is no need to limit literature describing sophisticated military techniques to a
period after it can be clearly demonstrated that
Israel was able to use those techniques.

But even if it is unnecessary to limit Dt 20:10-
20 to a period when Israel, in fact, used sophisticated military techniques, the institution of holy
war does not automatically become the setting of the
text. There are still many discrepancies between the
theologies of von Rad's war law texts in Deuteronomy,
and the Ancient Near Eastern institution.[246] For
example, von Rad's war law texts in Deuteronomy
assume the existence of military officers which
historically appear only after the kings established a
standing army. Likewise, von Rad's war texts consider
the holy war an offensive tactic; historically it was
defensive. Finally these war texts stress the importance of a central shrine, an emphasis which did
not appear in Israel until late in the monarchy.
Therefore, the war law texts which von Rad identifies
in Deuteronomy did develop early in Israel but only
after the founding of the monarchy.

The setting of Dt 20:10-20 is urban. Only an
urban people in an urban setting would be interested
in the effect of the command on recruiting cities or
the command to destroy cities. The passage presumes
a fully walled city and a highly technical siege, as
well as a fully urban economy with orchards and
forests. The form of the unit is legal instruction,

which presumes the existence of judicial instruments
which need to be explained, and uses case laws in
its distinctions. Throughout the unit, there is a
sense of arbitration. A city must be given the opportunity to capitulate. Its intentions must be
identified with words and actions. A city must
demonstrate its peaceful intentions, for example, by
word (*its answer to you is peace*) and action (*it opens
to you*). The setting of Dt 20:10-20 is Yahwist. The
distinguishing characteristic between cities to be
enjoyed and cities to be destroyed is their acceptance
or rejection of Yahweh worship. A sign of peace is
the service of Yahweh, just as surely as a sign of war
is the service of other gods. It is Yahweh himself
who gives the city to Israel to enjoy (Dt 20:14) or to
sacrifice (Dt 20:16). Ultimately, the setting of
Dt 20:10-20 is in the urban communities like Gibeon
and Shechem, Hebron and Shiloh, who were corporate
members of ancient Israel. It was in these communities that Israel was addressed by cities, and in
which membership was carefully determined by legal
means such as Dt 20:10-20 explains. For these communities the city was composed not only of a walled
settlement, but also surrounding orchards and forests.

Intention

Von Rad considers Dt 20:10-20 indicative of the
military piety with which the Levites developed
support for Josiah's efforts to raise a citizen
army.[247] But if the purpose of reinstating the
militia was to save the state money, it hard to understand why Dt 20:10-20 outlaws the alternative form of
payment for the soldier, viz., booty! Such a concept
of total war is extremely idealistic, and does not
explain how, in fact, Josiah kept his army pro-
visioned.[248]

But, even if Dt 20:10-20 is not part of an actual
reform, Deuteronomy as a whole considers the citizen
army the ideal manner of defense.[249] Mercenaries were
part of the painful legacy of feudalism in Canaan.
Neither enjoyed any hereditary connection with the
land, but sold their services to the highest bidder.
Only those who have a clear legal right to the land
can exercise any control over it. It is futile to try
and establish a claim on the land through force. The
land can only be deeded by Yahweh, and those who have

received such an inheritance are invincible. Practical matters, such as feeding an army in the field or paying its soldiers are of no consequence, since they enjoy the bounty of the land itself.

For Carmichael, Dt 20:10-20 stipulates the conditions Israel must fulfill in order to exercise her legal rights as heir to Canaan. To enjoy a final rest from war, Israel must first conquer the places of the other gods who are enemies of Yahweh.[250] The right to dwell in the land is contingent on the willingness of Israel to fight a total war for it. Coexistence or compromise of any kind makes one ineligible to inherit the land.

By destroying her enemies, Israel protects the purity of her worship, which is the overriding concern of Deuteronomy.[251] Deuteronomy 20:10-20 has no tactical interest as far as the destruction of the enemy is concerned, even though an army far away from home would have more use for booty, than one fighting near to home.

The intention of Dt 20:10-20 is to revise Israel's theology of the city.[252] Traditionally, cities were incorporated into Israel or annihilated on the basis of their response to the ultimatum in Dt 20:10. It is the intention of Dt 20:10-20 to limit this policy to specified cities, and to prohibit the devastation of the surrounding countryside. Deuteronomy 20:10-20 recognizes a distinction between its theology, and the traditional theology of the city in Israel. Traditionally, all cities were extended the same opportunity to join Israel. Deuteronomy 20:10 makes no distinction between cities near and cities far off. Deuteronomy 20:10-20, for its part, considers only certain cities eligible for membership. Furthermore, Dt 20:10-20 distinguishes between the city itself, and its orchards and woods. The theology which prohibits Dt 20:10-20 from including all cities in the gifts of Yahweh to Israel, makes a conscious exemption of the orchards and woods of these cities.

Aware that Israel has always included cities, and that Yahwism is not simply the religion of rural or herding peoples, Dt 20:10-20 is very careful to distinguish its criticism of urban life. Certain cities are eliminated from Israel on the same basis that certain classes of recruits are exempt from the

194

militia (Dt 20:2-8). Just as the presence of some recruits threatens the army, the presence of some cities
threatens the nation.[253] Only those cities which pose
no threat to the faith of Israel may be included.

What man is there that is fearful and faint-
hearted? Let him go back to his house,
lest the heart of his fellows melt as his
heart (Dt 20:8).

Deuteronomy 20:10-20 intends to harmonize Israel's
ambivalent traditions on cities. Both traditions consider the city as a gift of Yahweh, however one tradition expected Israel to offer the city as a sacrifice, and the other to enjoy it as a blessing.
Deuteronomy 20:10-20 explains that only cities which
join Israel can be enjoyed, all others are to be
destroyed.

The sacrifice offered after a victory varied.
Historically, warriors would commit all or a portion
of the spoil for a sacrifice before the battle. The
greater the commitment, the greater the warriors'
faith, and presumably the greater their need for
divine assistance. In Deuteronomy, the conquest of a
city is considered completely an act of Yahweh,
therefore Yahweh deserves all the spoil. But this
theological assessment contrasts with an urban tradition in which sacrifices varied. The annihilation
demanded in Dt 13:13-19 is the most absolute found
anywhere in Deuteronomy. Of the five places where the
ban (herem) is described or described in Deuteronomy,
only in Dt 13:13-19 are men, women, children,
buildings, beasts and booty all to be destroyed.[254]
Deuteronomy 20:10-20 uses this variation to explain
how cities survive in Israel. There is no reason to
consider the cities themselves men that they should be
besieged (Dt 20:19). Just as the trees in Dt 20:19-20
are spared because of their usefulness, cities which
show faith in Yahweh and are useful to Israel are
also spared.

Cities which are very far are also exempt from
interdict. This theology in Dt 20 is shared with the
etiology in Js 9 explaining how the Gibeonites survived
in Israel. This dichotomy between near and far is
used in Deuteronomy in the same way as the formula
When the Lord your God enlarges your territory. Both
allow Deuteronomy to preserve conflicting traditions.
Traditions in force now will be modified later. Faced

195

with the problem that Israel at one time destroyed
cities, and at another employed them, Deuteronomy
preserves both as valid. Generally the phrase *which
are very far* is considered a geographic description.[255] However in Dt 30:11-14, *far off (rāhaq)*
means *difficult*. Although this text is not in the
Deuteronomic mainstream, it suggests the geographic
interpretation of *far off* is too literal. Amnesty in
Dt 20:10-20 may be granted only to cities *too difficult*, rather than *too far*. The difficulty cannot be
military, because Deuteronomy considers the cities a
gift from Yahweh to Israel. Military questions are
irrelevant. If *far off* here in Dt 20:10-20 is the
opposite of *nearest* in Dt 21:1-9, then *far off* means
cities with whom Israel has no juridical connection.
Isaiah 50:8 may, in fact, define *near (qārôb)* as *he
who vindicates* or *ally*.[256] Therefore, Dt 20:10-20
distinguishes cities with whom Israel has treaties
(*the cities of these peoples that the Lord your God
gives you for an inheritance*) from those with whom she
has no treaties (*cities which are very far from you*).

Deuteronomy 20:10-20 is not a tactical
instruction in siege warfare, but a legal instruction
on the place of cities in Israel. The credentials of
a city are established through arbitration. The unit
is concerned with the standing a city will have in
Israel. The concern is theological. Therefore, the
audience need not be a king and his mercenaries or an
army in battle array, but simply Israelites uncertain
of whom to consider eligible for membership. The text
is conservative and humanitarian. The cities and their
produce are not inherently evil; both are useful to
Israel in her worship of Yahweh, and only after it can
be legally determined that there is no possible
harmony are either to be destroyed.

In the Deuteronomic History, the intention of
Dt 20:10-20 is tied both to Js 9 and Dt 13:13-19. It
was the considered opinion of the History that Israel
had been destroyed because it had not destroyed
pagans living in Canaan.[257] They had contributed to
the contaminations of Israel's worship, and thus
brought about Israel's destruction. Deuteronomy
13:13-19 is a clear statement that cities are to remain absolutely loyal to the liturgical demands set
down in Dt 12, or else they are to be destroyed. It
was clear to the Deuteronomic Historian that urban
communities like Gibeon were charter members of
ancient Israel, and therefore Js 9 is composed by the

196

CHART

Applications of *the ban (ḥērem)* in Deuteronomy

	men	women	children	build-ings	beasts	booty
Dt 2:24-27	x	x	x	n/a	free	free
Dt 3:1-11	x	x	x	n/a	free	free
Dt 13:13-19	x	x	x	x	x	x
Dt 20:10-14	x	free	free	n/a	free	free
Dt 20:15-18	x	x	x	n/a	n/a	n/a

Deuteronomic Historian to demonstrate that the membership of urban communities in ancient Israel was not
the result of the intention of Yahweh, but deception.
The deception is portrayed by the Deuteronomic
History through the editing of Dt 20:10-20 where a
commonly accepted tradition of membership through
alliance is limited to cities far off. Without the
Deuteronomist's additions, Dt 20:10-20 served as a
text encouraging cities in Josiah's time to recognize
the validity of their place as Yahwist communities.
They had responded to the call to join Israel with
word and deed, and continued that response with service
to the throne. Ultimately, Dt 20:10-20 was part of a
tradition stating the manner in which cities came
into Israel and the obligations of that treaty.

Deuteronomy 21:1-9

Genre

Structure analysis

<pre>
LEGAL INSTRUCTION concerning
  a corpus delicti discovered
  outside the jurisdiction of
  any particular city   Dt 21:1-9
  I. Protasis (sign: kî)   1
    A. Protasis proper   1a α
    B. Mitigating circumstances   1a β-b
      1. Place   1a β-ε
        a. In the land which the
           Lord your God gives
           you . . .   1a β-δ
          1) Circumstance proper   1a β
          2) Qualifications   1a γ-δ
            a) Land grant formula   1a γ
            b) Possession formula   1a δ
        b. lying in the open
           country   1a ε
      2. Suspect   1b
  II. Apodosis (sign: we)   2-9
    A. Deposition   2-8
      1. What-is-to-be-done Ritual   2-6
        a. Preparation   2-3
          1) Certification of city
             by elders and judges   2-3a
</pre>

       a) Determination of
          affected city   Dt 21:2
          (1) *shall come forth*   2a
          (2) *shall measure*   2b
       b) Statement concerning
          affected city   3a
    2) Choice of victim Rubric
       for elders only   3b
       a) Rubric proper   3b α
       b) Parallelism specifying
          heifer   3b β-γ
          (1) First member
              (sign: *'ašer)*   3b β
          (2) Second member
              (sign: *'ašer)*   3b γ
  b. Celebration   4-6
    1) Choice of Place Rubric
       for elders only   4a
       a) Rubric proper   4a α
       b) Parallelism specify-
          ing *valley*   4a β-γ
          1) First member
             (sign: *'ašer)*   4a β
          2) Second member
             (sign: *we)*   4a γ
    2) Slaying of Heifer
       Rubric for elders only   4b
    3) Installation of Wit-
       nesses Rubric for
       priests only   5
       a) Rubric proper   5a *a*
       b) Qualifications   5a β-
          1) Definition of
             priests   5a β
          2) Parallelism moti-
             vating definition   5a γ-b
             (a) First member
                 (sign: *kî*)   5a γ
             (b) Second member
                 (sign: *we)*   5b
    4) Washing of Hands Rubric
       for elders only   6
       a) Gloss   6a
          1) Gloss proper   6a α
          2) Consolidation marker   6a β
       b) Rubric proper   6b
  2. What-is-to-be-said formula
     for elders only   7-8
     a. Testimony   7
     b. Prayer   8

                 199

```
    B. Motivation                        Dt 21:9
       1. Purge formula                      9a
       2. Do good/evil formula               9b
```

Dt 21:1-9: Legal instruction

Although Driver, Mayes, Seitz and Liedke all
identify Dt 21:1-9 as *law* or *case law*, it is
neither.[258] Even though the passage is introduced by
if (kî) in Dt 21:1, has a protasis (Dt 21:1) and
apodosis (Dt 21:2-9) structure, it is not itself a
law, but an instruction on a law.[259]

Law establishes norms for behavior, while legal
instruction explains those norms, and encourages the
audience to observe them. For example, both explanation and encouragement are found in Dt 21:1+3+5
+9. In Dt 21:1, the authors remind their audience
that the land belongs to them only as stewards of
Yahweh, and therefore, it is a sacred inheritance.
They must not allow that inheritance to be sacri-
legiously contaminated by an unsolved murder. In
Dt 21:3, the requirement that measurements be made is
explained as necessary to determine into whose jurisdiction the responsibility for the ritual of
expiation falls. In Dt 21:5, the presence of the
priests is required, because, explains the text,
they have power as the result of their election by
Yahweh. The matter at hand is one of religious significance and political importance. Deuteronomy 21:9
assures the audience that the dutiful observance of
the ritual prescribed in Dt 21:2-8 will definitively
expiate the death which has contaminated the land.
Formulas assure the audience that following the
declaration of innocence made in the washing of the
hands and the deposition of the elders, the case is
closed. The fundamental division after Dt 21:1,
introduced by *then (we)* separates the initial verb--
is found--from the remaining verbs in the chain.

Dt 21:1: Protasis

Although Seitz refers to Dt 21:1 as a case *(ein
Rechtsfall)*, the expansions in Dt 21:aβ-γ
characterize it as the protasis of a legal
instruction, and not the case in a law.[260] As the
premise or condition dependent on the requirements of
the apodosis for its integrity, Dt 21:1 uses a form
found only in three other passages: Dt 17:2; 22:22

and 24:7. According to Daube, this construction is
used to shift the emphasis from the fearfulness of the
crime itself, to the fearfulness of the resulting
appearance of the defendant in the eyes of Yahweh.[261]
The impersonal construction does not indicate that the
defendant was caught in the act. Similarly,
Carmichael considers these passages characteristic of
the shame cultural aspect of D, which seeks to maintain public order not through any judicial process,
but through human respect.[262] With the shame cultural
factor, when shame is used as a sanction, the
judicial system becomes less important as a means of
social control. Religious pressures replace legal
penalties as a punishment for crimes. Daube and
Carmichael's evaluation of Dt 21:1-9 is too moralizing
and overlooks the simple fact that in Dt 21:1-9 the
murderer is not exposed to public humiliation.

The premise of Dt 21:1-9 is twofold. First, it
requires a body slain with a sword, or other sharp
instrument, i.e., an obvious victim of human violence
and not simply the victim of an act of God, a wild
animal, disease, illness or age. Such deaths from
natural causes did not pollute the land with the kind
of curse Dt 21:2-8 could handle. Second, it requires
the body to be discovered in the field, i.e., in the
arable land from which the citizens harvested their
crops or in which they grazed their herds and flocks.
If the body was found in the streets of a city or in
the house of a citizen, other norms than those given in
Dt 21:2-8 would be applicable.

The term *slain (hālāl)* occurs in only one other
place in Deuteronomy--the song of Moses (Dt 32:42).

> I will make my arrows drunk with blood,
>   and my sword shall devour flesh--
> with the blood of the slain and the captives,
>   from the long-haired heads of the enemy
>   (Dt 32:42).

Outside Deuteronomy *slain (hālāl)* is customarily used
with the phrase *with a sword*, as in Ez 35:8 . . . *in
all your ravines those slain by the sword shall fall.*
This use clearly emphasizes the meaning of *halal* as
pierced.

Although its character as case law is identifiable, Dt 21:1 has two unusual characteristics: the
use of *Nip'al (is found)*, rather than the *Qal (finds)*,

and the use of the participle (*lying*), rather than the
marker *'im* with a finite form of the verb to state the
mitigating circumstance.

When (*kî*) a man strikes his slave, male
or female, with a rod and the slave dies
under his hand, he shall be punished.
But if (*'im*) the slave survives a day or
two, he is not to be punished.
(Ex 21:20-21)

The classic pattern of the case in this genre is
stated in the active voice with the subject,
generally *anyone* (*'îs*) being the defendant. In case
law where the content is customary, rather than
criminal, the subject is the law-abiding Hebrew.
However, in this matter of an unsolved murder, there
seems to be no interest at all in the person who dis-
covers the corpse. No indication is given that such
a person may be a suspect, or that the person has
contracted personal impurity. It is interesting that
Nm 19:11-13, which concerns the personal impurity
which any Hebrew contracts by touching a corpse,
follows the ritual for sacrificing a heifer (Nm
19:1-10), whose ashes will be used to purify the
community of any combination presumably including that
brought on by a member of that community who has
touched a corpse!

Dt 21:1aγ: Land grant and possession formula

The land grant and possession formulas are used
here in Dt 21:1a to continue the Moabite perspective,
and not to give the exact location, which is described
in Dt 21:1aγ. These formulas are normally part of the
introduction to unit, as a comparison with Dt 19:1
shows.

Dt 21:2-9: Apodosis

The apodosis in Dt 21:2-9 details the requirements
which are to be met when the conditions in the
protasis are fulfilled. In case law, the consequence
is a succinct description of the punishment which the
defendant named in the case must undergo. Unlike the
very spartan consequence clauses in the Covenant Code,
Dt 21:2-9 reflects a very complex literary composition.
Introduced by the particle *then* (*we*), this consequence
consists of a liturgical deposition and a Deuteronomic parenesis.

202

Dividing Dt 21:2-8 after Dt 21:6 produces a liturgical deposition in two parts: what-is-to-be-done and what-is-to-be-said. The cumulative style of the traditional ritual in Dt 21:3b-4+6 is recognized in this structure, and the direct address portions of the passage are set apart from the narrative portions of the text.

Dt 21:2-8: Deposition

A *deposition* is testimony taken under oath by authorized witnesses. Elders and judges represent the local authority of all the cities in the vicinity of the crime. This local representation is strengthened by the presence of the priests who represent the central authority of Jerusalem. Not only the number of persons present but also their prestige emphasizes the publicity of the act.

The authority on which this deposition is based is provided by the Moabite perspective (Dt 21:2+5+9). However, it seems these verses, together with Dt 21:7, which was also added by the authors of Dt, may have called for some unsettling revisions of a well-known and widely-accepted form of worship (Dt 21:3b-4 +6). The presence of the parenesis in Dt 21:9 seeking to remove any subjective obstacles which the audience may have to fulfilling the requirements set down in Dt 21:2-8, suggests the Moabite perspective alone was not a powerful enough authority on which such a deposition could be promulgated.

The character of Dt 21:2-8 as worship is carried by the exorcism ritual (Dt 21:2b-4+6) and the prayer (Dt 21:8). Implicitly the exorcism ritual acknowledges that life, both of the slain and of the land, is not under the control of the cities. Explicitly the prayer admits that the shedding of innocent blood jeopardizes the status of Israel as Yahweh's redeemed people, and that only Yahweh can pardon such an act. The worshipping community envisioned by this text is remarkably large including all the surrounding cities.

Dt 21:2-6: Ritual

Ritual in Dt 21:2-6 identifies a specific series of actions intended to express a particular sentiment and accomplish a particular result. The actions in the ritual are indicated by the finite verbs in the *wāw* consecutive chain which belong to the narrative,

and not the direct address, portions of the text.
Thus the ritual expects the celebrants to select a
victim, take it to virgin soil, break its neck and
wash their hands over it.

Dt 21:7-8: What-is-to-be-said formula

A *formula* is a pattern of words for use in a
ceremony. Thus Dt 21:7-8 makes up the spoken element
intended to accompany the ritual in Dt 21:2-6. The
formula consists of a testimony and a prayer. In the
testimony, the elders declare their innocence (Dt
21:7) under oath (Dt 21:3b-4+6) before the
authorized magistrates of the state (Dt 21:5). The
oath implicit in the actions of Dt 21:3b-4+6 is
. . . *may my neck be broken like that of the heifer's
if what I say is not true*. The function of the
priests, the sons of Levi as witnesses is clearly
stated in Dt 21:5b: *by their words every dispute and
every assault shall be settled*.

Dt 21:2-3a: Certification of city

Schulz has reconstructed a pattern for the
sanctuary court.[263] Some of the elements of this
pattern are visible here in Dt 21:2-3. The pattern
was made up of three parts. First the sanctuary
court held the trial; second it recited the litanies
of capital offenses; third the court announced its
decision. The decision of the court made use of at
least five different formulas. One of these formulas,
the certification of the deed, e.g., *he has uncovered
his sister's nakedness* (Lv 20:17) is similar to the
statement concerning the affected city in Dt 21:3a.

Dt 21:3b: Choice of victim rubric

Although Driver has suggested reading *unmated
('br)* instead of *unworked ('bd)*, the qualification is
a parallelism, rather than two distinct specifications
of the heifer.[264]

The *prayer* in Dt 21:8 is a formal communication
with Yahweh, addressed to him in the second person
masculine singular force, requesting forgiveness.
Just how Dt 21:8, which like the ritual acts in Dt
21:3b-4, admits responsibility for the unsolved
murder and seeks to avoid its adverse effects, can be
reconciled with Dt 21:6-7 which denies any responsibility for the murder in the first place, is not

clear. Thus this deposition both admits the crime and
seeks to atone for it, while on the other hand, denies
any guilt for the crime and seeks to avoid punishment.
If the elders and their constituents have in fact done
nothing, then there is no need of the forgiveness
sought in Dt 21:8. If the presence of a corpse is the
responsibility of the entire community, whether or not
anyone in the community was involved in the murder,
then the testimony in Dt 21:7 is gratuitous. The
words *declare* and *say* are a fixed pair which occur in
Dt 25:9; 26:5; 27:14, 15, and elsewhere in the Hebrew
Bible.[265] They indicate a solemn declaration in
either a judicial or a liturgical setting.

Setting

The institutional or societal matrix of Dt 21:1-
9 is the diplomacy of Ancient Near Eastern cities.
According to Carmichael, it is this unit's use of
cities rather than *gates*, which points to the art and
practice of conducting negotiations between cities
without hostility as the setting for Dt 21:1-9,
rather than the practice of municipal court justice.[266]

Every urban culture in the Ancient Near East had
some method of resolving the crime without a suspect.
For example, the Code of Hammurabi required the
Babylonian city nearest the scene of the crime for
which there are no suspects to compensate the vic-
timized family or city for its loss.[267] In the Aqhat
literature of Ugarit, Dan'el goes to the place where
his son has been murdered, and there curses the
murderer, who is unknown, and the city nearest to the
scene of the crime.[268] At Nuzi, the city nearest the
carcass of a head of livestock must compensate the
owners, when a suspect cannot be found.[269] There are
Akkadian and Hittite parallels as well.[270]

The intellectual, ideological or theological
matrix of Dt 21:1-9 is urban. The *corpus delicti*
threatens the economy of the city by its presence in
the field. The participants are officials from
cities, which are the basic communities in which the
people affected live. The participants in the ritual
described in the text are all traditional or appointed
members of the judiciary. Their concern is a possible
conspiracy which would keep them from fulfilling their
judicial responsibilities as witness or as judge. The

genre of the unit is legal instruction which assumes the existence of the law *you shall not kill* and a process for dealing with murder: the municipal court. Yahweh is the landlord who has given Israel this urban land, and to whom the ritual now appeals. Israel is considered the people of Yahweh, who are unable to fulfill their fundamental obligations to him through the judicial process. These obligations acknowledge Yahweh as Israel's redeemer, and failing to fulfill them denies that sacred relationship.

Intention

The intention of Dt 21:1-9 is to transfer the unknown murderer from the jurisdiction of the city nearest the scene of the crime to Yahweh. By the ritual in Dt 21:2-6 and the formula in Dt 21:7-8, the city acknowledges that none of the sacral or judicial remedies by which it ordinarily keeps the peace is adequate to compensate the family or the city of the victim for its loss. Therefore, the city releases the unknown murderer from its jurisdiction, and appeals to Yahweh to intervene so that harmony may be restored. The ordinary remedies for murder are presented in Dt 19:1-13, which is also a city text.

There is no consensus among critics about how cities who used the procedure in Dt 21:1-9 understood the transfer. The effectiveness of the ritual may depend on magic or sacrifice or neither. If the ritual is sacrificial it may be connected with atonement or covenant renewal. If the ritual is not sacrificial it may be a judicial symbol connected with an oath, or a sacred symbol connected with reconciliation.

In 1921, Elhorst argued that the ritual was magic. It was effective because it brought supernatural forces to bear on the powers of nature through its charm or spell.[271] The intentions of this ritual in the magical and animistic tradition was to inoculate the land against the ill effects of bloodshed. The taboo paralyzed the cities so that they could no longer worship God; and without the ability to worship, the entire economy of the cities would collapse.[272] What Dt 19:1-13 regards as a social problem, the magical tradition in Dt 21:1-9 considers a sinister and independent power.[273] Most critics accept Elhorst's analysis, while stressing, as he did, that the present intention of the text is not magical![274] Nevertheless, the idea that the shedding of innocent blood makes the land an impossible place for Yahweh to live, appears again in the Deuteronomist's History as an explanation for why Yahweh turned Canaan over to the Babylonians.[275] As Yahweh's housekeeper, it was Israel's responsibility to keep everything in order.[276] This theology, although based on Israel's historical experience and concrete covenant obligations with Yahweh, does share the magic tradition's conviction that the shedding of innocent blood can make Canaan uninhabitable.

The intention of Dt 21:1-9, according to most, is to explain how the elders of the city nearest the scene of the crime can fulfill their obligations as *next of kin!*[277] The ordinary remedies for murder presented in Dt 19:1-13 limit prosecution to the suspect. His family and his city and for that matter, the city nearest to the scene of the crime, are immune. Neither Dt 19:1-13, nor Dt 21:1-9 assume community liability as an operating principle.[278] Since the city nearest the scene of the crime has no recourse through ordinary remedies, it must use the extraordinary remedy prescribed in Dt 21:1-9 to fulfill its responsibility *avenger (gō'ēl)* to the victim. According to this analysis of Dt 21:1-9, the elders prosecute the heifer in lieu of the defendant. Most early commentators considered the procedure liturgical or sacrificial.[279]

There are difficulties in considering the ritual prosecution in Dt 21:1-9 a genuine sacrifice.[280] In a sacrifice, the heifer would be slaughtered, not have its neck broken.[281] In a sacrifice, the priests, not the elders of the city, would be the principal celebrants of the rite. Therefore, the ritual is easier to understand as strictly a paraliturgical or symbolic act, similar to the practice of driving the scapegoat into the desert to die.

And when he has made an end of atoning for
the holy place and the tent of meeting and
the altar, he shall present the live goat;
and Aaron shall lay both his hands upon the
head of the live goat, and confess over him
all the iniquities of the people of Israel,
and all their transgressions, all their
sins; and he shall put them upon the head
of the goat, and send him away into the

wilderness by the hand of the man who is in
readiness. The goat shall bear all their
iniquities upon him to a solitary land; and
he shall let the goat go in the wilderness
(Lv 16:20-22).

Weinfeld further emphasizes the paraliturgical
character of the ritual in Dt 21:1-9 by arguing that
Deuteronomy never considers atonement the result of a
silent sacrifice by a priest. For Deuteronomy, only
confession and prayer bring about atonement.[282]
Breaking the heifer's neck and washing one's hands are
not magic rituals or sacrifices, but simple gestures
of innocence like those alluded to in Pss 24:4 and
26:6+10. Both actions are expressions of the confession and prayer of the citizens, nothing more.
Weinfeld's interpretation is part of his general argument that Deuteronomy proposes a thorough
secularization of life in Israel. This overall
analysis of Deuteronomy is incorrect: Deuteronomy
does not propose to substitute personal conversion
for public worship and sacrifice. However, Weinfeld's
interpretation of Dt 21:1-9 is very accurate: both
breaking the heifer's neck and washing one's hands
are gestures of innocence.

In Dt 21:1-9, the elders of the city, and in
later developments, the judges (Dt 21:2) and the
priests, the sons of Levi (Dt 21:5), as well as are not
fulfilling the responsibilities of *avenger (gō'ēl)*
to the victim, but testifying under penalty of death
that they cannot fulfill those responsibilities.
Boecker also uses this interpretation of Dt 21:1-9,
however, he considers the ritual an equivalent of a
judicial verdict of not-guilty, instead of an oath
of inadequacy.[283]

The oath is taken at a site clearly beyond the
jurisdiction of any of the cities summoned in Dt 21:1
to indicate they have no ability to prosecute. The
site requires running water so that the elders of the
city can wash their hands as a gesture of release, on
the grounds that they lack testimony on which to
prosecute. If they are guilty of perjury, they will
be executed like the heifer whose neck is then
broken.[284] Both the site for the ritual and the
victim are natural, untouched by civilization.

. . . and the elders of the city which is
nearest to the slain man shall take a

heifer which has never been worked and
which has not pulled the yoke. And the
elders of that city shall bring the
heifer down to a valley with running
water, which is neither plowed nor sown
. . . (Dt 21:3-4).

Through the due process of the municipal court,
the city protected and fed its citizens. Human life
and fertile fields were the blessings of
civilization. To signify that the case of the
corpus delicti is totally beyond the capability of
civilization, an uncivilized site and victim are
chosen for the ritual. The transfer of jurisdiction takes place at a site where human life and
the fertility of the field is totally dependent on
Yahweh. There is no irrigation, only wild water.
There is no cleared land, only virgin soil. There is
no tame animal, only one that is unbroken. The
heifer is not a substitute for the murderer. And although the ritual does lift the taboo which the
corpus delicti put on the field where it fell, it
does not move it to the wadi where the ritual is
carried out, cursing that land in its place. The
taboo is lifted when the jurisdiction for the case
is transferred to Yahweh. As long as adjudication
continues, life and fertility are possible, and the
ill effects of the taboo are off-set.[285] The use of
animals in oaths like this is not sacrificial, but
symbolic, as the treaty between Assurnirari VI and
Mati'ilu of Bit-Agusi clearly indicates.[286]

Thus, in Israel, the intention of Dt 21:1-9 is
to transfer the jurisdiction in a murder case
without suspects from the municipal court to Yahweh.
Only a complete lack of evidence exempts the city
from convening the municipal court. Therefore, the
oath in Dt 21:7 certifies that citizens who would
normally serve as witnesses and judges have absolutely
no testimony on which to render a judgment in this
matter. Once the possibility of a conspiracy is
ruled out by the oath, then the jurisdiction in the
case must be transferred.[287] For the leagues of
ancient cities in Canaan who entered early Israel,
the ritual in Dt 21:1-9 demonstrated their
acceptance of Yahweh as the ultimate judge and prosecutor in the land.

For those who opposed the monarchy, the matter
of a murder without a suspect could be handled

completely on the local level without recourse to the king, and his courts. That was the important point. There are ways within the Yahwist tradition for handling such important matters, ways older and more efficient than the central court established by the monarchy. The king is not the only means of protecting the life and the security of the nation. It is possible to do what is right in the sight of the Lord without the king!

An indication of the anti-monarchial tendency of Dt 21:1-9 is also seen in the do good/evil formula with which it concludes. The royal edition of Judges stresses that without the king *everyone did what was right in his own eyes* and that brought disaster to the nation. The implication of this interpretation of Israel's social structure before the monarchy was that only under a king could Israel do what was right in the sight of Yahweh. Deuteronomy 21:1-9 helped the anti-monarchists clearly attack that assumption. The elders of the cities are fully capable of seeing that the nation does what is right in the sight of Yahweh.

When Dt 21:1-9 was absorbed into the Deuteronomic reform it was placed under the close supervision of the judges and the Levitical priests. The ritual was not considered a sacrifice, or it would not have been preserved. As a procedure for transferring jurisdiction it did not affect the restriction of sacrifice which Dt 12 required.

Genre

Structure analysis

LEGAL INSTRUCTION concerning an incorrigible son from an urban family	Dt 21:18-21
I. Protasis (sign: *kî hāyâ*)	18
A. First offense	18a α
B. Second offense	18a β-b
1. Citation	18a β
2. Offense proper	18b
II. Apodosis (sign: *we*)	19-21
A. Arrest	19a
B. Arraignment for trial	19b
C. Testimony	20
1. Consequence proper	20a α
2. Example of testimony	20aβγ-b
a. Charge:	20a βγ
1) First offense	20a β
2) Second offense	20a γ
b. Charge	20b
D. Execution	21
1. Death sentence	21a α
2. Parenesis	21a β-*b*
a. Purge formula (2 sg)	21a β
b. Hear and fear formula	21b

Dt 21:18-21: Legal instruction

As a legal instruction, Dt 21:18-21 assumes a law which prohibits being *stubborn and rebellious.* The instruction points out the ramifications which the law has for the parents and the city of those who are stubborn and rebellious. Therefore the instruction begins *If anyone has a stubborn and rebellious son* and not *If anyone is stubborn and rebellious.* The instruction goes step by step through the process which parents are expected to take in cooperation with the municipal court. Finally, the instruction uses parenesis to encourage its audience to obey the law. Like most instructions, second and third person forms of the verb are combined. Although most commentators identify the genre of Dt 21:18-21 as law, it is not

law, but legal instruction.[289] By comparing the laws
in Ex 21:15 and Ex 21:17 with Dt 21:18-21, it is clear
that the instruction in Dt 21:18-21 contains explanations and motivations which the Exodus laws
lack.[290]

Dt 21:18: Protasis

The construction *If a man has* occurs in only
three places in Deuteronomy: 21:15-17; 18-21 and
22-23. The primary meaning of the construction is
married to (Dt 21:15; 24:2 25:5; Lv 22:12; Je 3:1;
Ez 44:25). Only in Lv 22:12 does the construction
appear in a case law: *If a priest's daughter is
married to an outsider, she shall not eat of the
offering of the holy things.* The construction does
not appear in Exodus or Numbers. A variation of the
construction appears in Dt 21:13; 22:19: *she becomes
a wife.* Here in Dt 21:18, the customary subject
which grammatically is masculine singular changes to
a common plural in order to accommodate both the
mother and the father. Thus the sense of the formula
becomes: *If a couple has . . . .*

Like the charge: *You have cursed God and the
king!* (1 K 21:10), which Jezebel the queen brings
against Naboth the vintager, the language in Dt
21:18a α is technical.[291]

The protasis (Dt 21:18) contains two offenses,
not one. Deuteronomy 21:18aβ-b does not simply give
the evidence on which the charge in Dt 21:18aα is
based. The parents are not charging their son with
stubborn and rebellious conduct *because* they have
counseled him and he refused to listen to their
advice. The procedure here in Dt 21:18-21 parallels
the procedure in the Code of Hammurabi for disinheriting an heir.[292] The Code of Hammurabi requires that
the father arraign his son for one serious offense
before he can disinherit him. Therefore, Dt 21:18aα
is the first offense; Dt 21:18β-b is the second
offense. The son is stubborn and rebellious (first
offense) and his parents punish him; he continues to
disobey his mother and father (second offense), therefore they arrest, try and execute him. The only
difference between the Code of Hammurabi and Dt 21:18-
21 is that Dt 21:18-21 allows the parents to punish
their son for the first offense, while the Code of
Hammurabi restricts punishment for the first offense
to the court.

212

Chart

Comparing Dt 21:18-21 with Ex 21:15 and Ex 21:17

	Dt 21:18-21	Ex 21:15	Ex 21:17
<u>Defendant</u>	*son*	*whoever*	*whoever*
<u>Allegation</u>	*stubborn and rebellious, who will not obey . . . give heed*	*strikes*	*curses*
<u>Victims</u>	*his father or . . . his mother*	*his father or mother*	*his father or mother*
<u>Recourse</u>	*chastise him . . . take hold of him and bring him out . . . and say*		
<u>Witnesses</u>	*father and mother . . .to the elders*		
<u>Exe- cutioners</u>	*all the men of the city*		
<u>Sentence</u>	*shall stone him . . .to death with stones*	*shall be put to death*	*shall be put to*
<u>Motivation</u>	*so you shall purge . . . and all shall hear and fear . . .*		

213

Dt 21:19-21:   Apodosis

In Ex 21:28, Je 34:3, 38:23 and Nm 15:13 *shall take hold of him* is technical, legal language meaning *arrest for the purpose of standing trial.*[293]   In Dt 17:15, 22:21, 22:24, *bring him* is also technical, legal language meaning *to appear for sentencing,* however, here in Dt 21:19b it means *to arraign the defendant to hear the charges brought against him.*[294]

Dt 21:20:   Testimony

Deuteronomy 21:20 uses *and they shall say* in the precise legal sense *and they shall testify.*   Examples of testimony follow.[295]   The first example is based on the conditions in Dt 21:18; thus parents might testify *This our son is stubborn and rebellious, he will not obey our voice . . .* (Dt 21:20a βγ).   The second example (Dt 21:20) is declaration or affidavit identifying a particular category of behavior parallel to *it is wickedness* (Lv 18:17) and *it is an abomination* (Lv 18:22).

Dt 21:21a: Death Sentence

The death sentence in Dt 21:21a specifies *stoning (rāgam),* although it uses a verb more common in the Holiness Code and the Priests' Tradition than in Deuteronomy.[296]   The common word for *stoning* in Deuteronomy is *sāqal.*[297]   When death sentences simply use the verb *die,* rather than specifying the manner of execution, they use the infinite.   When the death sentence uses the verb *die,* the standard construction is the infinitive absolute (*môt*) and the finite form of the verb (*yûmat*).[298]

Dt 21:21a β-b: Parenesis

Deuteronomy 21:21 is the only portion of Dt 21:18-21 which uses the second person forms of speech.   The remaining verses use the third person narrative forms. The purge formula is always used in connection with the death penalty, and so here in Dt 21:18-21 is connected directly to the command to execute, rather than to the entire unit.

214

Setting

The institutional or societal matrix for disinheriting one's son is the judicial system on which cities in the Ancient Near East were established. All adult males (*the men of the city* in Dt 21:21) were full citizens of these urban communities.[299] This legal status could be specified as a formal legal office.[300] Generally, those eligible for the office of *elder* (*the elders of his city* in Dt 21:19-20) were the landholders.[301] Among the legal rights of full citizens was that of designating or *adopting* their legal heir, who might be their natural and eldest son or another natural child or someone else's child. This heir carried the legal title *son* and enjoyed special privileges even during the life of his *father*.[302] The words *son (ben)*, *servant ('ebed)*, *brother ('āḥ)* are frequently used as technical, legal terms for covenant partners, people who are related to one another, not by kinship, but by legal agreement.[303] For example, Ahaz acknowledges his treaty with the Assyrian Tiglat-pileser by saying: *I am your servant ('ebed) and your son (ben)*. Tyre is indicted for betraying her covenant partners who are called *her brothers:*

> Thus says the Lord:
> "For three transgression of Tyre, and for four,
>   I will not revoke the punishment;
> because they delivered up a whole people to Edom,
>   and did not remember the covenant of brotherhood (Am 1:9).

Shechem is Israel's covenant partner or *son* (Gn 34:2; Jg 9:28), although the RSV translation: *and when Shechem the son of Hamor* (i.e., covenant partner) does not make that clear.[304]

Since in the cities of the Ancient Near East, designating an heir was a legal process, as opposed to a natural process derived simply from the fact of the heir's birth, it could be legally reversed. Either the superior (the father or parents) or the inferior (the son) could repudiate the covenant which bound them to one another. The repudiation consisted of both actions and declarations which were publically witnessed. The Code of Hammurabi provides for parallel procedures.[305]

The urban setting of Dt 21:18-21 is clear. Its
audience contains parents who live in cities, which
have municipal courts to whom they have recourse. The
elders in the text are urban elders, and the
executioners are citizens. The judicial setting of
Dt 21:18-21 is also apparent. The passage prescribes
a legal process through which parents must go before
they can disinherit their son.

But the setting of Dt 21:18-21 is not simply the
urban culture of Canaan or the Ancient Near East, it
is also Yahwist. The formulas in Dt 21:21 tag the
crime as directly affecting the relationship of Israel
to Yahweh, thus these cities are corporate members of
Israel. There is, then, at least one historical,
epochal or cultural setting for such a text, which is
the Deuteronomic reform. The reform was clearly
concerned with an Israel in which the corporate
members were cities, and the concern was with the
municipal courts. However, if Dt 21:18-21 has originated during the reform, certainly the officials who
appear in the municipal court would be the judges and
officers appointed in Dt 16:18--17:7, and not the
elders of the city.[306] In the setting of Dt 21:18-21,
parents, elders and citizens alone arbitrate the
matter.

In the history of Israel cities also played a
significant role during the struggle to restrain the
monarchy from completely taking over the traditions
of Israel; and when the priests at the Yahwist
sanctuaries in the ancient cities of Hebron, Shiloh,
Gibeon and Shechem, for example, would instruct the
pilgrims in their responsibilities to Yahweh. The
stress in Dt 21:18-21 on the ancient and venerable
institutions, rather than the novel demands of the
monarchy would well characterize the instruction at
these times. Finally, there are the covenant celebrations at which the urban leagues who had entered
early Israel praised Yahweh for having adopted them,
and recalled their own responsibilities to remain an
obedient and faithful heir.

Because the witnesses in this legal procedure
are *parents,* and the defendant is a *son,* some critics
like Boecker have argued that the setting for Dt
21:18-21 is the extended nomadic family.[307] According
to von Rad, Dt 21:18-21 represents a stage in the
development of the extended family when the absolute
jurisdiction of the father over the lives of his

wives and children has been curtailed.[308] At its
peak, the authority of a patriarch like Judah was
able to sentence his daughter-in-law to death.

About three months later Judah was told,
'Tamar your daughter-in-law has played
the harlot; and moreover she is with child
by harlotry.' And Judah said, 'Bring her
out, and let her be burned' (Gn 38:24).

In Dt 21:18-21, that power of life and death was to be
exercised only under the jurisdiction of the elders of
the city and the men of the city, after the consent of
the child's mother had been obtained.[309]

On the contrary, however, the roles of the mother
and the father in Dt 21:18-21 are taken for granted.
The text does not warn: *you shall not put your child
to death, but rather take him to the municipal court.*
The concern is not family discipline, but legal inheritance, which is a public, not a domestic matter.
Deuteronomy 21:18-21 does not reduce the prerogatives
of the father and mother to those of a marshall and
witness against their own son. The tradition
assumes that the parents do not have the right to put
their son to death without the court's approval.
Urban families may never have enjoyed that pre-
rogative. As the city texts show, arbitration through
the judicial process was an indispensable step in any
execution. For example, in Dt 13:13-19, cities are
not to be destroyed without carefully corroborating
the rumor of apostasy; in Dt 19:1-9, suspects are not
to be executed without verifying that the killing was
premeditated; in Dt 20:10-20, cities are not to be
destroyed without clear indications of their hostility
to Israel; and in Dt 21:1-9, due process is to be
pursued even when it seems clearly beyond the ability
of the municipal courts themselves to do so. The
judicial process is the indispensable means with which
the ancient cities in Israel fulfill their obligations
to Yahweh on every level. The family and the city are
not hostile to one another; both are subject to the
court.

Bellefontaine proposes a family setting for at
least part of the tradition in Dt 21:18-21.[310] Based
on the findings of various sociologists and anthropologists, she argues that a son who is a *glutton and
a drunkard* is liable to excommunication from tribal
society as a bad seed.[311] The bad seed is any

217

non-conformist who is incorrigible. The individual
may simply fail to observe the customs of the community on the one hand, or practice the more serious
sins of incest, witchcraft, or any other form of
sacrilege.

All Bellefontaine's examples are from simple
societies. The society reflected in Dt 21:18-21 is
far from simple. At least four classes of people are
mentioned: testators, heirs, citizens and elders.
The society has a complicated process for making and
revising wills, and a judicial system for enforcing
this and other such social controls. It is not an
arbitrary system, but one which follows due process.
There are warnings, witnesses, trials, mandatory
sentences and so on. The crimes Bellefontaine mentions are primarily liturgical crimes, and the setting
is not justice, but magic and taboo. She also does
not discuss the process by which the accused is tried
and executed.

Weinfeld suggested that the setting of Dt 21:18-
21 is wisdom.[312] He argues that the expression
glutton and drunkard is characteristic of wisdom
literature and that the relationship of a sage to his
pupil is often described as the relationship of a
parent to a child. What Weinfeld overlooks in his
argument, however, is that in Dt 21:18-21 the charge:
he is a glutton and drunkard is not the primary focus
of the text. The defendant is primarily *stubborn
and rebellious*. Furthermore, although the wisdom
tradition condemns gluttony and drunkenness, it considers both to be self-punishing. There is no need
for the community to intervene in the way Dt 21:18-21
describes.

> Be not among wine-bibers,
>   or among gluttonous eaters of meat;
> For the drunkard and the glutton will come to
>   poverty.
> And drowsiness will clothe a man in rags
>   (Pr 23:20-1).

Likewise, although *mother, father, son* are mentioned
in Dt 21:18-21, the intention of the text is to
regulate relationships between adults, not between
adults and children. The legal instruction is
parental only in the sense that it is authoritative.
It is not the audience which is addressed as a child
or a son and the setting of the text which considers

218

itself a father.

Intention

The intention of Dt 21:18-21 is to encourage the
full citizens of the cities of Israel to revise their
wills if their heirs have failed them. By the observance of this ancient custom, Israel will remain
conscious of her own status as the heir of Yahweh, and
the responsibility she has to be obedient and faithful.

The consideration in Dt 21:18-21 is not a more
sensitive attitude toward one's natural parents.[313]
What is prohibited is clearly identifiable, measurable
and punishable. The intention of Dt 21:18-21 is not
ethical, but legal. It does not promulgate law, but
it also is not preaching moral perfection. It is
encouraging the audience to observe the law because of
its effect on the common good. The evolution of a
spiritual principle which Merendino charts from Ex
21:15 where the crime is striking one's parents, to
Ex 21:17 where the crime is cursing one's parents, to
Dt 21:18-21 where the crime is refusing to listen to
one's parents is much too psychological for the
practical process which Dt 21:18-21 envisions.

Neither the Decalogue, nor Dt 21:18-21 envision
the son as a petulant child, though that interpretation appears frequently enough. In 1923, Schmidt
excluded the command: *Honor your father and your
mother* from the original Decalogue he was re-
constructing.[314] Schmidt made this decision for a
variety of reasons. Among them, Schmidt considered
this command for children out of place in a passage
addressed to adults, even if the Jewish tradition in
which a boy becomes a responsible person and hence a
man at 13 years of age reflects a more ancient
custom. The Decalogue is addressed not simply to
adults, but to adults who are the heads of households in Israel, and hence not only legally adult,
but also mature. In 1962, although Reventlow admitted
that the son in Dt 21:18-21 was an adult, the
virtues which Reventlow describes this adult as lacking are the virtues of a child![315] In the Decalogue
it is the heirs who are addressed; in Dt 21:18-21 it
is the landowners, but in both cases the passages are
dealing with the measurable and public relations

between these individuals as adults.

Narrative (Nm 20:10,24; 27:14; Dt 1:26,43; 9:7, 23-4; 31:27; 1 S 12:15; Ne 9:26-9), prophetic (Ho 9:15; Is 1:23; 63:8-10; 65:2; Je 4:17; 5:23; 6:28; Ez 5:6; 20:8,21) and poetic (Ps 5:11; 78:8; 105:28; 106:7) texts often describe Israel as *stubborn and rebellious*. The crime is never petulance. The crime is apostasy, which is measurable and public. For example, stubbornness is the reason Yahweh denied the desert generation access to the land of Canaan.

O that today you would hearken to his voice!
Harden not your hearts, as at Meribah,
On the day of Massah in the wilderness,
when your fathers tested me,
And put me to the proof, though they had seen my work.
For forty years I loathed that generation
And said, 'They are a people who err in heart,
And they do not regard my ways.'
Therefore I swore in my anger
that they should not enter my rest.
(Ps 95:7b-11)

Plöger is even more emphatic about the relationship between obedience, the opposite of stubbornness, and the land.[316] The use of capital punishment in Dt 21:18-21 against the disobedient acknowledges the importance of obedience as a public virtue. According to Plöger, Dt 21:18-21 is an instruction on the command: *Honor your father and mother*, which in both Dt 5:16 and Ex 20:12 is connected with the land.

Honor your father and your mother, as the Lord your God commanded you; that your days may be prolonged, and that it may go well with you, in the land which the Lord your God gives you (Dt 5:16).

Although this motivation is missing in Ex 21:15, 17 and Dt 27:16 as well as this text in Dt 21:18-21, Plöger's point that it is a public virtue, and not a private virtue under consideration, is still valid. The heir in Dt 21:18-21 is not honoring his obligations to his parents, his testators. When they designated him their heir, *their first born son*, they turned their estate, their *naḥalā*, over to him. In return he accepted certain religious, economic, and social obligations for the testators. A stubborn and

220

rebellious heir is one who is not fulfilling these
specific responsibilities. The formula, *stubborn and
rebellious*, does not refer to attitude, but to actions.
Likewise, when Israel is stubborn and rebellious, she
is not fulfilling her obligations to Yahweh, her
testator, who has legally willed his estate, Canaan,
to Israel. By accepting Canaan, Israel has accepted
certain religious, economic and social obligations
to Yahweh.

Tolerant parents were encouraged to confront their
heirs (Dt 21:18), and if they persisted to testify
against them (Dt 21:19-20). Such an instruction,
whether in the days of early Israel, or the period of
the monarchy or during the Deuteronomic reform emphasized that Israel did not enjoy an unconditional
right to the land, any more than heirs enjoyed an unconditional right to the inheritance of their testators. Although the entire Decalogue was to be observed
as a condition for long life in the land, it was
particularly the relationship between testator and
heir that allowed Israelites to enjoy their *naḥalâ*,
their inheritance.[317] Thus this testator-heir relationship became an important metaphor for understanding the relationship between Yahweh and Israel, who
inherited the land and its cities, but who could also
forfeit that inheritance by being stubborn and
rebellious.

Deuteronomy 22:13-21

Genre

Structure analysis

<pre>
LEGAL INSTRUCTION concerning
  charges of premarital promis-
  cuity against a daughter from
  an urban family   Dt 22:13-21
  I. Protasis (sign: kî)   13-14
     A. Marriage contracted   13a
     B. Marriage consummated   13b α
     C. Marriage contested   13b β-14
        1. spurns her   13b β
        2. charges her   14a α
        3. brings an evil name upon her   14a β-b
           a. Circumstance proper   14a β
           b. Citation   14b
              1) Grounds   14b αβ
                 a) Marriage contracted   14b α
                 b) Marriage consummated   14b β
              2) Charge proper   14b γ
 II. Apodosis   15-21
     A. Principal instruction
        (sign: we)   15-19
        1. Consequences for the
           plaintiffs   15-17
           a. Impound tokens of
              virginity (betûlîm)   15a
           b. Place tokens in custody   15b
           c. Identify tokens for court   16-17
              1) Introduction   16a
              2) Identification proper   16b-17
                 a) Testimony: marriage
                    contracted   16b α
                 b) Testimony: marriage
                    contested   16b β-17a
                    (1) Basic testimony   16b β
                    (2) Qualification of   17a αβ
                        (a) Generic
                            qualification   17a α
                        (b) Specific
                            qualification   17a β
                 c) Testimony: tokens
                    identified   17a γ-b
                    (1) Affidavit   17a γ
                    (2) Tokens displayed   17b
</pre>

222

Dt 22:13-21:   Legal instruction

Because of its protasis-apodosis structure and almost exclusive use of third person forms of the verb, most commentators identify Dt 22:13-21 as *case law*.[318]   However, Dt 22:13-21 is not law, it is *legal instruction*.   This legal instruction provides substantial explanations about these laws.   For example, the instruction discusses not only what to do if the husband is seeking to defraud the parents, but also what to do if the husband is defrauded.   There are examples of testimony to be given in the municipal court (Dt 22:14b, 16-17a).   These examples, in the first person, contrast with the remainder of the text which uses third person forms.   The only second person forms in the passage appear in the purge formula in Dt 22:21b.   Finally, the instruction provides motivations for the audience to observe the norms which these laws set for life in Israel.   Bringing perpetrators of fraud to justice, whether they are parents or husbands, is significant because it affects the national character of Israel.

Dt 22:13-14:   Protasis

The protasis in Dt 22:13 is introduced by *if (kî)*
and a noun verb (*yiqtōl-x*) construction.[319] Like the
structure of the entire instruction, it is the verbs
in the protasis which are most significant.[320] The
· chain of perfectly inflected verbs indicates that a
sequence of events is being described. The marriage
is contracted, then consummated, then an internal or
domestric problem develops between the man and his
wife, then an external and public accusation of her
by her husband. The language here is technical and
each element is important.

The contracting of the marriage includes the paying of the bride-price, the eight days of celebration,
etc., after which time the husband has intercourse
with his wife. Here in Dt 22:13, the verb *takes*
controls five verbs in the case and eight verbs in the
consequence.[321]

The premise set down in Dt 22:13-14 is threefold.
First, the man in question must have legally
contracted marriage with the woman. Rape, incest,
casual liaisons, concubinage and other forms of
heterosexual relationships are not the concern of this
legislation. Second, the marriage contract must have
been consummated by sexual intercourse. It is not
sufficient that the contract has been publically celebrated. Accusations against the virginity of a woman
cannot be a matter of speculation, but only of
evidence. Third, the husband must reject his wife.
Regardless of their feelings about the son-in-law, a
woman's parents cannot begin action against him until
rejection can be demonstrated. Since only this condition was subsequently qualified, there was no doubt
some difficulty determining just what constituted rejection.

The importance of the three conditions and their
priority in the development of the text is emphasized
by their repetition in both Dt 22:14b, 16b-17a. Only
when all three have been fulfilled does a matter
affecting the common good exist, and is the intervention of the city government required. Situations
lacking one or more of the conditions are presumably
handled by some other form of public sanction, or are
resolved by the members of the nuclear or extended

CHART

Diagram of consecutive chain of verbs
in Dt 22:13-19

consecutive verbs	anchor verb
Case	*takes* Dt 22:13
and goes in	13
and then spurns her	13
and charges her	14
and brings	14
saying	14
I took	14
when I came near	14
I did not find	14
Consequence	
shall take	15
and bring out	15
shall say	16
I gave	16
and he spurns her	16
has made	17
and they shall spread	17
shall take	18
and whip	18
they shall fine	19
and give	19

families concerned.

Dt 22:14: Charge

While in Dt 22:13b, the husband *hates* his wife,
in Dt 22:14 he accuses her of premarital promiscuity,
alleging she was not a virgin at the time of their
marriage.[322] The language in which these charges are
formulated is similar to that found in literature from
the Middle Assyrian period.[323] An example of the
complaint the husband makes is given in Dt 22:14b,
where the first person form clearly distinguish it
from the third person forms in the surrounding text.[324]

Dt 22:15-19: Principal instruction

The law of evidence invoked here in Dt 22:15-19
clearly seeks to protect the wife from a fickle and
malicious husband, whose calumny ostracizes her and
disgraces her parents. Deuteronomy frequently reflects a concern for human rights which was no doubt
characteristic of the reformers. However, the protection of the wife was not new. Even the Covenant
Code (Ex 20:22 -- 23:19) demanded that a husband provide his estranged wife with support and sexual fulfillment (Ex 21:7-11)! Deuteronomy 21:15-17 would not
let the husband exclude her son as first born from
his will. Deuteronomy 24:1-4 seems even to mitigate
the penalty prescribed in Dt 22:20-21a, by allowing
the husband only to divorce her for promiscuity (Dt
22:20b; Dt 24:1) and not to have her stoned in front
of her father's house.

This case regards the wife's parents as
plaintiffs and the elders of the municipal court as
having jurisdiction in the matter. The intention of
Dt 22:15-19 is to place both husband and wife squarely
before the control of the city government, and prevent the senseless deterioration of harmony as the
result of the lack of personal discipline on the part
of either. The stability of the city rested clearly
on the ability of its families to live in peace, and
the responsibility for those families was no longer
left to the unquestioned supervision of the husband.
Husband as well as wife could be guilty of ir-
responsible and punishable conduct: a legal pre-
sumption which Dt 22:15-21a wishes to make clear.

This interest in due process, evident not only
here in Dt 22:13-21 but in other city texts as well,

is probably characteristic of the municipal courts. As in Dt 21:18-21, the parents are considered responsible for the preliminary investigation, and the municipal court meets only to sentence the offender.[325]

Dt 22:17: Affidavit

The affidavit in Dt 22:17 is a formula or set pattern of words used in a ceremony or ritual to make an emphatic statement. The formula uses the demonstrative pronoun *this* or *these, that* or *those* with a noun. Classic examples of this formula are found in Lv 18: *it is your father's nakedness* (Lv 18:8); *for their nakedness is your own nakedness* (Lv 18:10); *for she is your mother's near kinswoman* (Lv 18:13). In both Dt 21:18-21 and Dt 22:13-21, the testimony includes affidavits which identify either the defendant or the evidence for the court. Like the examples in Lv, the formulas combine a demonstrative pronoun with a noun: *this is our son* (Dt 21:20a) and *these are the tokens of my daughter's virginity* (Dt 22:17a). The formula submits the individual or the evidence to the court making the person or thing in question no longer an exhibit, but evidence in a fully official sense.

Four directives outline the action of the plaintiff(s) in Dt 22:15-17. Although each is a third person verb, the context indicates the intention of each verb is instructional: *shall take* (Dt 22:15a); *and bring out* (Dt 22:15b); *and . . . shall say* (Dt 22:16); *and they shall spread* (Dt 22:17b). The directive character of the verbs should be more evident with second person verb forms.

Each of the directives concerns *the tokens of virginity (betûlîm).*[326] These were the blood-stained cloths on which the marriage had been consummated and which were delivered by the son-in-law to his wife's parents as a sign that he had consummated the marriage, and was preserved by her parents as evidence that in fact their daughter was a virgin at the time they contracted marriage for her with their son-in-law. The tokens are to be impounded, placed in the custody of the court, identified during the trial itself, and then displayed for all to see. Although Dt 22:17b could be a subsection of Dt 22:17a, it is not likely. Deuteronomy 22:16-17a contains the formal complaint of the woman's father in the first common

Comparison of Dt 22:15-17 with Dt 21:18-21

Dt 22:15-17		Dt 21:18-21
	SEIZURE	
shall take		*shall take hold of him*
the father of the young woman		*his father*
and her mother...		*and his mother*
	ARRAIGNMENT	
and bring out		*and bring...out*
the tokens of her virginity...		*him*
to the elders of the city...		*to the elders of his city...*
in the gate...		*at the gate of the place where he lives...*
and...shall say...		*and they shall say ...*
the father of the young woman...		
to the elders...		*to the elders of his city...*
	TESTIMONY	
Dt 22:16b-17a α		Dt 21:20aβ-b
	IDENTIFICATION	
these are...		*this*
the tokens of my daughter's virginity + Dt 22:17b		*our son*
	SENTENCE	
shall take...		*shall stone...*
the elders of that city... + Dt 22:18-19b		*Then all the men of the city...* + Dt 21:21a

228

singular form of the verb, while Dt 22:17b returns to the third person plural found in Dt 22:15a, 15b, 16. Therefore, it seems better to consider Dt 22:16b-17a as a subsection of *and . . . shall* in Dt 22:16a, and *and they shall spread* in Dt 22:17b as a separate directive. By definition a directive is any authoritative instrument issued by a high level body or official that serves to direct, guide and usually impel toward an action or goal. Besides this third person form of the verb, the imperative, and the second person verbs can also be used.

Dt 22:19-20: Consequences

A disposition is a settlement made by a court. As here in Dt 22:18-19, it consists in one or more consequences which affect the defendant and sometimes the plaintiff (Dt 22:19a β-γ). There are two reasons for limiting this subsection to Dt 22:18-19, even though Dt 22:20-21a also contains a disposition. First, the plaintiffs' action in Dt 22:15-17 results in the disposition of Dt 22:18-19 and not Dt 22:20-21a. If the parents of the woman can produce the tokens of virginity, the only disposition possible is Dt 22:18-19. Therefore Dt 22:15-17 is related to Dt 22:18-19, but not to Dt 22:20-21a. Second, the particle *but ('im)* generally introduces a modification of the consequence and is balanced with *then (we)*. Therefore, Dt 22:15-19 and Dt 22:20-21a are balanced with one another, not Dt 22:18-19 and Dt 22:20-21a. In fact, Dt 22:14, 20-21a can be read without losing any coherence.

The disposition is serious, but short of death. The requirements of Dt 19:16-19 evidently do not apply to the heads of households. Even the elders of the city do not have the authority to execute such powerful individuals in the community. According to Dt 19:16-19 if anyone falsely accuses another of a crime, then the false witness shall suffer the penalty of his own calumny. In this case, the husband should have been stoned to death, because that was the penalty his wife would have suffered if she were guilty of the crime of promiscuity before marriage with which he accused her.

If a malicious witness rises against any man
to accuse him of wrongdoing, then both
parties to the dispute shall appear before
the Lord, before the priests and the judges

229

who were in office in those days; the judges
shall inquire diligently and if the witness
is a false witness and has accused his
brother falsely, then you shall do to him
as he had meant to do to his brother
(Dt 19:16-19).

Deuteronomy 19:16-19 applies to the testimony of one
man against another. Evidently the testimony of a
man against a woman was accorded no such legal safe-
guards. The leniency has been attributed to the fact
that the judicial system is male dominated. In fact,
nowhere in the Ancient Near Eastern tradition is the
husband executed.[327] The perspective of the law,
however, may not be strictly chauvinistic. The husband is considered guilty of accusing the father of
fraud, rather than the wife of infidelity, since she
is not an independent legal person, but the ward of
her father. Hence, if the father is not guilty of
fraud, then the husband is arrested, flogged, fined,
and placed under an injunction, but not executed.

It is questionable whether *shall take that man*
(Dt 22:18a) represents a clear and distinct sentence
separate from Dt 22:18b-19. Damages and an injunction
are obviously sentences, however arrest may simply
indicate the persons who have jurisdiction in a matter.
For example, in Dt 22:13, it is the jurisdiction of
the husband to take a woman as his wife, and not vice
versa. In Dt 22:15 it is the jurisdiction of the
mother and father to impound the tokens of virginity.
Therefore, here in Dt 22:18a, it may simply be the
jurisdiction of the elders of the city to flog, to
impose damages, and to place the husband under an injunction.

Some commentators suggest that *whip (yissar)*
means *to punish, to penalize,* but that the verb does
not mean *to whip, flog.*[328] Therefore, here in Dt
22:18-19 means *shall penalize the man by fining him
a hundred shekels of silver . . .:* a general statement followed by the specifications, viz., damages
and an injunction. Nonetheless, corporal punishment
appears in Je 20:2, 29:26; 2 C 16:10; Pr 19:18 as
well as in Middle Assyrian and Babylonian laws for
false accusations of fraud.[329] Therefore, Driver,
Craigie, Phillips, Weinfeld and von Rad consider *flog*
the proper translation of *weyissrû* in Dt 22:18.[330]

Deuteronomy 22:19a β-γ is a qualification of the sentence of damages. It explains what the court will do with the money paid to it by the convict. If Dt 11:19a β-γ were part of the sentence proper, it would direct that the convict himself pay the damages to his father-in-law. Each of the other four sentences are directed toward the convict, only this qualification is directed toward the plaintiff. Damages are imposed upon the convict in a criminal suit, while fines are imposed upon convicts in a civil suit. Both involve the payment of money as compensation for the harm done.[331]

The injunction *and she shall be his wife; he may not put her away all his days* could reflect the intentions of Ex 21:7-11:

> When a man sells his daughter as a slave,
> she shall not go out as the male slaves do.
> If she does not please her master, who has
> designated her for himself, then he shall
> let her be redeemed; he shall have no right
> to sell her to a foreign people since he
> had dealt faithlessly with her. If he
> designates her for his son, he shall deal
> with her as with a daughter. If he takes
> another wife to himself, he shall not
> diminish her food, her clothing, or her
> marital rights. And if he does not do
> these three things for her, she shall go
> out for nothing, without payment of money
> (Ex 21:7-11).

However, Ex 21:7-11 is concerned with a slave sold for the purpose of being her master's wife, whereas Dt 22:13-21 is concerned with a free woman. Nonetheless both are concerned that a wife, slave or free, not be placed in permanent jeopardy as the result of a change in her husband's sexual attraction.

Daube considers Dt 22:19b a distinct genre similar to Dt 12:17; 16:5; 17:5; 21:16; 22:3,9; 24:4.[332] He argues that as a form it stands halfway between wisdom advice and statutory injunction. However, Daube is analyzing only the intention of these texts, and nothing which will distinguish them from a general prohibition, which Gerstenberger in 1965 had already argued may have originated not in a legal but in a family or wisdom setting.[333] Here in Dt 22:19b, however, there is no reason to assume that the intention

of the court is simply to *advise* the defendant to keep
his wife; the court is ordering him to do so. Ad-
mittedly, as both Phillips and Carmichael have noted,
there is a desire on the part of the laws governing
the breaking of contracts to deter imposters from
attempting to do so.[334] The laws are binding, not
simply admonishing.

Dt 22:20-21: Companion instruction

Deuteronomy 22:13-19 is complete in itself. The
instruction is concerned with the question of fraud.
As a companion instruction, however, Dt 22:20-21 introduces another consideration: premarital promiscuity.

L'Hour considers Dt 22:20 the protasis of a purge
law.[335] However, Dt 22:20 is meaningless without the
information in Dt 22:13-14.[336] It is better, as
Liedke does, to consider Dt 22:13-14 a principal case
(*Hauptfall*) and Dt 22:20 a companion case (*Unterfall*).
The particle *but* (*'im*) in Dt 22:20 indicates that
this case is subordinate to the case in Dt 22:13-
14.[337]

Dt 22:20: Verdict

A verdict is a decision of a judicial tribunal on
a matter submitted in trial. Here in Dt 22:20a, the
declaratory formula *the thing is true* introduces the
verdict. The declaratory formula proper does not include the words *But if*.

In Dt 22:20b, the verdict proper uses the word
were not found. Although this may indicate that a
physical search resulted in nothing, it is more likely
that the term is technical and refers to a legal
process of discovery. However, in Dt 21:1, the discovery seems physical, while in 22:22, as here, the
discovery seems physical.

Dt 22:21: Death sentence

The formula in Dt 22:21 is technical and used to
impose the death penalty. It consists of four elements: the verb, the subject (*all the men of her
city*, the adverb (*with stones*), and the modifying
clause (*to death*). Just as in Dt 21:21, the
executioners of the rebellious and stubborn son are
the men of *his city*; the executioners of the woman who
has created a folly are the men of *her city*. Stoning
required every citizen to notarize the decision of the

municipal court to execute the convict.[338]

Setting

The judicial system of Ancient Near Eastern cities is the setting for Dt 22:13-21.[339] This system had jurisdiction over contracts of marriage and divorce. The Code of Hammurabi, for example, has several laws governing divorce.[340]

The judicial system also had jurisdiction over matters of calumny. Lipit-Ishtar fines anyone convicted of calumny; the Code of Hammurabi sentences them to flogging.[341] The setting of Dt 22:13-21 is urban. The trial takes place in a city before urban elders. The defendants are citizens and the executioners are men of her city. The setting of Dt 22:13-21 is judicial. The municipal court has jurisdiction over the question of illicit sexual intercourse, and the text has great confidence in the ability of the municipal court to bring about a just resolution to even such an overwhelmingly explosive issue as alienation of affection. The text explains a judicial process, and makes use of the laws of evidence. It assumes there is a law prohibiting illicit intercourse, as well as false witness. The setting of Dt 22:13-21 is Yahwist. The importance of the tokens of virginity in Dt 22:13-19, and the explanation given for the severity of the sentences for both calumny in Dt 22:18-19 and adultery in Dt 22:21 is the status of the woman as an Israelite. The crime in both cases is *evil*, a technical expression for an irregularity in the relationship between Israel and Yahweh.

The setting of Dt 22:13-21 is not limited to the social institution of making and breaking marriage contracts, but also reflects the understanding which the cities in early Israel had of their relationship to Yahweh. The do good/evil (foolishness) formula reflects a very early period in Israel.[342] Another indication of the pre-Deuteronomic setting for Dt 22:13-21 is the role of the elders in the administration of justice. This traditional system of justice administered by the elders was practiced in the cities of early Israel; the Deuteronomic reform instituted a system of justice administered by professional

judges.[343] Israel did not limit herself to a single
judicial system, nor were the various systems of
justice integrated with one another.[344] However, the
court system officiated by the elders was connected
with the ancient cities which were corporate members
of early Israel.[345] Hence laws associated with the
elders are more clearly urban laws, than those connected with judges and officers. Although these
municipal laws would have been operative in Israel
from the beginning, instructions like Dt 22:13-21
stressing the significance of traditional legal procedures, as opposed to the royal innovations, would
have developed during the early monarchy as Gibeon,
Shiloh, Hebron, and Shechem. As part of the literature of the Deuteronomic reform, instructions like Dt
22:13-21 authorize the municipal courts to supervise
marriage contracts, a responsibility which, according
to the reform, is not a purely secular pursuit. The
administration of justice in such matters is of importance to the welfare of the entire nation.

Intention

        The intention of Dt 22:13-21 is to convince the
full citizens of Israel that they have a particular
responsibility to treat marriageable women or married
women with deference because they represent Israel--
a community with a marriage bond to Yahweh. Words or
actions which question the existence of that relationship are intolerable. Of particular interest in
Dt 22:13-21 is the role of the city. The city is the
corporate member of Israel, whose elders and whose
citizens are responsible for the fulfillment of her
obligations to Yahweh. These obligations to Yahweh
are to be fulfilled through the municipal court.

        Deuteronomy 22:13-21 protects marriage and sexual
intercourse by establishing its proper place in
Hebrew life.[346] Without a doubt, long established traditions in Canaan prevented husbands from defrauding
their fathers-in-law. A husband could not simply
accuse his wife of premarital promiscuity, send his
wife home disgraced, and recover the bride price which
he paid to her father.[347] Likewise, parents are not
to defraud their sons-in-law by arranging marriages
for daughters whose reputations for chastity are
questionable.[348] Full citizens of Israel--husbands
and parents--have the responsibility to confront

imposters in the municipal court. The role of the mother and father in Dt 22:13-21 as in Dt 21:18-21 is not educational, but legal.[349]

The city-as-a-woman tradition in West Semitic cultures gives instructions like Dt 22:13-21, Dt 22:23-27 and Dt 25:5-10 special importance. In this tradition cities were bound to their gods by marriage contracts. Prophetic literature used this tradition in identifying the city of Jerusalem as a woman whose unfaithfulness to Yahweh was called adultery.[350] This city-as-a-woman tradition is influential in those three city texts from Deuteronomy as well.

The status of royal women in Israel is clearly significant. In 2 S 13:1-39 Amnon, David's son, wants to have intercourse with Tamar, David's daughter. But *she was a virgin, and it seemed impossible to Amnon to do anything to her* (2 S 13:2). Tamar's status as a virgin is indicated by her clothing: *Now she was wearing a long robe with sleeves; for thus were the virgin daughters of the king clad of old* (2 S 13:18). The social significance of her status is also indicated in her attempt to reason with her attacker: *. . . do not force me for such a thing is not done in Israel, do not do this wanton folly* (2 S 13:12).

Not only the natural children of the king, but his wives enjoyed a status of social significance. Diplomatic marriages were common enough in the families of kings. To ratify a treaty, the signatories would marry women from each other's cities. These women would serve as hostages, guaranteeing the terms of the treaty would be met, and as ambassadors promoting the interests of their natural parents' cities in the cities of their husbands. Only the covenant sovereign was permitted to have intercourse with these women. Intercourse with any other person destroyed the covenant. Thus when Absalom has intercourse with the ten women David left in his Jerusalem palace, the crime is not only adultery, it is treason (2 S 15:16; 16:20-3).

By the use of terms such as *virgin of Israel* (Dt 22:19) and *folly in Israel* (Dt 22:21), Dt 22:13-21 extends the significance of the instruction from the city to Israel.[351] The city-as-a-woman tradition makes this extension possible. The relationship between Yahweh and Israel, just as the relationship

235

between the city and its god, is reflected in the
public treatment of the marriage contract. This
status is applicable not only to the women in the
household of the king, but to all women. Thus the intention of Dt 22:13-21 is not only to regulate the
marriage contract itself, but also to emphasize the
importance of the marriage contract for understanding
the contract between Yahweh and the cities of Israel.

Deuteronomy 22:23-7

Genre

Structure analysis

```
LEGAL INSTRUCTION concerning
   the rape of a fiancee from
   an urban family                          Dt 22:23-27
   I. Primary instruction:
      when the fiancee is
      executed                              23-24
      A. Protasis (sign:  kî
         yihyeh)                            23
         1. Status of the woman             23a
         2. Location of the crime           23b α
         3. Nature of the act               23b β
      B. Apodosis (sign:  we)               24
         1. Command to transfer (2 pl)      24a α
         2. Death sentence                  24a β-b
            a. Command (2 pl)               24a β
            b. Qualifications               24a γ-b
               1) Basic qualifications      24a γδ
                  a) Specification of
                     her crime              24a γ
                  b) Specification of
                     his crime              24a δ
               2) Purge formula            24b
   II. Companion instruction:  when
       the fiancee is acquitted             25-27
       A. Protasis (sign:  'im)             25a
          1. Location of the crime          25a α
          2. Status of the woman            25a β
          3. Nature of the act              25a γ
```

```
B. Apodosis (sign: we)              Dt 22:25b-27
   1. Restricted death sentence,
      i.e., for man only (only)          25b
   2. Acquittal for woman               26-27
      a. Command (2 sq)                  26a α
      b. Qualifications                  26a β-27
         1) Declaration of
            Innocence                    26a β
         2) Citation of Dt
            19:1-13                      26b-27
            a) Citation proper           26b
            b) Qualification             27
```

Dt 11:23-7: Legal instruction

Although Dt 22:23-7 is generally identified as
law, it is *legal instruction*.[352] The instruction explains the difference between rape and adultery on the
basis of where it occurs, and how that affects the
victims. In the city, the victim must resist or be
considered a partner to adultery; Dt 22:25-7 explains
that in the country the victim need not resist because
help is unavailable. The instruction also explains the
particular acts by which adultery is to be identified,
as well as those by which rape is characterized. A
precedent is cited for the interpretation.

Deuteronomy 22:23-7 also encourages its audience
to accept and obey the laws it is explaining. In the
first case the purge formula is used, and in the
second a precedent is cited and then explained. Expansion, explanation, encouragement are characteristic
not of law, but of legal instruction.

Dt 22:23-4: Primary instruction

Dividing Dt 22:23-7 after Dt 22:24 produces a two
part instruction. The primary instruction in Dt
22:23-4 is introduced by *if (kî)* and the companion case
is introduced by *but if (we'im)*. The coherence of the
primary instruction is further emphasized by the verb
chain consisting of six verbs anchored on *if there is*
(Dt 22:23).[353] The coherence of the companion case is
emphasized by the three verbs in the chain anchored
on *meets (yimṣâ)* in Dt 22:25. Only the companion case
itself is included in the chain. The commentary which
begins in Dt 22:26 uses independent finite verbs.

The verb chain develops the protasis using a technique called *ennumeration (enumerative Redeweise)*.[354] Although Liedke sees no logic in the verb chains, but only an effort to provide additional information on the circumstances surrounding the allegation, in both chains the verbs follow a chronological order.[355]

Dt 22:23: Protasis

The protasis in the primary instruction (Dt 22:23-4) presents two circumstances: *if a man meets . . . and lies with*. The first circumstance has two qualifications, one concerning the status of the woman, the other concerning the location of the crime. The protasis in the companion instruction (Dt 22:25-7), however, presents three circumstances: *if a man meets . . . seizes her . . . lies with her . . . .* Again the first circumstance is qualified, with information about the status of the woman and the location of the crime. These qualifications form a chiasm with those found in the primary instruction:

A.   *a betrothed virgin*
B.   *in the city*
B'   *in the country*
A'   *a betrothed virgin*

The phrase *betrothed to a man* is unusual.[356] Likewise, the word *virgin* is in apposition to *young woman*, so that literally the verse reads: *If there is a young woman, a virgin betrothed to a man*. This suggests that *a virgin betrothed to a man* is a gloss defining *young woman*. However, the phrase *betrothed to a man* occurs in Dt 20:7 and 23:30 as well as here, and there is no indication that the phrase is secondary. Yet there is nothing to indicate that *to a man* is essential to the construction, since it is absent from Ex 22:15; Dt 22:25, 27, 28. In fact, since the phrase *betrothed young woman* occurs in the companion case in Dt 22:25-7, it should be presumed that both the principal and companion cases dealt with a *betrothed young woman* and not just a *young woman*. Therefore the phrase is original to each text. Only *virgin* remains as a possible gloss to explain *young woman* which without punctuation could mean either a young man or a young woman.

Hosea and Deuteronomy share many of the same traditions, one of which is understanding marriage as a

CHART

Diagram of the consecutive verb
chains in Dt 22:23-7

Principal case: Dt 22:22-4

	consecutive verbs	anchor verbs	
		if there is	Dt 22:22
	meets her		23
	and lies		24
	you shall bring		24
	and you shall stone		24
	to death		24
	you shall purge		24

Companion case: Dt 22:25

		if . . . meets	25
	and siezes		25
	and lies		25
	then . . . shall die		25

metaphor by which the relationship of Yahweh and
Israel can be understood.[357]

Dt 22:23b α: Circumstance

The emphasis in Dt 22:23b is on *in the city*, in
contrast to *in the field* in Dt 22:25a. By placing *in
the field* first in the companion instruction, the
community indicated that this was the principal circumstance with which it was concerned. Even the use of
force, mentioned explicitly in Dt 22:25a is not considered the important variable between the two cases
in Dt 22:23-4 and Dt 22:25-7.[358]

Setting

The societal or institutional matrix for Dt
22:23-7 is the judicial system of contracts by which
marriages were governed in the cities of the Ancient
Near East. Similar texts concerned with when to
execute the woman as well as the man, when a
marriage contract has been broken, appear in Babylonian and Assyrian laws.[359] Hittite Law #197 also
deals with the seduction of an engaged woman.[360]
The case appears again in the Laws of Eshnunna #26.[361]
The tradition was ancient and urban. The setting for
Dt 22:23-7 is clearly urban. The walled settlement
and the fields are the two basic components of the
city in Canaan, and thus the distinction made in the
primary and companion instructions would be of
interest only to an urban audience. Furthermore, the
defendants are citizens, and the place of execution is
the city gate.

The setting for Dt 22:23-7 is judicial. The
instruction presumes the existence of a law prohibiting intercourse between a woman who is engaged
and any other man except her fiance. However, there
is a noticeable lack of reference to the municipal
court found in the other city texts. Nonetheless, the
reference to Dt 19:1-9 in Dt 22:27 may want the
audience to assume that the process described in Dt 19
is to be followed for Dt 22. In fact, there is some
textual tradition reading *they shall bring them* rather
than *you shall bring them* in Dt 22:24. Merendino considers the mother and father, mentioned in Dt 21:18-21
and Dt 22:13-21 as the subjects of this verb.[362]
Seitz, however, patterns the text after city texts in

which the execution is handled by the elders and men of the city.363

It is the purge formula in Dt 22:24b which identifies the setting of the passage as Yahwist. According to Phillips, the only cultural, historical or epochal matrix in Israel for such a text is the Deuteronomic reform. No other period of history considered a woman a legal person, and thus able to be protected or prosecuted. She was a ward of her husband, who alone was a full citizen.364 But the presence of similar laws in other Mesopotamian codes indicates that adultery was often distinguished from rape. If the distinction was original to the reform, the procedure for deciding the case would probably have involved the judges and officials, and perhaps the central court--none of which appear here in Dt 22:23-7.

Finally, the judicial traditions of the Ancient Near East were initially very democratic; there is no reason to presume that women were not legal persons. In other city texts, the mother and father of a woman initiate a judicial proceeding on her behalf (Dt 22:13-21); likewise the mother and father are both called to testify at a hearing to revise their will and disinherit their heir (Dt 21:18-21). The presence of women in the municipal court is a characteristic of the antiquity of a text, not of its contemporeity. Ancient cities which joined early Israel would have brought traditions like those in Dt 22:23-7 with them. The security of the woman in the city is a development of the tradition which regards the city herself as a married woman.

Intention

In Dt 22:24a, as in Dt 22:25b-7, the man is executed because he violated the wife of his neighbor with cold and calculated premedication. His guilt rests on the violation of the Decalogue prohibition: *You shall not commit adultery* Dt 5:18). The man had violated his neighbor's wife and whether he did that in the city or in the country made no difference: he was to be executed.

The young woman in Dt 22:24a was to be executed not because she had or did not have intercourse with

241

her assailant, but because she failed *to cry out*
(sā'aq). In the final form of Dt 22:23-7, *crying out*
identifies the critical difference between a young
woman who is to be executed (Dt 22:24a) and the young
woman who is to be spared (Dt 22:27). The text takes
a very literal view of the woman's responsibility. If
she cries out in the city, her noise will be heard by
someone and she will be rescued, whereas, her sister
in the countryside could never make enough noise to
attract the attention of a deliverer.

Theologically *crying out* was possible only for a
people who believe in the responsibility of one human
being for another, and in a God who cares.[365] Both
were tenets of Yahwism. The Deuteronomist punctuated
his history of Israel and Judah with the sentence:
*But when the people of Israel cried to the Lord, the
Lord raised up a deliverer for the people of
Israel . . . (Jg 3:9).* The similarity between the
statements is striking.

The intention of Dt 22:23-7 for the ancient
cities of early Israel was to provide for observance
of their commitment to Yahweh through the structure
of their municipal court. Though the protection of
women in the city was a venerable tradition in the
Ancient Near East, for the cities of early Israel it
was particularly significant, since the status of the
woman and the status of Israel herself were so
similar. Having herself been delivered by crying out,
Israel was particularly indebted to those who, like
the endangered woman, cry out. The intention of
Dt 22:23-7 for the anti-monarchial movement in cities
like Shechem, Hebron, Shiloh and Gibeon was to stress
the importance of urban solidarity in the face of the
monarchy. Only if the citizens of these urban communities responded to the calls of one another for
protection could they hope to defend themselves from
the expanding powers of the king. Only in the cities
was there strength. In the open fields, help is
impossible.[366]

The intention of Dt 22:23-7 for the Deuteronomic
reform was to authorize the municipal courts to deal
with matters of family and marriage law. Affirming
the jurisdiction of these local courts in such
matters was part of an effort during the reform to
strengthen the outlying cities' responsibilities for
non-liturgical matters. Since the liturgy had been
appropriated by the king, the cities had lost a sense

of their identity as Yahwist communities. By using
the instructions which had been developed by the
ancient cities in Israel who had initially opposed the
monarchy, the reform attempted to restore some of
that identity. Yahwism was not limited to liturgy,
but was a pervading influence in the entire culture of
Israel.

Deuteronomy 25:5-10

Genre

Structure analysis

```
LEGAL INSTRUCTION concerning the
  obligations of a brother-in-
  law to a sonless widow from
  an urban family                      Dt 25:5-10
  I. Protasis (sign:  kî)              5
     A. Case                           5a α-δ
        1. Condition:  proximity       5a α
        2. Condition:  kinship         5a β
        3. Condition:  death           5a γ
        4. Condition:  heirlessness    5a δ
     B. Consequence                    5a ε-b
        1. Negative                    5a ε
        2. Positive                    5b
           a. shall go in              5b α
           b. take her                 5b β
           c. perform the duty         5b γ
 II. Apodosis (sign:  wehayah)         6-10
     A. Principal instruction:
        paternity accepted             6
        1. Negative consequence        6a
        2. Positive consequence        6b
     B. Companion instruction:
        paternity rejected             7-10
        1. Qualification (sign:
           we'im)                      7a
        2. Apodosis proper (sign:
           we)                         7b-10
           a. Judicial remedy          7b-8
              1) Remedy proper         7b-8a
                 a) Consequences for
                    the plaintiff      7b
```

243

Dt 25:5-10: Legal instruction

Deuteronomy 25:5-10 follows the same pattern as
the legal instructions in Dt 20:10-20 and Dt
22:13-21. The instruction proper, introduced by *if*
(kî) and the verb-noun (yiqtōl-x) construction, consists of a protasis and an apodosis.[367] The protasis
cites the case law in question; the apodosis
instructs the audience on how to respond in two
different situations: when the brother-in-law accepts
paternity, and when he does not. The apodosis is
introduced by *if (kî)*. In both the instruction in
Dt 25:5-10 and in Dt 20:10-20 the major concern is
what to do when the response is negative, hence the
discussion of this result is longer in both.

Generally, legal instruction encourages its
audience with second person verb forms and a variety
of formulas. Since there are no second person verb
forms in Dt 25:5-10, some commentators identify the

genre as *law*.[368] But the protasis of Dt 25:5-10 explains the purpose of the levirate (Dt 25:6) as well
as the disinvestment (Dt 25:10). The text gives an
example of the complaint which the plaintiff should
lodge in Dt 25:7b; and quotes the defendant's
position in Dt 25:8b. Finally, Dt 25:5-10 does not
intend to establish guidelines, which is the purpose
of law, but to encourage its audience to accept the
reasonableness of these laws and appreciate the
effect which observing them has on the future of
Israel--which is the purpose of instruction.

Dt 25:5: Protasis

The protasis in Dt 25:5-10 cites four conditions.
In case law each condition applies to the same
defendant. Here in Dt 25:5a both brothers are required to live together, but only one dies and is
heirless. In case law the defendant to whom the
conditions apply is punished in this consequence.
Here in Dt 25:6-10, the apodosis is not a punishment
but a responsibility, and it is fulfilled by only one
of the two parties mentioned in the protasis. Like
Dt 25:5-10, Ex 21:18-19 and Ex 21:22 involve two
defendants. This characteristic may indicate a
different kind of case law is at the basis of this
particular instruction than the more general pattern
in which only one defendant is concerned.

Kinship can be close or distant. Onan in Gn
38:8-10 is the natural brother of the deceased, while
in Ruth, neither Boaz, nor the original relative
responsible for the women (Ru 3:12) is from the
immediate family. Hebrew has a special term for the
relationship; it is an established institution in
Israel and throughout Canaan as well.[369]

Seitz considers kinship and proximity as a
single circumstance.[370] Although in Hebrew, the kinship circumstance is sandwiched between the two parts
of the circumstance proximity, i.e., *dwell . . .
together* they are distinct. For example, the
brother-in-law's responsibilities of Naomi and Ruth's
relative does not begin until the two women move
back to Israel from Moab.

As in Dt 21:18-21, the word *son* is technical,
and refers to the legal heir of the deceased.[371]
Without an heir, the property of the deceased went
first to his widow, then to his father, and then to

his brother-in-law. However, if his wife remarried, her husband became the legal heir. The concern of Dt 25:5a is to prevent just such an outsider from entering the picture.

Dt 25:5a-6: Consequence

The. phrase *outside the family to a stranger* is the opposite of *brothers dwelling together*. This technical term (*lĕ'îš zār*) occurs here as well as in Dt 32:16, Pr, Is, Nm, Ex, Ez and Jr. The term refers to an Israelite, not a foreigner; but the Israelite is a member of a household other than that to which the widow's husband belonged.[372]

The concern with what should not be done in Dt 25:5a is balanced by a concern with what should be done. The structure here uses three verbs.[373] There is some development in meaning between one verb and the next. The idiom *shall go to her (yābo')* refers to sexual intercourse; the idiom *take her as his wife (leqāhâ l'o le'iššâ)* refers to marriage. Therefore, Samson *goes to* the prostitute at Gaza (Jg 16:1); the Nephalim *go to* the daughters of human beings (Gn 6:4) and Abraham *goes to* his wife's maid (Gn 16:2). There is no connotation of either marriage or paternity. In Dt 25:5, the idioms are used together, as they are in Dt 22:13-21, another city text. What is unusual about the construction of the idioms in Dt 25:5 is that it says: *he shall have intercourse with her (go to her), and then marry her (take her as his wife)*. Deuteronomy 22:13-21 has the more normal construction: *He shall marry her and then have intercourse with her*. Evidently the brother-in-law could not marry his brother's widow until he demonstrated that, in fact, he could conceive a child with her. This would prevent the woman from being a partner in yet another sterile marriage. The official term for the obligations of a brother-in-law (*yābām* or *levir*) were not identical to those of a husband, although they included sexual intercourse and marriage. In some cases, the widow would become the brother-in-law's second wife.

Genesis 38:26 notes *And he* [Judah] *did not lie with her* [Tamar, his widowed daughter-in-law] *again*. At least in Gn 38, the brother-in-law was allowed intercourse with his sister-in-law, only until she conceived and/or gave birth to an heir. After that, his obligations were strictly financial, insofar as he had to support her, manage her deceased husband's property, and grace her with the social status of a married woman. Unlike Dt 25, however, Gn 38 considers declining the responsibility of a brother-in-law a crime, not simply a disgrace.[374]

In Rt 4, Boaz not only has the obligation of a *brother-in-law (yābām or levir)*, he is also the *avenger (gō'ēl)* for the household of Elimelech and Naomi. Therefore, it is unclear under what role any one of his actions falls. Furthermore, Boaz is not closely related to Ruth, and her brother-in-law by marriage is dead.[375] Examples of this institution appear in most Near Eastern cultures.[376]

Dt 25:6-10: Apodosis

The particle *and (wehāyâ)* and the switch in perspective from that of the brother-in-law to that of the widow emphasize the division between Dt 25:5 and Dt 25:6.[377] There is a conscious parallel between Dt 25:6 and 10.[378]

Both verses stress the concern of the text with *names*. *Name* here in Dt 25:5-10 has the sense of *posterity* or *heir from one's own family* so that the property of the father may remain intact.[379] The theme appears not only in both these conclusions (Dt 25:6 & 10), but also in the complaint of the widow (Dt 25:7b).

The importance of the phrase *in Israel* can be seen in such passages as 2 S 13:12. There, Tamar attempts to discourage her brother from having intercourse with her by reminding him: *such a thing is not done in Israel!* The phrase identifies venerable Hebrew traditions. The phrase also appears in the purge formula, e.g., Dt 22:22.

Dt 25:7-10: Companion instruction

Deuteronomy 25:7-10 is much longer than Dt 25:6, however, both belong to the same subdivision. The marker *and (wehāyâ)* in Dt 25:6 introduces the subdivision and the marker *and if (we'im)* opens this companion instruction, consisting of two remedies available to the widow. The principal instruction (Dt 25:6) simply stated the positive and negative results of accepting the paternity demanded by the law. Unlike the parallel structure in Dt 20:11, Dt 25:6

247

CHART

Comparison of Dt 25:6b with Dt 25:10

Deuteronomy 25:6b	Deuteronomy 25:10
may not be blotted out	*shall be called*
his name	*its name*
of Israel	*in Israel*
	The house of him that had his sandal pulled off

does not use a protasis-apodosis structure, viz., *if the brother-in-law goes to . . . then, . . .* The principal instruction simply comments on the cooperative brother-in-law as the companion instruction will comment on the remedies in case of an uncooperative brother-in-law.

The brother-in-law in Dt 25:7-10 has inherited his responsibilities by reason of the same four conditions mentioned in Dt 25:5: proximity, kinship, death and heirlessness. The brother-in-law could decline the responsibility because the children would not be his heirs, but his brother's, and because he had to forfeit his right to inherit the property directly from his widowed sister-in-law.

If a man dies, and has no son, you shall cause his inheritance to pass to his daughter. And if he has no daughter, then you shall give his inheritance to his brothers. And if he has no brothers, then you shall give his inheritance to his father's brothers, then you shall give his inheritance to his kinsman that is next to him of his family, and he shall possess it . . . (Nm 27:8-11).

The verb *does not wish (yahpoṣ)* which the brother-in-law uses to explain his unwillingness to sire a son for his deceased brother, indicates one of two things. It may indicate that he does not find his sister-in-law sexually attractive. As the verb is used in Gn 34:19 and Dt 21:14, that seems to be the obvious connotation. However, *delight (yahpoṣ)* does not only indicate sexual attraction. In Nm 14:8, it is Yahweh who *delights* in Israel and in Jg 13:23 it is Yahweh again who *accepted* the offering of Samson's parents. Therefore, it is possible that the brother-in-law has the same grounds for declining as the brother-in-law in Rt 4:6. *I cannot redeem it for myself, lest I impair my own inheritance.* Thus whether here in Dt 25, the widow is undesirable for physical or financial reasons, it is not clear.

But even if the brother-in-law declines his responsibility to the widow, she cannot marry outside the family. This was the plight of Tamar in Gn 38. Although Judah did not fulfill his promise to her, she could not leave his family and marry into another. This also is the obligation from which Naomi dispensed

249

Orphah and Ruth (Rt 1:12). Deuteronomy 25:7-10 offers
the woman faced with this situation two remedies by
which her husband's right to an heir can be enforced,
and her own right to support will not be violated.
One remedy is judicial (Dt 25:7-8); the other is
ritual (Dt 25:9-10).

Dt 25:7-8: Judicial remedy

The structure of Dt 25:7-8 is similar to Dt
21:19-20 and Dt 22:15-16. Each reflects a municipal
court process. The term *submit* is technical meaning
to commit to the discretion of another.

In Dt 25:7-8, it is the elders of the defendant's
city who have jurisdiction. They have the power to
subpoena the defendant and to hold a hearing on the
matter. However, in Dt 25:9-10, these same elders act
only as witnesses of the action taken by the plaintiff
against the defendant. Whether or not these two
different functions of the elders are characteristic
of their office or whether a development in the
function has taken place is questionable. Perhaps at
one period the plaintiff herself was expected to confront her brother-in-law in public, while at
another all that was permitted was that she turn the
matter over to the elders of her brother-in-law's
city, and let them handle it. This second function
is described by Boecker as *notarial.*[380]

There is an addition to the text, also concerned
with the installation of witnesses:

> And the priests the sons of Levi shall come
> forward, for the Lord your God has chosen
> them to minister to him and to bless in the
> name of the Lord, and by their word every
> dispute and every assault shall be settled
> (Dt 21:5).

The phrase *in the presence of the elders* in Dt 25:9a
is also secondary. If Dt 25:9-10 and 7-8 were
originally part of the same text, the reference to
the elders would not have been repeated. The phrase
before the eyes of the elders does not refer to
location but to authorization. Thus Dt 25:9aα is set
apart from the rest of the ritual in Dt 25:9a.

The role of the elders in the judicial remedy is
more conciliatory than authoritative. Köhler has

argued that originally this was the only role which
the municipal court in Canaan enjoyed.[381] These courts
did not hand down verdicts, but simply attempted,
through dialogue, to mediate for the parties.[382]

Dt 25:9-10: Ritual remedy

Although the remedy in Dt 25:9-10 seems more
radical than that in Dt 25:7-8, it presumably allowed
someone other than the brother-in-law to marry the
widow. This seems to be the purpose of the rite in
Rt 4. In addition to the procedure given in Dt 25:9-
10, the widow could also entrap the brother-in-law to
recover her right of an heir. Both Tamar (Gn 38) and
Ruth (Rt 3:6-15) use the method with success. It
should be noted that technically the remedy is not
part of the action, nor does remedy include the
action. Remedy is the result of the action, and the
reason for the litigation in the first place. By
appealing to the court, and by confronting the
brother-in-law, the widow in Dt 25:7-10 seeks a
remedy.

The order of the text (judicial, then ritual) is
intended to establish the order in which the two
remedies in Dt 25:7-10 are to be used. The
character of the ritual in Dt 25:9-10, so full of
ceremony and symbol, combining both things-to-be-done
(Dt 25:9a) and things-to-be-said (Dt 25:9b) contrasts
starkly with the bland suggestions that the elders
try to talk the brother-in-law into cooperating (Dt
25:8a).[383]

In Rt 4:1, it is Boaz, and not the court who
summons the brother-in-law with the words: *Turn
aside friend; sit down here.* In Rt 4:2, part of the
subpoena formula is repeated: *Sit down here.*

The liturgy in Dt 25:9-10 consists of a ritual to
be performed (Dt 25:9a) and a formula to be recited
(Dt 25:9b). The same structure is found in Dt 21:2-9,
also a city text. A liturgy is a public act of worship whose rubrics have been established by custom
or authority for use by a religious community. The
public nature of this liturgy, like that of Dt 21:2-9,
is emphasized by the requirement that it be performed
in the presence of the elders (Dt 25:9a). Ritual,
here in Dt 25:9a and Dt 21:2-6, identifies a
specific series of religious actions intended to express a particular sentiment and accomplish a

CHART

Comparison of Dt 25:7 with Dt 25:9

Deuteronomy 25:7	Deuteronomy 25:9
shall go up	*shall go up*
his brother's wife	*his brother's wife*
to the gate	*to him*
to	*in the presence of*
the elders	*the elders*

particular result. Ritual is one of the elements of
liturgy, a more comprehensive term. Sometimes, ritual
is limited to acts alone, as it is here. When a
ritual is combined with a formula, the what-is-to-be-
said portion, the result is a liturgy.

During the ritual, the widow spits on the
brother-in-law. There is no question that this
gesture is humiliating.[384]

And Moses cried to the Lord, 'Heal her
[Miriam], O God, I beseech thee.' But
the Lord said to Moses, 'If her father
had but spit in her face, should she not
be shamed seven days? Let her be shut up
outside the camp seven days, and after
that she may be brought in again (Nm
12:13-14).

However, the significance of the widow removing the
brother-in-law's sandal is not so clear.[385] If the
ritual is using sexual symbolism, the foot is a
symbolic penis, the sandal a symbol vagina, which are
publically disengaged. The rite is thus re-enacting
the coitus interruptus for which Onan, an unwilling
brother-in-law was executed. In the Hebrew Bible,
feet are occasionally a euphemism for the sexual
organs, e.g., Ex 4:25, Is 6:2 and Is 7:20. However,
there are no examples of the sandal as a metaphor for
the vagina. As a symbol of power, removing the
sandal may be a symbolic act of castration, by which
the widow curses the brother-in-law with the same
sterility which he is imposing upon her.

The formula in Dt 25:9b implies a humiliation, but
the meaning of *The house of him that had his sandal
pulled off* is not clear. Like many etiologies, the
formula may be a later attempt to explain something,
even the formula did not clearly understand.
Divestiture, as a public humiliation is often practiced by societies who wish to punish members for
dishonorable conduct or cowardice. Clerics are
stripped of their vestments and soldiers of their
uniforms. The problem with the theory of humiliation
is that in Rt 4:7, there is no indication the cere-
money is more than a transfer of power. Furthermore,
the final form of the text makes no express reference
to the ceremony as a humiliation. In contrast Dt 25:3
contains a prohibition against giving the convict more
than forty lashes with the whip *lest . . . your*

253

brother be degraded. It is difficult to see how forty
lashes would be more degrading than having your
sister-in-law pull off your sandal and spit in your
face in front of all the important people in your home
town. Although, there is no doubt that the passage as
a whole wishes to humiliate the brother-in-law who
declines to accept the paternity of his deceased
relative, removing the sandal is not in itself
humiliating. In Gn 13:17, Yahweh tells Abraham to
establish his ownership over the land of Canaan by
pacing it off. Removing one's sandal renounced any
legal claim to the land over which its wearer had
walked.[386]

Dt 25:9b: What-is-to-be-said-formula

The phrase: *thus shall it be done,* according to
Rowley, indicates that the formula in the liturgy
explains the meaning of the acts. Nonetheless, there
is no guarantee that the formula in every ritual
originated at the same time as the ritual itself or
that the formula preserved an authentic interpretation
of the ritual. Thus Rowley's observation should be
understood with one caution: formulas interpret
rituals; but not always correctly.[387]

Setting

The setting of Dt 25:5-10 is urban. The plaintiff
has recourse to the municipal court, and her case is
under the jurisdiction of the elders of the city.
Their jurisdiction allows them to summon the defendant
and conduct a hearing. The city is the corporate
member of Israel and is concerned about the ramifications of refusing to care for widows on its common
good. The genre of the unit is legal instruction,
presuming laws which it seeks to explain. Deuteronomy
25:5-10 also considers the municipal court to have
ordinary jurisdiction in resolving disputes, and is
familiar with a particular legal process by which this
is accomplished. The municipal court is instrument
through which obligations to Yahweh are paid. The
primary concern of the text is the impact of the
levirate law on Israel, the community of Yahweh. There
is a concern that the names of those whom Yahweh has
assembled as his own be perpetuated.

The institutional or societal matrix of Dt 25:5-10

is a system of transferring deeds or contract to
property in the cities of the Ancient Near East.
During the lifetime of the testator, changes in one's
will were made by the procedure outlined in Dt 21:18-
21. However, after the death of the landowner, his
executor or brother-in-law was expected to see to his
property. Deuteronomy 25:5-10 assumes a legal and
ritual remedy by which the testator's widow can have
a new executor of her husband's will designated.

The cultural, epochal or historical matrix of
Dt 25:5-10 would initially have been the ancient
cities which joined early Israel. As newly instated
landowners, they would not only have been preoccupied
with the security of their inheritance, but also concerned that the process by which this *inheritance*
(nahala) was passed on from one generation to the next
eliminate the traditional horrors of feudalism in
Canaan. In the early monarchy, these ancient cities
would find Dt 25:5-10 an aid in resisting the king
who felt free to appropriate the property of those
who died without heirs. The levirate tradition,
according to Dt 25:5-10 was both a venerable and
Yahwist custom for caring for the land, which did not
require the intervention of the king. Finally in the
Deuteronomic reform, Dt 25:5-10 stressed the very
important role which the outlying cities had in preserving the culture of Yahwism--apart from the
liturgy. Traditions like that in Dt 25:5-10 recovered
a very significant, but thoroughly non-liturgical way
for these cities to maintain their identity as
Yahwist communities.

Intention

The intention of Dt 25:5-10 is to instruct its
audience on how the custom of the levirate marriage
keeps the property of the *names in Israel* intact.[388]
Names were an essential means of identification in
Israel. Names were the way the founding members of
Israel were recognized, and genealogies were developed
to prevent the names of Israel from becoming confused
or disappearing altogether, thus destroying the legal
claim of the families to their land. During the
monarchy, the kings used the names as the basis of the
census on which armies were built and taxes were
collected. The phrase *in Israel* underlines the importance of preserving family inheritances intact for

255

the whole community. It is the municipal court which
has the primary responsibility for maintaining this
unity in Israel.

In feudalism only the *feudal lords (ḥazannu)* had
any legal claim to the land; the *serfs (ḥupshu)* simply
worked that land for them. Therefore, through the
conscientious maintenance of the family ownership of
the land in early Israel, it would be difficult, if
not impossible, for any one person to take control of
the land again. If there was a single and emphatic
difference between Israel and the feudalism which she
replaced in Canaan, it was in land ownership. Under
Israel, Yahweh alone was the landlord, and the
families of Israel his tenants. To allow anyone else
to exercise the kind of exclusive control of property
which Canaan had experienced under the feudal lords
was to destroy the meaning of Israel altogether.

When the hereditary monarchy appeared in Israel
herself, the ancient cities resisted the territorial
imperative which these monarchs exercised. The custom
of the levirate marriage was a strong check and
balance which the priests encouraged the pilgrims to
exercise. So long as the people themselves safe-
guarded their legal right to the land, the power of
the king would remain in balance. If the names in
Israel became hopelessly confused because of the personal greed of the families for the land of one
another, the king would benefit. By their faithful
exercise of jurisdiction over such matters as the inheritance of property, the cities promoted the stability of the ancient families on their ancestral lands.
Following the period of Manassah, the reconstruction
of the names in Israel was an important contribution
to the nationalism of Josiah's reform. It was in
this particular manner that the reform wished to encourage the cities to participate, hoping, of course,
to distract them from their concern for the liturgy of
Yahweh, which had been centralized in the city of
Jerusalem

FOOTNOTES - CHAPTER III

[1]Form criticism studies *literary forms* in theory where they are called *genres,* and in texts where they are called *structures.* (See IDB, "Criticism.")

[2]Peter C. Craigie, The Book of Deuteronomy (Grand Rapids, MI.: William B. Eerdmans Publishing Company, 1976), p. 173.

[3]Liedke, Gestalt, p. 26.

[4]Rosario P. Merendino, Das Deuteronomische Gesetz: Eine literarkritische, gattungs- und überlieferungs- geschichtliche Untersuchung zu Dt 12--26 (Bonn: Peter Hanstein Verlag, 1969), p. 115.

[5]Norbert Lohfink, Das Hauptgebot: eine Unter- suchung literarischer Einleitungsfragen zu Dtn 5--11 (Romae: E. Pontificio Instituto Biblico, 1963), p. 114. See Tiffany, "Parenesis," p. 111.

[6]Tiffany, "Parenesis," p. 111. The definition is from Gerhard von Rad, "Ancient Word and Living Word: The Preaching of Deuteronomy and our Preaching," trans. Lloyd Gaston, Int 15 (1961):7.

[7]Weinfeld, Deuteronomy, pp. 320-65.

[8]"Genre File of the Form Critical Project from the Institute of Antiquity and Christianity at the Claremont Graduate School," s.v. "Catalogue," "List," "Series," and "Register," by Rolf P. Knierim.

[9]Gerhard von Rad, Deuteronomy, A Commentary (Philadelphia: Westminster Press, 1966), p. 64. See Gerhard von Rad, Das fünfte Buch Mose: Deuteronomium (Göttingen: Vandenhoeck & Ruprecht, 1964), p. 46.

[10]Buis, Deutéronome, p. 133.

[11]Baltzer, Formulary, pp. 20-1 and Jean Nougayrol,

Le palais royal d'Ugarit (Paris: Impr. Nationale, 1955), no. 16 138, 16 204, 17 340.

[12]Josef G. Plöger, Literarkritische, form-geschlichtliche und stilkritische Untersuchungen zum Deuteronomium (Bonn: Peter Hanstein, 1967), pp. 87-9.

[13]"Genre File," s.v. "Catalogue."

[14]Dt 8:10,12;11:15; 14:29; 26:12; 31:20; Lv 26:26; Jo 2:26; Ps 22:27; 78:29; Ne 9:25; 2 C 31:10. See Merendino, Gesetz, p. 102.

[15]Primarily on the basis of content, rather than form, Driver, Deuteronomy, p. 95 and others have made the same division of the unit.

[16]See Merendino, Gesetz, pp. 14-15 on the use Deuteronomy makes of to do ('āśâ) as in Dt 6:14.

[17]Seitz, Studien, pp. 72-3.

[18]Handbook of Biblical Criticism, s.v. "Chiasmus," by Richard N. Soulen.

[19]Lohfink, Hauptgebot, p. 8. See Ex 12:25; 13:5;13:11;23:23; Lv 14:34; 19:23; 23:10; 25:2; Nu 15:2; 15:18; 33:51; 34:2; 35:10; Dt 7:1; 8:7; 11:29; 11:31; 12:20; 12:29; 17:14; 18:9; 19:1; 26:1; 27:2.

[20]Weinfeld, Deuteronomy, pp. 320-65.

[21]Carmichael, Deuteronomy, p. 94.

[22]Tiffany, "Parenesis," pp. 107-8.

[23]See "Genre File of the Form Critical Project from the Institute of Antiquity and Christianity," s.v. "Motive Clause," by Roland E. Murphy. See: B. Gemser, "The Importance of the Motive Clause in Old Testament Law," SVT 1 (1953):50-66.

[24]Von Rad, Deuteronomy, p. 64 and Seitz, Studien, p. 72.

[25]Lohfink, Hauptgebot, p. 156. See also
Merendino, Gesetz, p. 18.

[26]Tiffany, "Parenesis," p. 89.

[27]So Seitz, Studien, p. 72; Weinfeld,
Deuteronomy, pp. 83 & 332; Tiffany, "Parenesis," pp.
89-97.

[28]Rolf Knierim, Die Hauptbegriffe für Sünde im
Alten Testament (Gerd Mohn: Gütersloher Verlagshaus,
1965), p. 139.

[29]For a discussion of the difference between
Deuteronomy's use of *territory* (*'ereṣ*) and *farmland*
(*'adāmâ*), see Josef G. Plöger, "Die Aussagen über
ארץ und אדמה im Dt und ihre theologische Interpretation," in Untersuchungen, pp. 60-129. See:
Merendino, Gesetz, p. 235.

[30]Lohfink, Hauptgebot, p. 95.

[31]E. Kautzsch, ed., Gesenius' Hebrew Grammar,
rev. A. E. Cowley (Oxford: At the Clarendon Press,
1910), p. 342 (#113,n).

[32]See, for example, W. L. Moran, "The Ancient Near
Eastern Background of the Love of God in Dt," CBQ 25
(1963):77-87, who argues that *love* is a technical
term in ANE treaties. Tiffany, "Parenesis," p. 104.

[33]Plöger, Untersuchungen, p. 79n.

[34]Douglas A. Knight, "The Understanding of Sitz
im Leben in Form Criticism," in SBL Seminar Papers,
vol. 1, ed. Paul J. Achtmeier (Chico, CA.: Scholars
Press, 1976), pp. 107-8.

[35]Weinfeld, Deuteronomy.

[36]See Tiffany, "Parenesis," pp. 85-97.

[37]Nicholson, Deuteronomy, pp. 28-9. See von Rad,

Studien, pp. 54 ff.

[38]Rolf P. Knierim, "The Nature of the Decalogue and its function in Israelite Society," unpublished lecture: Theologische Hochschule, Sankt Georgen, Frankfurt/Main and Universities of Heidelberg and Munich, 1974. Revised manuscript, Institute of Antiquity and Christianity at the Claremont Graduate School, Claremont, CA., 1976.

[39]Wolff, Hosea, pp. 79-80. See also: Hans Walter Wolff, "Hoseas geistige Heimat," ThLZ 81 (1956):90-94 and Andre Neher, L'essence du prophetisme (Paris: Presses Universitaires de France, 1955), pp. 166-75.

[40]Joseph Blenkinsopp, "Are there traces of the Gibeonite Covenant in Deuteronomy?" CBQ 28 (1966):207-19. See also: I. M. Grintz, "The Treaty with the Gibeonites," Zion 26 (1960/61):69-84 and McCarthy, Treaty, p. 125.

[41]George Mendenhall, "Law," pp. 3-24 and I. Lewy, "The Puzzle of Dt XXVII: blessings announced, but curses noted," VT (1962):207-11.

[42]Blenkinsopp, "Traces," p. 215.

[43]James W. Flanagan, "The Relocation of the Davidic Capital," JAAR 47 (1979):223-44.

[44]Ibid., p. 236. See Walter Beltz, Die Kaleb-Traditionen im Alten Testament (Stuttgart: W. Kohlhammer, 1974).

[45]Tiffany, "Parenesis."

[46]See, for example, C. Steuernagel, Die Entstehung des deuteronomischen Gesetzes kritisch und biblisch-theologisch untersucht (Halle: J. Krause, 1896).

[47]Wellhausen, Prolegomena.

[48]Noth, Studien.

[49]Lohfink, Hauptgebot.

[50]IDB, supplementary vol., s.v. "Deuteronomy."

[51]Childs, Introduction, pp. 215-17.

[52]Achtmeier, Deuteronomy, p. 29.

[53]See Interpreter's Dictionary of the Bible, s.v. "Milk," by J. F. Ross.

[54]Theologisches Handwörterbuch zum Alten Testament, s.v. "gadōl," by E. Jenni.

[55]Theologisches Handwörterbuch zum Alten Testament, s.v. "tob," by H. J. Stoebe.

[56]Jean L'Hour, "Une legislation criminelle dans le Deuteronome," Bib 44 (1963):11-14.

[57]Ibid., pp. 3-4; Alt, Kleine Schriften, vol. 1; Alfred Jepsen, Untersuchungen zum Bundesbuch (Stuttgart: W. Kohlhammer, 1927).

[58]See, for example, Harry W. Gilmer, The If-You Form in Israelite Law (Chico, CA.: Scholars Press, 1975).

[59]L'Hour, "Legislation," pp. 7-8.

[60]L'Hour, "Legislation," p. 11n.

[61]Seitz, Studien, p. 146. Liedke, Gestalt, p. 21 classifies Dt 13:13-19 as If-you law (wenn-du Rechtsatz), while admitting it has a number of characteristics of standard case law (kasuistische Rechtssatz) as well.

[62]Weinfeld, Deuteronomy, pp. 91-100.

[63]The worship of other gods is always forbidden, e.g., Ex 20:3, 22:19, 23:18, etc.), but only here in Deuteronomy are the occasions of apostasy identified.

[64]McCarthy, Treaty, p. 171n.

[65]Johannes Friedrich, Staatsverträge des Hatti Reiches (Leipzig: Mitteilungen der Vorderasiatisch-Agyptischen Gesellsschaft, 1926).

[66]Patrick D. Miller, "The Gift of God. The Deuteronomistic Theology of the Land," Int 23 (1969): 461.

[67]Hubert Junker, Deuteronomium (Würzburg: Echter-Verlag, 1952), p. 41.

[68]Von Rad, Deuteronomy, p. 19, for example.

[69]Tiffany, "Parenesis," pp. 7-8.

[70]Merendino, Gesetz, p. 69.

[71]See Interpreter's Dictionary of the Bible, supplementary vol., s.v. "War, Holy," by Norman K. Gottwald and De Vaux, Israel, pp. 258-70.

[72]Buis, Deutéronome, pp. 243-4 considers the juridical and the holy war procedures complementary and sets them both in the period of the settlement.

[73]Von Rad, Studies, p. 15. See Tiffany, "Parenesis," p. 11.

[74]Dale Patrick, "The rights of the Under-privileged," in SBL Seminar Papers, vol. 1, ed. Paul J. Achtemeier (Chico, CA.: Scholars Press, 1975), pp. 1-6.

[75]Driver, Deuteronomy, p. 153.

[76]The phrase *in one of your cities* explains where the apostasy occurred, not where the report was

made. See, for example, George A. Smith, The Book of
Deuteronomy (London: Cambridge University Press,
1950).

[77]Merendino, Gesetz, pp. 73-4.

[78]Von Rad, Deuteronomy, p. 96. So also
Carmichael, Laws, p. 73. Craigie, Deuteronomy, pp.
221-2.

[79]Seitz, Studien, p. 303 and Merendino, Gesetz,
p. 81 disagree on just how Dt 17:2-7 and Dt 13 are
related. Seitz argues that originally Dt consisted
of two collections of centralization laws; some
casuistic laws and some war laws. When these sources
were combined, the redactor used parts of Dt 13 to
compose Dt 17:2-7 which he needed to introduce the
case laws. Merendino, on the other hand, considers
Dt 17:2-7 and Dt 13 to have been part of one tradition, viz., Dt 17:2-7+Dt 13:2-6+14-17. According
to Merendino, Dt 13 was separated from Dt 17 and used
as an example of the temptations Israel faced in
Canaan, and Dt 17 was used to introduce a series of
laws monitoring the behavior of officials of state,
who might easily allow worship of other gods for
political reasons.

[80]Buis, Deutéronome, p. 239. See also, p. 243 n
21.

[81]De Vaux, Israel, p. 156.

[82]On the translation of nākôn as a technical
term meaning certain, trustworthy, sure, see, for
example, G. Rinaldi, "KWN" BeO 10 (1968):206.

[83]Merendino, Gesetz, p. 70 argues that Dt
13:14ab+16ab is the original apodosis for three
reasons: 1) it contains 11 poetic feet (rhythmischen
Worten); 2) no admonitions; 3) a casuistic structure.

[84]A. D. H. Mayes, Deuteronomy (Greenwood, SC.:
Attic Press, 1979), p. 141.

[85]Merendino, Gesetz, p. 69 and Carl Steuernagle,

Deuteronomium (Göttingen: Vandenhoeck & Ruprecht, 1900), p. 104.

[86]Weinfeld, Deuteronomy, p. 210. See Dt 33:10 and 1 S 7:9.

[87]Seitz, Studien, p. 148.

[88]Mayes, Deuteronomy, p. 237. See Seitz, Studien, p. 149.

[89]Merendino, Gesetz, p. 70.

[90]Gottwald, Tribes, pp. 63-128.

[91]Weinfeld, Deuteronomy, pp. 59-178. Weinfeld himself, however, associates the covenant genre with scribes, not priests!

[92]Buis, Deutéronome, p. 244.

[93]Craigie, Deuteronomy, p. 221.

[94]See Childs, "Formulae."

[95]Von Rad, Problem.

[96]Noth, Studien.

[97]Gottwald, Tribes, pp. 34-5.

[98]J. Maxwell Miller, The Old Testament and the Historian (Philadelphia: Fortress Press, 1976), p. 54.

[99]Malamat, "Aspects."

[100]Peter Machinist, "Literature as Politics: The TIKULTI-NINURTA epic and the Bible," CBQ 38 (1976):455-52.

[101]Buis, Deutéronome, pp. 243-4.

[102]So also Nu 25:4-9.

[103]Paul Koschaker, Quellenkritische Untersuchungen zu den "altassyriche Gesetzen" (Leipzig: J. C. Hinrichs, 1921). So also Anton Jirku, Das weltliche Recht im Alten Testament (Gütersloh: C. Bertelsmann, 1927) who distinguishes *law code (Gesetzeskodex)* from *law book (Rechtsbuch)*.

[104]Weinfeld, Deuteronomy, pp. 59-178.

[105]J. J. Finkelstein, "Some New Misharum Material and its implications" in Studies in Honor of Benno Landsberger on his 75th Birthday (Chicago: University of Chicago Press, 1965), p. 243 ff.

[106]W. E. Lambert, "Nebuchadnezzer, King of Justice," Iraq 27 (1965):8.

[107]The Babylonian Laws, vol. 1, ed. G. R. Driver and J. C. Miles (Oxford: Clarendon Press, 1952), p. 20.

[108]Otto Eissfeldt, The Old Testament: An Introduction, trans. Peter R. Ackroyd (New York: Harper and Row, Publishers, 1965), p. 220.

[109]Von Rad, Deuteronomy and Studies.

[110]McCarthy, Treaty.

[111]Friedrich Horst, Das Privilegrecht Jahres (Göttingen: Vandehoeck & Ruprecht, 1930).

[112]Merendino, Gesetz.

[113]Hermann Schulz, Das Todesrecht im Alten Testament (Berlin: Töpelmann, 1969).

[114]Weinfeld, Deuteronomy, p. 91. So also, for example, von Rad, Deuteronomy, p. 96; Driver, Deuteronomy, pp. 150-1; Seitz, Studien, pp. 146-8.

[115]See Je 7:30-1.

[116]Driver, Deuteronomy, pp. 137-8.

[117]Childs, Exodus, pp. 468-9.

[118]The categorical identification of paganism is made with the phrase *'elōhî nēkār hā'āreṣ* (Dt 31:16). See Theologisches Handwörterbuch zum Alten Testament, s.v. "*nekar*," by R. Martin-Achard.

[119]Theology Dictionary of the Old Testament, s.v. "*'acher*," by Seth Erlandsson.

[120]Horst, Privilegrecht.

[121]Hayes and Miller, History, pp. 356-8.

[122]Von Rad, Deuteronomy, p. 19.

[123]Von Rad, Deuteronomy, p. 18.

[124]Liedke, Gestalt, p. 21n.

[125]Seitz, Studien, p. 226.

[126]Brueggemann, "Study," pp. 99-101. See Theological Dictionary of the Old Testament, s.v. "*bdl*," by Benedikt Otzen.

[127]Theologisches Handwörterbuch zum Alten Testament, s.v. "*bhr*," by H. Wildberger and Theological Dictionary of the Old Testament, s.v. "*bachar*," by Jan Berman, Helmer Ringgren and Horst Seebass.

[128]Brueggemann, "Study," p. 100.

[129]Steuernagel, Deuteronomium. So also Buis, Deutéronome, pp. 292-3, and Mayes, Deuteronomy, pp. 285-6.

[130]See James B. Pritchard, ed., Ancient Near
Eastern Texts relating to the Old Testament, 3rd ed.
(Princeton, NJ.: Princeton University Press, 1969),
p. 189, especially Hittite Laws #3-4.

[131]The Babylonian Laws, ed., G. R. Driver and
John C. Miles, vol. 1 (Oxford: At the Clarendon
Press, 1952), p. 315n.

[132]George Albert Cooke, A Text-book of North
Semitic Inscription (Oxford: At the Clarendon Press,
1903), p. 17.

[133]Henning Graf Reventlow, Gebot und Predigt im
Dekalog (Gerd Mohn: Gütersloher Verlagshaus, 1962),
p. 73.

[134]Johann J. Stamm and Maurice E. Andrew, The
Ten Commandments in Recent Research (London: SCM
Press, Ltd., 1967), p. 99.

[135]See Ludwig Köhler, "Der Dekalog," ThR, 1
(1929):182.

[136]English from New American Bible. Translated
by the Catholic Biblical Association. RSV does not
translate wehu.

[137]Friedrich Horst, "Recht und Religion im Bereich
des Alten Testaments," in Gottes Recht, Studien zum
Recht im Alten Testament (1961), pp. 260-91; Knierim,
"Hauptbegriffe," pp. 67-73.

[138]Liedke, Gestalt, p. 118.

[139]See Seitz, Studien, pp. 112, 168.

[140]Mayes, Deuteronomy, p. 286.

[141]A. Phillips, Ancient Israel's Criminal Law
(New York: Schocken Books, 1971), pp. 103-4.

[142]Liedke, Gestalt, p. 85.

[143]Boecker, Redeformen, p. 133.

[144]Hayes and Miller, History, p. 350.

[145]Whitelam, King.

[146]Hayes and Miller, History, p. 432.

[147]Nicholson, Deuteronomy, p. 10. See also,
Frank Moore Cross and David Noel Freedman, "Josiah's
Revolt against Assyria," JNES 12 (1953):56-8 and W.
H. Dubberstein, "Assyrian-Babylonian Chronology,"
JNES 3 (1944):38-46.

[148]Alt, "Gaue."

[149]See Childs, Exodus, p. 610 and Otto Kaiser,
Introduction to the Old Testament. A Presentation of
its Results and Problems, trans. John Study
(Minneapolis, MN.: Augsburg Publishing House, 1975).

[150]Paul F. Jacobs, "The Life Motif in Deuteronomy:
a study of its stylistic and redactional use," paper
presented at SBL Southwest Regional Meeting, Waco,
TX.: March, 1979.

[151]Buis, Deutéronome, p. 294.

[152]Johannes Hempel, Die Schichten des Deuteronomiums: ein Beitrag zur israelitischen Literatur-
und Rechtsgeschichte (Leipzig: R. Voigtländer, 1914),
p. 219.

[153]Steuernagel, Deuteronomium, p. 122.

[154]Von Rad, Deuteronomy, p. 90.

[155]L'Hour, "Legislation," p. 16.

[156]Daube, Studies, p. 111.

[157]Nicholson, Deuteronomy, p. 51.

[158] See N. M. Nicolsky, "Das Asylrecht in Israel," _ZAW_ 48 (1930):157-8 and John L. McKenzie, "The Elders in the Old Testament," _Bib_ 40 (1959):522-40.

[159] Rolf P. Knierim, "Exodus 18 and die Neuordnung der mosaischen Gerichtsbarkeit," _ZAW_ 73 (1961):146-71.

[160] Kurt Galling, _Die Bücher der Chronik_ (Göttingen: Vandenhoeck & Ruprecht, 1954) and Erhard Junge, _Der Wierderaufbau des Heerwesens des Reiches Juda unter Josia_ (Stuttgart: Kohlhammer Verlag, 1937).

[161] "Genre File of the Form Critical Project from the Institute of Antiquity and Christianity at the Claremont Graduate School," s.v. "Etiology," by Rolf P. Knierim and Gene M. Tucker.

[162] Is 1:21-6; Is 3:2ff; Is 3:14; Mi 3:1,2a,9-11; Dt 1:9-18; Dt 16:18ff, Dt 19:19ff.

[163] Mi 3:1.

[164] Junge, _Wiederaufbau_.

[165] Georg Christian Macholz, "Die Stellung des Königs in der israelitischen Gerichtsverfassung," _ZAW_ 84 (1972):157-82; "Zur Geschichte der Justiz-organization in Juda," _ZAW_ 84 (1972):314-40; L'Hour, "Legislation."

[166] See "Chart: City texts and L'Hour's _Législation criminelle_" below.

[167] Alt, "Origins," pp. 101-181.

[168] See "CHART: Comparison of Israelite apodictic law and Municipal case law" below.

[169] Von Rad, _Theology_, p. 264n.

[170] L'Hour, "Legislation," p. 8.

[171] L'Hour, "Legislation," pp. 15, 17 + n.

[172] L'Hour, "Legislation," p. 22 . . . *en ces matières si importantes, la cohésion même de la famille et de la cité était en jeu.*

[173] See "CHART: Comparison of L'Hour's *Legislation criminelle* with Merendino's list below of purge laws.

[174] Merendino, Gesetz, p. 400.

[175] Clark, "Law," p. 121.

[176] Alt, "Origins."

[177] Gerstenberger, Wesen.

[178] Seitz, Studien, p. 131.

[179] Lohfink, Hauptgebot, p. 104.

[180] See "CHART: *Une legislation criminelle* and the Covenant Code" below.

[181] Horst, "Privilegrecht," pp. 17-54.

[182] Lohfink, Hauptgebot.

[183] Macholz, "Stellung," p. 178.

[184] Ludwig Köhler, Hebrew Man (New York: Abingdon Press, 1956), p. 128.

[185] Thorkild Jacobsen, "Primitive Democracy in Ancient Mesopotamia," JNES 2 (1943):159-88.

[186] Anton Jirku, "Drei Fälle von Haftpflicht in altorientalischen Palästina-Syrien und Dt cap 21," ZAW 59 (1967):159-88.

[187]H. Gressmann, Altorientalische Texte und Bilder zum Alten Testament, vol. 1 (Berlin: W. de Gruyter, 1926), p. 154.

[188]Nougayrol, Palais, vol. 4, p. 154.

[189]Ibid., p. 146.

[190]Knierim, "Nature."

[191]L'Hour, "Legislation," pp. 27-8.

[192]Knierim, "Decalogue," p. 46.

[193]Knierim, "Decalogue," pp. 43-4.

[194]Knierim's argument that the Decalogue is addressed to *individual, adult males* finds more support among certain directives in the Decalogue than others. For example, Dt 5:21 supports his position. The prohibition reads: *Neither shall you covet your neighbor's wife,* and not *Neither shall you covet your neighbor's husband or wife.* However, if Dt 5:14 addresses only individual adult males, it is unusual that wives are not listed among those to whom the sabbath rest is extended: ... *the seventh day is a sabbath to the Lord your God; in it you shall not do any work, you [or your wife ?] or your son, or your daughter, or your manservant and your maidservant or your ox or your ass or any of your cattle, or the sojourner who is within your gates . . . .* It is not likely that the wife was expected to work on the sabbath if the servants and the cattle rest!

[195]Interpreter's Dictionary of the Bible, s.v. "Number, Numbering, Numbers," by M. H. Pope.

[196]Carmichael, Laws, p. 112.

[197]Mayes, Deuteronomy, p. 285. See: Moshe Greenberg, "The Biblical Concept of Asylum," JBL 78 (1959):125-32.

[198]Von Rad, Deuteronomy, p. 11.

[199]So Seitz, Studien, pp. 225-7; Phillips, Law, pp. 101-2.

[200]L'Hour, "Legislation," p. 5.

[201]The use of this example involving trees is interesting. In Dt 20:19-20, there is a law against cutting trees during a siege. The legislators were interested in trees.

[202]Von Rad, Deuteronomium, p. 38; von Rad, Deuteronomy, p. 51. Gottwald, Tribes, p. 53 identifies Ju 10:1-2+ 3-5; 12:7, 8-10, 11-12, 13-5 as notations, brief analistic notes. S. Mittmann, Deuteronomium 1:1--6:3 literarkritisch und traditionsgeschichtlich untersucht (Berlin: DeGruyter, 1975); 130-1 identifies Dt 4:41-3 as ein Kurzbericht or ein knapper Bericht. So also Craigie, Deuteronomy, p. 144. Hayes and Miller, History, p. 491 identify Ez 1:9-11a as a notice.

[203]Ju 1:16-17 are examples of reports.

[204]Mittmann, Deuteronomium, p. 129 calls Dt 4:41 a Situationshinweis.

[205]Carmichael, Laws, p. 111.

[206]Mayes, Deuteronomy, p. 159. See Aharoni, Land, pp. 308, 375, 383, and Nelson Glueck, "Ramoth-Gilead," BASOR 92 (1943):10-16.

[207]Kenyon, Cities, pp. 54-5.

[208]Mayes, Deuteronomy, p. 159. Henri Cazelles, Deutéronome (Paris: Les Editions du Cerf, 1950), p. 816 considers Dt 4:41-3 a Yahwist or Elohist tradition joined to Dt 4:1-10 when Deuteronomy was separated from the Deuteronomist's History and joined to Gn--Nm. Steuernagel, Deuteronomium, p. 69 considers the Priests' Tradition (P) responsible for joining the Deuteronomist's History to Gn--Nm and for composing

Dt 4:41-3. Buis, Deutéronome, p. 103 agrees, but considers Dt 4:41-3 a misplaced section of Nm 32. Noth, Studien, pp. 189 + 195-6 after comparing Nm 35; Dt 19; Js 20 and Dt 4:41-3 concludes that all share a common Deuteronomic tradition. Seitz, Studien, p. 27 agrees.

[209]Driver, Deuteronomy, p. 78. Weinfeld, Deuteronomy, p. 237n, for example, considers *set apart (bdl)* a word indicative of the secular trends of Deuteronomy. A priestly text would have used *make holy (qds)* to indicate how Moses designated certain cities.

[210]Noth, Studien, pp. 27-87 assigns the following material to the Deuteronomist: 1:1--3:29; 4:1-2, 5-8, 10-14, 22-23a, 25-28.

[211]Mittmann, Deuteronomium, p. 6 returns to an earlier position argued by Alt that originally Deuteronomy began at Dt 6:4. (See Alt, Schriften, vol. 2, p. 253n) Mittmann considers Dt 1:1--6:3 to be an introduction to both the code of Deuteronomy, and the Deuteronomist's History.

[212]Driver, Deuteronomy, 78-79, and Carmichael, Laws, pp. 110-13.

[213]Driver, Deuteronomy, p. 78.

[214]Carmichael, Laws, p. 111.

[215]Von Rad, Deuteronomy, p. 51.

[216]See Seitz, Studien, p. 27.

[217]Mittmann, Deuteronomium, p. 130.

[218]Seitz, Studien, p. 33. Buis, Deutéronome, p. 102 also considers Dt 4:41-49 a single unit, identified as *Introduction d'un discours*.

[219]So Craigie, Deuteronomy, p. 145.

[220]The New American Bible translation of Dt 1:46

shows the causality needed here: *That is why you had to stay as long as you did at Kadesh.*

[221]Brueggemann, Land, pp. 69-70.

[222]Achtmeier, Deuteronomy, p. 29.

[223]Interpreter's Dictionary of the Bible, Supplementary Vol., s.v. "Inheritance in the NT," by P. L. Hammer.

[224]Harold O. Forshey, "The Hebrew Root NHL and its Semitic Cognates" (Ph.D. dissertation, Harvard, 1973).

[225]Frick, City, pp. 111-13.

[226]Von Rad, Deuteronomy, p. 131. So, also, Driver, Deuteronomy, p. 236; Bächli, Israel, pp. 92-3; Weinfeld, Deuteronomy, p. 167; Seitz, Studien, p. 159; Carmichael, Laws, p. 130; Craigie, Deuteronomy, p. 271; and Mayes, Deuteronomy, p. 293.

[227]Von Rad, Studies, pp. 45 ff. and Der Heilige Krieg im alten Israel (Zurich: Zwingli Verlag, 1958), pp. 68 ff.

[228]Von Rad, Deuteronomy, pp. 132-3.

[229]Alt, "Origins," p. 112. So, Liedke, Gestalt, pp. 31-4.

[230]So, Jirku, Recht, p. 37, and Gilmer, Form, p. 3.

[231]Mayes, Deuteronomy, p. 293.

[232]Carmichael, Laws, p. 34.

[233]Craigie, Deuteronomy, p. 270; Buis, Deutéronome, p. 300; Von Rad, Deuteronomy, p. 131.

234Pritchard, Texts, p. 240.

235Ibid., 276.

236Harold H. Nelson and Uvo Holscher, Medinet Habu Reports (Chicago: University of Chicago Press, 1931), p. 32.

237Craigie, Deuteronomy, pp. 276-77.

238So Craigie, Deuteronomy, p. 277n.

239Von Rad, Deuteronomy, p. 131.

240Blenkinsopp, "Traces," p. 209.

241Von Rad, Deuteronomy, p. 133.

242Fritz Stolz, Jahwes and Israels Kriege (Zurich: Theologischer Verlag, 1972), p. 27.

243Buis, Deutéronome, pp. 300-1.

244Negotiations also appear in Js 11:19, 2 S 10:19 and 2 K 18:19.

245Carmichael, Laws, pp. 130-1 considers the laws in Dt 12--26 organized according to the narrative material in Dt 1--4, but he is careful to point out that Moses did not deal precisely according to the stipulation in Dt 20:10-20.

246Nicholson, Deuteronomy, p. 52.

247Von Rad, Deuteronomy, pp. 24-26.

248Because he sets Dt 20:1-20 in the Mosaic period, Craigie, Deuteronomy, pp. 270-1, considers this idealism due to Israel's lack of experience. Once the grim realities of war and the cost of battle had matured Israel, she would no longer think of war in such sweeping generalities.

[249]Buis, Deutéronome, p. 301.

[250]Carmichael, Laws, pp. 118-33. Carmichael's use of the *rest* motif here emphasizes the conviction he shares with Weinfeld, Deuteronomy, p. 33, that Deuteronomy has significant connections with the wisdom tradition in Israel.

[251]Bächli, Israel, pp. 11-14, & 94.

[252]Mayes, Deuteronomy, pp. 293-7.

[253]The use of *'ām* for both *army* (Dt 20:1) and *nation* (Dt 28:32) appears in the Hebrew Bible and the Qumran literature. See, for example, von Rad, Krieg, pp. 70ff and Gottwald, Tribes, pp. 241-2.

[254]See "CHART" Applications of *the ban (herem)* in Deuteronomy" below.

[255]Von Rad, Deuteronomy, pp. 132-3. So also, Carmichael, Laws, p. 131.

256

[257]Bächli, Israel.

[258]Driver, Deuteronomy, p. 241; Mayes, Deuteronomy, p. 277; Seitz, Studien, p. 115, and Liedke, Gestalt, p. 21.

[259]So von Rad, Deuteronomy, p. 135 who defines the unit as *instructions regarding the ritual to be observed in the event of a murder by an unknown hand* . . . .

[260]Seitz, Studien, p. 116.

[261]David Daube, "To be Found Doing Wrong," in Studi in onore di Volterra, vol. 2 (Rome, 1961), pp. 3-12.

[262]Carmichael, Laws, pp. 46-7.

[263]Schulz, Todesrecht.

[264]G. R. Driver, "Three Notes," VT 2 (1952): 356-7.

[265]Merendino, Gesetz, p. 238.

[266]Carmichael, Laws, pp. 261-2.

[267]Pritchard, Texts, s.v. "Code of Hammurabi, sections 23-4," p. 167.

[268]John Gray, The Legacy of Canaan (Leiden: E. J. Brill, 1957), pp. 122 & 241.

[269]Cyrus Gordon, "Biblical Customs and the Nuzu Tablets," in The Biblical Archeologist Reader, vol. 2, ed. David Noel Freedman and E. F. Campbell (1964), p. 31.

[270]Cyrus Gordon, "An Akkadian Parallel to Deuteronomy 21:1ff," RA 33 (1936): 1-6 and Harry A. Hoffner, "Some Contributions of Hittitology to Old Testament Study," TB 20 (1969):39.

[271]H. J. Elhorst, "Eine verkannte Zauberhandlung (Dtn 21,1-9)," ZAW 39 (1921):64.

[272]So von Rad, Deuteronomy, p. 135.

[273]Buis, Deutéronome, p. 308.

[274]So, for example: Alexander Roifer, "The Breaking of the Heifer's Neck," Tarbiz 31 (1961):119-43; von Rad, Deuteronomy, pp. 135-7; Buis, Deutéronome, pp. 307-9; Seitz, Studien, pp. 115-17; Weinfeld, Deuteronomy, p. 211n; H. McKeating, "The Development of the Law on Homicide in Ancient Israel," VT 25 (1975):46-68; Mayes, Deuteronomy, pp. 297-8.

[275]Driver and Miles, Babylonian Laws, p. 316.

[276]Carmichael, Laws, p. 129.

[277]Driver and Miles, Babylonian Laws, p. 317.

[278]Daube, Studien, p. 101. Phillips, Law, p. 34, on the other hand, admits that only the defendant can be prosecuted, but still considers the humanity responsible!

[279]For example, Alfred Bertholet, Deuteronomium (Berlin: Evangelische Verlangsanstalt, 1956), p. 64; Steuernagel, Deuteronomium, p. 128. But also, Ziony Zevit, "The EGLA ritual of Dt 21:1-9," JBL (1976):377-90, who argues that Deuteronomy changes the ritual from sacrifice to symbol to keep from contradicting the restriction of all sacrifice to a single sanctuary.

[280]Weinfeld, Deuteronomy, pp. 210-11 summarizes the most frequently listed difficulties, and points out that although the site of the ritual in Dt 21:1-9 is not a sanctuary, that does not prohibit the ritual from being a sacrifice. In Nm 19, a genuine sacrifice is offered outside a sanctuary.

[281]Seitz, Studien, p. 115 that neither in Ex 13:13; 34:20 where the neck of an ass is broken, nor in Is 66:3 where the neck of a dog is broken, is break ('rp) a liturgical term.

[282]Weinfeld, Deuteronomy, pp. 210-11.

[283]Hans Joachim Boecker, Redeformen des Rechtslebens im Alten Testament, 2nd ed. (Neukirchen: Neukirchener Verlag, 1970), pp. 124-4.

[284]Mayes, Deuteronomy, p. 299 says the animal is killed to guarantee it will not wander back into the community and thus contaminate it all over again.

[285]Phillips, Law, pp. 11-12.

[286] E. F.Weidner, "Der Staatsvertrag Assurniraris VI von Assyrien mit Mati'ilu von Bit Agusi, *AfO* 8 (1932-3):17-27.

[287] McKeating, "Development," p. 62.

[288] Merendino, *Gesetz*, p. 245, reconstructs this law from Dt 21:18-21a. Schulz, *Todesrecht*, p. 51, argues that no such law ever existed!

[289] Von Rad, *Deuteronomy*, p. 138, identifies Dt 21:18-21 as a rule. Buis, *Deutéronome*, p. 304, and Craigie, *Deuteronomy*, p. 277, calls Dt 21:18-21 law (*loi*). Liedke, *Gestalt*, p. 21, and Seitz, *Studien*, p. 118, specify that it is case law (*ein kasuistischer Rechtssatz*) to which two formulas have been added (*Über die kasuistische Form des Gesetzes besteht kein Zweifel. Lediglich am Ende begegnen wieder zwei formelhafte Zusätze.*) For Merendino, Dt 21:18-21 *Gesetz*, p. 402, Dt 21:18-21 is a purge law (*bi'arta Gesetz*).

[290] See "Chart comparing Dt 21:18-21 with Ex 21:15 and Ex 21:17," below.

[291] Boecker, *Redeformen*, p. 90.

[292] CH 169:25-31. See *Babylonian Laws*, p. 348.

[293] Boecker, *Redeformen*, p. 107n.

[294] Ibid., p. 75n.

[295] So, for example, Buis, *Deutéronome*, p. 312: *la deposition des parents et un exemple de ce qu'ils peuvent dire.* Boecker, *Redeformen*, p. 75, identifies Dt 21:20a as *die Formulierung du Anklage.*

[296] So Mayes, *Deuteronomy*, p. 305.

[297] So Phillips, *Law*, p. 24. The analysis of the relationship of these two terms for *stoning* made by Boecker, *Redeformen*, pp. 148-9 argues that *saqal* means only to stone an animal, and that *ragam* is rare

because it was replaced by *môt yûmat* which implies stoning a human being. Liedke, Gestalt, pp. 49-53 points out the specific limitations of Boecker's argument.

[298]Schulz, Todesrecht, pp. 83-4.

[299]C. U. Wolf, "Traces of Primitive Democracy in Ancient Israel," JNES 6 (1947):99.

[300]E. A. Speiser, "'Coming' and 'Going' at the 'City' Gate," in Oriental and Biblical Studies. Collected Writings of E. A. Speiser, ed. J. J. Finkelstein and Moshe Greenberg (Philadelphia: University of Pennsylvania Press, 1967), pp. 83-8 and G. Evans, "'Coming' and 'Going' at the City Gate—a Discussion of Professor Speiser's Paper," BASOR 150 (1958):28-33.

[301]McKenzie, "Elders."

[302]Weinfeld, Deuteronomy, pp. 80-1.

[303]McCarthy, Treaty, pp. 222, 279n, 288.

[304]F. Willesen, "Die Eselsöhne von Sichem als Bundesgenossen," VT 4 (1954):216-17.

[305]CH 192. See Babylonian Laws, p. 403.

[306]Mayes, Deuteronomy, p. 305.

[307]Boecker, Redeformen, p. 75n.

[308]Von Rad, Deuteronomy, p. 138. So, also, Buis, Deutéronome, p. 311; Liedke, Gestalt, p. 40.

[309]Whitelam, King, p. 42. See, also, J. Salmon, "Judicial Authority in Early Israel: An Historical Investigation of Old Testament Institutions" (Th.D. dissertation, Princeton Theological Seminary, 1968).

[310]Elizabeth Bellefontaine, "Deuteronomy 21:18-21: Reviewing the Case of the Rebellious Son," JSOT 13 (1979):13-31.

[311]Bellefontaine cites the following social scientists: M. Gluckmann, Politics, Law and Ritual in Tribal Society (Oxford: Basil Blackwell, 1965); E. R. Service, Origins of the State and Civilization (New York: W. W. Norton, 1975); A. R. Radcliffe-Brown, Preface to African Political Systems, eds. M. Fortes and E. E. Evans-Pritchard (London: Oxford University Press, 1970); K. N. Llewellyn and E. Adamson Hoebel, The Cheyenne Way: Conflict and Case Law in Primitive Jurisprudence (Norman, OK.: University of Oklahoma Press, 1941); and Ralph M. Linton, The Study of Man (New York: Century Press, 1936).

[312]Weinfeld, Deuteronomy, p. 303. So, also, Driver, Deuteronomy, p. 248, and Craigie, Deuteronomy, p. 284.

[313]Merendino, Gesetz, p. 337. Weinfeld, Deuteronomy, p. 241 also considers Dt 21:18-21 a moral development of Ex 21:15.

[314]Hans Schmidt, "Mose und der Dekalog," in Eucharisterion. Studien zur Religion und Literatur des Alten and Neuen Testaments. Hermann Gunkel zum 60. Geburtstage, vol. 1, ed. Hans Schmidt (Göttingen: Vandenhoeck & Ruprecht, 1923), pp. 78-119.

[315]Reventlow, Gebot, pp. 64-5.

[316]Plöger, Untersuchungen, pp. 91-5. So also Stamm, Commandments, pp. 95-8.

[317]J. Gamberoni, "Das Elterngebot im Alten Testament," BZ 8 (1964):161-90.

[318]Liedke, Gestalt, p. 21, identifies Dt 22:13-21 as case law (kasuistische Rechtssatz); Seitz, Studien, p. 119 agrees (kasuistische Gesetz). Because it deals with a capital offense, presumes an urban context and concludes with the purge formula, L'Hour, "Legislation,"

p. 23, considers Dt 22:13-21 a purge law. Merendino, Gesetz, pp. 257-9 considers Dt 22:20 a case law (*Rechtssatz*) and refers to Dt 22:13-21 in his reconstruction of the Ur-text as marriage law (*Eherecht*), but never identifies the genre of the canonical passage. Von Rad, Deuteronomy, p. 141, calls Dt 22:13-21 an *ordinance*.

[319]Liedke, Gestalt, p. 35.

[320]Seitz, Studien, p. 119.

[321]See "CHART: Diagram of consecutive chain of verbs in Dt 22:13-19," below.

[322]CH 142-3. See Babylonian Laws, p. 299.

[323]Weinfeld, Deuteronomy, p. 292n.

[324]Seitz, Studien, p. 119, identifies Dt 22:14b as a *citation of the complaint (ein Zitat der Anklage)*. Boecker, Redeformen, p. 77, calls it *a carefully worded complaint (eine wörtliche formulierte Anklagrede)*. Boecker, Redeformen, pp. 71-94 gives full treatment to the genre *complaint Anklagereden)*.

[325]See "CHART: Comparison of Dt 22:15-17 with Dt 21:19-21," below.

[326]August Knobel, Die Bücher Numeri, Deuteronomium and Josua (Leipzig: S. Hirzel, 1861) reviews the literature on the Ancient Near Eastern practice of the tokens of virginity. See, also, Theological Dictionary of the Old Testament, s.v. *"betûlîm,"* by M. Tsevat.

[327]See Pritchard, Texts, #181; The Assyrian Laws, eds. G. R. Driver and John C. Miles (Oxford: At the Clarendon Press, 1952), pp. 18-19, 68; Babylonian Laws, pp. 275-83.

[328]Mayes, Deuteronomy, p. 310.

[329]See Assyrian Laws and Babylonian Laws.
Flogging is the only penalty in the Babylonian laws;
in the Middle Assyrian laws both flogging and
damages appear. Carmichael, Laws, p. 236, argues
that Dt 25:1-3 which allows flogging to be required
by a municipal court was developed from Dt 22:13-21.
However, Carmichael does not explain why Dt 25:1-3
used a different word for flogging than Dt 22:13-21.

[330]So, for example, Driver, Deuteronomy, p. 256
who cites Josephus, Antiquities 4:8,23 as his source;
Craigie, Deuteronomy, p. 293; Phillips, Law, p. 115;
Weinfeld, Deuteronomy, p. 293n., and von Rad,
Deuteronomy, p. 142.

[331]Liedke, Gestalt, pp. 44-5.

[332]David Daube, "The Culture of Deuteronomy,"
Orita (Ibadan) 3 (1969):41-3.

[333]Gerstenberger, Wesen.

[334]Phillips, Law, p. 113; and Carmichael, Laws,
pp. 46-7.

[335]L'Hour, "Legislation," p. 23.

[336]Merendino, Gesetz, p. 259.

[337]Liedke, Gestalt, pp. 31-4.

[338]Pedersen, Israel, vols. 1-2, p. 428 argues
that stoning prevented the victim from being interred
in the family tomb. Köhler, Man, p. 112 is of the
same opinion. Julian Morgenstern, "The Book of
the Covenant, Part II," HUCA, 7 (1930):146 + 196
claims that stoning prevents the executioners from
becoming ritually unclean. See Seitz, Studien, p. 125n.

[339]Weinfeld, Deuteronomy, p. 188.

[340]CH 137-49. See Babylonian Laws, pp. 290-306.

283

[341]Lipit-Isthar 33. See Miguel Civil, "Lipit-Ishtar," _AS_ (1962):4. CH 127. See _Babylonian Laws_.

[342]Noth, _System_, pp. 104-106.

[343]Mayes, _Deuteronomy_, p. 309; Phillips, _Law_, p. 19.

[344]

[345]Charles Mabee, "The Problem of Setting in Hebrew Royal Judicial Narrative" (Ph.D. dissertation: Claremont Graduate School, 1977), p. 28.

[346]Merendino, _Gesetz_, pp. 257 + 271; Phillips, _Law_, p. 155. So, also, Buis, _Deutéronome_, p. 316; _Ce groupe de lois est centre sur la repression de l'adultere._

[347]Mayes, _Deuteronomy_, p. 309; Craigie, _Deuteronomy_, p. 293n.

[348]According to Phillips, _Law_, p. 133, the injunction in Dt 22:19b prevents the accused wife from the humiliation of living an unmarried life and also keeps her husband from passing her off as a virgin to another unsuspecting husband!

[349]According to Weinfeld, _Deuteronomy_, pp. 305-6, Dt 21:18-21 and Dt 22:13-21 stress the educational role of the father. Buis, _Deutéronome_, p. 317, on the other hand, emphasizes that the father's role in this instruction is legal (. . . _toute la procédure est conduite par son père, qui était son responsable légal avant la mariage.)._

[350]Fitzgerald, "Background." See Am 5:2;. Je 18:13; Je 31:4,21, for example.

[351]Although there is a technical quality to both terms, neither is exclusively technical, not even very precisely defined. See G. J. Wenham, _Bethulah--a girl of marriageable age_," _VT_ 22 (1972):326-48; _Interpreter's Dictionary of the Bible_, s.v. "Virgin,"

by O. J. Baab and the translation of the Septuagint
here: επι παρθενον Ισραηλιτιν, which simply means *upon an
Israelite virgin* (Septuaginta, vol. 3 Deuteronomium,
ed. John W. Wevers (Göttingen: Vandenhoeck &
Ruprecht, 1977). See also Anthony Phillips,
"NEBALAH--a term for serious disorderly and unruly conduct," VT 25 (1975):237-42, and von Rad, Deuteronomy,
p. 142.

[352]L'Hour, "Législation," p. 23, for example.
Seitz, Studien, p. 120, calls Dt 22:23-7 *a regulation
(eine gesetzliche Regelung)* even though he treats it
in the chapter dealing with *laws (die Gesetze)*.

[353]See "CHART: Diagram of the consecutive verb
chains in Dt 22:23-7," below.

[354]Carl Brockelman, Hebräische Syntax (Neukirchen: Neukirchener Verlag, 1956), #135.

[355]Liedke, Gestalt, pp. 38-9.

[356]Merendino, Gesetz, p. 262; *The apositive in
Dt 22:23 is superfluous. (So ist die Apposition nach
v. 23 überflüssig).*

[357]Wolff, Hosea, p. 52.

[358]Seitz, Studien, p. 120.

[359]Babylonian Laws, p. 282. In Middle Assyrian
Law #12, the case deals with a woman's cry for help in
the city that went unanswered. See Pritchard, Texts,
p. 181.

[360]Pritchard, Texts, p. 196.

[361]Ibid., p. 162.

[362]Merendino, Gesetz, p. 263.

[363]Seitz, Studien, p. 120.

[364] Phillips, Law, p. 110.

[365] Theologisches Handwörterbuch zum Alten Testament, s.v. "ṣāʾaq," R. Albertz.

[366] Von Rad, Deuteronomy, p. 142.

[367] Liedke, Gestalt, p. 35.

[368] Mayes, Deuteronomy, p. 328. Merendino, Gesetz, p. 318, identifies Dt 25:5-10 as law (Gesetz); Seitz, Studien, p. 124, and Liedke, Gestalt, p. 21, as case law (Rechtssatz).

[369] See de Vaux, Israel, pp. 37 ff., Gray, Legacy, p. 271, discusses the same root in Ugaritic.

[370] Seitz, Studien, p. 124.

[371] Driver, Deuteronomy, p. 282.

[372] Gottwald, Tribes, pp. 303-4. See also, pp. 298-315.

[373] Merendino, Gesetz, p. 319.

[374] Mayes, Deuteronomy, p. 328.

[375] So von Rad, Deuteronomy, p. 155, and Driver, Deuteronomy, p. 285.

[376] H. M. Snaith, "The Daughters of Zelophehad, Deut 25:5-10," VT 16 (1966):124-7; Pritchard, Texts, p. 182: #30-1, 33; Assyrian Laws, pp. 240ff.

[377] Seitz, Studien, p. 125.

[378] See "CHART: Comparison of Dt 25:6b with Dt 25:10" below.

[379] Cooke, Text-Book, p. 197ff.

^{380}Boecker, Gestalt, pp. 163-4.

^{381}Köhler, Man.

^{382}Boecker, Gestalt, p. 16.

^{383}See "CHART: Comparison of Dt 25:7 with Dt 25:9" below.

^{384}See also Jb 30:10 and Is 50:6.

^{385}See Maurice H. Farbridge, Studies in Biblical and Semitic Symbolism (New York: E. P. Dutton, 1923), p. 274, and Karl H. Rengstorf, Die Re-Investitur des verlorenen Sohnes in der Gleichniserzählung Jesu Luk 15, 11-32 (Köln, Opladen: Westdeutscher Verlag, 1967), pp. 46ff.

^{386}So Mayes, Deuteronomy, p. 329; Theodor H. Gaster, Myth, Legend and Custom in the Old Testament (New York: Harper and Row Publishers, 1975), p. 447; Driver, Deuteronomy, p. 283.

^{387}H. H. Rowley, Worship in Ancient Israel: its form and meaning (London: SPCK, 1967), p. 135.

^{388}Mayes, Deuteronomy, p. 328.

CHAPTER IV

CONCLUSIONS

Chapter I: Introduction

In the Ancient Near East, the city is a community whose members live in a single complex of buildings surrounded by a wall. Less than half the community produces enough food for everyone, so trades and arts --such as writing--flourish. In some cities the government is feudal; in others it is retribalized. A single landowner (*ḥazannu*) governs a feudal city; all the other citizens (*ḥopshu*) work for him. Feudal cities enjoy a strong surplus economy and control much more territory than the community needs for its own survival. The most important social institution in a feudal city is liturgy which maintains the divine right of the king to govern and educates the people in their role as his obedient servants. The retribalized city is self-governing. Its subsistence economy controls little territory beyond that needed for farms, pastures, orchards and timberlands. The most important social institution in retribalized cities is the judicial system which uses an elaborate process of arbitration to teach its citizens how to maintain their own independence and to prevent their differences from destroying the community.

From the very beginning, Israel was an alliance, not only of tent and village communities, but of cities as well. Therefore, the first cities in Israel were not the feudal cities conquered during the 10th century BCE by the imperial armies of David, but rather the retribalized cities like Gibeon, Shechem, Shiloh and Hebron converted to Israel's self-governing way of life during the 13th century BCE.

Deuteronomy 4:41--26:19 is the nucleus of Israel's canon and it contains more than one urban tradition. For example, there is a major urban tradition characterized by the place (*māqôm*) formula and a concern for the capital city of Jerusalem which has been regularly studied. *Deuteronomy and City Life*, on the other hand, studies the urban tradition developed by the retribalized cities of the 13th century BCE. This tradition is characterized by the word *city* (*'îr*) and a concern, not only for Jerusalem, but for the other cities of Israel as well. The tradition of the retribalized cities reflects those aspects of city life which played important roles in the foundation of Israel during the 13th century BCE, as well as in the control of the Hebrew monarchy during the 10th century BCE and the centralization of the liturgy during the Deuteronomic reform in the 7th century BCE.

During the monarchy, the tradition of the retribalized cities continued to stress the simplicity and equality of a retribalized way of life, while the tradition of the monarchy spoke of Israel in more and more feudal terms to guarantee the uniqueness and supremacy of Jerusalem and the king. The Deuteronomic reformers used the tradition of the retribalized cities as part of their rationale for centralizing the liturgy. The reform argued that liturgical centralization did not deprive the outlying cities of Judah of their status as Yahwist communities. They still enjoyed the prerogatives of the retribalized cities who were corporate members of early Israel. The Yahwist character of the city of Jerusalem was liturgical; the Yahwist character of the remaining cities of Judah was legal.

This tradition of the retribalized cities makes no claim to be the exclusive interpretation of Israel's identity as the people of Yahweh. It neither affirms nor denies the validity of the traditions of the tent and village communities on the one hand, nor the feudal cities of the Israelite kings on the other. However, the tradition of the retribalized cities clearly considers it possible to be both thoroughly urban and at the same time authentically Yahwist, because it considers the city as Israel's inheritance (*naḥalâ*) and therefore a model of the Yahwist way of life.

Chapter II: Review of Scholarship

According to 18th century CE Romanticism, the ideal human society was nomadic. Settled life was decadent and cities were the most decadent examples of settled life. Inevitably, nomadic societies age, settle down and decay. Israel was an example of an ideal, and therefore nomadic, society overwhelming an urban, and therefore a decadent, society in Canaan.

Since 1950, one social scientist after the other has repealed the nomadic ideal. Nomads move out of cities, not into them; and nomadic societies are far from ideal. Some nomads are non-conformists fleeing persecution, but most are fugitives from justice and victims of collapsing urban economies. In any case, it was not until after the appearance of Israel in the 13th century BCE that the domestication of the camel in the 10th century BCE allowed these urban refugees to flee into the deep deserts to form the earliest nomadic societies in the Ancient Near East. Therefore, Israel is an example of the ideal settled life, not of the ideal nomadic life.

It is the mobile elements of a settled society which are most idealistic. Some of idealists are itinerant; others migrate to found new settlements. Itinerants move in order to work--soldiers (*'apiru*) go off to war, herders (*Shoshu*) to pastures. Successful cities send out expeditions to exploit or to settle new territory. Egypt exploited Canaan from the south, but it was Mesopotamia sending in expeditions from the north which founded the cities of Canaan.

Specialization and trade are keys to settled life. Specialists in the same community must trade with one another to meet their basic needs; cities must trade with one another to acquire luxuries. The exploitation of one group by another leads to revolution; the exploitation of one city by another leads to war. In the Ancient Near East revolution and war destroy cities, nomads do not.

Israel was a revolution by the segments of Canaan's urban society, which were being exploited by their fellow citizens to create a surplus economy. Thus it is the exploitation of one group of citizens in Jerusalem by another that Jeremiah condemns, and not the eccentric nomadic lifestyle of the Rechabites which he celebrates (Jr 35). For a short period of time Israel restored an idealistic subsistence economy in Canaan.

Literary critics deferred to the nomadic ideal longer than social scientists. Nonetheless they implicitly acknowledged the urban character of early Israel by the models they used to analyze the forms and settings of the literature in the Hebrew Bible, especially Deuteronomy. Genres such as covenant, law and parenesis; settings such as liturgy, monarchy,

prophecy and wisdom have clearly urban origins.
Covenants, for example, are treaties between major
metropolitan cities *(mothers)* and their urban
colonies *(daughters)*. Law is the instrument by which
cities protect and govern their citizens. *Liturgy*
is the expression of a city's relationship with her
god-husband, who guarantees the fertility of her land.

Thus the nomadic ideal is too simple; it distorts
both the established social conditions in Canaan
during the 13th century BCE and the development which
Israel represents. Feudalism brought prosperity to
Canaan, but it also brought slavery. Among the
victims of feudal oppression were ancient cities like
Gibeon, Shechem, Shiloh and Hebron. When Israel re-
dedicated herself to a simpler and more self
determining way of life, converts from every oppressed
level of Canaanite society appeared. Retribalized
cities were among the converts. Each convert had a
special story telling how its encounter with Yahweh
had set it free; and each renewed the structures of
its common life to reflect the commitment it made
upon joining Israel to protect that freedom. The traditions of the tent and village Yahwists from the 13th
century BCE as well as the traditions of the royal
cities of David and Solomon from the 10th century BCE
have been generously studied; the traditions of the
Yahwists living in retribalized cities during the 13th
century BCE have not.

Chapter III: The City Texts

As a form critical study, *Deuteronomy and City
Life* is interested not only in what life in a retribalized city was like, but also why its citizens
considered their life style particularly Yahwist.

Deuteronomy 6:10-19

Deuteronomy 8:7-10 catalogues the natural resources of Canaan. Deuteronomy 6:10-11a, on the other
hand, catalogues the human improvements which made
settled life in Canaan possible; safe places to live
(cities); things to eat *(barns full of goods)*; water
to drink *(cisterns)*; raw materials to manufacture for
trade *(vines and olive trees)*. These were essentials

for an urban economy. To provide these amenities for themselves, feudal kings enslaved their populations (Ex 1:11). The feudal city is a sweat shop (*house of bondage* Dt 6:12); the retribalized city, on the other hand, is an oasis in the desert where *you eat and are full* (Dt 6:11b). Retribalized cities are not manmade (Dt 6:10-11), they are *great and godly* which is the trademark of Yahweh carried by the cosmos and the exodus as well. Retribalized cities are the property of Yahweh, leased to Israel (Dt 6:10), but with clear deed restrictions (Dt 6:13-14) allowing her to enjoy, but not to exploit city life.

As communities organized by consent rather than coercion, retribalized cities developed various forms of persuasive literature such as parenesis and legal instruction. Each parenesis in Dt 6:12-19 combines directives which cite commands (Dt 6:13,17) and prohibitions (Dt 6:14,16) with motivations such as gratitude (Dt 6:12), fear (Dt 6:15) and materialism (Dt 6:18) to remove whatever objections these Yahwists living in cities had to simply enjoy their inheritance. The parenesis encourages these Yahwists not to exploit city life by shifting from a retribalized to a feudal economy.

Deuteronomy 13:13-19

Deuteronomy 13:13-19 is one of eight legal instructions in Dt 4:41--26:19 based on traditions developed in the retribalized cities. Legal instruction is a genre which combines citation of the law and a commentary. The citation may be direct or paraphrased. The commentary contains definitions of technical terms, explanations of legal procedures, examples of testimony, specifications and parenesis. The commentary uses both second and third person verb forms. Municipal courts in the retribalized cities developed legal instruction; other teaching institutions, like the households, royal courts and sanctuaries, eventually adopted it. The municipal courts used legal instruction to prepare citizens to serve as witnesses and members of the jury; other teaching institutions used legal instruction to introduce citizens to their public responsibilities or the ramifications of social reforms.

Deuteronomy 13:13-19 tells how to settle major

landlord-tenant disputes. The wealth and power of feudal cities often tempted ambitious citizens (*base fellows* Dt 13:13) to exploit their neighbors, thus destroying the retribalized way of life and violating the deed restrictions set by Yahweh on Israel's enjoyment of the city (Dt 6:13-14). An inquest is to be made of reported (*If you hear* Dt 13:13) violations. There is to be a pre-trial hearing (*you shall inquire* Dt 13:15), a formal study of the evidence to uncover any pertinent information necessary to rule in the matter (*and make search* Dt 13:15), and finally an examination carried out for the purpose of exposing the weaknesses of the report (*and ask diligently* Dt 13:15). If the findings show (*it is true* Dt 13:15) that Yahweh's property is being used for purposes other than those intended, the city is interdicted (*it shall not be built again* Dt 13:16). Deuteronomy 13:13-19 is not an instruction on holocaust or holy war, but on the legal process by which the lease on a retribalized city can be cancelled and the city and its goods returned to Yahweh, its owner.

In the 7th century BCE, the Deuteronomic reformers used Dt 13:13-19 to indict the ancient cities, along with the prophets (Dt 13:1-5) and the leading families in Judah (Dt 13:7-12) who opposed the efforts of the monarchy to impose feudalism on Judah. By indicting the ancient cities for not participating in the royal program of centralization, which prohibited additional sanctuaries (*other gods* Dt 13:13) to Yahweh outside Jerusalem, the reformers placed the blame for the destruction of Jerusalem on their opponents.

Deuteronomy 19:1-13

Any three retribalized cities could make a treaty with one another and form an urban league. Deuteronomy 19:1-13 is a legal instruction on two institutions which these treaties made possible: the right of a citizen to a change of venue (*who by fleeing there may save his life* Dt 19:4) and the extradition of criminals from one city to another (*send and fetch him from there and hand him over* Dt 19:12). The instruction points out that unless the use of these two institutions is coordinated culpable killing (*innocent blood* Dt 19:10) will destroy the league. Deuteronomy 19:1-13 is a part of a larger discussion of just how deceiving legal appearance can be. Just as fortune tellers, soothsayers, charmers, diviners and casters of spells can appear to be prophets (Dt 18:9-22), and squatters can appear to be property owners (Dt 19:4), the execution of a killer connected only with accidental death can appear to be justice; in reality the execution is murder (Dt 19:1-13).

Deuteronomy 19:1-13 demonstrates the sophistication of the judicial system in these retribalized cities by the way it distinguishes homicide due to the accidental and non-culpable nature of the circumstances from murder (Dt 19:5-6). The instruction provides three other insights into the social structure of the retribalized city. First, the citizens of retribalized cities are legally related to one another as *neighbors* (Dt 19:4). Second the *forest* (Dt 19:5) is as important a part of the urban economy as the *cities, barns, cisterns, vines and olive trees* catalogued in Dt 6:10-11. And third, although the neighbors live together inside the wall, they go outside the wall to make their livings.

Deuteronomy 4:41-3

Ancient Israel honored Moses as the architect of her way of life by connecting all her important social institutions with him. Accordingly Moses inaugurates the first retribalized cities (Dt 4:41). Retribalized cities are not conquered like those of Sihon and Og (Dt 4:46-9); they are acquired by treaty (*set apart* Dt 4:41). Kings build feudal cities to garrison troops (1 K 9:19) and to collect taxes (Gn 41:48); Moses does not build, but rather inaugurates retribalized cities to administer justice. Moses grants these cities jurisdiction, and he establishes due process by which they are to administer justice.

When the treaty inaugurating these cities (Dt 5:41--11:32) was extended from these three originally retribalized cities in East Jordan to a larger Israel on both sides of the river, its superscription (Dt 4:41+44-9) was revised. The treaty in Dt 4:44--11:32 was absorbed into the core literature of Deuteronomy (Dt 5:1--26:19 + 28:1-68); the notice in Dt 4:41 which originally restricted the treaty to the cities of Beser, Ramoth and Golan was attached to Dt 1:1--4:40 as a supplement.

Deuteronomy 20:10-20

Deuteronomy 13:13-19 reflects a tradition governing the internal affairs of retribalized cities in an
urban league. Deuteronomy 20:10-20, on the other hand,
is a legal instruction reflecting a tradition governing the foreign relations of a retribalized city with
cities out of its league. The same concern for due
process characterizes the traditions in both
instructions.

External and internal forces both brought about
changes of government in ancient cities. These times
of transition gave cities with more stable governments
the opportunity to expand. However, the uncontrolled
military expansion vital for the growth of a feudal
city would destroy the subsistence economy of a retribalized city. Feudal cities built empires containing hundreds of cities (1 K 11:3); retribalized cities
formed leagues with as few as three cities (Dt 4:41-3;
19:1-13). Therefore, retribalized cities carefully
limited their options for military expansion by out-
lawing war against cities outside the league until
they had been served with an ultimatum (*offered terms
of peace* Dt 20:10) and had responded in both word
(for example, *its answer to you is peace* Dt 20:11)
and action (for example, *it opens to you* Dt 20:11).

Served with an ultimatum, a city chose either to
settle with the league or to fight against it. A
settlement, however, did not entitle the city to full
membership in the league; it became a colony. Nonetheless, a settlement did allow the city to preserve
its culture and, like Gibeon (Js 9:3-26), to be clearly
distinguished from the majority culture of the league
itself. Thus this tradition checked the appetite for
empire in a retribalized city. This tradition also
limited the conduct of war by carefully redefining
technical terms such as *war, peace, siege, interdict,
plunder.* For example, in the tradition of the retribalized cities, *siege* exempted both the orchard
industry and the standing timber of a city from the
wholesale destruction common in feudal wars (Dt 20:19-
20).

Because it coincided with the limitations they
set on their own expansion, retribalized cities in the
13th century BCE celebrated the willingness of both
Moses (Dt 2:25--3:11) and Joshua (Js 10:1-2) to

negotiate with foreign cities rather than to conquer them outright. Early Israel made only modest claims to the cities of Canaan, assuming that the cities which Yahweh leased to Israel, and hence which were eligible for full membership in Israel, were few. In contrast, the early monarchy in the 10th century BCE pursued a more aggressive policy of incorporating virtually every city in Canaan into Israel. Claiming that it was simply exercising its right and responsibility as Yahweh's heir to Canaan, the monarchy defended itself against charges of uncontrolled feudal expansion. In the 7th century BCE the Deuteronomic reformers turned the monarchy's apology into an indictment by arguing that by failing to take full possession of cities like Gibeon and by allowing them to remain distinct colonial cities, Israel in the 13th century BCE had defaulted in her responsibilities to Yahweh, and thus jeopardized her own existence. According to the reformers only cities to which Israel had no clear legal claim (*cities which are very far from you* Dt 20:15; See Dt 21:3; Dt 30:14; Is 50:8) were eligible for colonial status; all others (*the cities of these peoples that the Lord your God gives you for an inheritance* Dt 20:16) were to be completely absorbed into Israel.

Deuteronomy 21:1-9

Before the municipal court in a retribalized city could prosecute a defendant for a capital crime, two witnesses were required. Inside the walls of the city it was a simple matter to meet this requirement; victims only had to *cry out* (Dt 22:24) and witnesses were readily available. However, the jurisdiction of the retribalized city extended beyond the walls to the farms (*field* Dt 21:1; 22:25), pastures, orchards (*vineyards and olive trees* Dt 6:11; *trees for food* Dt 20:20) and forests (Dt 19:5; *trees* Dt 20:20) where its citizens made their livings. Therefore every urban culture in the Ancient Near East had some method of resolving an unwitnessed crime, because, witnessed or not, capital crimes jeopardized the league in which the victim was a citizen (*the cities which are around him* Dt 21:2) and the relationship between the league and their landlord (Dt 21:8).

Deuteronomy 21:1-9 is a legal instruction reflecting a tradition in which the responsibility for prosecuting a murderer is transferred from the city which has jurisdiction in the case (*which is nearest to the slain man* Dt 21:3) to the landlord. The instruction explains how to conduct a deposition consisting of ritual (Dt 21:3b-4+6) and a prayer (Dt 21:7-8). The transfer of jurisdiction takes place at a site where human life and the fertility of the field are totally dependent on the landlord (Dt 21:4). There is no irrigation, only wild water (Dt 21:4). There is no cleared land, only virgin soil (Dt 21:4). There is no tame animal, only one that is unbroken (Dt 21:3). At this site which is beyond the jurisdiction of any of the cities in the league, the elders in whose jurisdiction the *corpus delicti* was found wash their hands and swear they lack the testimony necessary to prosecute the case (*Our hands did not shed this blood, neither did our eyes see it shed* Dt 21:7). If the elders are guilty of perjury, they will be executed like the heifer whose neck is then broken (Dt 21:6). Once the possibility of a conspiracy by the citizens who would normally serve as witnesses and judges has been ruled out by this procedure, jurisdiction is transferred to the landlord who becomes responsible for prosecuting the case.

In the 13th century BCE the cities which were corporate members of early Israel continued the practice explained in Dt 21:1-9 to acknowledge that Yahweh was their landlord and the custodian of city life. In the 10th century BCE when the monarchy inaugurated a judicial system of its own arguing that royal courts were necessary to safeguard the rights of citizens in cases where the municipal courts could not function, traditions like that in Dt 21:1-9 stressed the judicial systems of the retribalized cities could meet those needs. In the 7th century BCE the Deuteronomic reform cited this tradition as an example of how the judicial system of the outlying cities of Judah clearly identified them as Yahweh communities, and therefore they did not need to have sanctuaries to Yahweh to be recognized as his people.

Deuteronomy 21:18-21

The *inhabitants* (Dt 13:13) of a retribalized city who enjoyed the legal status of full citizens were called *men of the city* (Dt 21:21); if they held public office they were called *elders of the city*

(Dt 21:19-20). Among the legal rights of full citizens was that of designating or adopting an heir, who might be their natural and eldest male-child or another natural child or someone else's child. This heir carried the legal title *son* (Dt 21:18) and the testators were called *father and mother* (Dt 21:18). Since designating an heir was a legal process, as opposed to a natural process derived simply from the fact of the child's birth, it could be legally reversed. Deuteronomy 21:18-21 is a legal instruction explaining how to disinherit an heir while the testators are still alive. The traditions on which it is based are common among cities in the Ancient Near East.

In retribalized cities, wills became effective on the retirement of the testator, not at the time of the testator's death. The heir was responsible for seeing that the testator received an adequate annuity on which to live. A *stubborn and rebellious* heir (Dt 21:18; See Nm 20:10; Ho 9:15; Ps 5:11) *squandered his property in loose living* (Lk 15:13) thus sentencing the testators to death by poverty and starvation. To disinherit their heir the testators first put the heir on notice (*chastise* Dt 21:18) that they intend to take legal action. If the heir continued to default, the testators arrested the heir for the purpose of standing trial (*take hold of* Dt 21:19); arraigned him to hear the charges brought against him (*bring* Dt 21:19) and testified against him (*say* Dt 21:20). If guilty, the heir was executed for intending to kill the testators, who then recovered control of the property which the heir was misusing. To guarantee the heir a fair and impartial judgment by his peers, the trial was held in the city where he was a citizen (*at the gate of the place where he lives* Dt 21:19), and not in the domicile of his testators.

By observing this tradition, retribalized cities in the 13th century BCE acknowledged their own status as heirs of Yahweh to whom they owed an annuity. The misuse of Yahweh's inheritance made them liable to disinheritance. The conditional nature of the relationship between the retribalized cities and Yahweh stood in stark contrast with the monarchy's claim in the 10th century BCE to be Yahweh's unconditional and irremovable heir (2 S 7:12-16). In the 7th century BCE the Deuteronomic reformers used the tradition to intimidate the outlying cities of Judah. According to the reformers, these cities would continue to enjoy their inheritance from Yahweh only as

299

long as they were not *stubborn and rebellious* about
their responsibilities to their testator in
Jerusalem.

Deuteronomy 22:13-21

West Semitic culture was unique in considering
cities as women. Phoenician coins always depict
cities as women and the title *mistress* is interchangeable with *goddess* and *city*. All goddesses,
and therefore all cities, were married and often took
their husbands' names in the feminine form (Js 9:10;
15:9). References to prominent cities as *mothers*
and the towns within their spheres of influence as
daughters in the Hebrew Bible also illustrate Israel's
use of the city-as-a-woman tradition (Js 15:45-7;
Jg 1:17).

Likewise, marriageable and married women were as
respected as the city herself. In retribalized
cities, women whose marriages ratified major business
transactions which significantly affected the
economy of the city enjoyed the special status of
virgin (Dt 22:19). In feudal cities, these were
called *princesses* (1 K 11:3) or *concubines* (2 S 15:16;
16:20-3). The way these women were treated was an
index of the city's economy. The intention of legal
instructions like Dt 22:13-21 and Dt 22:23-7 is not
only to regulate the marriage contract, but also to
emphasize the importance of such contracts for understanding the relationship between Yahweh and the
cities which were corporate members of early Israel
during the 13th century BCE.

Deuteronomy 22:13-21 is a legal instruction on
what to do if either party in a business transaction
is defrauded. Neither party can sue for damages
without grounds. The contract must be official (*takes
a wife* Dt 22:13), ratified (*goes in to her* Dt 22:13)
and terminated (*spurns her* Dt 22:13) before it can
be contested. As plaintiffs, the parents impound
(*take* Dt 22:15) the cloths on which their daughter
and her husband consummated their marriage; place them
in evidence (*bring out* Dt 22:15) and testify (*say*
Dt 22:16) that they have not defrauded their
daughter's husband. A husband guilty of fraud is
flogged (*whip* Dt 22:18) and placed under an injunction
(*he may not put her away all his days* Dt 22:19

300

See Ex 21:7-11; Dt 21:15-17). The parents are awarded damages by the court (*fine* Dt 22:19). Parents guilty of fraud, on the other hand, must witness their daughter's execution (Dt 22:21).

In highly competitive feudal economies, women were frequently victims of violence. The traditions of the retribalized cities outlaw the use of brute force and aggression as means of economic growth. Thus during the 10th century BCE the retribalized cities were staunch opponents of the efforts of the monarchy to introduce violence and aggression into Israel's economy (2 S 11:1-5; 13:1-22; 15:16; 16:20-3). In the 7th century BCE the Deuteronomic reformers used these same urban traditions to argue that the outlying cities of Judah did not need a Yahweh sanctuary to acknowledge their covenant relationship with Yahweh. According to the reformers, the outlying cities could acknowledge that relationship with Yahweh just as well by their supervision of the economy and the protection of the woman whose marriages marked major economic developments.

Deuteronomy 22:23-7

The woman in Dt 22:13-21 and the woman in Dt 22:23-7 are both *virgins* (Dt 22:19,23): people whose marriages ratify such important business transactions in a retribalized city that they enjoy the same status as the city itself. Furthermore, both the traditions reflected in Dt 6:10-19; 19:1-12; 20:10-20; 21:1-9 and the tradition reflected in Dt 22:23-7 identify two distinct sectors in retribalized cities: first, the community inside the walls (*in the city* Dt 22:24) and second, the farms, pastures, forests, orchards and vineyards outside the walls (*in the open country* Dt 22:25). In the city a *virgin* must *cry out* (Dt 22:24) or be considered an accomplice to the breach of contract; in the country she is exonerated from any complicity. Although the standards for judging a crime vary between the two sectors, both are subject to the jurisdiction of the municipal court (*the gate of the city* Dt 22:24). As in Dt 22:13-21, the plaintiffs in Dt 22:23-7 are the parents of the woman (*you shall bring them both* Dt 22:24; *you shall [they shall* according to the variant readings] *do nothing* Dt 22:26). The man is the defendant (Dt 22:23,25).

301

Cry out is not only a call for help, but a technical term meaning to litigate. The integrity of a retribalized city rested on the willingness of its citizens to support the legal system and to settle disputes through arbitration rather than force or violence. To begin a lawsuit the plaintiff stood at the gates of the city as the citizens left or returned from work outside the walls and cried out for justice (2 S 15:1-6). In Judges the formula: the people of Israel cried out to the Lord (Jg 3:9) marks the turning point in the heroic indicating Israel's conversion. Only by acknowledging their need for one another was the solidarity of the retribalized city guaranteed.

During the 13th century BCE the retribalized cities stressed the importance of their municipal courts for maintaining the democratic ideals of early Israel. The municipal court was a suitable vehicle for believers in Yahweh to express their faith. By using the municipal court the city would remain a free and safe place in which to enjoy the blessings of Yahweh. During the 10th century BCE the kings of Israel tried to replace the municipal court as the keepers of the peace by garrisoning troops through the empire (1 K 9:17-19) and then by inaugurating their own system of royal courts (Ex 18:13-27; 2 S 12:1-6; 1 K 3:16-18). The retribalized cities opposed this development. They preferred the municipal court system in which a jury reached a consensus through arbitration to the royal court system in which a magistrate handed down a ruling after a hearing. The intention of the legal instruction in Dt 22:23-7 during the 7th century BCE was to demonstrate to the outlying cities of Judah how they could maintain their identity as Yahwist communities even without a Yahweh sanctuary. By delivering the powerless from the powerful the municipal courts in these cities revealed Yahweh as a liberating god.

Deuteronomy 25:5-10

Deuteronomy 21:18-21 reflects a tradition which testators in retribalized cities used to disinherit their heirs while they were still alive. The estate of a citizen who dies before adopting an heir and retiring is cared for by an executor (husband's brother Dt 25:5,7). Deuteronomy is a legal

302

instruction explaining the requirements which must be met before one citizen in a retribalized city can enjoy power of attorney over the estate of another citizen (Dt 25:5-6) and how to remove an executor who is delinquent (Dt 25:7-10).

The executor must be a person who is officially designated (*brother* Dt 25:5) and establish the same domicile as the testator (*dwell...together* Dt 25:5). However, unlike an heir, the power of the executor does not take effect until the testator *dies* (Dt 25:5) and only in the absence of an heir (*son* Dt 25:5). The executor is to sire an heir with the widow of the testator (*shall go in to her, and take her as his wife, and perform the duty of a husband's brother to her* Dt 25:5). Once that heir was old enough to manage the estate, the executor had to turn it over (Dt 25:6). The executor enjoyed the usufruct of this property as long as there was no heir. He had the personal use of his brother's property and could keep any profit that he realized from that property while he was executor. Therefore, unscrupulous executors would try to keep their brother's beneficiaries as clients for as long as possible. In such cases where the executor was delinquent, the testator's widow (*wife of the dead* Dt 25:5) lodged a complaint with the municipal court, which subpoenaed (*call* Dt 25:8) the executor and tried to mediate (*speak to* Dt 25:8), the disagreement. If the executor remained incorrigible (*persists* Dt 25:8), the widow decommissioned him using a ritual and formula remedy (Dt 25:9-10) with the same structure as found in Dt 21:1-9.

Under feudalism only the lord had any legal title (*name* Dt 25:6-7) to the land; everyone else simply worked the land for him. In retribalized communities, the land was owned by households whose titles were recorded in genealogies. During the 13th century BCE the retribalized cities made it difficult if not impossible for any one lord to control all the land, by their conscientious maintenance of the titles by which the households owned land. In early Israel, Yahweh alone was the landlord. To allow anyone else to exercise exclusive control of property was to destroy Israel altogether.

During the 10th century BCE when the hereditary monarchy appeared in Israel herself, the retribalized cities resisted the territorial imperative which these monarchs exercised to gain exclusive control of the

303

land (1 K 21:1-29). So long as the people safe-
guarded their legal right to the land, the power of
the king would remain in balance. If the property
titles (*names* Dt 25:6-7) were not properly protected because of the personal greed of the households for each other's land then the king would
confiscate the property. During the 7th century BCE
the Deuteronomic reformers encouraged the outlying
cities to fulfill their obligations to Yahweh by
seeing that his estate remained in the hands of the
heirs to whom he had leased it. The responsibility
of the cities for the real estate of Judah was considered by the reformers to be a substitute for the
liturgical responsibilities the king had taken away
from the outlying cities and limited to the city of
Jerusalem.

Having form critically studied the city texts in
Dt 4:41--26:19, *Deuteronomy and City Life* concludes
that they do reflect an urban tradition which
endorses city life as one setting in which early
Israel encountered and served Yahweh. In this urban
tradition cities are gifts from Yahweh which Israel
is to enjoy; cities are responsible for preserving
Yahweism by their administration of justice.

Cities like Gibeon, Shechem, Shiloh and Hebron,
who were corporate members of early Israel, were the
custodians of this urban tradition. Government in
these cities was *retribalized*, i.e., democratic, not
the typical *Asiatic mode of production*, i.e., feudal.
This retribalized government made these cities
eligible for membership in Israel which was part of a
general upheaval in the 13th century BCE against the
feudalism which the Hyksos had imposed on city life
in Canaan.

Retribalized cities experimented with hereditary
monarchs like Abimelek (Jg 9) and Saul (1 S 8), but
found hereditary monarchy incompatible with Yahwism.
Therefore, during the 10th century BCE these cities
opposed the royal Yahwism which supported hereditary
monarchies at Jerusalem and Samaria. Royal Yahwism
stressed Israel's obligation to acknowledge Yahweh
in the liturgy, while retribalized cities emphasized
her obligation to honor Yahweh by the way she

administered justice in the municipal courts.
Eventually during the 7th century BCE, the hereditary
monarchy at Jerusalem neutralized the opposition of
these cities and absorbed their traditions into the
Deuteronomic reform. Now this tradition appears in
Deuteronomy as part of the hereditary monarchy's
rationale for centralizing the liturgy. The reform
argued that liturgical centralization did not deprive
the outlying cities of Judah of their status as
Yahwist communities. They still enjoyed the prerogatives of the Yahwist cities who were corporate
members of early Israel. The Yahwist character of
the city of Jerusalem was liturgical; the Yahwist
character of the remaining cities of Judah was legal.

Because there is an urban tradition in the city
texts of Dt 4:41--26:19 which goes all the way back to
Yahwists who lived together in cities during the 13th
century BCE, then Biblical histories and theologies
can no longer consider early Israel to be completely
non-urban! According to this tradition of the retribalized cities in Dt 4:41--26:19 it was possible
from the very beginning, and not simply after the
time of David and Solomon, to be both thoroughly urban
and authentically Yahwist.

APPENDIX

BIBLIOGRAPHY

OF WORKS CITED

Achtemeier, Elizabeth. Deuteronomy Jeremiah.
    Proclamation Commentaries. Philadelphia, PA.:
    Fortress Press, 1978.

Aharoni, Yohanan. The Land of the Bible: a historical
    geography. Translated by A. F. Rainey. London:
    Burns and Oates, 1968.

Ahlstrom, Sydney E. A Religious History of the
    American People. 2 vols. Garden City, NY.:
    Doubleday and Company, 1975.

Albright, William Foxwell. "Abraham the Hebrew: a
    New Archeological Interpretation." BASOR 163
    (1961):36-54.

_____. "Canaanite ḥapšî and Hebrew ḥofšî."
    JPQS 6 (1926):107.

_____. From the Stone Age to Christianity:
    monotheism and the historical process. 2nd ed.
    Baltimore, MD.: The Johns Hopkins Press, 1940;
    Doubleday Anchor Books, 1957.

_____. "The List of Levitic Cities." In
    American Academy for Jewish Research Louis
    Ginzburg Jubilee Volume, pp. 49-73. Philadelphia:
    Jewish Publication Society of America, 1945.

_____. "New Canaanite Historical and
    Mythological Data." BASOR 63 (1936):29.

_____. Yahweh and the gods of Canaan: an
    historical analysis of two contrasting faiths.
    Garden City, NY.: Doubleday & Company, 1968;
    reprint ed. Winona Lake, IN.: Eisenbrauns, 1978.

Alt, Albrecht. "The Formation of the Israelite State
    in Palestine." In Essays on Old Testament
    History and Religion, pp. 222-309. Translated by
    R. A. Wilson. Garden City, NY.: Doubleday &
    Company, Inc., 1967; Anchor Books, 1968.

Alt, Albrecht. "Die Heimat des Deuteronomium." In
      Kleine Schriften zur Geschichte des Volkes
      Israel. Vol. 2, pp. 250-75. München: Beck,
      1968.

_____. "Judas Gaue unter Josia." In Kleine
      Schriften zur Geschichte des Volkes Israel.
      Vol. 2, pp. 276-88. München: Beck, 1968.

_____. Kleine Schriften zur Geschichte des
      Volkes Israel. 2 vols. München: C. H. Beck,
      1968.

_____. "The God of the Fathers." In Essays on
      Old Testament History and Religion, pp. 1-100.
      Translated by R. A. Wilson. Garden City, NY.:
      Doubleday & Company, Inc., 1967; Anchor Books,
      1968.

_____. "The Origins of Israelite Law." In
      Essays on Old Testament History and Religion,
      pp. 101-72. Translated by R. A. Wilson. Garden
      City, NY.: Doubleday & Company, Inc., 1967;
      Anchor Books, 1968.

Anderson, David E. "Theologians Clash Over Bible's
      Stance on Cities." Los Angeles Times, 21
      January 1978.

The Assyrian Laws. Edited by G. R. Driver and John C.
      Miles. Oxford: At the Clarendon Press, 1952.

The Babylonian Laws. Edited by G. R. Driver and
      John C. Miles. Oxford: At the Clarendon Press,
      1952.

Bächli, Otto. Israel und die Völker: eine Studie
      zum Deuteronomium. ATANT. Vol. 41. Zurich:
      Zwingli Verlag, 1962.

Baltzer, Klaus. The Covenant Formulary: in Old
      Testament, Jewish and early Christian writings.
      Translated by David E. Green. Philadelphia:
      Fortress Press, 1971.

Baly, Denis. "The Geography of Monotheism." In
      Translating and Understanding the Old Testament:
      essays in honor of Herbert Gordon May, pp. 253-
      78. Edited by Harry Thomas Frank and William L.
      Reed. New York: Abingdon Press, 1970.

Barth, Hermann, and Steck, Odil Hannes. <u>Exegese des</u>
<u>Alten Testaments: Leitfaden der Methodik</u>. 2nd
ed. Neukirchen Vluyn: Neukirchener Verlag,
1971.

Baumgartel, Friedrich. "The Hermeneutical Problem of
the Old Testament." In <u>Essays on Old Testament</u>
<u>Hermeneutics</u>, pp. 134-59. Edited by Claus
Westermann. Translated by James Luther Mayes.
Richmond, VA.: John Knox Press, 1960.

Begrich, J. "Das Priesterliche Heilsoraken." In
<u>Gesammelte Studien</u>, pp. 217-31. München:
Kaiser Verlag, 1964.

_____. "Die Priestliche Tora." In <u>Gesammelte</u>
<u>Studien</u>, pp. 232-60. München: Kaiser Verlag,
1964.

Bellefontaine, Elizabeth. "Deuteronomy 21:18-21:
Reviewing the Case of the Rebellious Son." <u>JSOT</u>
13 (1979):13-31.

Beltz, Walter. <u>Die Kaleb-Traditionen im Alten</u>
<u>Testament</u>. Stuttgart: W. Kohlhammer, 1974.

Bentzen, Aage. <u>Die Josianische Reform und Ihre</u>
<u>Voraussetzungen</u>. Copenhagen: P. Haase & Söhne
Verlag, 1926.

Bernhardt, K.-H. <u>Das Problem der altorientalischen</u>
<u>Königsideologie im Alten Testament</u>. Leiden:
Brill, 1961.

Bertholet, Alfred. <u>Deuteronomium</u>. Berlin:
Evangelische Verlangsanstalt, 1956.

Blenkinsopp, Joseph. "Are there traces of the
Gibeonite Covenant in Deuteronomy?" <u>CBQ</u> 28
(1966):207-19.

Boecker, Hans Joachim. <u>Redeformen des Rechtslebens</u>
<u>im Alten Testament</u>. 2nd ed. Neukirchen:
Neukirchener Verlag, 1970.

Bottero, J. "Le probleme des Habiru." <u>Cahiers de la</u>
<u>Societe Asiatique</u> 12 (1954):192-8.

Bright, John. <u>A History of Israel</u>. 2nd ed.
Philadelphia: Westminster Press, 1972.

Brockelmann, Carl. Hebräische Syntax. Neukirchen:
    Neukirchener Verlag, 1956.

Bronner, Leah. "The Rechabites, a sect in Biblical
    Times." In De Fructu Oris Sui: essays in honor
    of Adrianus van Selms, pp. 10-16. Edited by
    I. H. Eybers, F. C. Fensham, C. J. Labuschagne,
    W. C. van Wyk and A. H. van Zyl. Leiden: Brill,
    1971.

Brownlee, William Hugh. "Ezekiel's Copper Caldron and
    blood on the rock (Chapter 24:1-14)." In For me
    to live: essays in honor of James Leon Kelso,
    pp. 21-43. Edited by Robert A. Coughenour.
    Cleveland: Dillon/Liederbach Books, 1972.

Brueggemann, Walter. The Bible Makes Sense. Winona,
    MN.: St. Mary's College Press, 1978.

_____. "A Form Critical Study of the Cultic
    Material in Deuteronomy: an analysis of the
    nature of the cultic encounter in the Mosaic
    tradition." Th.D. dissertation, Union Theology
    Seminary, 1961.

_____. The Land: Place as gift, promise and
    challenge in Biblical faith. Overtures to
    Biblical Theology. Edited by Walter Brueggemann
    and John R. Donahue. Philadelphia: Fortress
    Press, 1977.

Buccellati, Giorgio. "'Abīru and Munnabtutu--The
    stateless of the first cosmopolitan age." JNES
    36 (1977):

_____. Cities and Nations of Ancient Syria:
    An Essay on Political Institutions with special
    reference to the Israelite Kingdoms. Studi
    Semetici, No. 26. Rome: Instituto di Studi del
    Vinino Oriente, University of Rome, 1967.

Budde, Karl. "The Nomadic Ideal in the Old Testa-
    ment." New World 4 (1895):726-45.

Buis, Pierre. Le Deutéronome. Verbum Salutis,
    Ancien Testament. Vol. 4. Paris: Beauchesne,
    1969.

Bultmann, Rudolf. "Prophecy and Fullment." In Essays on Old Testament Hermeneutics, pp. 50-75. Edited by Claus Westermann. Translated by James Luther Mays. Richmond, VA.: John Knox Press, 1960.

Burn, A. R. The Pelican History of Greece. Baltimore: Penguin Books, 1966.

Carmichael, Calum N. The Laws in Deuteronomy. Ithaca, NY.: Cornell University Press, 1974.

Causse, Antonin. Du groupe ethnique a la communaute religieuse. Etudes d'histoire et de philosophie religieuse. Paris: F. Alcan, 1937.

Cazelles, Henri. Deutéronome. Paris: Les Editions du Cerf, 1950.

Childe, V. Gordon. "Civilization, Cities and Towns." Antiquity 31 (1957):36-8.

_____. What Happened in History? Rev. ed. New York: Penguin Books, 1954.

Childs, Brevard S. The Book of Exodus, a critical, theological commentary. Old Testament Library. Philadelphia: The Westminster Press, 1974.

_____. "Deuteronomic Formulae of the Exodus Traditions." In Hebräische Wortforschung, pp. 30-9. Edited by Benedikt Hartmann, et. al. Leiden: Brill, 1967.

_____. Introduction to the Old Testament as Scripture. Philadelphia: Fortress Press, 1979.

Civil, Miguel. "Lipit-Isthtat." Asiatische Studien 16 (1962):1-7.

Claburn, William E. "Deuteronomy and Collective Behavior." Ph.D. dissertation, Princeton University, 1968.

Clark, W. Malcolm. "Law." In Old Testament Form Criticism. Edited by John H. Hayes. San Antonio, TX.: Trinity University Press, 1974.

Clements, Ronald E. Abraham and David: Genesis XV and its Meaning for Israelite Tradition. Naperville, IL.: Alec R. Allenson, Inc., 1967.

_____. Old Testament Theology: a fresh approach. Atlanta, GA.: John Knox Press, 1978.

Cooke, George Albert. A Text-book of North Semitic Inscriptions. Oxford: At the Clarendon Press, 1903.

Cox, Harvey. The Secular City: secularization and urbanization in theological perspective. New York: The Macmillan Company, 1965.

Craigie, Peter C. The Book of Deuteronomy. Grand Rapids, MI.: William B. Eerdmans Publishing Company, 1976.

Cross, Frank Moore. Canaanite Myth and Hebrew Epic: Essays in the History and Religion of Israel. Cambridge, Ma.: Harvard University Press, 1973.

Cross, Frank Moore, and Freedman, David Noel. "Josiah's Revolt Against Assyria." JNES 12 (1953):56-58.

Danell, Gustaf Adolf. Studies in the Name "Israel" in the Old Testament. Uppsala: Appelbergs boktryckeri-a.-b., 1946.

Daube, David. "The Culture of Deuteronomy," Orita (Ibadan) 3 (1969):41-43.

_____. Studies in Biblical Law. Cambridge: The University Press, 1947; reprint ed., New York: KTAV, Inc., 1969.

_____. "To be Found Doing Wrong." In Studi in onore di Volterra, vol. 2. Rome, 1961, pp. 3-12.

Delitzsch, Friedrich. Die grosse Täuschung. 2 vols. Stuttgart: Deutsche Verlags Anstalt, 1920-21.

DeWette, W. M. L. Dissertatio critica qua Deuteronomium a prioribus Pentateuchi libris diversum alius suisdam recentioris opus esse monstratus. Jena, 1803.

Dictionary of Biblical Theology. 2nd ed. S.v.
"City," by Pierre Grelot.

Dictionary of the Bible. S.v. "Jerusalem," by John L.
McKenzie.

_____. S.v. "Shechem," by John L. McKenzie.

Dix, Gregory. The Shape of the Liturgy. London:
Dacre Press, 1945.

Dodd, C. H. The Bible and the Greeks. London:
Hodder and Stoughton, 1935.

Doughty, C. M. Travels in Arabia Deserta. 2 vols.
Boston: J. Cape, 1888; reprint ed., Leiden:
Brill, 1979.

Dreyer, H. J. "The Roots QR, 'R, GR and S/TR =
'Stone Wall, City, etc." In De Fructu Oris Sui:
essays in honor of Adrianus van Selms, pp. 17-
25. Edited by I. H. Eybers, F. C. Fensham,
C. J. Labuschagne, W. C. van Wyk and A. H. van
Zyl. Vol. 9: Pretoria Oriental Series.
Leiden: Brill, 1971.

Driver, S. R. A Critical and Exegetical Commentary on
Deuteronomy. 3rd ed. The International Critical
Commentary. Edinburgh: T. & T. Clark, 1895.

_____. "Three Notes." VT 2 (1952):356-7.

Dubberstein, W. H. " Assyrian-Babylonian Chronology."
JNES 3 (1944):38-46.

Dumermuth, F. "Zur deuteronomischen Kulttheologie und
ihren Voraussetzungen." ZAW 70 (1958):59-98.

Dürr, Lorenz. Ursprung und Ausbau der israelitsche-
jüdischen Heilandserwartung. Berlin: C. A.
Schwetschke & Sohn, 1925.

Dus, Jan. "Moses or Joshua? On the Problem of the
Founder of the Israelite Religion." In The Bible
and Liberation: Political and Social
Hermeneutics, pp. 26-41. Edited by Norman K.
Gottwald and Antoinette C. Wire. Berkeley, CA.:
Radical Religion, 1976.

Eichrodt, Walther. Theology of the Old Testament.
2 vols. Translated by J. A. Baker.
Philadelphia: The Westminster Press, 1961.

Eissfeldt, Otto. The Old Testament: An Introduction.
Translated by Peter R. Ackroyd. New York:
Harper and Row, 1965.

Elhorst, H. J. "Eine verkannte Zauberhandlung (Dtn
21,1-9)." ZAW 39 (1921):58-67.

Ellul, Jacques. The Meaning of the City. Translated
by Dennis Pardee. Grand Rapids, MI.: William B.
Eerdmans Publishing Co., 1970.

Emerton, J. A. "The Riddle of Genesis XV." VT 21
(1971):403-39.

_____. "Some False Clues in the Study of
Genesis XIV." VT 21 (1971):24-71.

Engnell, Ivan. Studies in Divine Kingship in the
Ancient Near East. Uppsala: Almquist &
Wiksells Bokt, 1943.

Evans, G. "'Coming' and 'Going' at the City Gate--a
Discussion of Professor Speiser's Paper."
BASOR (1958):28-33.

Farbridge, Maurice H. Studies in Biblical and Semitic
Symbolism. New York: E. P. Dutton & Co., 1923.

Finkelstein, J. J. "Some New Misharum Material and its
implications." In Studies in Honor of Benno
Landsberger on his 75th Birthday, pp. 243ff.
Chicago: University of Chicago Press, 1965.

Fitzgerald, Aloysius. "The Mythological Background for
the presentation of Jerusalem as a queen and
false worship as adultery in the Old Testament."
CBQ 34 (1972):403-16.

Flanagan, James W. "The Relocation of the Davidic
Capital." JAAR 47 (1979):223-44.

Flight, John W. "The Nomadic Idea and Ideal in the
OT." JBL 42 (1923):158ff.

Fohrer, Georg. Studien zur alttestamentlichen
Prophetie. Berlin: A. Topelmann, 1967.

Fohrer, Georg. Theologische Grundstrukturen des Alten Testaments. Berlin: DeGruyter, 1972.

Forshey, Harold O. "The Hebrew Root NHL and its Semitic Cognates." Ph.D. Dissertation, Harvard University, 1973.

Fraine, J. DE. L'aspect religieux de la royaute Israelite: l'institution monarchique dans l'ancien Testament et dans les Textes mesopotamiens. Rome: Pontifical Biblical Institute, 1954.

Frankfort, Henri. The Birth of Civilization in the Near East. Bloomington, IN.: Indiana University Press, 1951.

Frick, Frank S. The City in Ancient Israel. SBL Dissertation Series, no. 36. Chico, CA.: Scholars Press, 1977.

_____. "The Rechabites Reconsidered." JBL 90 (1971):379-87.

Friedrich, Johannes. Staatsverträge des Hatti Reiches. Leipzig: Mitteilungen der Vorderasiatisch-Agyptischen Gesellsschaft, 1926.

Galling, Kurt. Die Bücher Chronik. Gottingen: Vandenhoeck & Ruprecht, 1954.

Gamberoni, J. "Das Elterngebot im Alten Testament." BZ 8 (1964):161-90.

Gaster, Theodor H. Myth, Legend and Custom in the Old Testament. New York: Harper & Row Publishers, 1975.

Gemser, B. "The Importance of the Motive Clause in Old Testament Law." SVT 1 (1953):50-66.

"Genre File of the Form Critical Project from the Institute of Antiquity and Christianity at the Claremont Graduate School." S.v. "Catalogue," by Rolf P. Knierim.

"Genre File of the Form Critical Project from the Institute of Antiquity and Christianity at the Claremont Graduate School." S.v. "Etiology," by Rolf P. Knierim and Gene M. Tucker.

"Genre File of the Form Critical Project from the
    Institute of Antiquity and Christianity at the
    Claremont Graduate School." S.v. "List," by
    Rolf P. Knierim.

"Genre File of the Form Critical Project from the
    Institute of Antiquity and Christianity at the
    Claremont Graduate School." S.v. "Motive
    Clause," by Roland E. Murphy.

"Genre File of the Form Critical Project from the
    Institute of Antiquity and Christianity at the
    Claremont Graduate School." S.v. "Register,"
    by Rolf P. Knierim.

"Genre File of the Form Critical Project from the
    Institute of Antiquity and Christianity at the
    Claremont Graduate School." S.v. "Series," by
    Rolf P. Knierim.

Gerstenberger, Erhard. Wesen und Herkunft des
    apodiktischen Rechts. Neukirchen-Vluyn:
    Neukirchener Verlag, 1965.

_____. "Zur alttestamentlichen Weisheit."
    Verkundigung und Forschung 14 (1969):28-44.

Gese, Harmut. "Der Dekalog als Ganzheit betractet."
    ZTK 9 (1964):121-58.

Gilmer, Harry W. The If-You Form in Israelite Law.
    Chico,CA.: Scholars Press, 1975.

Gluckmann, M. Politics, Law and Ritual in Tribal
    Society. Oxford: Basil Blackwell, 1965.

Glueck, Nelson. "Ramoth-Gilead." BASOR 92 (1943):10-
    16.

Gordon, Cyrus. "Abraham and the Merchants of Ura."
    JNES 12 (1958):28-31.

_____. "An Akkadian Parallel to Deuteronomy
    21:1ff." RA 32 (1936):1-6.

_____. "Biblical Customs and the Nuzu Tablets."
    In The Biblical Archeological Reader. Vol. 2,
    pp. 21-33. Edited by David Noel Freedman and
    E. F. Campbell. Garden City, NY.: 1964.

Gottwald, Norman K. "Early Israel and 'The Asiatic Mode of Production in Canaan'." In SBL Seminar Papers. Vol. 1, pp. 145-53. Edited by Paul J. Achtemeier. Chico, CA.: Scholars Press, 1976.

_____. The Tribes of Yahweh. Maryknoll, NY.: Orbis Books, 1979.

Gray, John. The legacy of Canaan. The Ras Shamra texts and their relevance to the Old Testament. 2nd revised and enlarged edition 1965. Vetus Test Suppl. V. Leiden: E. J. Brill.

Greenberg, Moshe. "The Biblical Concept of Asylum." JBL 78 (1959):125-32.

Gressmann, H. Altorientalische Texte und Bilder zum Alten Testament. Vol. 1. Berlin: W. de Gruyter, 1926.

Grintz, I. M. "The Treaty with the Gibeonites." Zion 26 (1960/61):69-84.

Gunkel, Hermann. Genesis. 3rd ed. Gottingen: Vandenhoeck & Ruprecht, 1969.

Hahn, Eduard. Von der Hacke zum Pflug. Leipzig: Quelle and Meyer, 1914.

Halligan, John Martin. "A Critique of the City in the Yahwist Corpus." Ph.D. Dissertation. University of Notre Dame, 1975.

_____. "The Role of the Peasant in the Amarna Period." In SBL Seminar Papers. Vol. 1, pp. 154-69. Edited by Paul J. Achtemeier. Chico, CA.: Scholars Press, 1976.

Hals, Ronald M. "Is there a Genre of Preached Law?" In SBL Seminar Papers. Vol. 1, pp. 1-12. Ed. Paul J. Achtemeier. Chico, CA.: Scholars Press, 1973.

Hammond, Mason. The City in the Ancient World. Cambridge, MA.: Harvard University Press, 1972.

Handbook of Biblical Criticism. S.v. "Chiasmus," by Richard N. Soulen.

Handbook of Biblical Criticism. S.v. "Credo," by
    Richard N. Soulen.

Harnack, Adolf von. Marcion: Das Evangelium vom
    fremdem Gott. Darmstadt: Wissenschaftliche
    Buchgesellschaft, 1960.

Hasel, Gerhard F. Old Testament Theology: Basic
    Issues in the Current Debate. Revised ed. Grand
    Rapids, MI.: William B. Eerdmans Publishing
    Company, 1975.

Hayes, John H., ed. Old Testament Form Criticism.
    San Antonio, TX.: Trinity University Press,
    1974.

Hayes, John H., and J. Maxwell Miller, eds.
    Israelite and Judean History. Philadelphia:
    The Westminster Press, 1977.

Heltzer, Michael. "Problems of the Social History of
    Syria in the Late Bronze Age." In La Siria nel
    Tardo Bronzo, pp. 31-46. Edited by M. Liverani.
    Rome: Orientis Antiqui Collectio, 1969.

Hempel, Johannes. Die Schichten des Deuteronomiums:
    ein Beitrag zur israelitischen Literatur- und
    Rechtsgeschichte. Leipzig: R. Voigtlander,
    1914.

Hesse, Franz. Das Alte Testament als Buch der Kirche.
    Gütersloh: C. Mohn, 1966.

Hirsch, Emanuel. Das Alte Testament und die Predigt
    des Evangeliums. Tübingen: Mohr, 1936.

Hölscher, Gustav. "Komposition und Ursprung des
    Deuteronomiums." ZAW 40 (1922):61-225.

Hoffner, Harry A. "Some Contributions of Hittitology
    to Old Testament Study," TB 20 (1969):27-55.

Hooke, Samuel Henry, ed. Myth and Ritual: Essays on
    Myth and Ritual of the Hebrews in relation to the
    Cultural Pattern of the Ancient East. London:
    Oxford University Press, 1933.

Horst, Friedrich. Das Privilegrecht Jahves.
    Gottingen: Vandenhoeck & Ruprecht, 1930.

Horst Friedrich. "Recht und Religion im Bereich des
Alten Testaments." In Gottes Recht, Studien zum
Recht im Alten Testament, pp. 260-91. Edited by
Hans Walter Wolff. Munchen: C. Kaiser, 1961.

Interpretation 27 (1973):387-468.

Interpreter's Dictionary of the Bible. S.v. "Bethel,"
by J. L. Kelso.

Interpreter's Dictionary of the Bible. S.v. "Camel,"
by J. A. Thompson.

Interpreter's Dictionary of the Bible. S.v. "Milk,"
by J. F. Ross.

Interpreter's Dictionary of the Bible. S.v. "Number,
Numbering, Numbers," by M. H. Pope.

Interpreter's Dictionary of the Bible. S.v. "Shechem,"
by W. L. Reed and L. E. Toombs.

Interpreter's Dictionary of the Bible. S.v. "Virgin,"
by O. J. Baab.

Interpreter's Dictionary of the Bible. Supplementary
Vol. S.v. "Deuteronomic History, The," by David
Noel Freedman.

Interpreter's Dictionary of the Bible. Supplementary
Vol. S.v. "Form Criticism, O.T." by Gene M.
Tucker.

Interpreter's Dictionary of the Bible. Supplementary
Vol. S.v. "Deuteronomy," by Norbert Lohfink.

Interpreter's Dictionary of the Bible. Supplementary
Vol. S.v. "Nomadism," by Norman K. Gottwald.

Interpreter's Dictionary of the Bible. Supplementary
Vol. S.v. "Rechabites," by Frank S. Frick.

Interpreter's Dictionary of the Bible. Supplementary
Vol. S.v. "Torah," by James A. Sanders.

Interpreter's Dictionary of the Bible. Supplemetary
Vol. S.v. "Typology," by Elizabeth Achtemeier.

Interpreter's Dictionary of the Bible. Supplementary
Vol. S.v. "War, Holy," by Norman K. Gottwald.

The Interpreter's One Volume Commentary on the Bible.
    S.v. "Ezekiel," by William Hugh Brownlee.

Jacobs, Paul F. "The Life Motif in Deuteronomy: a
    study of its stylistic and redactional use."
    Paper presented at SBL Southwest Regional
    Meeting. Waco, TX.: March, 1979.

Jacobsen, Thorkild. "Primitive Democracy in Ancient
    Mesopotamia." JNES 2 (1943):159-88.

Jepsen, Alfred. Untersuchungen zum Bundesbuch.
    Stuttgart: W. Kohlhammer, 1927.

Jirku, Anton. "Drei Fälle von Haftpflicht in alt-
    orientalischen Palästina-Syrien und Dt cap 21."
    ZAW 59 (1967):159-88.

_____. Das weltliche Recht im Alten Testament.
    Gütersloh: C. Bertelsmann, 1927.

Johnson, A. R. Sacral Kingship in Ancient Israel.
    Cardiff: University of Wales Press, 1967.

Jolles, Andre. Einfache Formen, Legende, Sage, Mythe,
    Rätsel, Spruch, Kasus, Memorabile, Märchen, Witz.
    Halle: M. Niemeyer Verlag, 1930.

Junge, Erhard. Der Weideraufbau des Heerwesens des
    Reiches Juda under Josia. Stuttgart:
    Kohlhammer Verlag, 1937.

Junker, Hubert. Deuteronomium. Wurzburg: Echter-
    Verlag, 1952.

Kaiser, Otto. Introduction to the Old Testament. A
    Presentation of its Results and Problems. Trans-
    lated by John Sturdy. Minneapolis, MN.: Augsburg
    Publishing House, 1975.

Kautzsch, E. Gesenius' Hebrew Grammar. Revised by
    A. E. Cowley. Oxford: At the Clarendon Press,
    1910.

Kempinski, Aharon. "Israelite Conquest or Settlement?
    New Light from Tell Mosos." BAR 2 (1976):25-30.

_____. The Rise of an Urban Culture: the
    urbanization of Palestine in the early bronze
    age, 3000-2150 BC. Israel Ethnographic Studies.

Vol. 4. Edited by Heda Jason. Jerusalem:
Israel Ethnographic Society, 1978.

Kenyon, Kathleen. Archeology in the Holy Land. New
York: Frederick A. Praeger, 1960.

_____. Digging up Jericho. New York: Praeger,
1957.

_____. Digging up Jerusalem. New York:
Praeger, 1974.

_____. Royal Cities of the Old Testament.
New York: Schocken Books, 1971.

Klengel, Horst. "Probleme einer politischen
Geschichte des spätbronzeitlichen Syrien." In
La Siria nel Tardo Bronzo, pp. 15-30. Edited
by M. Liverani. Rome: Orientis Antiqui
Collectio, 1969.

Kline, Meredith G. Treaty of the Great King: the
covenant structure of Deuteronomy. Grand Rapids,
MI.: William B. Eerdmans Publishing Company,
1963.

Klostermann, August. Der Pentateuch: Beiträge zu
seinem Verständnis und seiner Entstehungs-
geschichte. 2 vols. Leipzig: A. Deichert,
1907.

Knierim, Rolf P. "Exodus 18 und die Neuordnung der
mosiaschen Gerichtsbarkeit." ZAW 73 (1961):146-
71.

_____. Die Hauptbegriffe für Sünde im Alten
Testament. Gerd Mohn: Gutersloher Verlagshaus,
1965.

_____. "The Nature of the Decalogue and its
function in Israelite Society." Unpublished
lecture: Theologische Hochschule, Sankt Georgen,
Frankfurt/Main and Universities of Heidelberg
and Munich, 1974. Revised Manuscript, Institute
of Antiquity and Christianity at the Claremont
Graduate School, Claremont, CA., 1976.

_____. "Old Testament Form Criticism Re-
considered." Interpretation 27 (1973):435-68.

Knight, Douglas A. "The Understanding of Sitz im Leben in Form Criticism." in SBL Seminar Papers. Vol. 1, pp. 103-25. Edited by Paul J. Achtemeier. Chico, CA.: Scholars Press, 1976.

Knobel, August. Die Bücher Numeri, Deuteronomium und Josua. Leipzig: S. Hirzel, 1861.

Koch, Klaus. The Growth of the Biblical Tradition. Translated by S. M. Cupitt. 2nd German ed. New York: Charles Scribner's Sons, 1969.

Köhler, Ludwig. "Der Dekalog." ThR 1 (1929):182.

_____. Die hebräische Rechtsgemeinde. Zurich: Jahresbericht der Universität Zurich, 1930.

_____. Hebrew Man. New York: Abingdon Press, 1956.

Korosec, Viktor. Hethitische Staatsverträge: ein Beitrag zu ihrer juristischen Wertung. Leipziger rechtswissenschaftliche Studien, no. 60. Leipzig: T. Weicher, 1931.

Koschaker, Paul. Quellenkritische Untersuchungen zu den "altassyriche Gesetzen." Leipzig: J. C. Hinrichs, 1921.

Kraus, Hans Joachim. Geschichte der historisch-kritischen Erforschung des Alten Testaments. Neukirchen: Neukirchener Verlag, 1969.

Kuenen, Abraham. Historisch-kritisch Onderzoek naar het ontstaan en de verzameling van de boeken des Ouden Verbonds. Leiden: Brill, 1861-65.

Kupper, Jean R. Les nomades en Mesopotamie au temps des rois de Mari. Paris: Musee national du Louvre, 1957.

Lambert, W. E. "Nebuchadnezzar, King of Justice." Iraq 27 (1965):1-11.

_____. "The Domesticated Camel in the Second Millenium--Evidence from Alalath and Ugarit." BASOR 160 (1960):42ff.

LaPointe, R. "La valeur linguistique du Sitz im Leben." Biblica 52 (1971):469-87.

Lapp, Paul. "The Conquest of Palestine in the Light of Archeology." Concordia Theological Monthly 38 (1967):298-9.

_____. "Tel el-Ful." BA 28 (1965):2-10.

Lattimore, Owen. Studies in Frontier History. New York: Oxford University Press, 1962.

Levenson, Jon D. "On the Promise to the Rechabites." CBQ 38 (1976):508-14.

Lewy, I. "The Puzzle of Dt XXVII: blessing announced, but curses noted." VT (1962):207-11.

L'Hour, Jean. "Une legislation criminelle dans le Deutéronome." Bib (1963):1-28.

Liedke, Gerhard. Gestalt und Bezeichung Alttestamentlicher Rechtssätze: Eine Formgeschichtlich-terminologische Studie. WMANT. No. 39. Neukirchen-Vluyn: Neukirchener Verlag, 1971.

Lindars, Barnabas. "Torah in Deuteronomy." In Festschrift for D. W. Thomas, pp. 117-36. New York: Cambridge University Press, 1968.

Linton, Ralph M. The Study of Man. New York: Century Press, 1936.

Littauer, M. A., and J. H. Crouwel. Wheeled Vehicles and Ridden Animals in the Ancient Near East. Leiden: Brill, 1979.

Liverani, M. "L'estradizione dei rifugiati in At." RSO 39 (1964):111-15.

Llewellyn, K. N., and E. Adamson Hoebel. The Cheyenne Way: Conflict and Case Law in Primitive Jurisprudence. Norman, OK.: University of Oklahoma Press, 1941.

Loersch, Sigrid. Das Deuteronomium und seine Deutungen. Stuttgarter Bibelstudien. No. 22. Stuttgart: Verlag Katholisches Bibelwerk, 1967.

Loewenstein, Susan Fleiss. "The Urban Experiment in the Old Testament." Ph.D. Dissertation, Syracuse University, 1971.

Lohfink, Norbert. Das Hauptgebot: eine Untersuchung literarischer Einleitungsfragen zu Dtn 5--11. Romae: E Pontificio Instituto Biblico, 1963.

_____. "Lectures in Deuteronomy." Rome, 1968 (Mimeographed).

Luke, John T. "Pastoralism and Politics in the Mari Period: A Reexamination of the Character and Political Significance of the Major West Semitic Tribal Groups on the Middle Euphrates, ca. 1828-1758 BC." Ph.D. Dissertation, University of Michigan, 1965.

Mabee, Charles. "The Problem of Setting in Hebrew Royal Judicial Narrative." Ph.D. Dissertation, Claremont Graduate School, 1977.

McCarthy, Dennis J. Treaty and Covenant, a study in form in the Ancient Oriental Documents and in the Old Testament. Rev. ed. Analecta Biblica. Vol. 21A. Rome: Biblical Institute, 1978.

_____. Covenant in the Old Testament: a survey of current opinions. Richmond, VA.: John Knox Press, 1972.

McKay, J. W. "A Decalogue for the Administration of Justice at the City Gate." VT 21 (1971):311-25.

McKeating, H. "The Development of the Law on Homicide in Ancient Israel." VT 25 (1975):46-68.

McKenzie, John L. "The Elders in the Old Testament." Bib 40 (1959):522-40.

_____. A Theology of the Old Testament. New York: Doubleday & Company, 1974.

Machinist, Peter. "Literature as Politics: The TUKULTI-NINURTA epic and the Bible." CBQ 38 (1976):455-82.

Macholz, Georg Christian. "Die Stellung des Königs in der israelitischen Gerichtsverfassung." ZAW 84 (1972):157-82.

Macholz, Georg Christian. "Zur Geschichte der Justizorganization in Juda." ZAW 84 (1972):314-40.

MacKenzie, R. A. F. "The City and Israelite Religion." CBQ 25 (1963):60-70.

Mahaffy, J. P. Social Life in Greece from Homer to Menander. London: Macmillan, 1888.

Malamat, A. "Aspects of the Foreign Policies of David and Solomon." JNES 22 (1963):1-17.

Martin, Keith. Perspectives on an Urban Theology. Washington, D.C.: Center for Theology and Public Policy, 1977.

Mayes, A. D. H. Deuteronomy. Greenwood, SC.: Attic Press, 1979.

Mendelsohn, Isaac. "The Canaanite Term for *Free Proletarian*." BASOR 83 (1941):36-9.

_____. "New Light on the HUPSU." BASOR 139 (1955):9-11.

Mendenhall, George E. "Ancient Oriental and Biblical Law." In Biblical Archaeologist Reader. Vol. 3, pp. 3-24. Edited by Edward F. Campbell, Jr., and David Noel Freedman. Garden City, NY.: Doubleday & Company, 1970.

_____. "The Hebrew Conquest of Palestine." In Biblical Archaeologist Reader. Vol. 3, pp. 76-99. Edited by Edward F. Campbell, Jr., and David Noel Freedman. Garden City, NY.: Doubleday & Company, 1970.

_____. "Migration theories vs Culture Change as an Explanation for Early Israel." In SBL Seminar Papers. Vol. 1, pp. 131-43. Edited by Paul J. Achtemeier. Chico, CA.: Scholars Press, 1976.

Merendino, Rosario P. Das Deuteronomische Gesetz: Eine literarkritische, gattungs-und überlieferungsgeschichtliche Untersuchung zu Dt 12-26. Bonn: Peter Hanstein Verlag, 1969.

Miller, J. Maxwell. _The Old Testament and the Historian_. Philadelphia: Fortress Press, 1976.

Miller, Patrick D. "The Gift of God. The Deuteronomistic Theology of the Land." _Int_ 23 (1969):451-65.

Mittmann, S. _Deuteronomium 1:1--6:3 literarkritisch und traditionsgeschichtlich untersucht_. Berlin: DeGruyter, 1975.

Moore, George F. _Judaism in the First Centuries of the Christian Era_. 3 vols. Cambridge: Harvard University Press, 1950-54.

Moran, W. L. "The Ancient Near Eastern Background of the Love of God in Dt." _CBQ_ 25 (1963):77-87.

_____. Review of _Israel and die Völker_, by Otto Bächli. _Biblica_ 44 (1963):375-77.

Morgenstern, Julian. "The Book of the Covenant, Part II." _HUCA_ 7 (1930):19-258.

Mowinckel, Sigmund. _The Psalms in Israel's Worship_. 2 vols. New York: Abingdon Press, 1962.

Muilenburg, James. "The Gains of Form Criticism in Old Testament Studies." _The Expository Times_ 71 (1960):229-33.

Mumford, Lewis. _The City in History: its origins, its transformations, and prospects_. New York: Harcourt, Brace and World, 1961.

Muntingh, L. M. "The City which has foundations: Hebrews 11:8-10 in light of the Mari Texts." In _De Fructu Oris Sui: essays in honor of Adrianus van Selms_, pp. 108-20. Edited by I. H. Eubers, F. C. Fensham, C. J. Labuschagne, W. C. van Wyck and A. H. van Zyl. Vol. 9. Pretoria Oriental Series. Leiden: Brill, 1971.

National Federation of Priests' Councils. _Hear the Cry of Jerusalem: a national urban pastoral statement_. Chicago: National Federation of Priests' Councils, 1979.

Neher, Andre. L'essence du prophetisme. Paris: Presses Universitaires de France, 1955.

Nelson, Harold H., and Uvo Holscher. Medinet Habu Reports. Chicago: University of Chicago Press, 1931.

Neuhaus, Richard John. Christian Faith and Public Policy. Minneapolis, MN.: Augsburg Publishing, 1977.

New Catholic Encyclopedia. S.v. "Marcion," by A. A. Stephenson.

Nicholson, E. W. Deuteronomy and Tradition. Philadelphia: Fortress Press, 1967.

_____. Exodus and Sinai in History and Tradition. Richmond, VA.: John Knox Press, 1973.

Nicolsky, N. M. "Das Asylrecht in Israel." ZAW 48 (1930):146-75.

Noth, Martin. "Gott, König, Volk im Alten Testament (Eine methodologische Auseinandersetzung mit einer gegenwartigen Forschungsrichtung)." ZTK 47 (1950):157-91.

_____. The History of Israel. 2nd Ed. New York: Harper and Row Publishers, 1960.

_____. Das System der Zwölf Stämme Israels. Stuttgart: Kohlhammer, 1930.

_____. Uberlieferungsgeschichtliche Studien. Vol. 1: Die sammelnden und bearbeitenden Geschichtswerke im Alten Testament. Tübingen: Max Niemeyer Verlag, 1943 (2nd ed., 1957).

Noygayrol, Jean. Le palais royal d'Ugarit. Paris: Impr. Nationale, 1955.

Nystron, Samuel. Beduinentum und Jahwismus. Eine soziologischreligionsgeschichtliche Untersuchung zum Alten Testament. Lund: C. W. K. Gleerup, 1946.

Oppenheim, A. Leo. Ancient Mesopotamia. Portrait of a Dead Civilization. Chicago: University of

Chicago Press, 1977.

Ostborn, Gunnar. Tora in the Old Testament: a semantic
study. Lund: Ohlsson, 1945.

Patrick, Dale. "The Rights of the Underprivileged."
In SBL Seminar Papers. Vol. 1, pp. 1-6. Edited
by Paul J. Achtemeier. Chico, CA.: Scholars
Press, 1975.

Paulys Real-Encyclopaedie der klassischen Altertumswissenschaft. S.v. "Amphiktyonia," by F.
Cauer.

Pedersen, Johannes. Israel, its Life and Culture.
4 vols. Translated by A. Møller and A. I.
Fausbøll. London: Cumberlege, 1946-7.

Pettinato, Giovanni. "The Royal Archives of Tell
Mardikh-Ebla." BA 39 (1976):44-52.

Phillips, Anthony. Ancient Israel's Criminal Law.
New York: Schocken Books, 1971.

_____. "NEBALAH--a term for serious disorderly
and unruly conduct." VT 25 (1975):237-42.

Ploger, Josef G. Literarkritische, formgeschichtliche
und stilkritische Untersuchungen zum
Deuteronomium. Bonn: Peter Hanstein, 1967.

Pritchard, James B., ed. Ancient Near Eastern Texts
relating to the Old Testament. 3rd ed.
Princeton, NJ.: University Press, 1969.

Pulgram, Ernest. "Linear B, Greek, and the Greeks."
Glotta 38 (1960):171-81.

Rad, Gerhard von. "Ancient Word and Living Word: The
Preaching of Deuteronomy and our Preaching."
Translated by Lloyd Gaston. Interpretation 15
(1961):3-13.

_____. Deuteronomy, A Commentary. Philadelphia:
The Westminster Press, 1966.

_____. "Das formgeschichtliche Problem des
Hexateuch." In Gesammelte Studien zum Alten
Testament. Vol. 2, pp. 9-88. Edited by Rudolf
Smend. München: Chr Kaiser Verlag, 1961.

Rad, Gerhard von. Das fünfte Buch Mose: Deuteronomium.
Göttingen: Vandenhoeck & Ruprecht, 1964.

_____. "Das Gottesvolk im Deuteronomium." In
Gesammelte Studien zum Alten Testament. Vol. 2,
pp. 9-108. Edited by Rudolf Smend. München:
Chr Kaiser Verlag, 1973.

_____. Der Heilige Krieg im alten Israel.
Zurich: Zwingli Verlag, 1958.

_____. Old Testament Theology. Translated by
David Stalker. New York: Harper and Row
Publishers, 1962.

_____. "The Problem of the Hexateuch." In
The Problem of the Hexateuch and other essays,
pp. 1-78. Translated by E. W. Trueman Dicken.
New York: McGraw Hill Book Company, 1966.

_____. Studies in Deuteronomy. Translated by
David Stalker. Chicago: H. Regnery Co., 1953.

Radcliffe-Brown, A. R. Preface to African Political
Systems. Edited by M. Fortes and E. E. Evans-
Pritchard. London: Oxford University Press,
1970.

Rengstorf, Karl H. Die Re-Investitur des verlorenen
Sohnes in der Gleichniserzählung Jesu Luk. 15,
11-32. Koln, Opladen: Westdeutscher Verlag,
1967.

Riemann, Paul A. "Desert and Return to Desert in the
Pre-exilic Prophets." Ph.D. Dissertation,
Harvard University, 1964.

Die Religion in Geschichte und Gegenwart. 3rd ed.
S.v. "Stadtkult," by F. C. Grant and W. von Soden.

Reventlow, Henning Graf. Gebot und Predigt im Dekalog.
Gerd Mohn: Gutersloher Verlagshaus, 1962.

Richter, Wolfgang. Recht und Ethos: Versuch einer
Ortung des Weisheitlichen Mahnspruches. München:
Kösel Verlag, 1966.

Rinaldi, G. "KWN." BeO 10 (1968):206.

Roifer, Alexander. "The Breaking of the Heifer's Neck." <u>Tarbiz</u> 31 (1961):119-43.

Rowley, H. H. <u>Worship in Ancient Israel: its form and meaning.</u> London: SPCK, 1967.

Rowton, M. B. "Autonomy and Nomadism in Western Asia." <u>Orientalia</u> NS 42 (1973):247-58.

_____. "Dimorphic Structure and the Problem of the <i>'Apîru-'Ibrîm.</i> <u>JNES</u> 35 (1976):13-20.

Rudolph, W. <u>Jeremia.</u> 3rd ed. Tubingen: J. C. B. Mohr-Paul Siebeck, 1968.

Salmon, J. "Judicial Authority in Early Israel: An Historical Investigation of Old Testament Institutions." Th.D. Dissertation. Princeton Theological Seminary, 1968.

Sanders, James A., ed. <u>Near Eastern Archeology in the Twentieth Century: Essays in honor of Nelson Glueck.</u> Garden City, NY.: Doubleday & Company, 1970.

_____. "Adaptable for Life: The nature and function of Canon." In <u>Magnalia Dei: The Mighty Acts of God; Essays on the Bible and Archaeology in Memory of G. Ernest Wright,</u> pp. 531-60. Edited by F. M. Cross, W. E. Lemke and P. D. Miller. Garden City, NY.: Doubleday and Company, 1976.

_____. <u>Torah and Canon.</u> 2nd ed. Philadelphia: Fortress Press, 1974.

Schmidt, Hans. "Mose und der Dekalog." In <u>Eucharisterion. Studien zur Religion und Literatur des Alten und Neuen Testaments. Hermann Gunkel zum 60. Geburtstage.</u> Vol. 1, pp. 78-119. Edited by Hans Schmidt. Göttingen: Vandenhoeck & Ruprecht, 1923.

Schmidt, Werner H. <u>Alttestamentlicher Glaube in seiner Geschichte.</u> Neukirchener Studienbücher. No. 6. Neukirchen-Vluyn: Neukirchener Verlag, 1975.

Schulz, Hermann. <u>Das Todesrecht im alten Testament.</u> Berlin: Topelmann, 1969.

Seitz, Gottfried. Redaktionsgeschichtliche Studien zum Deuteronomium. Stuttgart: Kohlhammer, 1971.

Septuaginta. Vol. 3. Deuteronomium. Edited by John W. Wevers. Gottingen: Vandenhoeck & Ruprecht, 1977.

Service, E. R. Origins of the State and Civilization. New York: W. W. Norton, 1975.

Sinclair, L. "An Archaeological Study of Gibeah: Tel el-Ful." AASOR 34-5 (1954-6):1-52.

Sjoberg, Gideon. The Preindustrial City: Past and Present. Glencoe, IL.: The Free Press, 1960.

Skinner, John A. Prophecy and Religion. Cambridge: The University Press, 1922.

Sklba, Richard J. The Faithful City. Herald Biblical Booklets. Chicago: Franciscan Herald Press, 1976.

Smith, George A. The Book of Deuteronomy. London: Cambridge University Press, 1950.

Snaith, H. M. "The Daughters of Zelophehad (Deut 25:5-10)," VT 16 (66):124-7.

Soggin, J. Alberto. Introduction to the Old Testament. Philadelphia: The Westminster Press, 1976.

Speiser, E. A. "'Coming' and 'Going' at the 'City' Gate." In Oriental and Biblical Studies. Collected Writings of E. A. Speiser, pp. 83-8. Edited by J. J. Finkelstein and Moshe Greenberg. Philadelphia: University of Pennsylvania Press, 1967.

Stamm, Johann J., and Maurice E. Andrew. The Ten Commandments in Recent Research. London: SCM Press, Ltd., 1967.

Steuernagel, Carl. Deuteronomium. Göttingen: Vandenhoeck & Ruprecht, 1900.

_____. Die Entstehung des deuteronomischen Gesetzes kritisch und biblisch-theologisch untersucht. Halle: J. Krause, 1896.

Stolz, Fritz. _Jahwes und Israels Kriege_. Zürich: Theologischer Verlag, 1972.

Talmon, Shemaryahu. "The 'Desert Motif' in the Bible and Qumran Literature." In _Biblical Motifs_, pp. 31-63. Edited by A. Altmann. Cambridge, MA.: Harvard University Press, 1966.

Theological Dictionary of the New Testament. S.v. "νομος ," by W. Gutbrod.

Theological Dictionary of the New Testament. S.v. "πολις,πολιτις,πολιτευομαι,πολιτεια,πολιτευμα," by Hermann Strathmann.

Theological Dictionary of the Old Testament. S.v. "'_acher_," by Seth Erlandsson.

Theological Dictionary of the Old Testament. S.v. "_bachar_," by Jan Bergman, Helmer Ringgren and Horst Seebass.

Theological Dictionary of the Old Testament. S.v. "_bdl_," by Benedikt Otzen.

Theological Dictionary of the Old Testament. S.v. "_betulim_," by M. Tsevat.

Theologisches Handwörterbuch zum Alten Testament. S.v. "_bhr_," by H. Wildberger.

Theologisches Handwörterbuch zum Alten Testament. S.v. "_sā'aq_," by R. Albertz.

Theologisches Handwörterbuch zum Alten Testament. S.v. "_tōb_," by H. J. Stoebe.

Theologisches Handwörterbuch zum Alten Testament. S.v. "_gadōl_," by Ernst Jenni.

Theologisches Handwörterbuch zum Alten Testament. S.v. "_nēkār_," by R. Martin-Achard.

Theologisches Handwörterbuch zum Alten Testament. S.v. "'_ir_," by A. R. Hulst.

Thomson, T., and D. "Some legal problems in the Book of Ruth." _VT_ 18 (1968):79-100.

Tiffany, Frederick Clark. "Parenesis and Deuteronomy 5 - 11 (Deut 4:45; 5:2-11:29): a form critical study." Ph.D. Dissertation, Claremont University, 1978.

Tucker, Gene M. Form Criticism of the Old Testament. Guides to Biblical Scholarship. Old Testament Series. Edited by J. Coert Rylaarsdam. Philadelphia: Fortress Press, 1971.

Turner, Ralph H., and Lewis M. Killian. Collective Behavior. Englewood Cliffs, NJ.: Prentice-Hall, 1957.

Van Seters, John. Abraham in History and Tradition. New Haven, CT.: Yale University Press, 1975.

Vaux, Roland De. Ancient Israel: Its Life and Institutions. Translated by John McHugh. New York: McGraw Hill Book Company, Inc., 1961.

Waldow, H. Eberhard Von. "Social Responsibility and Social Structure in Early Israel." CBQ 32 (70):182-204.

Wallis, G. "Die Stadt in den Uberlieferungen der Genesis." ZAW 78 (1966):133-48.

Walz, R. "Zum Problem des Zeitpunktes der Domestifikation der altweltlichen Cameliden." Zeitschrift der Deutschen Morgenländischen Gesellschaft 100 (1951):29-51.

Weidner, E. F. "Der Staatsvertrag Assurniraris VI von Assyrien mit Mati-ilu von Bit Agusi." AfO 8 (1932-3):17-27.

Weinfeld, Moshe. "The Covenant of Grant in the Old Testament and in the Ancient Near East." JAOS 90 (1970):184-203.

_____. Deuteronomy and the Deuteronomic School. Oxford: Clarendon Press, 1972.

Wellhausen, Julius. Prolegomena to the History of Israel. Translated by M. Menzies and M. Black. New York: World Publishing, Times Mirror, 1957. Reprint ed. Gloucester, MA.: Peter Smith, 1973.

Wenham, G. J. "Betulah--a girl of marriageable age."
    VT 22 (1972):326-48.

Westermann, Claus. Genesis. Vol. 1: Biblischer
    Kommentar. Neukirchen: Erziehungsverein, 1966.

Whitelam, Keith W. The Just King: Monarchial Judicial
    Authority in Ancient Israel. Sheffield, England:
    Journal for the Study of Old Testament Press,
    1979.

Willesen, F. "Die Eselsöhne von Sichem als
    Bundesgenossen." VT 4 (1954):216-17.

Wirth, Louis. "Urbanism as a Way of Life." In Cities
    and Society: The Revised Reader in Urban
    Sociology, pp. 46-63. Edited by Paul K. Hatt
    and Albert J. Reiss. Glencoe, IL.: Free Press,
    1957.

Wolf, C. U. "Traces of Primitive Democracy in Ancient
    Israel." JNES 6 (1947):98-108.

Wolff, Hans Walter. Hosea. Philadelphia: Fortress
    Press, 1974.

_____. "Hoseas geistige Heimat." ThLZ 81
    (1956):90-4.

_____. "The Kerygma of the Deuteronomic
    Historical Work." In The Vitality of the Old
    Testament Traditions. Edited by Walter
    Brueggemann and Hans Walter Wolff. Atlanta, GA.:
    John Knox Press, 1975.

Wright, G. Ernest. "Cult and History." Int 16
    (1962):3-20.

_____. The Old Testament Against its Environ-
    ment. Chicago: H. Regnery Co., 1950.

Wurthwein, E. "Der Sinn des Gesetzes im AT." ZThK
    55 (1958):255-70.

Yadin, Yigael. The Art of Warfare in Biblical Lands in
    the Light of Archeological Discovery. London:
    Weidenfeld and Nicolson, 1963.

Zevit, Ziony. "The EGLA (עגלה) ritual of Dt 21:1-9." JBL 95 (1976):377-90.

Zuber, Beat. Vier Studien zu den Ursprüngen Israels: Die Sinaifrage und Probleme der Volks- und Traditionsbildung. Göttingen: Vandenhoeck & Ruprecht, 1976.

INDEX OF BIBLICAL REFERENCES

GENESIS

1--11	28,180
4:16	150
4:17	5,11,27,180
6:4	246
10:10	27
11:1-9	3,5,182-3
11:31	7
12--50	61
12	44
12:1-9	58
13:2-18	58,150,254
14	45,79
16:2	246
18	5
24:6	100
26:22	144
31--33	44
31:24	100
31:53	39
33:18-20	58
34:2	215
34:19	249
38	217,245-7,249,251
41:48	295
48:6	182

EXODUS

1--5	61
2:15	142,149
4:25	253
12:25	258
13:1-16	258,278
18	152-4,302
19--24	48-9,59,132,144-6
20:1-21	24,163,168,220,262
20:22---23:33	121,131-2,226
21:2-6	136
21:7-11	226,231,301
21:12-14	142,149,162-4
21:15	162-4,213,220,279,281
21:16	162-4
21:17	213,220,279
21:18-19	245
21:20-1	202
21:22-3	186,245
21:28-32	214

EXODUS (cont'd)

22:19	262
22:20	117,119
23:1-3+6-8	52,168
23:14-17	169
23:18	262
23:20-33	258
25:31	131
32	125,131,182
34:12	100
34:18-24	144,169,278
34:28	142
34:29--Lv 16 + Nm	131

LEVITICUS

14:34	258
16:20-2	208
17--26	131,155
18:6-18	168-9,214,227
18:22	214
19:20-2	122
19:23-5	258
20:17	204
22:12	212
23:10	258
25:2	258
25:29-31	26
26:26	258

NUMBERS

12:13-14	253
14:8	249
15:1-12	258
15:13	214
15:17-21	258
16:14	182
19:1-10	202,278
19:11-13	202
20:10	220,299
20:24	220
21:25	25,85
25:4	125
26:52-6	182
27:8-11	249
27:14	220
31:10	25
32	85,182
33:50-6	182,258

NUMBERS (cont'd)

34:1-15	182,258
35:10-14	176-7,258
36:2	182

DEUTERONOMY

1--11	59,177
1--4	49,60,107-8,177-83,273,275
1:1	108
1:5	90
1:6-8	179
1:9-19	183
1:26-38	179-80,220
1:28	180
1:29-36	179,183
1:34-6	179,220,273-4
2:24--3:11	192,197,296
2:33-5	124
2:36	180-1
3:1-11	3-4,26,103,124,180-1,197
3:12-22	103,177-8,180-1
4:1-40	49,100,142,174,182
4:41-26:19	24,289,293,304-5
4:41-3	12,171,173-83,272-3,289-305
4:44-9	83,89-90,108,174,178
4:45+5:2 --11:29	107
5--28	48,108,177,295
5--11	83,107-10,165,295
5	24
5:6-21	93,140-1,155,158,165,168,171, 220,241,271
6:4	93,273
6:10-19	6,12,24,41,91-11,156,289-305
7:1-11	258
7:16-26	110,185
8:1-5	109-10
8:6-20	96-7,100,102,109-10,258,292
9:1-6	185
9:7	220
9:23-4	220
10:1-11	142
10:12-22	111
11:1-17	59,100,109
11:18-25	186,231
11:26-32	258
12--26	17,107-8,127, 129-32,155,162 165,179,186,275
12--18	132,140,151,165

DEUTERONOMY (cont'd)

22:13-21	12,24,64,67,118,156-8,160-1, 212,214,226-36,238,244,246, 250,281-4,289-305
22:22	156,158,161,163-4,200,247
22:23-7	12,15,24,64,67,156,158,161, 214,235-43,285,289-305
22:28-9	238
23:10-15	141,185
23:16--24:18	160
24:1-4	156,158,161,182,212,226,231
24:5	185
24:7	114,156,158,161,163-4,201
25:5-10	12,24,64,67,156,158,161,205, 212,235,243-56,286,289-305
25:17-19	182,185
26 1	141,182,258
26:5-9	47,66-7,128,205
26:12-15	258
26:16-19	132
27	55-59,106
27:1-8	258
27:11-13	51
27:14-26	50,205,220
28:1-2+15	49
28:1-6	97
28:32	276
28:49+52-3	6
28:69--30:20	49,60
29--32	108
30:11-14	196,297
31:1-6	186
31:9-13	49,60,90
31:16-22	136,258
31:24-9	220
32:1-44	201,246
33:1-29	70,108,144

JOSHUA

1:1-11	64,87
1:12-18	300
6:2	180
7:26	125
8:1-29	59,180
8:30-35	55
9:1-27	57,106,296,300
10:1-27	118,180,191,296
11:12	25
13:7	182

JOSHUA (cont'd)

14:2	182
15	18,57,300
15:13-19	4
15:20-63	85,300
19	18,182
20:1-9	151,177
24	58-9,106

JUDGES

1	4,85,144,175
3--16	61
3:7-11	242-302
3:12-30	4,118
4:15	118
6:3	118
7:2	118
9:1-57	55,58,215,304
10:1-5	272
11:39	58
12:7-15	272
13:23	249
16:1	246
19--20	55,130,132
19:1-30	26-7
20:14	132
21:21	58

RUTH   245,249-53

I SAMUEL

1--2	58
7:10	118
8	304
9	58
12:15	220
14:6	118
15:1-35	26,124
20:1-42	58
21:6	118
23:15	149
27:11	143
28:6	118
30:7	118
30:29	26

ISAIAH (cont'd)

JEREMIAH

EZEKIEL

INDEX OF GENRES